TUNNEL TO HELL

THE LAKE ERIE TUNNEL DISASTERS : TALES OF HEROISM AND TRAGEDY

A Graphic Novel

WRITTEN BY SCOTT MACGREGOR
ILLUSTRATED BY GARY DUMM

INTRODUCTION BY PAUL BUHLE

Tunnel To Hell/The Lake Erie Tunnel Disasters/Tales of Heroism and Tragedy
A Graphic Novel

Published by
EOI Media Press Inc.
P.O. Box 35491
Cleveland, Ohio 44135
eoimediapress.com

Production Assistance: Laura Dumm
Cover Illustrations Front and Back: Gary Dumm

ISBN: 9781619847804
ISBN: 9781619847811
eISBN: 9781619847743

Library of Congress Control Number: 2017953714

This book is a work of fiction based on real events and was drawn from a variety of sources. For dramatic and narrative purposes, the book contains fictionalized scenes, composite and representative characters, dialogue, and time compression. The views, actions, and opinions portrayed in the book are those of the characters only and do not necessarily reflect or represent the views and opinions held by individuals on which those characters are based.

Printed in the United States of America

Tunnel To Hell

The Lake Erie Tunnel Disasters
Tales of Heroism and Tragedy

Table of Contents

Introduction: A Real Life Tunnel to Hell
By Paul Buhle

This graphic novel brilliantly explores a historical moment within a much misunderstood and maligned phenomena: working class life in the USA. Blue collar experience seems often like a world unto itself, subject to endless caricature, most of it unfriendly or at least condescending. Sensitive film critics suggest that among a recent cinematic crop, including *Manchester By the Sea* and *Fences*, ignorance seems to be leavened with sympathy. Just as likely, the fog generated by journalists' discussion of the blue collar votes for Donald Trump will overwhelm empathetic efforts. Since at least the emergence of the modern novel and theatrical drama, heroism and even subjectivity belong elsewhere, with the heroic, rising middle class and the remnants of an often melancholy nobility. Anarchist, socialist, communist, feminist and race-conscious projects in many arts sought to shift the balance, but these were all but swept away in the Cold War era. American individualism returned with a vengeance.

A newly sympathetic effort in both arts and scholarship took form during the 1960s-70s. A young, radical generation sought to rewrite labor history, for instance, away from the "history of union leaders" that had dominated the field, along with the saga of "labor-industrial relations" in which the calming of working class tempers and acceptance of elite economic rule would be understood as both permanent and proper. Daniel Bell's totemic *End of Ideology (1960)* explained that social conflict, at least in the US, had turned out benevolently for almost everyone, nonwhites aside. The future blue collar generations hereafter would mainly face boredom, due to an excess of leisure. Corporations were, as he had explained earlier explained in Fortune magazine, were now largely owned by the public, through assorted investment funds, and for that matter, the fortunes of the great families (Rockefellers, Carnegies and so on) had mainly become major sources of philanthropy. Looking back from this happy present, the difficult and unhappy moments of American past had been only a way station, anyway.

Newer historians of race and community...their work linked, in turn, to specific ethnic histories-- saw things differently. Rich, dense historical studies connected and found support in the work of older scholars such as David Montgomery and Herbert Gutman, themselves influenced by E. P. Thompson and his totemic *Making of the English Working Class (1966)*. A new scholarship of African American life, followed by work on Latinos, Asians-Americans and Native Americans, told a story of exploitation, repression and upward struggle. Ruthless plunder had been an ever-present reality of the nation's rise to global supremacy. Gains on the part of ordinary folks had been made not through philanthropy but from struggle and sacrifice, rarely without sacrifice, often enough blood sacrifice. The history lessons did not point to a happy present or future, but one of continued conflicts ranging from social and health conditions to the very sustainability of life.

This vital, if unhappy tale, occupies most of Tunnel to Hell. Comics prodducer and scriptwriter of this comic, Scott MacGregor, lays out the basics in his Preface. We can usefully say a bit more about historical context and then pass on to the uniqueness of the art form.

Looking at Cleveland working class life of the nineteenth and early twentieth centuries requires a somewhat broader compass than the city proper. Burgeoning with growth, building an economy with a vital, accessible water supply from the Great Lakes while treating Erie as a dumping ground for refuse of every kind, Cleveland repeated an old ecological tragedy. The results were predictable as those of vanished cities across the world (and as close to Ohio as Cahokia Village in Illinois) that built up a population with commerce, cut down the surrounding green zones, slaughtered nearby game for the tastes of the ruling group, then faced fevers and ultimately decimation of the protein-starved poorer classes. American technology in the swift rise of industrialism allowed an escape of this dire fate, but at a great cost.

Let us set the scene a little more firmly. Here, for starters, race could only be central. Ohio, a veritable border state with the Southern-oriented Kentucky, whose population moved northward for jobs, became a racial battleground long before the era of this comic. The "Butter Nut" districts of the state openly sympathized with the Confederacy, and after the Civil War, as white and black regional in-migrants met a growing stream of Europeans looking for work, a dire pattern emerged. Scholars of Cleveland have analyzed how the differentiation made between white and nonwhite in-migrants, setting "skilled" categories of better work by race rather than the skill itself, relegated jobs, housing, and all the rest to the supposedly superior race. Racial segregation crossed all lines of work and domestic life, established earlier for Irish and native-born, then reinforced with the newer arrivals of the 1870s from Central and Southern Europe. Whites, including the families of European immigrant workers, scarcely escaped their own suffering, often in the worst of conditions at the lowest standards of living. The fortunate and well placed managed to rise somewhat, but never in proportion to the majority. When necessary, the threat of black labor to replace them was used to drive their wages and conditions downward.

Meanwhile, the "public works" required for urban life, infrastructure, public transportation, and so on, played a central role in the rapid growth of cities, and therefore a central role for the urban workforce. Indeed, the upbuilding of such necessities constituted an overarching expense of further growth. European cities needed to be reinvented; American cities grew up from frontier basis, and the expanse of presumably available land (often snatched up in preparation of public purchase), offered room for vast as well as hasty experiments. What Mac-Gregor describes as the work of municipal visionaries after the turn of the century to create miles of tunnels offshore, beneath the lake, would be a shining triumph of engineering wisdom if not a tragedy of human sacrifice to make it possible — and the stupidity of needless pollution in the first place.

Something similar could be said, of course, for private industry, the creation of railroads and of urban architecture growing into skyscrapers. The sacrifice of human life was viewed as a small cost, one of the least valuable of expenses.

Titans of industry guided these efforts and milked the public tax rolls for profits. Often enough, at the near-lowest levels of labor, the building trades unions-- among the first successfully organized to win contracts and endure in late nineteenth century America--traded favors with politicians while locking out all potential workers except their own (male) relatives. Older established ethnic groups, Germans, Welsh or Irish, often took full advantage of their positions. "Sandhogs" at the bottom, meanwhile, experienced few benefits and often the shortest life spans, as their betters played the role of supervisors. In Manhattan and Brooklyn, with the vast creation of subways, the Irish-American sandhogs were so numerous, their roles so continuous over generations until displaced by technology, that they became ethnic legend. They were "fortunate" (by race but also connections to relatives, for job entry) enough to risk their lives on a daily basis and earn a miserly salary. Such is the life brilliantly depicted in these pages.

Drop down a half-century without leaving Cleveland. Here, during the 1960s-80s, the city is losing its historic industries. "Urban decay" is the subject of endless journalism and editorializing, most of it sympathetic to business rather than the real victims. As if to compensate, the setting gained its vernacular prose and visual storytellers: Harvey Pekar and a small circle of local comics artists, most especially Gary Dumm. This artist "owns" Cleveland and Cleveland owns him, not only by virtue of personal residence but the location of his Irish-and-other, blue collar family stretching as far away as Pennsylvania but not much further, for several generations. An illustrator for his community-college newspaper, prolific artist (with his wife, fellow artist Laura Dumm) of local scenes and interests, Gary has the feeling for the city and its residence in his very bones.

Enter Harvey Pekar (1939-2011), fellow blue collar native, Yiddish-speaker with a childhood three-decker house and son of hard-pressed bodega owners. Pekar was not Jerry Siegel, that comic strip writer of a previous generation and different Cleveland Jewish neighborhood, who with artist Joe Shuster, invented Superman (also mistakenly sold off the rights cheap) in the 1930s. Pekar, the jazz buff and friend of Robert Crumb, had something different in mind, not Superhero escapism at all. Instead, Pekar stylized Cleveland reality, his own Cleveland reality. The funky blue collar life of the post-industrial age was at once so piquant and difficult to understand that nighttime TV Comedian David Letterman brought on Harvey to ridicule Cleveland as pathetic and "out of it" to the hip world. Cleveland in decline was real enough for the residents. The VA hospital staffer who met with other workers, white and black, on a basis of absolute equality, while trying to keep together failing marriages (until Joyce Brabner), keep friends, watch Indian games and otherwise develop his own writing, reviewing (jazz) to comics, Harvey made himself into an icon of an art form coming of age.

Recounting in comic art form local blue collar life, that is his own, the life's work that screen actress Helen Mirren described as opening readers to a new way to understand comic art: this was Pekar's gift. He could not have done this without the collaboration of his friend and collaborator, Gary Dumm. Thanks to this latest work, Dumm's art has spanned the distances in Cleveland life, found dignity and purpose in the worlds of ordinary folk, and offered to us in forms both instructive and artistic. The scriptwriter of Tunnel to Hell, who initiated the project, is a suitable partner in the work. A native Clevelander and talented photographer, Scott MacGregor began a long-term friendship and intermittent collaboration with Gary Dumm in 1976, and produced his own one-shot comic (drawn by Gary and others) four years later. In the decades following, MacGregor wrote essays on local history, illustrated by Dumm and collaborator Greg Budgett, for the alternative press, and placed his photos in the Irish-American press. In retirement after four decades as a medical practice manager (thus sharing part of Harvey Pekar's world), he submitted a story outline of Tunnel to Hell to a regional arts council and won the fellowship used to create this work.

We can say that MacGregor has made the graphic novel a model study in the world of work and of its perils, also the "black history" so long forgotten and in the last forty years, just beginning to be remembered properly, in public ways. These characters come alive in their travails, and true to the work of labor historian Herbert Gutman back in the 1950s-70s, these come alive in their daily habits, their home lives, their lingo and above all, their very willingness to risk life and limb for a wage. (MacGregor's own great grandfather, an Irish immigrant, was himself a sandhog.) MacGregor has also captured the corruption innate to the political-economic system of the burgeoning Gilded Age metropolis, as one hand dirties another and fortunes are made almost but not quite in public sight.

These sandhogs, like most American workers in the "unskilled" categories, never had the opportunity to resist collectively and demand better pay with safer conditions. Their resistance, however, can be found in personal acts of courage and self-sacrifice for their fellow wage-earners, the common decency that proves the cynics about blue collar life wrong, generation after generation. The keenness of the narrative, no less than the illuminating art-work, show us what comic art can do, when freed from the limits of the superhero model and used to tell the story of one city, inside and out. In my view, Tunnel to Hell will stand as an outstanding example of how to tell history so that all can understand it.

-Paul Buhle April, 2017

Select Bibliography:
- William H. Auburn and Miriam R. Auburn, *This Cleveland of Ours*. Cleveland: S.J. Clarke Publishing Co, 1933.

- John Stark Bellamy, II, *They Died Crawling, and Other Tales of Cleveland Woe*: Cleveland: Gray and Company, 1995.

- Herbert Gutman, *Work, Culture and Society in Industrializing America. Essays in America's Working Class and Social History*. New York: Vintage, 1977.

- David Montgomery, *The Fall of the House of Labor: The Workplace, the State and American Labor Activism*, 1865-1925. New York: University of Cambridge Press, 1987.

- Mary N. Oluony, *Garrett Augustus Morgan: Businessman, Inventor, Good Citizen*. Bloomington, IN: Author House, 2008.

- David D. Van Tassel and John J. Grabowski., eds., *The Encyclopedia of Cleveland History*. Second Edition. Bloomington, IN: Indiana University Press, 1996.

- On Line:Jim Dubelko, *"The 1916 Waterworks Disaster,"* Clevelandhistorical.org/items/show/736#. WPeJryMrJGE

Scott MacGregor dedicates this book to:

Kate, Patrick, and Maureen...

*...and to Gary Dumm who traversed his own "tunnel to hell"
while battling cancer during the creation of this book
and bravely won back the daylight.*

Gary Dumm dedicates this book to:

The memory of my parents, Margaret and George Dumm, who both, in vastly different ways, allowed and gave me the strength to dream big.

Laura Dumm, who's helped me to recover from cancer while in the middle of our four year journey, working together on the nuts-and-bolts of producing this big graphic novel.

Scott MacGregor, who trusted me implicitly to collaborate artistically and lend shape and definition to his dream.

Preface

Cleveland was a wicked little town back in the day. A popular jumping off point on the railway between New York and Chicago, the well situated city had earned its nickname as "the best location in the nation". Then as now, Cleveland is symbiotically tethered to Lake Erie, its invaluable water mother and the conduit most responsible for bringing the world to its doorstep. The city's serpentine Cuyahoga River, though infamously polluted for decades, has survived and remains an integral resource for the city's hopeful present and future.

Cleveland is one of those great American cities that grew up during the industrial era personalized by self-made tycoons. Their smoke belching industries turned buildings and respiratory systems black with soot and banks green with money. Success in steel, oil, and manufacturing translated into significant enviromental pollution which triggered a mammoth struggle for this Great Lakes city to provide clean drinking water for its growing population. Though generally forgotten, well into the 20th century Clevelanders were sickened or died from outbreaks of typhoid fever, cholera, and other illnesses stemming from the same waters its very existence depended upon.

Long before effective pollution controls were in place, the city's water supply was fed from long intake pipes that were placed incrementally further and further away from its fetid Erie shoreline. They worked like big hypodermic needles sucking lake water of hideous quality back toward the thirsty masses onshore. To simply clean up and restrict the pollution had never entered into the prevailing wisdom of the day much less threaten the conventions of those in power and control. Instead, the municipal visionaries ordered the construction of intake tunnels originating miles offshore and *underneath* the lake in order to channel relatively potable water toward the city's filtration plants.

The tunnel projects attracted waves of Irish, Italian, and Bohemian immigrants from places with names like Achill Island, Mezzogiorno, and Krakow. Among their ranks were experienced European tunnel men who had dug through the Alps, cut coal mines in Wales, or built the New York subways. Many of the workers were just fellas living far away from home and trying to feed their families anyway they could. They were desperate to have *any* job no matter how dangerous it was. It's important to understand that there was no such thing as a "safety net" during the ruthless times in which these stories dwell. If you didn't work, you didn't eat.

Forever optimistic and expert on the rules of calamity, the tunnel workers (aka "sandhogs") had the right stuff. They were affable, willing to work for low wages, and their vulnerable circumstances were fully exploited by the potentates that controlled the city. In Cleveland for the long run, these immigrant groups settled into urban neighborhoods and ramshackle villages that grew up along the city's river underbelly. The ghettos they created were sharply divided along ethnic lines and known by names that sound romantic today. And yet, Big Italy, Dutch Hill, and Irishtown Bend were not the types of neighborhoods where you would bump into a Rockefeller. They were the dank, desperate enclaves of the blue collar working poor who would eventually become the bedrock of Cleveland's future.

"Water, water everywhere nor any drop to drink"
- Samuel Taylor Coleridge

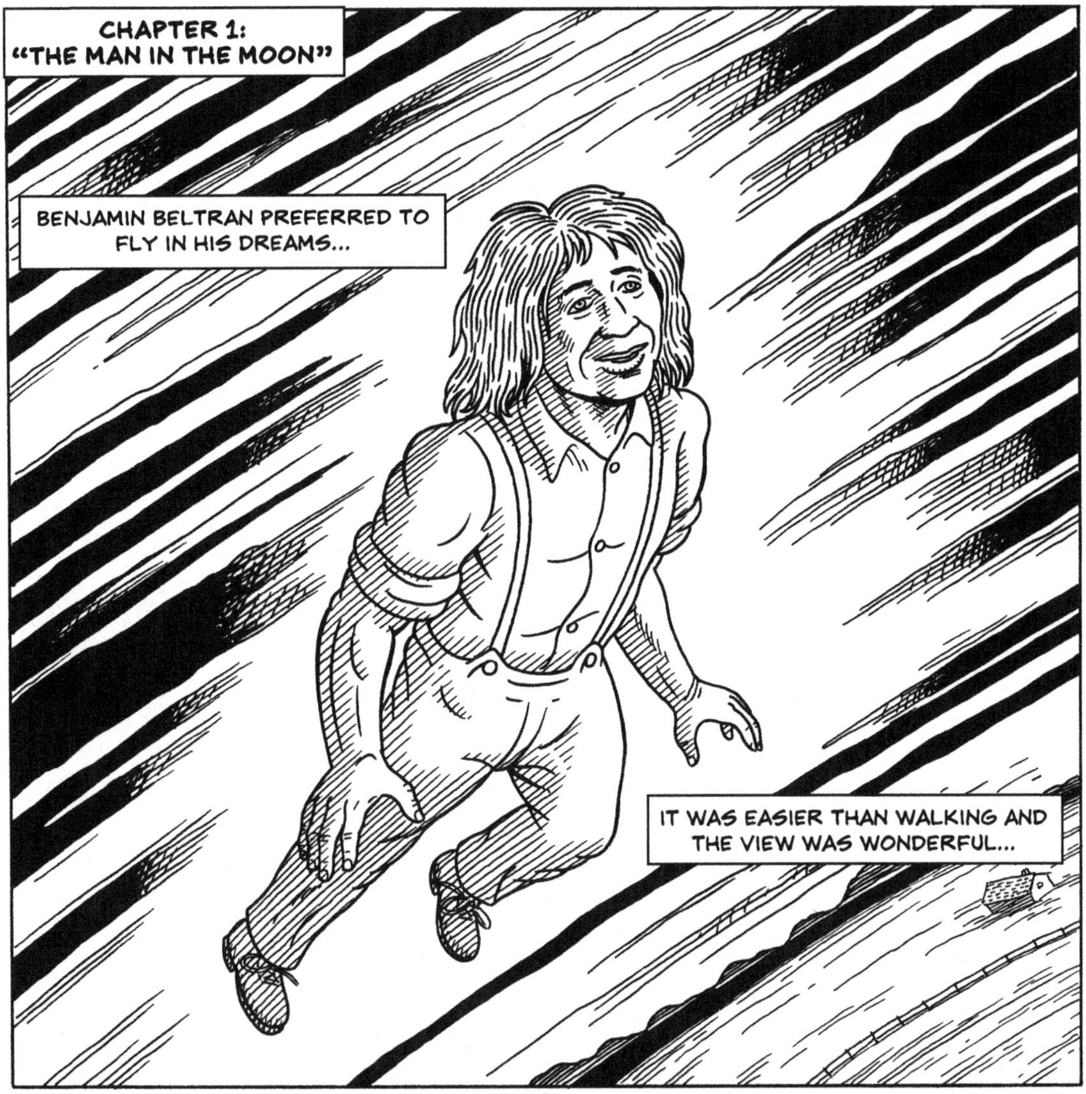
CHAPTER 1:
"THE MAN IN THE MOON"
BENJAMIN BELTRAN PREFERRED TO FLY IN HIS DREAMS...
IT WAS EASIER THAN WALKING AND THE VIEW WAS WONDERFUL...

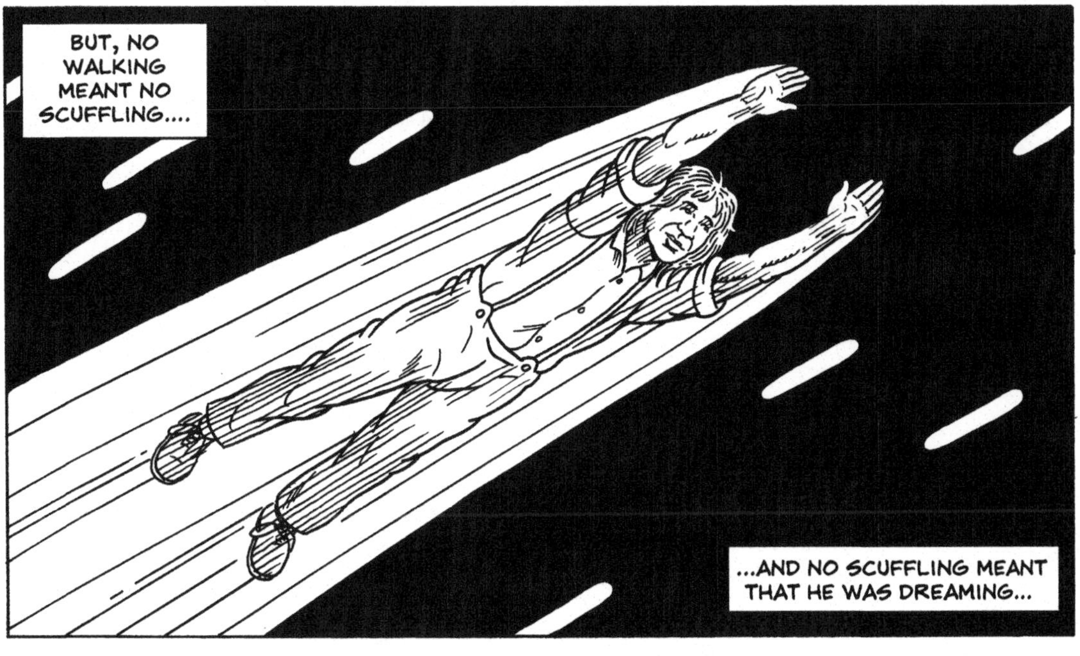
BUT, NO WALKING MEANT NO SCUFFLING....
...AND NO SCUFFLING MEANT THAT HE WAS DREAMING...

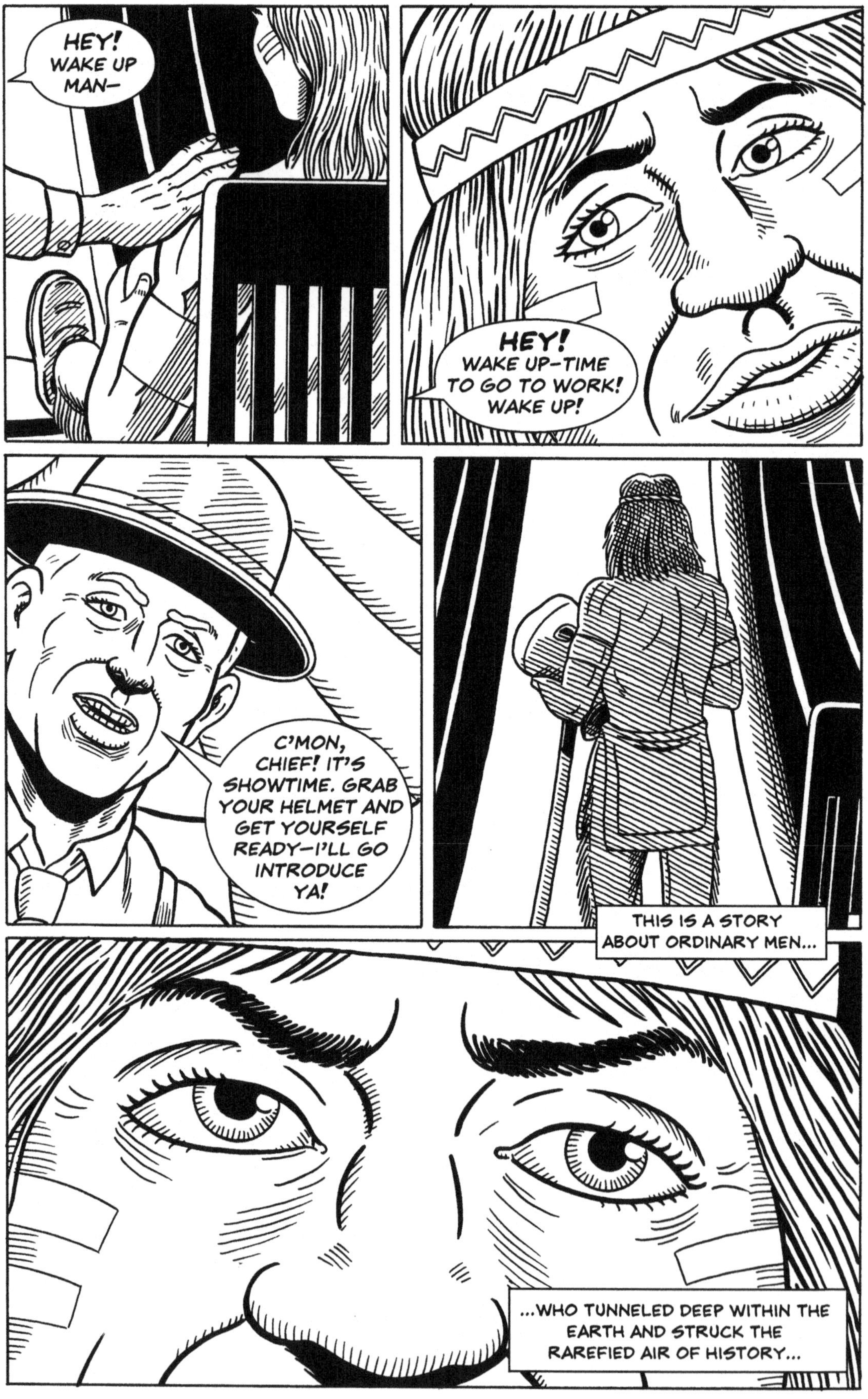
HEY! WAKE UP MAN—
HEY! WAKE UP—TIME TO GO TO WORK! WAKE UP!
C'MON, CHIEF! IT'S SHOWTIME. GRAB YOUR HELMET AND GET YOURSELF READY—I'LL GO INTRODUCE YA!
THIS IS A STORY ABOUT ORDINARY MEN...
...WHO TUNNELED DEEP WITHIN THE EARTH AND STRUCK THE RAREFIED AIR OF HISTORY...

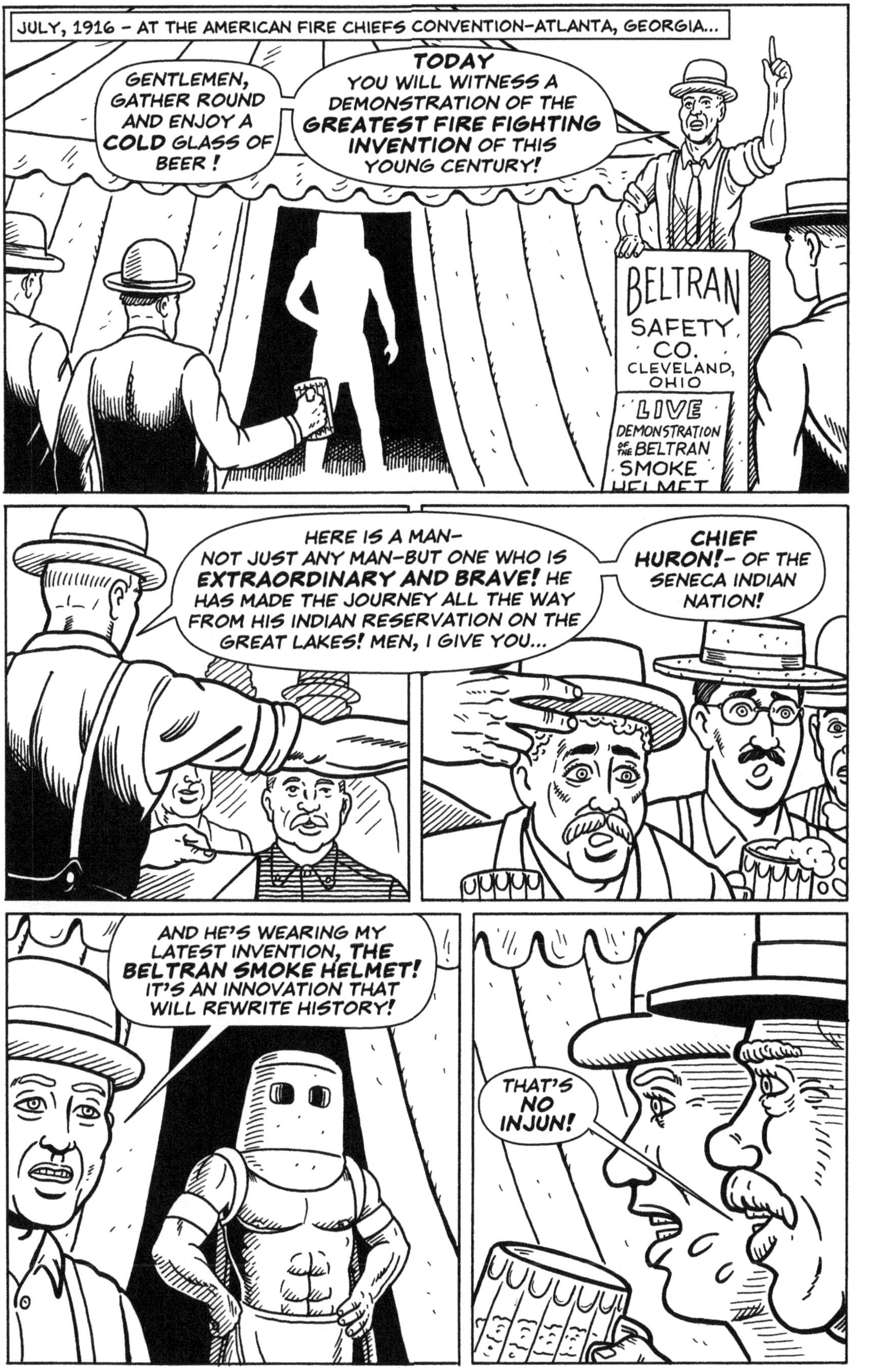
JULY, 1916 – AT THE AMERICAN FIRE CHIEFS CONVENTION–ATLANTA, GEORGIA...
GENTLEMEN, GATHER ROUND AND ENJOY A COLD GLASS OF BEER!
TODAY YOU WILL WITNESS A DEMONSTRATION OF THE GREATEST FIRE FIGHTING INVENTION OF THIS YOUNG CENTURY!
BELTRAN SAFETY CO. CLEVELAND, OHIO
LIVE DEMONSTRATION OF THE BELTRAN SMOKE
HERE IS A MAN– NOT JUST ANY MAN–BUT ONE WHO IS EXTRAORDINARY AND BRAVE! HE HAS MADE THE JOURNEY ALL THE WAY FROM HIS INDIAN RESERVATION ON THE GREAT LAKES! MEN, I GIVE YOU...
CHIEF HURON!– OF THE SENECA INDIAN NATION!
AND HE'S WEARING MY LATEST INVENTION, THE BELTRAN SMOKE HELMET! IT'S AN INNOVATION THAT WILL REWRITE HISTORY!
THAT'S NO INJUN!

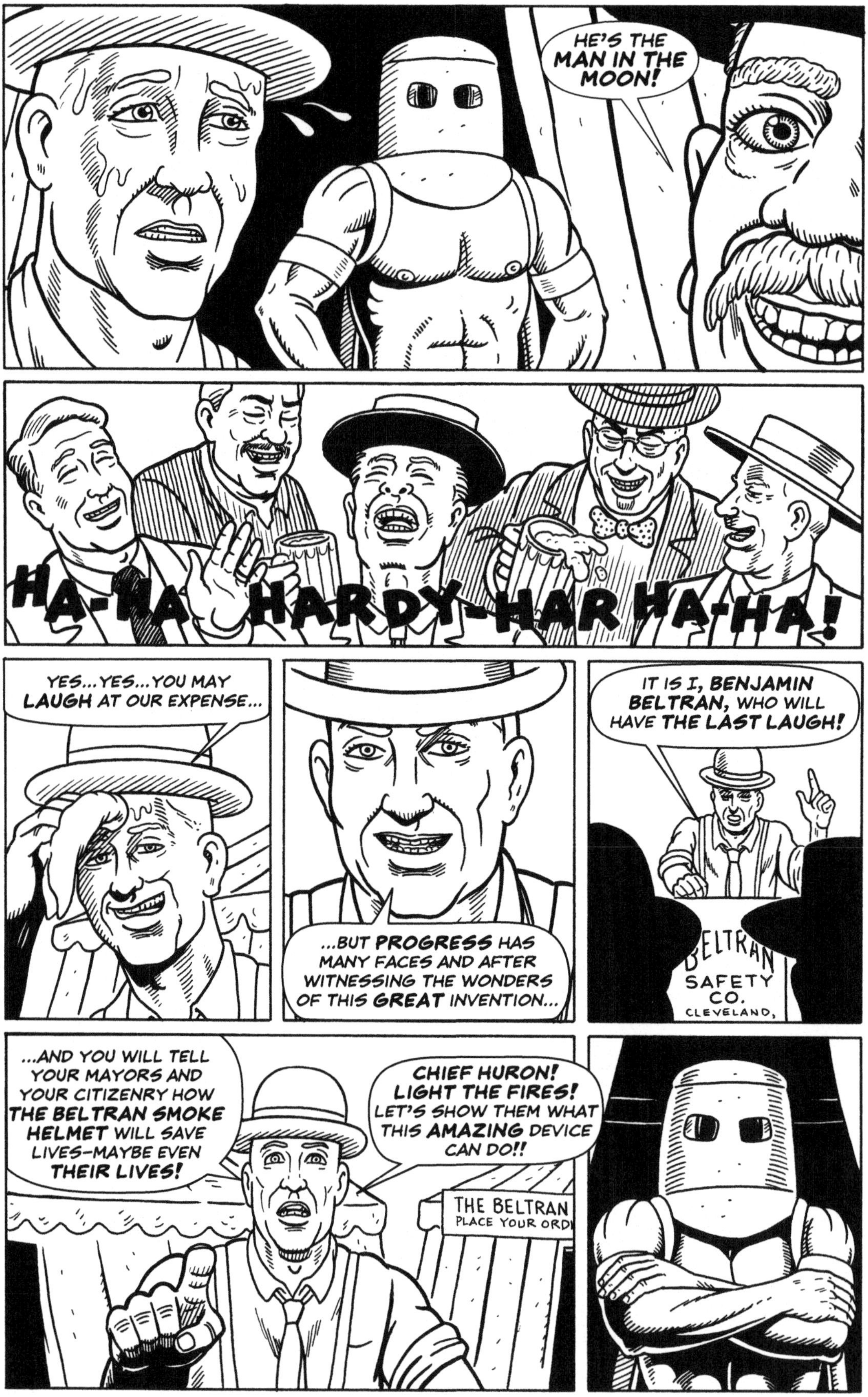
HE'S THE MAN IN THE MOON!
HA-HA HARDY-HAR HA-HA!
YES...YES...YOU MAY LAUGH AT OUR EXPENSE...
...BUT PROGRESS HAS MANY FACES AND AFTER WITNESSING THE WONDERS OF THIS GREAT INVENTION...
IT IS I, BENJAMIN BELTRAN, WHO WILL HAVE THE LAST LAUGH!
BELTRAN SAFETY CO. CLEVELAND,
...AND YOU WILL TELL YOUR MAYORS AND YOUR CITIZENRY HOW THE BELTRAN SMOKE HELMET WILL SAVE LIVES–MAYBE EVEN THEIR LIVES!
CHIEF HURON! LIGHT THE FIRES! LET'S SHOW THEM WHAT THIS AMAZING DEVICE CAN DO!!
THE BELTRAN
PLACE YOUR ORD

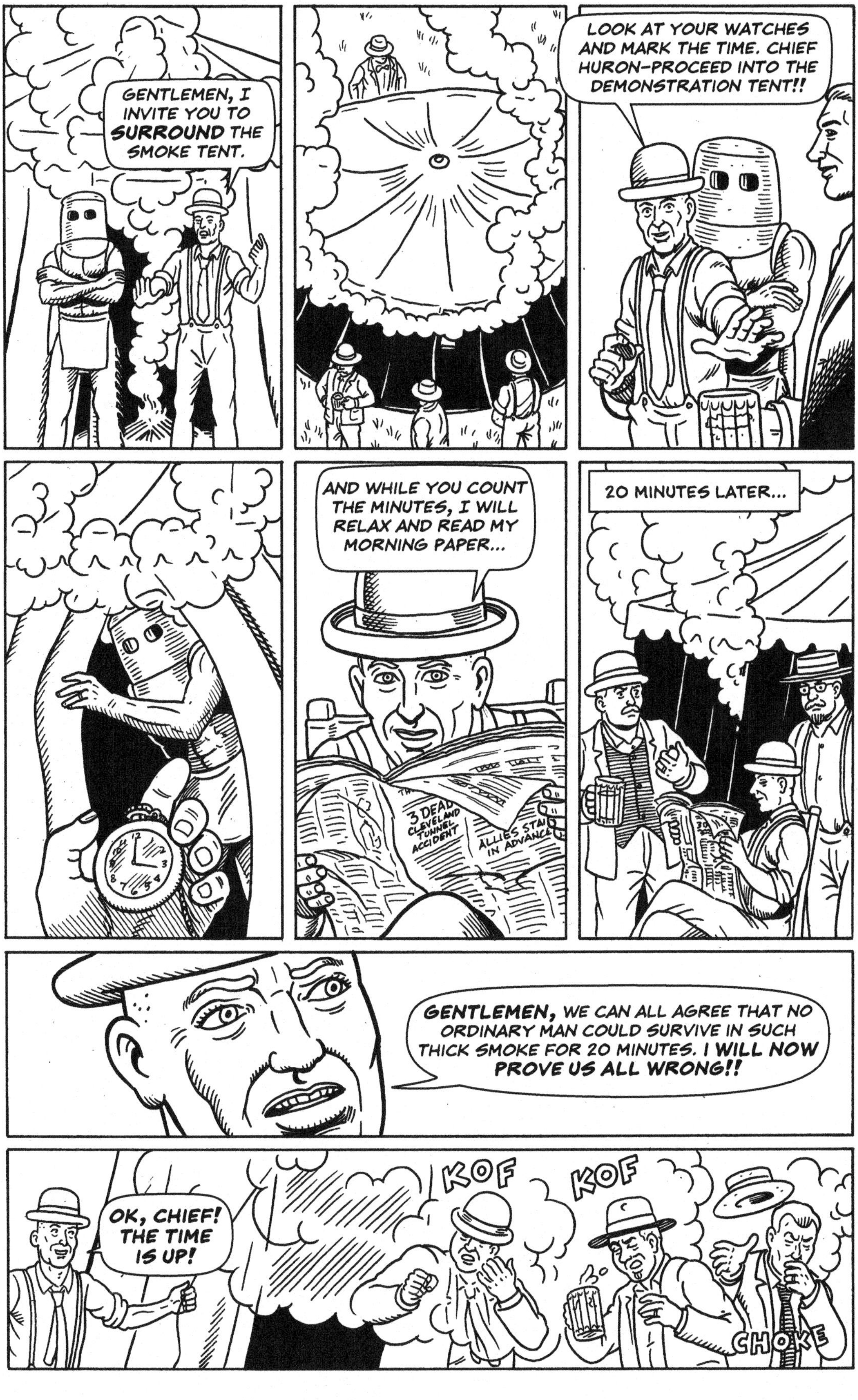
GENTLEMEN, I INVITE YOU TO **SURROUND** THE SMOKE TENT.
LOOK AT YOUR WATCHES AND MARK THE TIME. CHIEF HURON–PROCEED INTO THE DEMONSTRATION TENT!!
AND WHILE YOU COUNT THE MINUTES, I WILL RELAX AND READ MY MORNING PAPER...
3 DEAD CLEVELAND TUNNEL ACCIDENT
ALLIES STA IN ADVANC
20 MINUTES LATER...
GENTLEMEN, WE CAN ALL AGREE THAT NO ORDINARY MAN COULD SURVIVE IN SUCH THICK SMOKE FOR 20 MINUTES. I **WILL NOW PROVE US ALL WRONG!!**
OK, CHIEF! THE TIME IS UP!
KOF
KOF
CHOKE

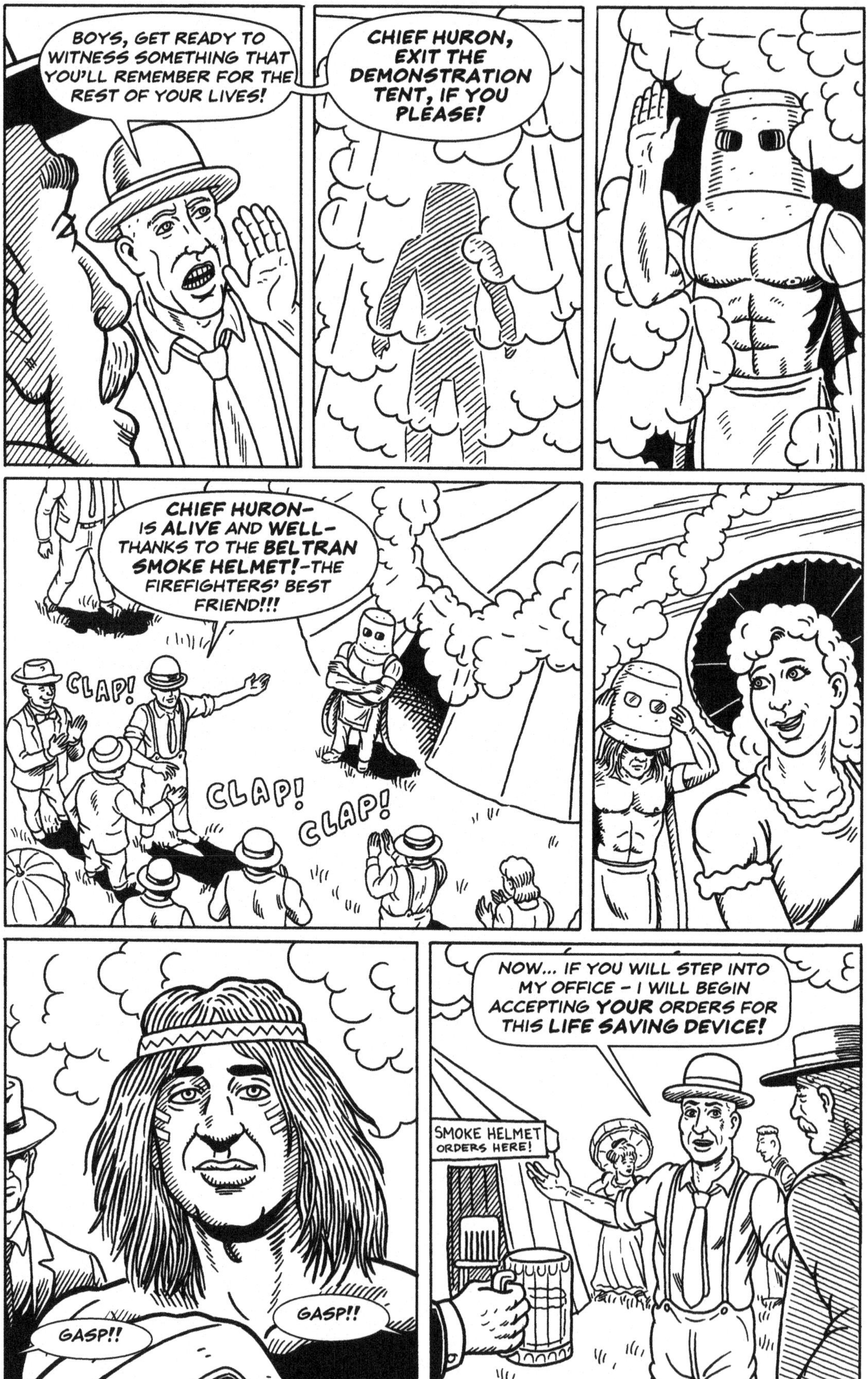
BOYS, GET READY TO WITNESS SOMETHING THAT YOU'LL REMEMBER FOR THE REST OF YOUR LIVES!
CHIEF HURON, EXIT THE DEMONSTRATION TENT, IF YOU PLEASE!
CHIEF HURON- IS ALIVE AND WELL- THANKS TO THE BELTRAN SMOKE HELMET!-THE FIREFIGHTERS' BEST FRIEND!!!
CLAP!
CLAP!
CLAP!
GASP!!
GASP!!
NOW... IF YOU WILL STEP INTO MY OFFICE - I WILL BEGIN ACCEPTING YOUR ORDERS FOR THIS LIFE SAVING DEVICE!
SMOKE HELMET
ORDERS HERE!

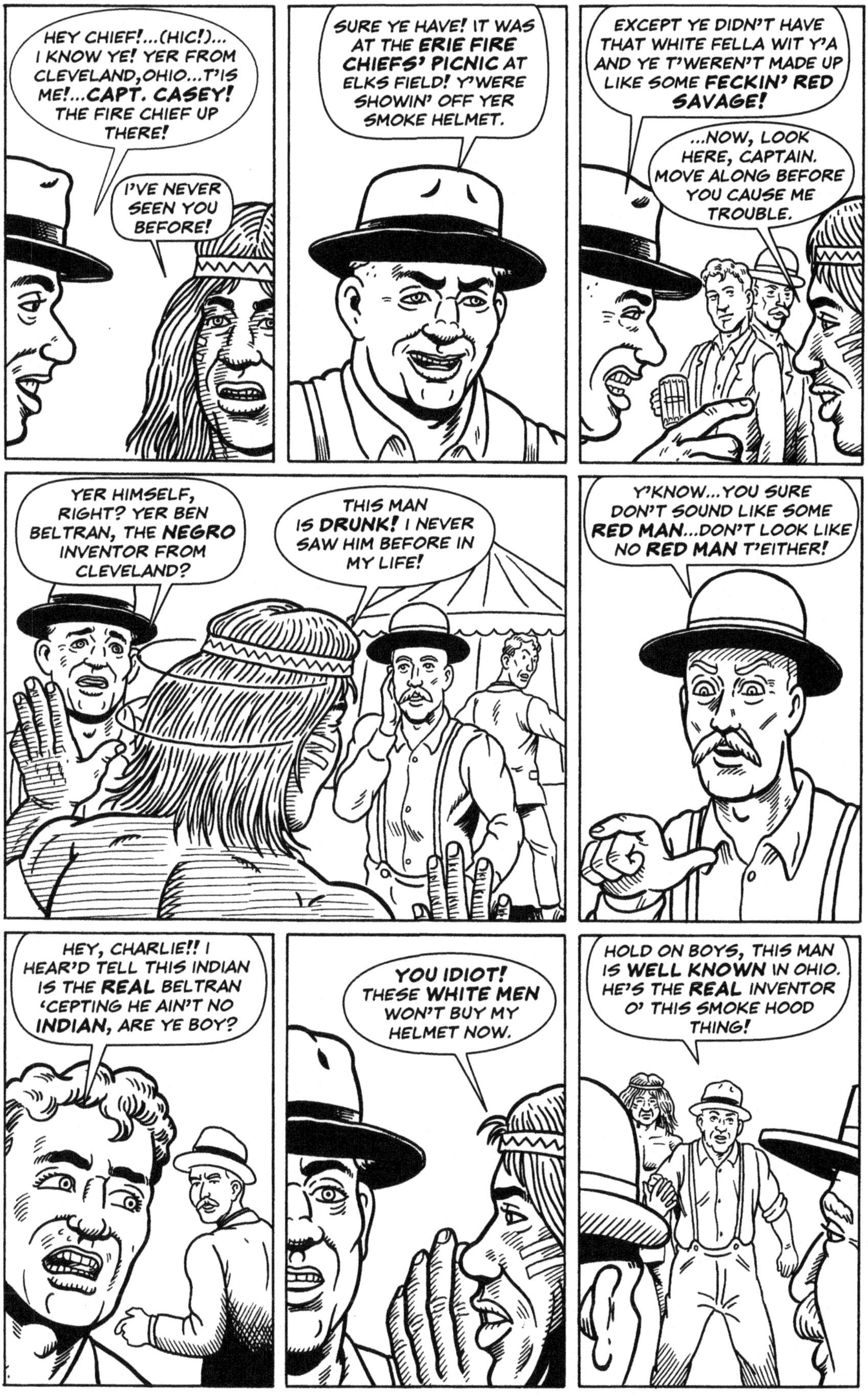
HEY CHIEF!...(HIC!)... I KNOW YE! YER FROM CLEVELAND,OHIO...T'IS ME!...CAPT. CASEY! THE FIRE CHIEF UP THERE!
I'VE NEVER SEEN YOU BEFORE!
SURE YE HAVE! IT WAS AT THE ERIE FIRE CHIEFS' PICNIC AT ELKS FIELD! Y'WERE SHOWIN' OFF YER SMOKE HELMET.
EXCEPT YE DIDN'T HAVE THAT WHITE FELLA WIT Y'A AND YE T'WEREN'T MADE UP LIKE SOME FECKIN' RED SAVAGE!
...NOW, LOOK HERE, CAPTAIN. MOVE ALONG BEFORE YOU CAUSE ME TROUBLE.
YER HIMSELF, RIGHT? YER BEN BELTRAN, THE NEGRO INVENTOR FROM CLEVELAND?
THIS MAN IS DRUNK! I NEVER SAW HIM BEFORE IN MY LIFE!
Y'KNOW...YOU SURE DON'T SOUND LIKE SOME RED MAN...DON'T LOOK LIKE NO RED MAN T'EITHER!
HEY, CHARLIE!! I HEAR'D TELL THIS INDIAN IS THE REAL BELTRAN 'CEPTING HE AIN'T NO INDIAN, ARE YE BOY?
YOU IDIOT! THESE WHITE MEN WON'T BUY MY HELMET NOW.
HOLD ON BOYS, THIS MAN IS WELL KNOWN IN OHIO. HE'S THE REAL INVENTOR O' THIS SMOKE HOOD THING!

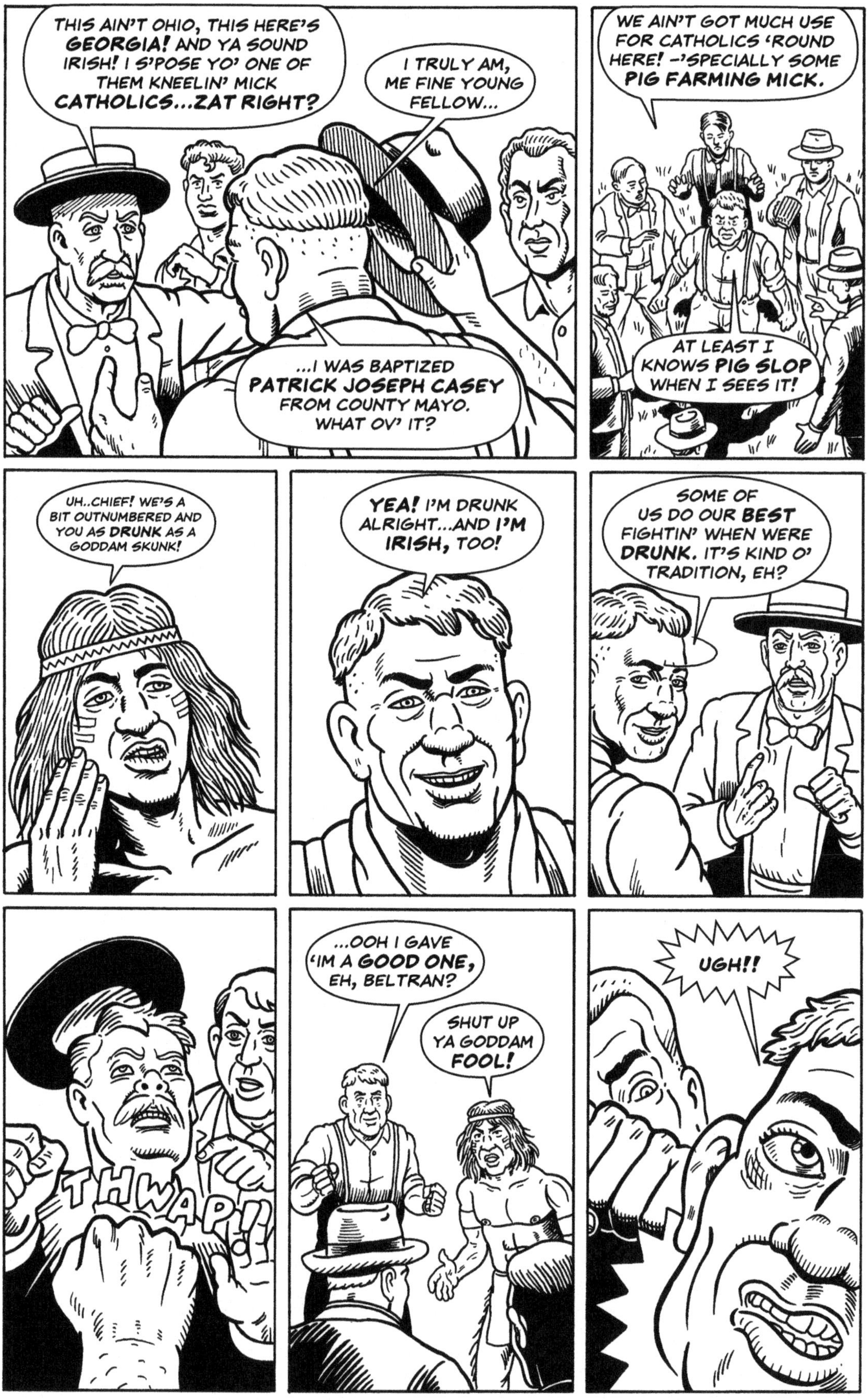
THIS AIN'T OHIO, THIS HERE'S GEORGIA! AND YA SOUND IRISH! I S'POSE YO' ONE OF THEM KNEELIN' MICK CATHOLICS...ZAT RIGHT?
I TRULY AM, ME FINE YOUNG FELLOW...
...I WAS BAPTIZED PATRICK JOSEPH CASEY FROM COUNTY MAYO. WHAT OV' IT?
WE AIN'T GOT MUCH USE FOR CATHOLICS 'ROUND HERE! –'SPECIALLY SOME PIG FARMING MICK.
AT LEAST I KNOWS PIG SLOP WHEN I SEES IT!
UH..CHIEF! WE'S A BIT OUTNUMBERED AND YOU AS DRUNK AS A GODDAM SKUNK!
YEA! I'M DRUNK ALRIGHT...AND I'M IRISH, TOO!
SOME OF US DO OUR BEST FIGHTIN' WHEN WERE DRUNK. IT'S KIND O' TRADITION, EH?
THWAP!!
...OOH I GAVE 'IM A GOOD ONE, EH, BELTRAN?
SHUT UP YA GODDAM FOOL!
UGH!!

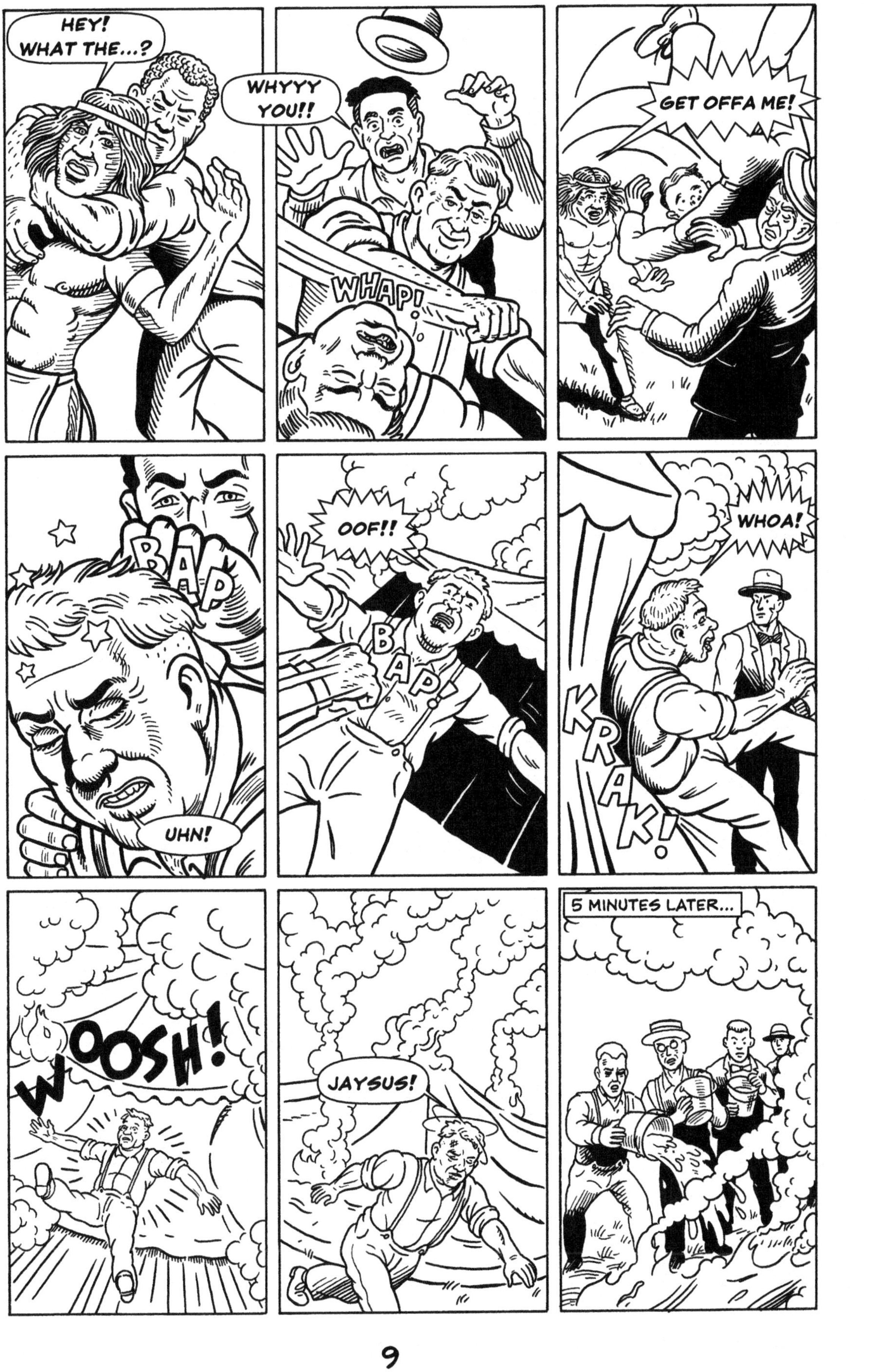
HEY! WHAT THE...?
WHYYY YOU!!
WHAP!
GET OFFA ME!
BAP
UHN!
OOF!!
BAP!
WHOA!
KRAK!
WOOSH!
JAYSUS!
5 MINUTES LATER...

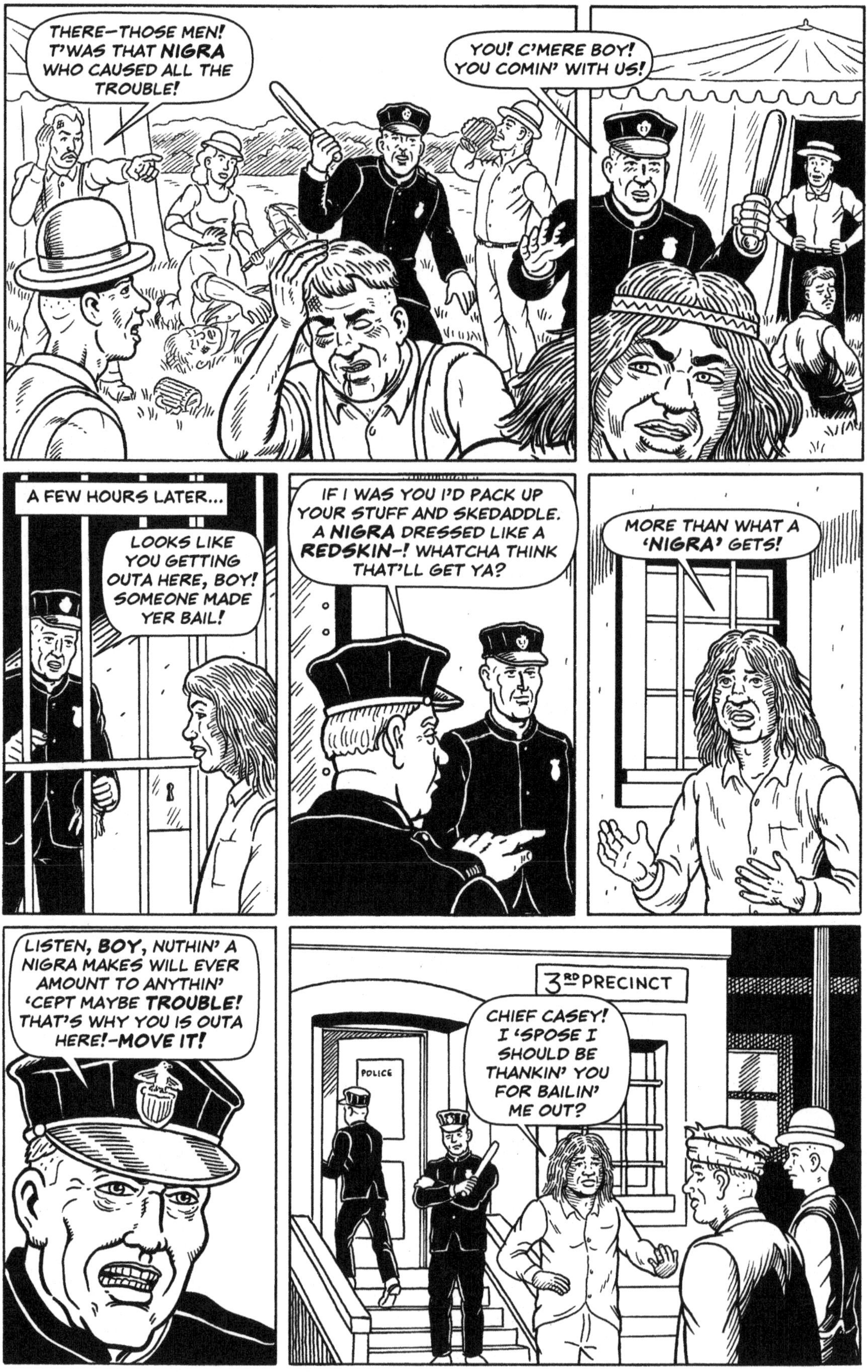
THERE–THOSE MEN! T'WAS THAT NIGRA WHO CAUSED ALL THE TROUBLE!
YOU! C'MERE BOY! YOU COMIN' WITH US!
A FEW HOURS LATER...
LOOKS LIKE YOU GETTING OUTA HERE, BOY! SOMEONE MADE YER BAIL!
IF I WAS YOU I'D PACK UP YOUR STUFF AND SKEDADDLE. A NIGRA DRESSED LIKE A REDSKIN–! WHATCHA THINK THAT'LL GET YA?
MORE THAN WHAT A 'NIGRA' GETS!
LISTEN, BOY, NUTHIN' A NIGRA MAKES WILL EVER AMOUNT TO ANYTHIN' 'CEPT MAYBE TROUBLE! THAT'S WHY YOU IS OUTA HERE!–MOVE IT!
3RD PRECINCT
POLICE
CHIEF CASEY! I 'SPOSE I SHOULD BE THANKIN' YOU FOR BAILIN' ME OUT?

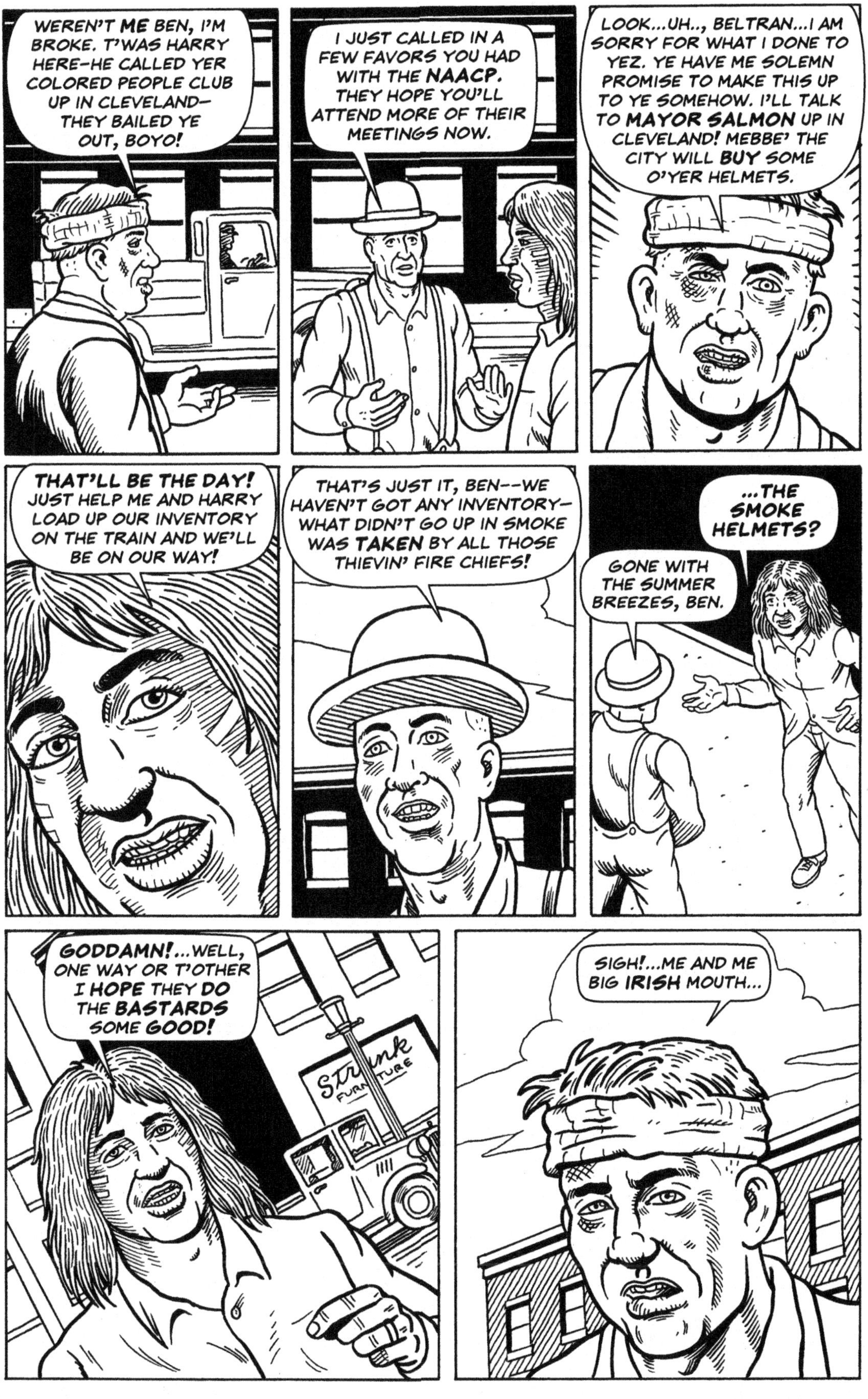
WEREN'T ME BEN, I'M BROKE. T'WAS HARRY HERE-HE CALLED YER COLORED PEOPLE CLUB UP IN CLEVELAND-THEY BAILED YE OUT, BOYO!
I JUST CALLED IN A FEW FAVORS YOU HAD WITH THE NAACP. THEY HOPE YOU'LL ATTEND MORE OF THEIR MEETINGS NOW.
LOOK...UH.., BELTRAN...I AM SORRY FOR WHAT I DONE TO YEZ. YE HAVE ME SOLEMN PROMISE TO MAKE THIS UP TO YE SOMEHOW. I'LL TALK TO MAYOR SALMON UP IN CLEVELAND! MEBBE' THE CITY WILL BUY SOME O'YER HELMETS.
THAT'LL BE THE DAY! JUST HELP ME AND HARRY LOAD UP OUR INVENTORY ON THE TRAIN AND WE'LL BE ON OUR WAY!
THAT'S JUST IT, BEN--WE HAVEN'T GOT ANY INVENTORY-WHAT DIDN'T GO UP IN SMOKE WAS TAKEN BY ALL THOSE THIEVIN' FIRE CHIEFS!
...THE SMOKE HELMETS?
GONE WITH THE SUMMER BREEZES, BEN.
GODDAMN!...WELL, ONE WAY OR T'OTHER I HOPE THEY DO THE BASTARDS SOME GOOD!
Strunk FURNITURE
SIGH!...ME AND ME BIG IRISH MOUTH...

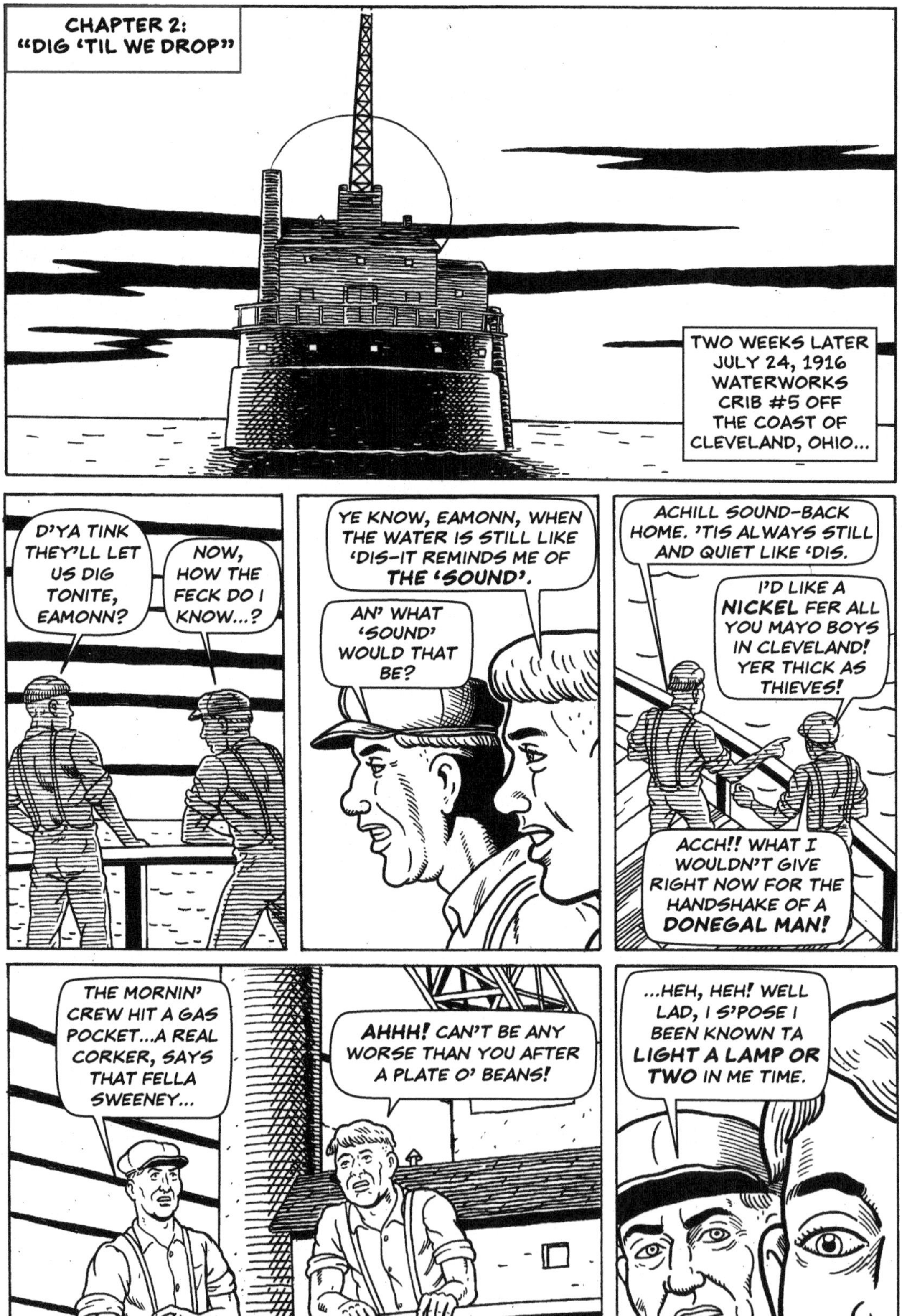
CHAPTER 2: "DIG 'TIL WE DROP"
TWO WEEKS LATER JULY 24, 1916 WATERWORKS CRIB #5 OFF THE COAST OF CLEVELAND, OHIO...
D'YA TINK THEY'LL LET US DIG TONITE, EAMONN?
NOW, HOW THE FECK DO I KNOW...?
YE KNOW, EAMONN, WHEN THE WATER IS STILL LIKE 'DIS–IT REMINDS ME OF THE 'SOUND'.
AN' WHAT 'SOUND' WOULD THAT BE?
ACHILL SOUND–BACK HOME. 'TIS ALWAYS STILL AND QUIET LIKE 'DIS.
I'D LIKE A NICKEL FER ALL YOU MAYO BOYS IN CLEVELAND! YER THICK AS THIEVES!
ACCH!! WHAT I WOULDN'T GIVE RIGHT NOW FOR THE HANDSHAKE OF A DONEGAL MAN!
THE MORNIN' CREW HIT A GAS POCKET...A REAL CORKER, SAYS THAT FELLA SWEENEY...
AHHH! CAN'T BE ANY WORSE THAN YOU AFTER A PLATE O' BEANS!
...HEH, HEH! WELL LAD, I S'POSE I BEEN KNOWN TA LIGHT A LAMP OR TWO IN ME TIME.
JAYSUS MAN, YE COULD LIGHT UP A WHOLE VILLAGE!

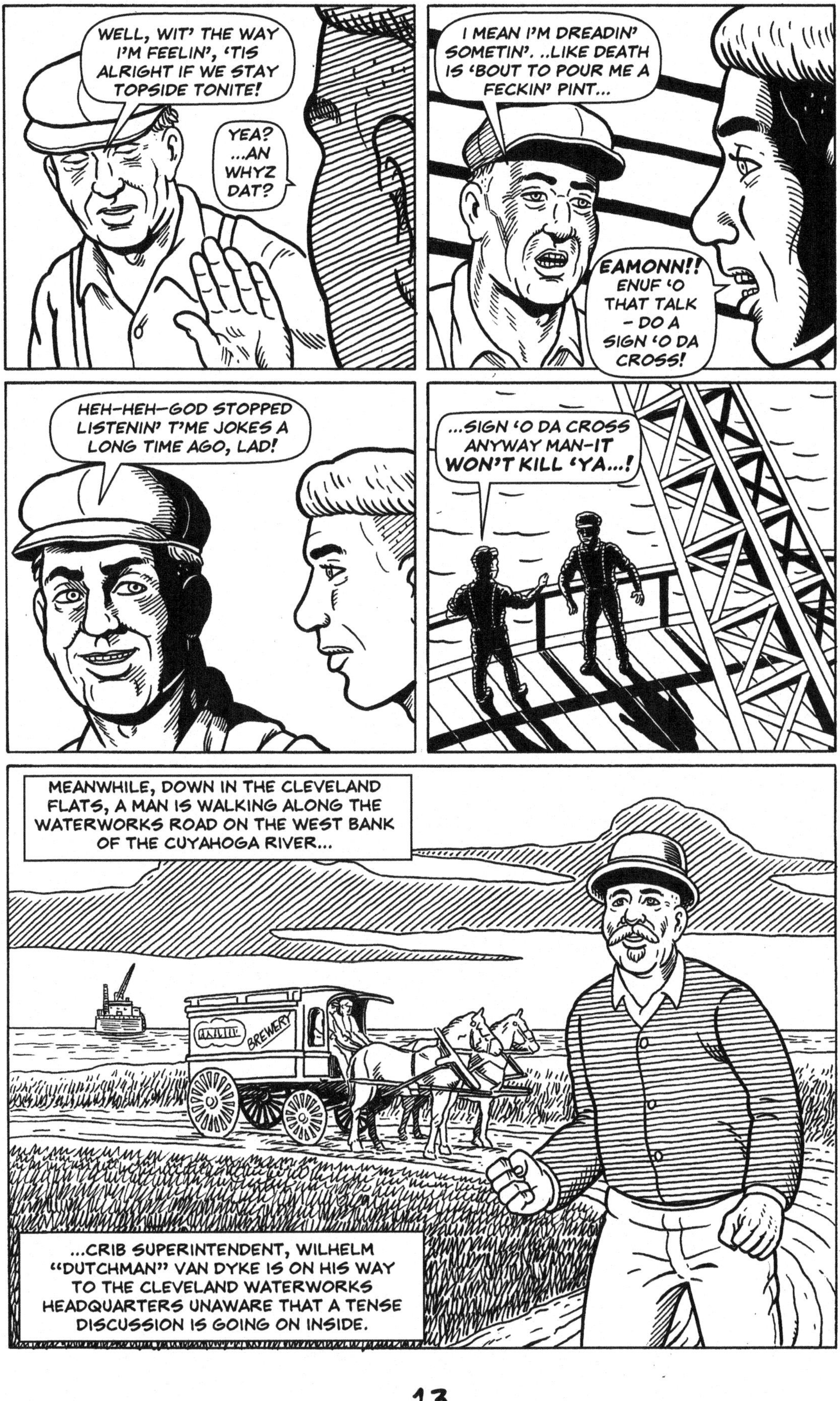

WELL, WIT' THE WAY I'M FEELIN', 'TIS ALRIGHT IF WE STAY TOPSIDE TONITE!
YEA? ...AN WHYZ DAT?
I MEAN I'M DREADIN' SOMETIN'. ..LIKE DEATH IS 'BOUT TO POUR ME A FECKIN' PINT...
EAMONN!! ENUF 'O THAT TALK - DO A SIGN 'O DA CROSS!
HEH-HEH-GOD STOPPED LISTENIN' T'ME JOKES A LONG TIME AGO, LAD!
...SIGN 'O DA CROSS ANYWAY MAN-IT WON'T KILL 'YA...!
MEANWHILE, DOWN IN THE CLEVELAND FLATS, A MAN IS WALKING ALONG THE WATERWORKS ROAD ON THE WEST BANK OF THE CUYAHOGA RIVER...
BREWERY
...CRIB SUPERINTENDENT, WILHELM "DUTCHMAN" VAN DYKE IS ON HIS WAY TO THE CLEVELAND WATERWORKS HEADQUARTERS UNAWARE THAT A TENSE DISCUSSION IS GOING ON INSIDE.

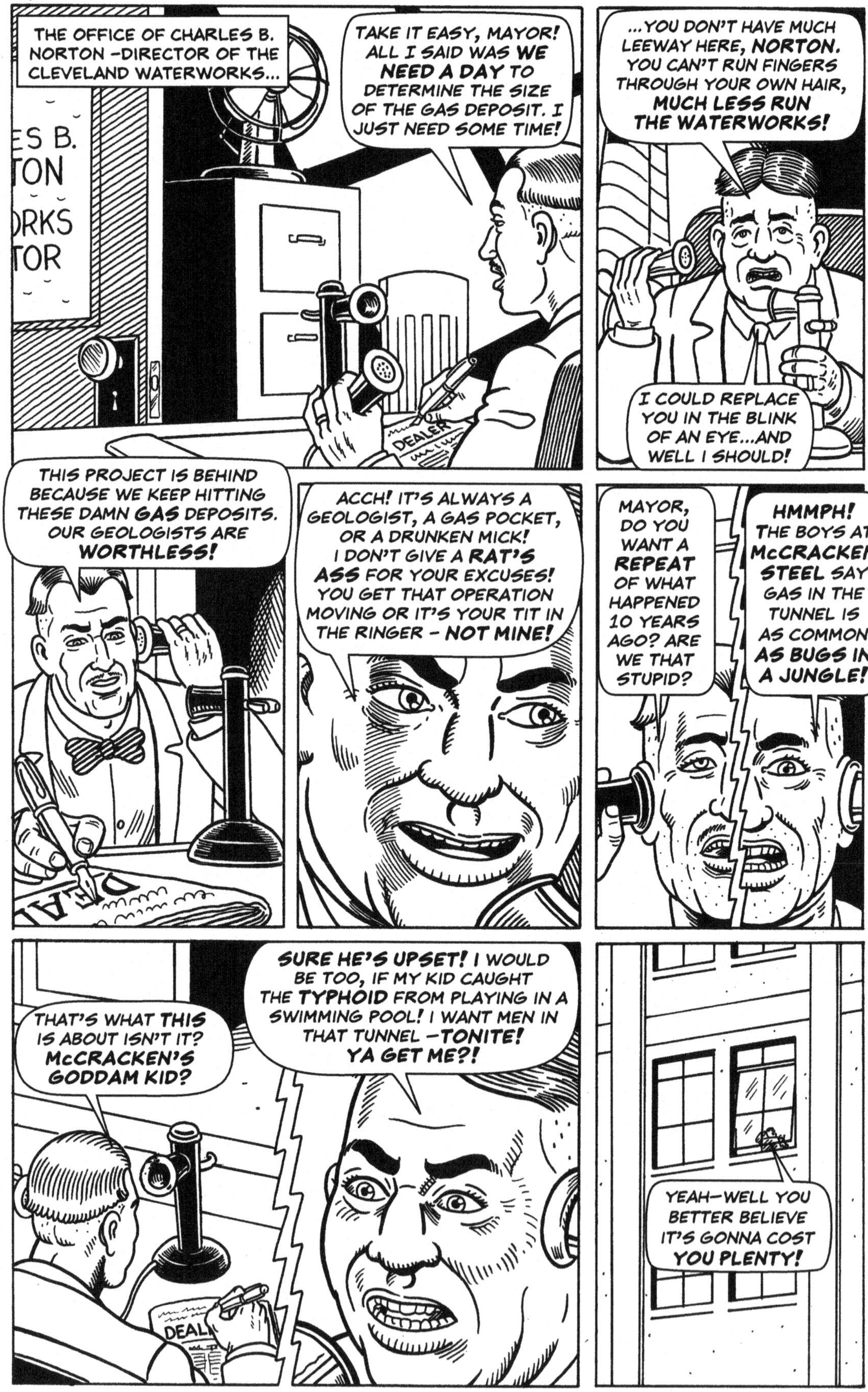
THE OFFICE OF CHARLES B. NORTON –DIRECTOR OF THE CLEVELAND WATERWORKS...
ES B.
TON
ORKS
TOR
TAKE IT EASY, MAYOR! ALL I SAID WAS WE NEED A DAY TO DETERMINE THE SIZE OF THE GAS DEPOSIT. I JUST NEED SOME TIME!
DEALER
...YOU DON'T HAVE MUCH LEEWAY HERE, NORTON. YOU CAN'T RUN FINGERS THROUGH YOUR OWN HAIR, MUCH LESS RUN THE WATERWORKS!
I COULD REPLACE YOU IN THE BLINK OF AN EYE...AND WELL I SHOULD!
THIS PROJECT IS BEHIND BECAUSE WE KEEP HITTING THESE DAMN GAS DEPOSITS. OUR GEOLOGISTS ARE WORTHLESS!
ACCH! IT'S ALWAYS A GEOLOGIST, A GAS POCKET, OR A DRUNKEN MICK! I DON'T GIVE A RAT'S ASS FOR YOUR EXCUSES! YOU GET THAT OPERATION MOVING OR IT'S YOUR TIT IN THE RINGER – NOT MINE!
MAYOR, DO YOU WANT A REPEAT OF WHAT HAPPENED 10 YEARS AGO? ARE WE THAT STUPID?
HMMPH! THE BOYS AT McCRACKEN STEEL SAY GAS IN THE TUNNEL IS AS COMMON AS BUGS IN A JUNGLE!
THAT'S WHAT THIS IS ABOUT ISN'T IT? McCRACKEN'S GODDAM KID?
SURE HE'S UPSET! I WOULD BE TOO, IF MY KID CAUGHT THE TYPHOID FROM PLAYING IN A SWIMMING POOL! I WANT MEN IN THAT TUNNEL –TONITE! YA GET ME?!
DEAL
YEAH—WELL YOU BETTER BELIEVE IT'S GONNA COST YOU PLENTY!

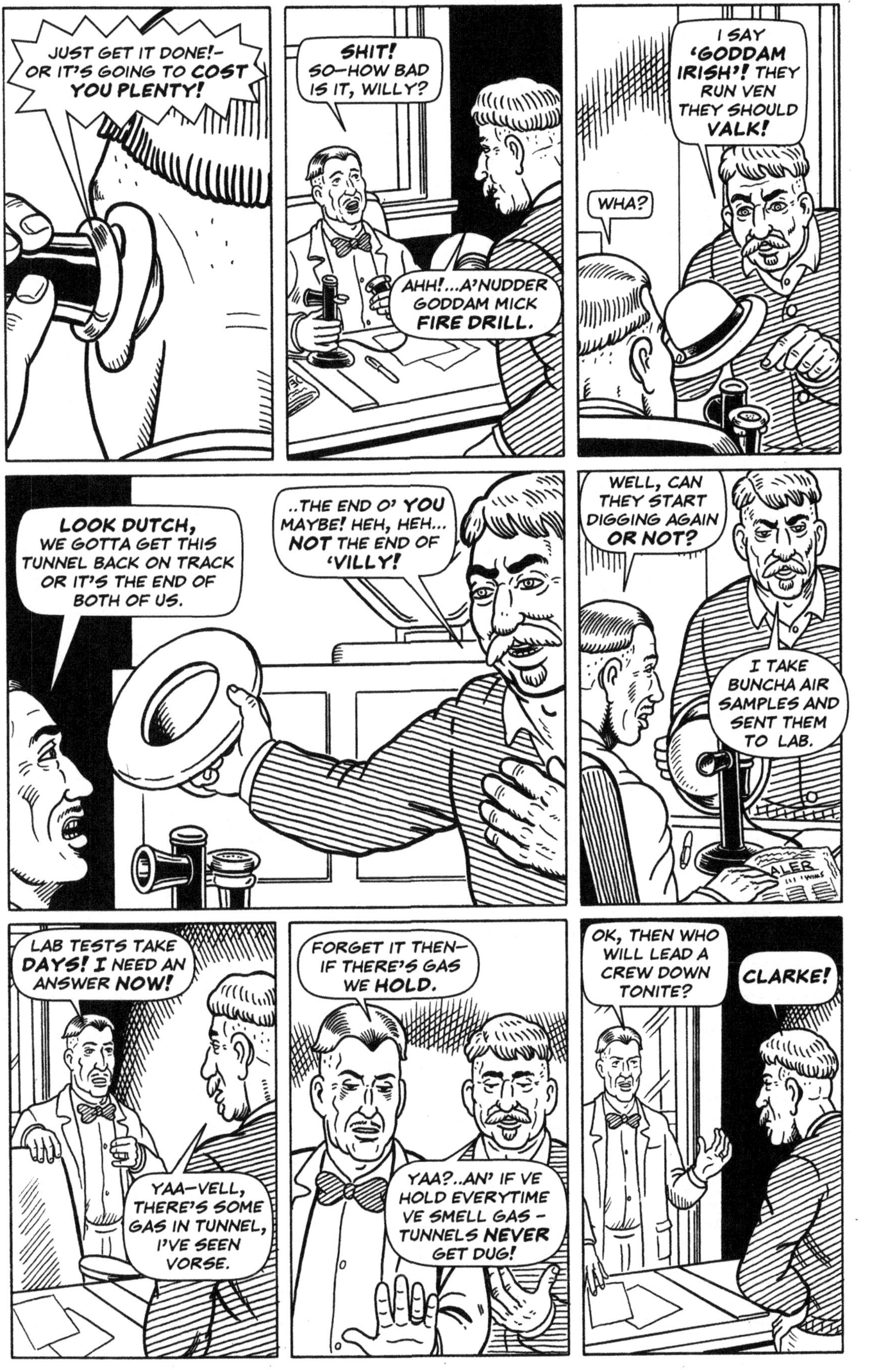

JUST GET IT DONE!- OR IT'S GOING TO COST YOU PLENTY!
SHIT! SO—HOW BAD IS IT, WILLY?
AHH!...A'NUDDER GODDAM MICK FIRE DRILL.
I SAY 'GODDAM IRISH'! THEY RUN VEN THEY SHOULD VALK!
WHA?
LOOK DUTCH, WE GOTTA GET THIS TUNNEL BACK ON TRACK OR IT'S THE END OF BOTH OF US.
..THE END O' YOU MAYBE! HEH, HEH... NOT THE END OF 'VILLY!
WELL, CAN THEY START DIGGING AGAIN OR NOT?
I TAKE BUNCHA AIR SAMPLES AND SENT THEM TO LAB.
LAB TESTS TAKE DAYS! I NEED AN ANSWER NOW!
YAA—VELL, THERE'S SOME GAS IN TUNNEL, I'VE SEEN VORSE.
FORGET IT THEN— IF THERE'S GAS WE HOLD.
YAA?..AN' IF VE HOLD EVERYTIME VE SMELL GAS - TUNNELS NEVER GET DUG!
OK, THEN WHO WILL LEAD A CREW DOWN TONITE?
CLARKE!

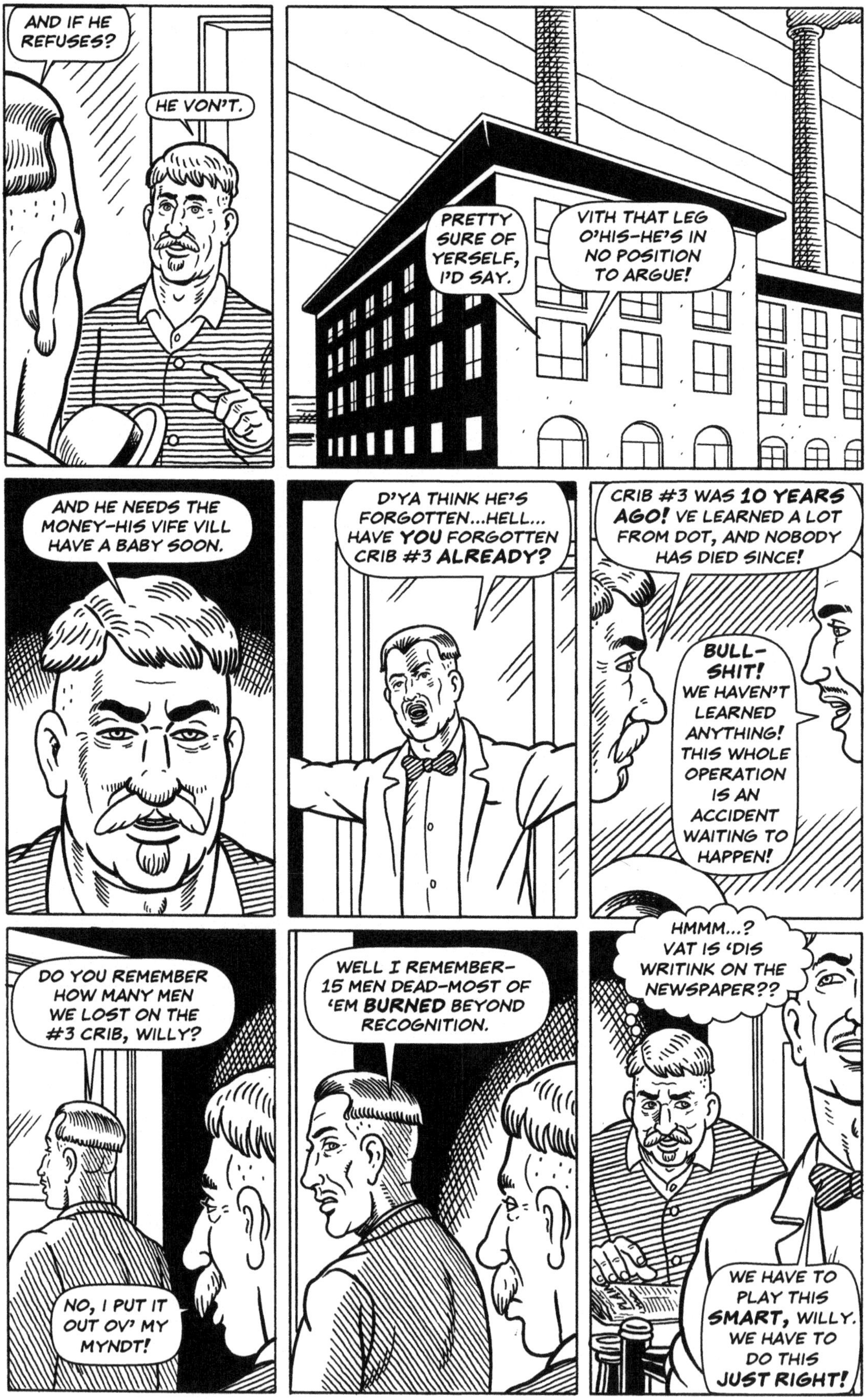
AND IF HE REFUSES?
HE VON'T.
PRETTY SURE OF YERSELF, I'D SAY.
VITH THAT LEG O'HIS–HE'S IN NO POSITION TO ARGUE!
AND HE NEEDS THE MONEY–HIS VIFE VILL HAVE A BABY SOON.
D'YA THINK HE'S FORGOTTEN...HELL... HAVE YOU FORGOTTEN CRIB #3 ALREADY?
CRIB #3 WAS 10 YEARS AGO! VE LEARNED A LOT FROM DOT, AND NOBODY HAS DIED SINCE!
BULL-SHIT! WE HAVEN'T LEARNED ANYTHING! THIS WHOLE OPERATION IS AN ACCIDENT WAITING TO HAPPEN!
DO YOU REMEMBER HOW MANY MEN WE LOST ON THE #3 CRIB, WILLY?
NO, I PUT IT OUT OV' MY MYNDT!
WELL I REMEMBER– 15 MEN DEAD–MOST OF 'EM BURNED BEYOND RECOGNITION.
HMMM...? VAT IS 'DIS WRITINK ON THE NEWSPAPER??
WE HAVE TO PLAY THIS SMART, WILLY. WE HAVE TO DO THIS JUST RIGHT!

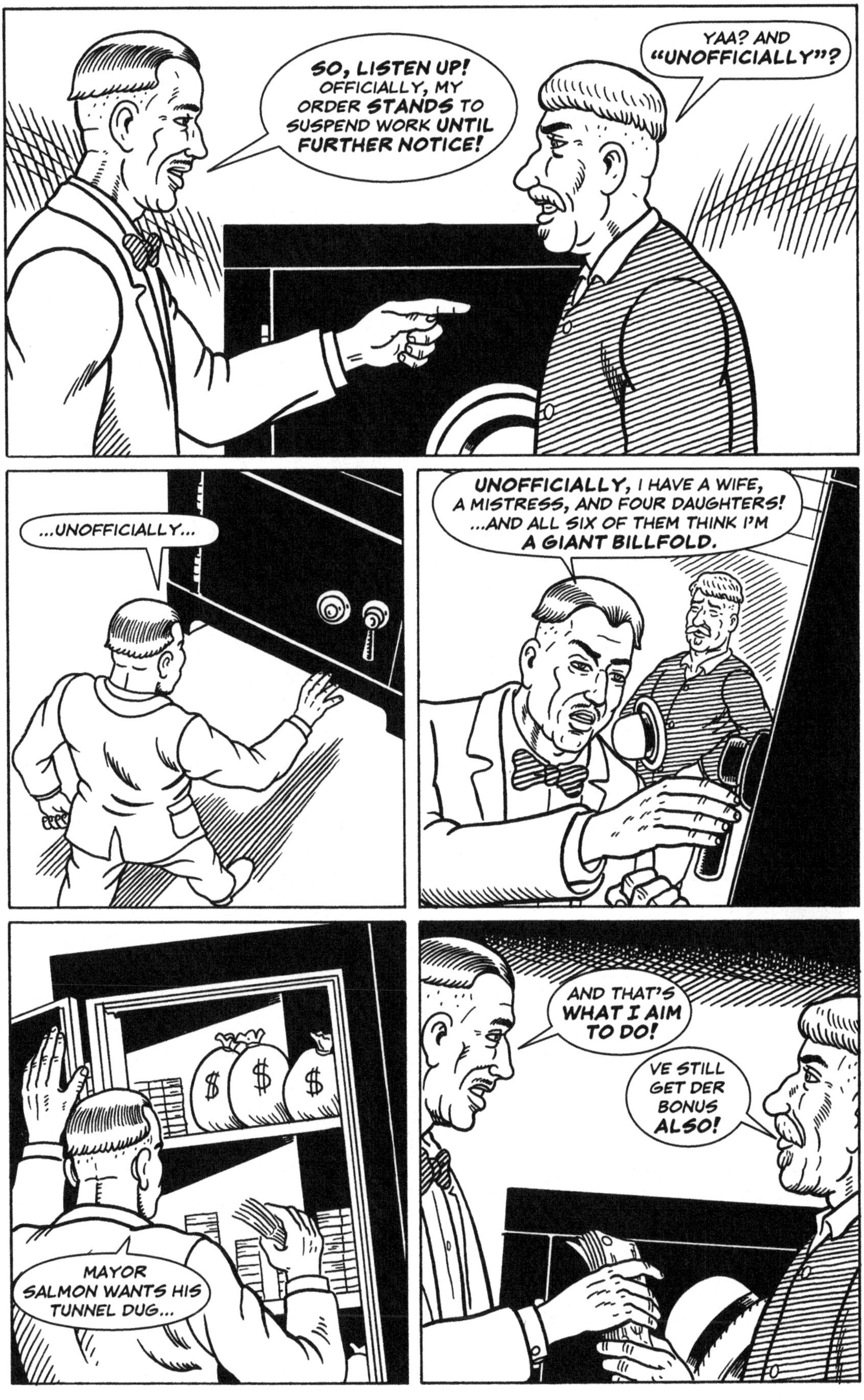
SO, LISTEN UP! OFFICIALLY, MY ORDER STANDS TO SUSPEND WORK UNTIL FURTHER NOTICE!
YAA? AND "UNOFFICIALLY"?
...UNOFFICIALLY...
UNOFFICIALLY, I HAVE A WIFE, A MISTRESS, AND FOUR DAUGHTERS! ...AND ALL SIX OF THEM THINK I'M A GIANT BILLFOLD.
MAYOR SALMON WANTS HIS TUNNEL DUG...
AND THAT'S WHAT I AIM TO DO!
VE STILL GET DER BONUS ALSO!

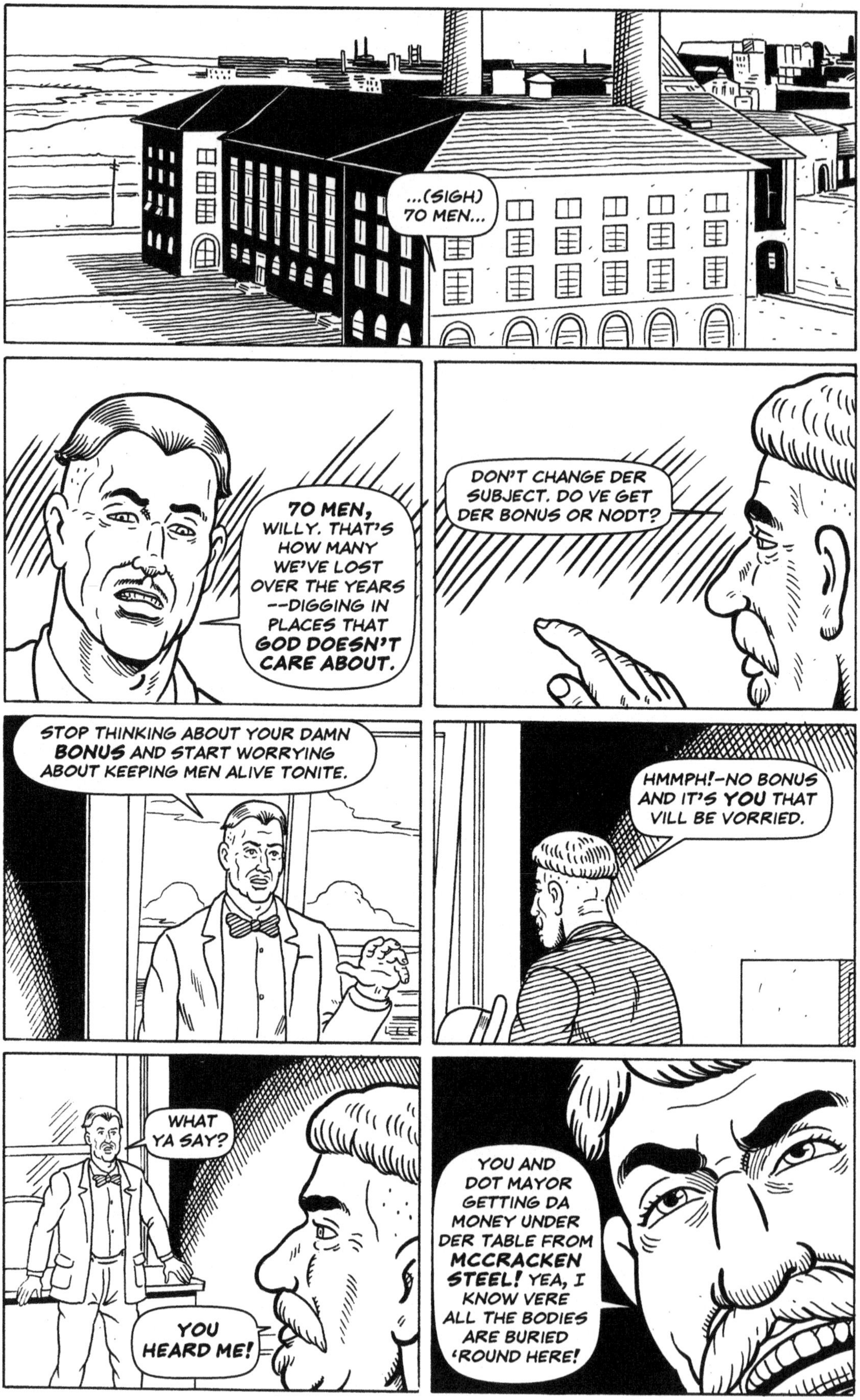
...(SIGH) 70 MEN...
70 MEN, WILLY. THAT'S HOW MANY WE'VE LOST OVER THE YEARS --DIGGING IN PLACES THAT GOD DOESN'T CARE ABOUT.
DON'T CHANGE DER SUBJECT. DO VE GET DER BONUS OR NODT?
STOP THINKING ABOUT YOUR DAMN BONUS AND START WORRYING ABOUT KEEPING MEN ALIVE TONITE.
HMMPH!-NO BONUS AND IT'S YOU THAT VILL BE VORRIED.
WHAT YA SAY?
YOU HEARD ME!
YOU AND DOT MAYOR GETTING DA MONEY UNDER DER TABLE FROM MCCRACKEN STEEL! YEA, I KNOW VERE ALL THE BODIES ARE BURIED 'ROUND HERE!

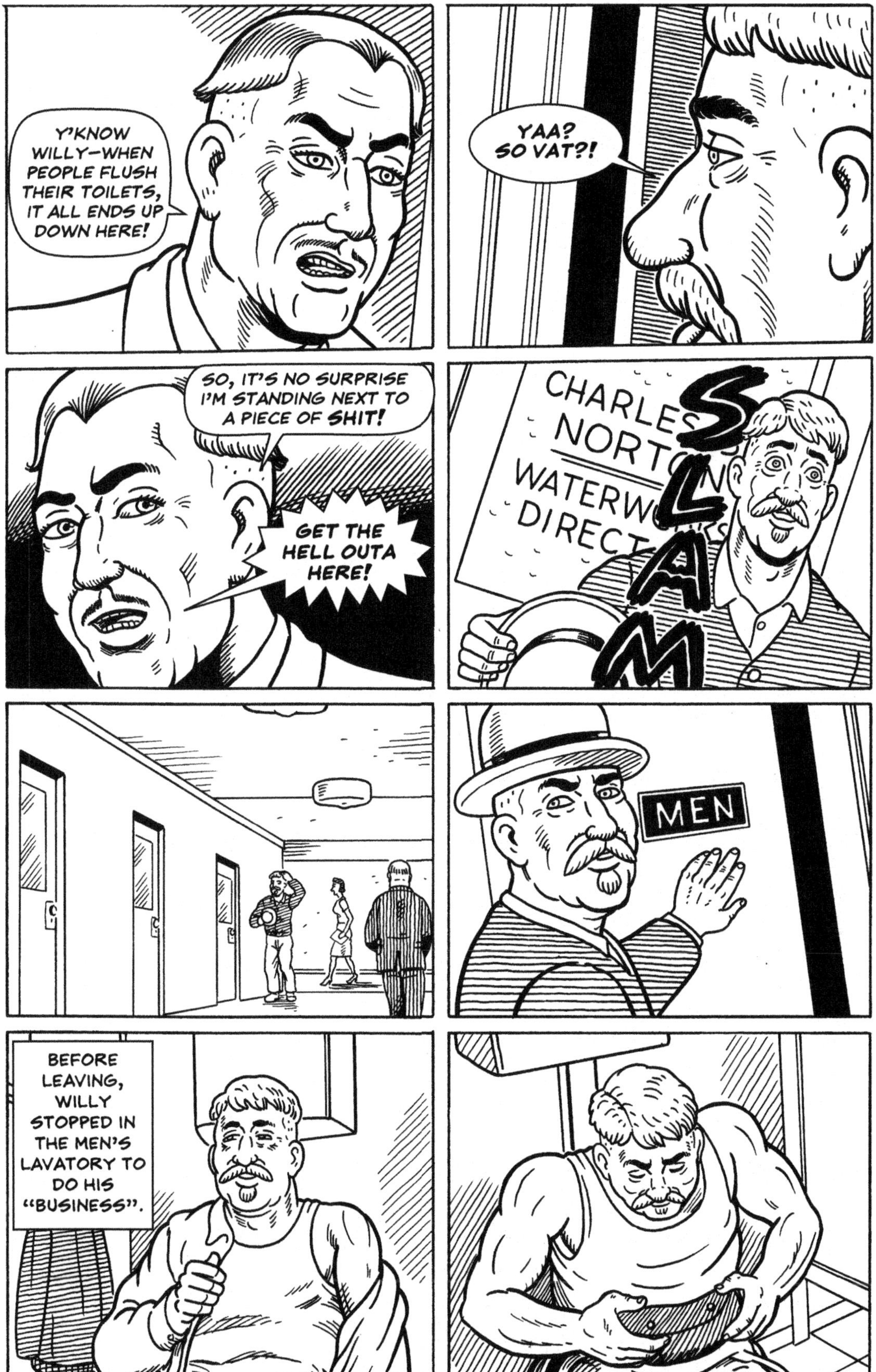

Y'KNOW WILLY—WHEN PEOPLE FLUSH THEIR TOILETS, IT ALL ENDS UP DOWN HERE!
YAA? SO VAT?!
SO, IT'S NO SURPRISE I'M STANDING NEXT TO A PIECE OF SHIT!
GET THE HELL OUTA HERE!
CHARLES NORTON WATERWORKS DIRECTOR
SLAM
MEN
BEFORE LEAVING, WILLY STOPPED IN THE MEN'S LAVATORY TO DO HIS "BUSINESS".

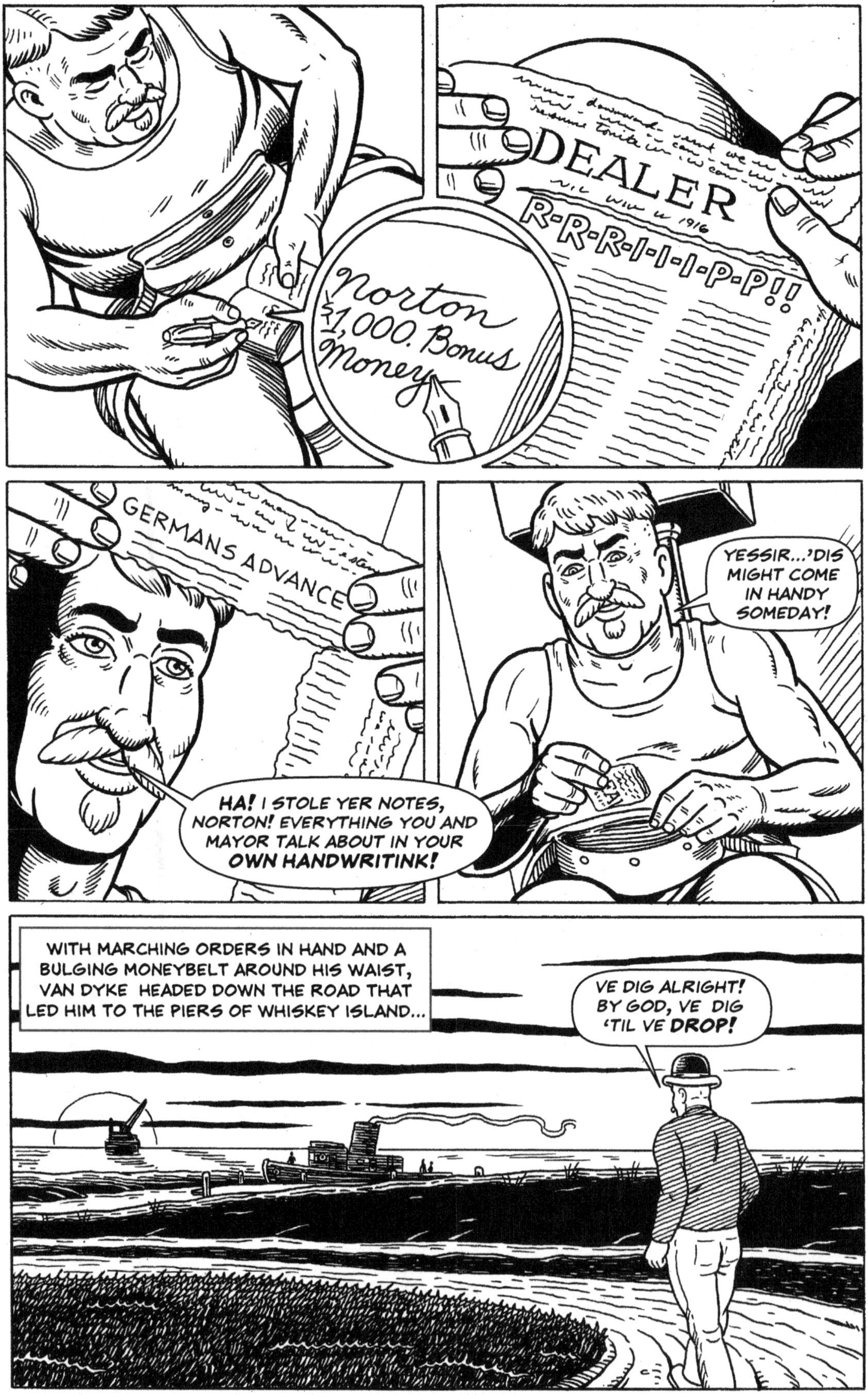
DEALER
R-R-R-I-I-I-P-P!!
Norton
$1,000. Bonus
Money
GERMANS ADVANCE
HA! I STOLE YER NOTES, NORTON! EVERYTHING YOU AND MAYOR TALK ABOUT IN YOUR OWN HANDWRITINK!
YESSIR...'DIS MIGHT COME IN HANDY SOMEDAY!
WITH MARCHING ORDERS IN HAND AND A BULGING MONEYBELT AROUND HIS WAIST, VAN DYKE HEADED DOWN THE ROAD THAT LED HIM TO THE PIERS OF WHISKEY ISLAND...
VE DIG ALRIGHT! BY GOD, VE DIG 'TIL VE DROP!

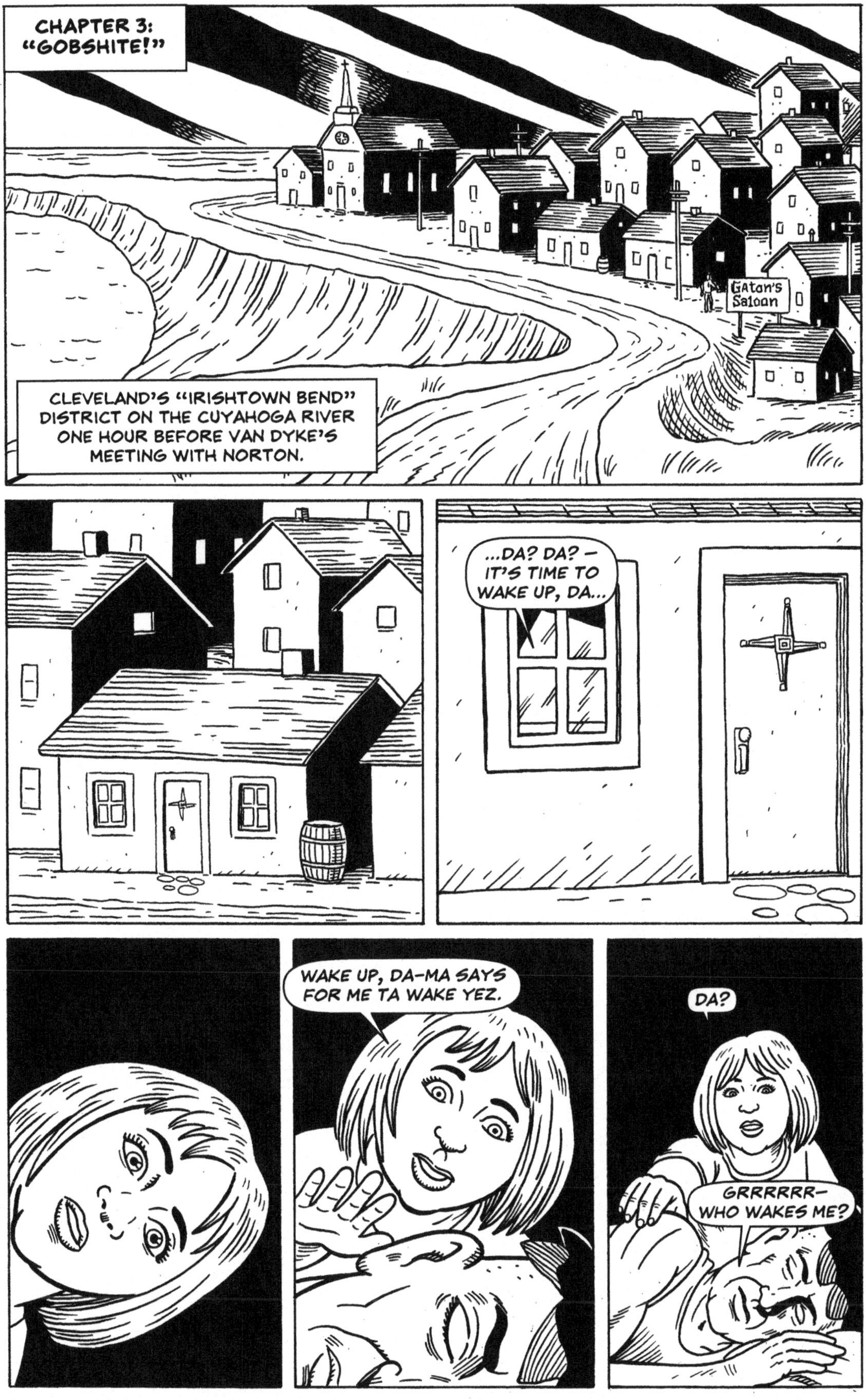
CHAPTER 3: "GOBSHITE!"
Gatan's Saloon
CLEVELAND'S "IRISHTOWN BEND" DISTRICT ON THE CUYAHOGA RIVER ONE HOUR BEFORE VAN DYKE'S MEETING WITH NORTON.
...DA? DA? — IT'S TIME TO WAKE UP, DA...
WAKE UP, DA—MA SAYS FOR ME TA WAKE YEZ.
DA?
GRRRRRR— WHO WAKES ME?

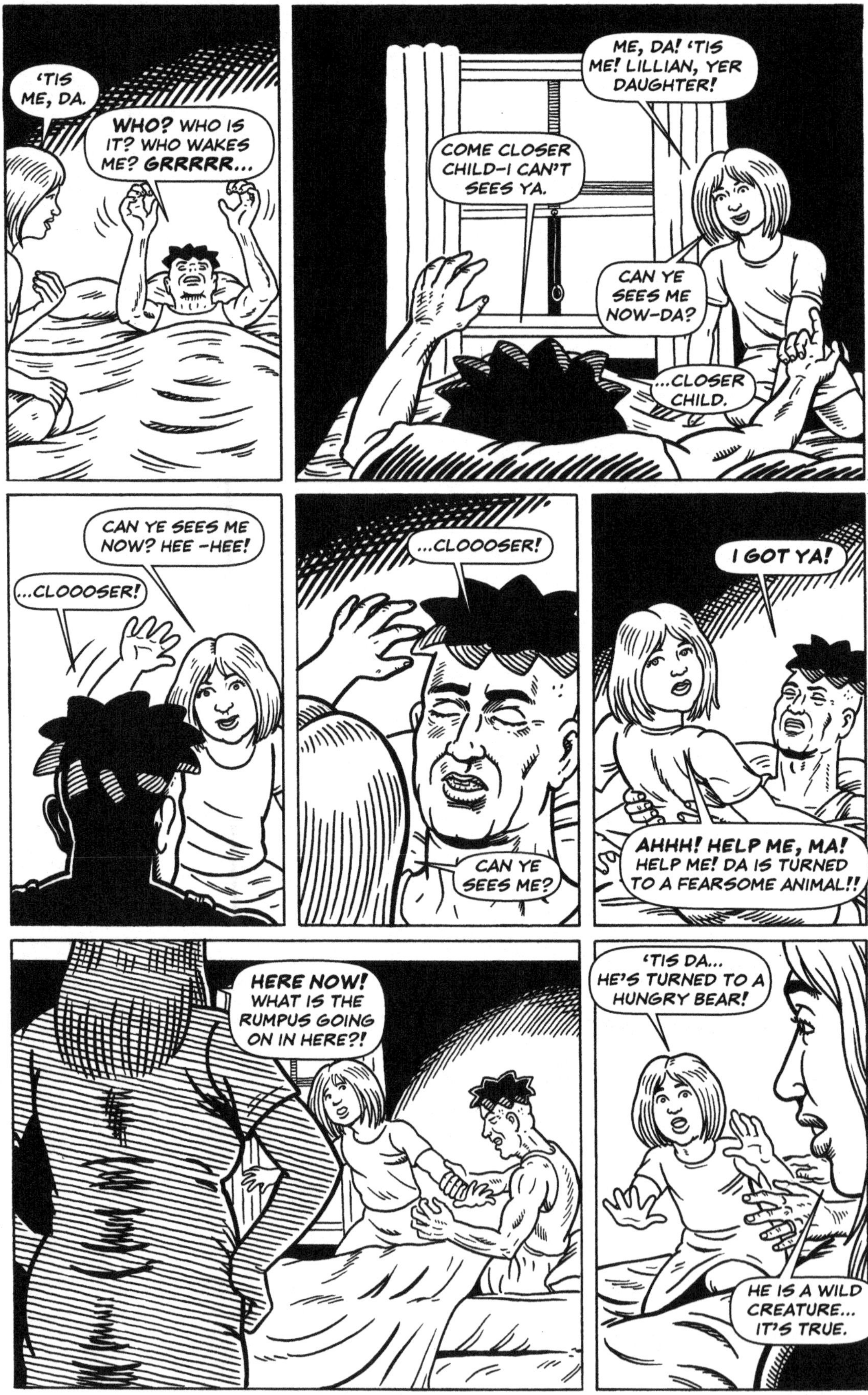
'TIS ME, DA.
WHO? WHO IS IT? WHO WAKES ME? GRRRRR...
ME, DA! 'TIS ME! LILLIAN, YER DAUGHTER!
COME CLOSER CHILD-I CAN'T SEES YA.
CAN YE SEES ME NOW-DA?
...CLOSER CHILD.
CAN YE SEES ME NOW? HEE -HEE!
...CLOOOSER!
...CLOOOSER!
CAN YE SEES ME?
I GOT YA!
AHHH! HELP ME, MA! HELP ME! DA IS TURNED TO A FEARSOME ANIMAL!!
HERE NOW! WHAT IS THE RUMPUS GOING ON IN HERE?!
'TIS DA... HE'S TURNED TO A HUNGRY BEAR!
HE IS A WILD CREATURE... IT'S TRUE.

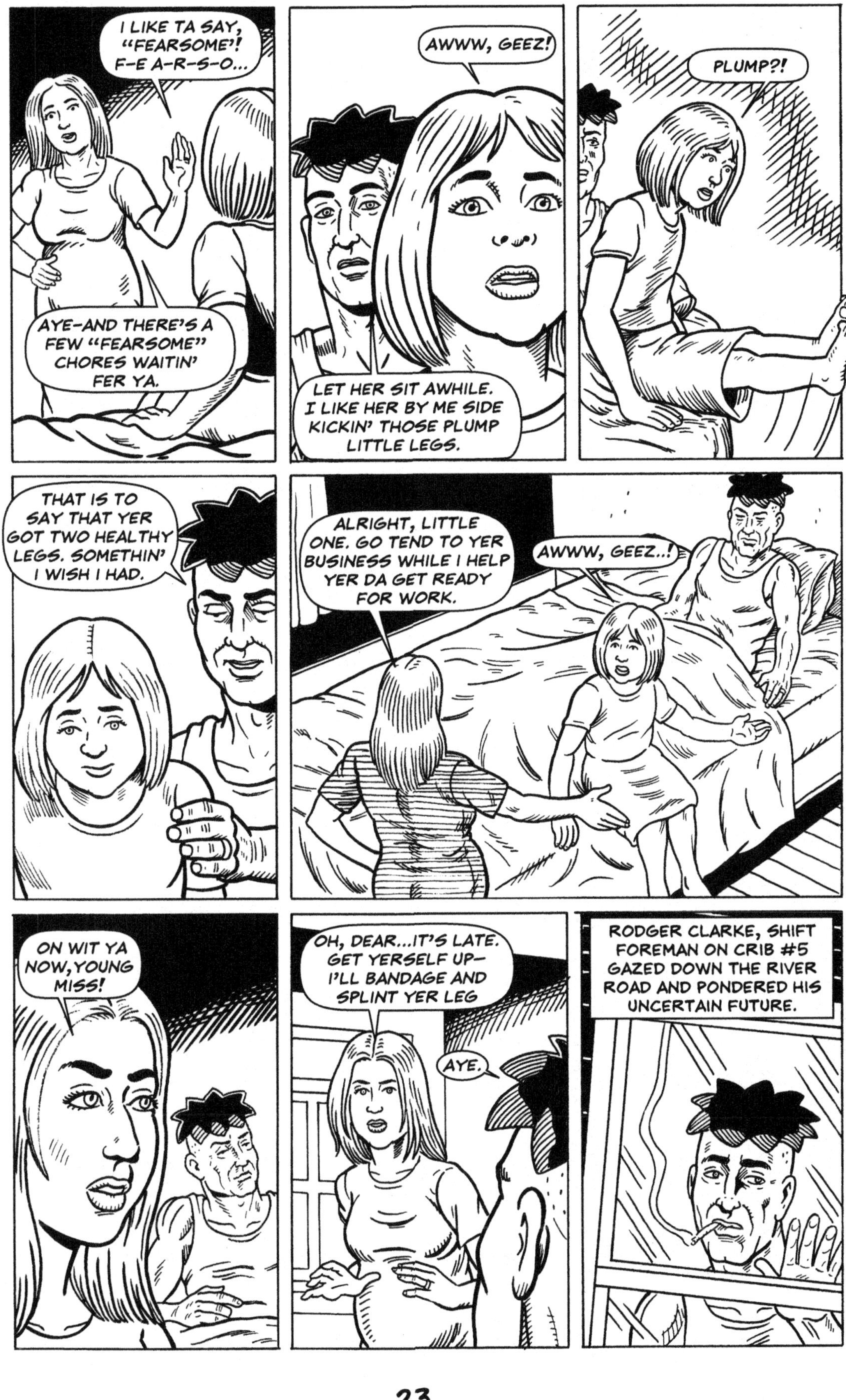
I LIKE TA SAY, "FEARSOME"! F-E A-R-S-O...
AYE-AND THERE'S A FEW "FEARSOME" CHORES WAITIN' FER YA.
AWWW, GEEZ!
LET HER SIT AWHILE. I LIKE HER BY ME SIDE KICKIN' THOSE PLUMP LITTLE LEGS.
PLUMP?!
THAT IS TO SAY THAT YER GOT TWO HEALTHY LEGS. SOMETHIN' I WISH I HAD.
ALRIGHT, LITTLE ONE. GO TEND TO YER BUSINESS WHILE I HELP YER DA GET READY FOR WORK.
AWWW, GEEZ...!
ON WIT YA NOW, YOUNG MISS!
OH, DEAR...IT'S LATE. GET YERSELF UP- I'LL BANDAGE AND SPLINT YER LEG
AYE.
RODGER CLARKE, SHIFT FOREMAN ON CRIB #5 GAZED DOWN THE RIVER ROAD AND PONDERED HIS UNCERTAIN FUTURE.

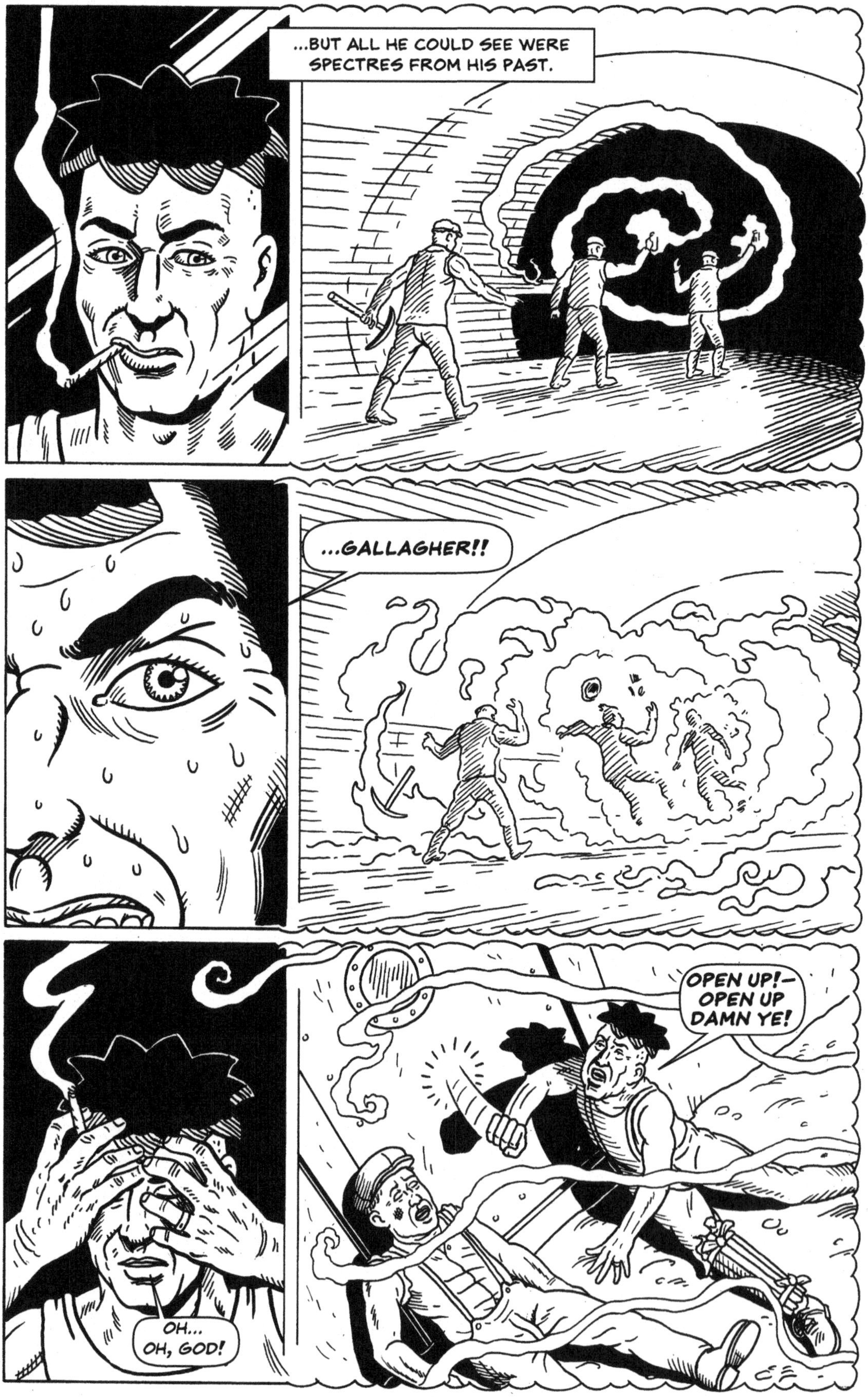
...BUT ALL HE COULD SEE WERE SPECTRES FROM HIS PAST.
...GALLAGHER!!
OH... OH, GOD!
OPEN UP!— OPEN UP DAMN YE!

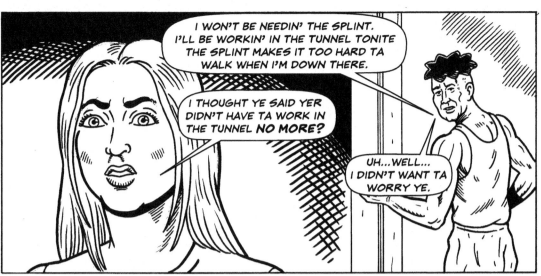

I WON'T BE NEEDIN' THE SPLINT. I'LL BE WORKIN' IN THE TUNNEL TONITE THE SPLINT MAKES IT TOO HARD TA WALK WHEN I'M DOWN THERE.

I THOUGHT YE SAID YER DIDN'T HAVE TA WORK IN THE TUNNEL **NO MORE?**

UH...WELL... I DIDN'T WANT TA WORRY YE.

YE SHOULDN'T LIE ABOUT IT. IT **HURTS** ME WHEN YE DO.

AHH...**NOT TA WORRY**...WE'RE BEHIND SCHEDULE AND **DUTCH** NEEDS ME TO KEEP A CLOSE EYE ON THE MEN. --IT'S THE EASIEST JOB ON THE CRIB!

AHH, I MIGHTA KNOWN IT WAS **THAT CREATURE.**

THERE'S NOTHIN' I CAN SAY...**HE'S THE BOSS.**

HE'S A GOBSHITE! HE COMES FROM THE LOWER REGIONS...

WELL, THAT MAY BE SO, BUT HE'S MY **GOBSHITE.** I WOULDN'T BE HERE IF IT WEREN'T FOR HIM.

AYE...AND HE'LL NEVER LET YE FORGET IT **WILL HE?** TELL ME...WHAT'S IN IT FER YA?

WELL... THERE IS TALK OF MONEY, YES.

THERE'S ALWAYS TALK...THE CRIB IS FULL OF TALK...FER THE LOVE O' PETE, YER LEG ISN'T FIT FER TUNNEL WORK!...

I DON'T LIKE IT WHEN YOU ARE MAD-**BOTH OF YOU!**

25

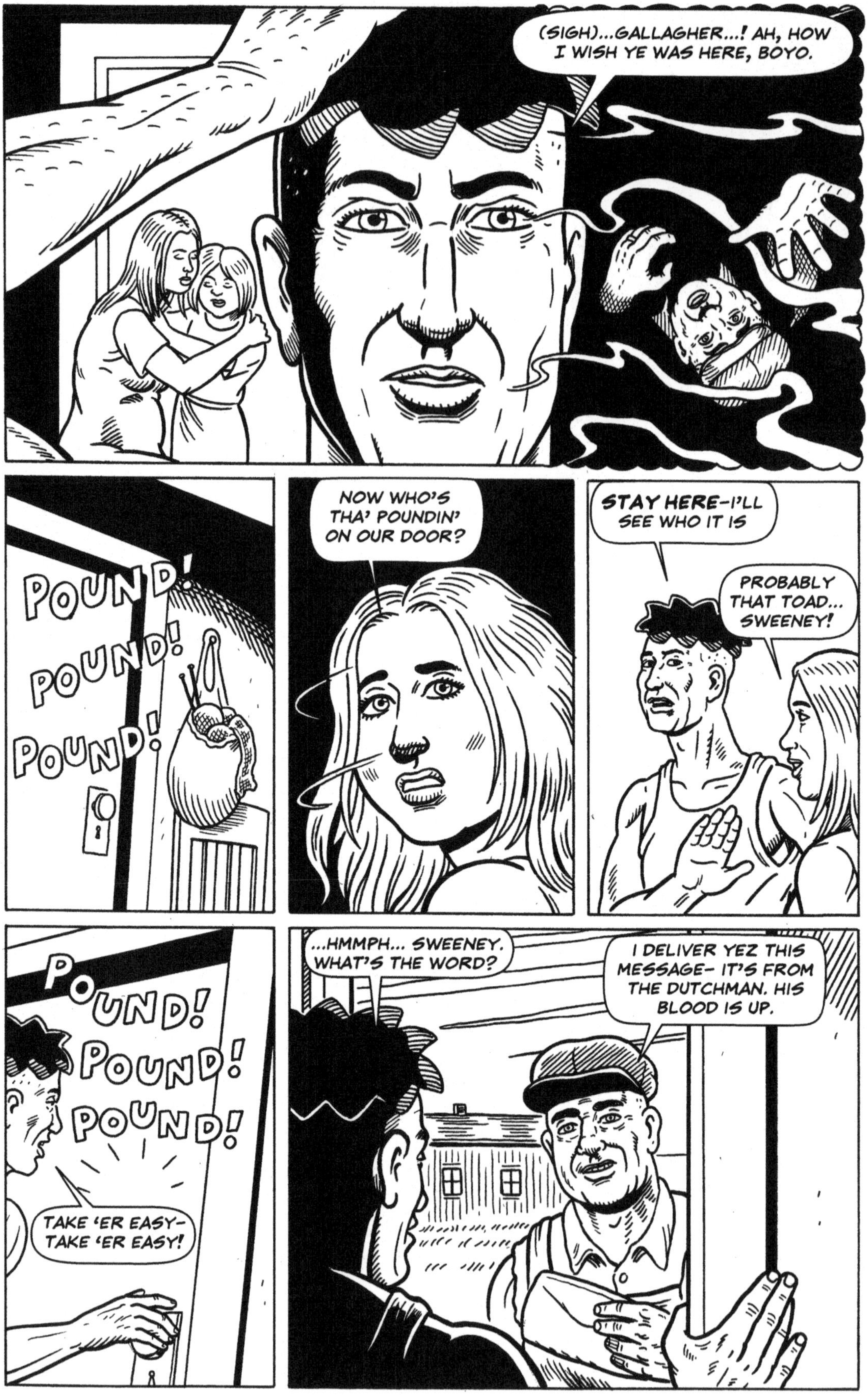
(SIGH)...GALLAGHER...! AH, HOW I WISH YE WAS HERE, BOYO.
POUND! POUND! POUND!
NOW WHO'S THA' POUNDIN' ON OUR DOOR?
STAY HERE-I'LL SEE WHO IT IS
PROBABLY THAT TOAD... SWEENEY!
POUND! POUND! POUND!
TAKE 'ER EASY-TAKE 'ER EASY!
...HMMPH... SWEENEY. WHAT'S THE WORD?
I DELIVER YEZ THIS MESSAGE- IT'S FROM THE DUTCHMAN. HIS BLOOD IS UP.

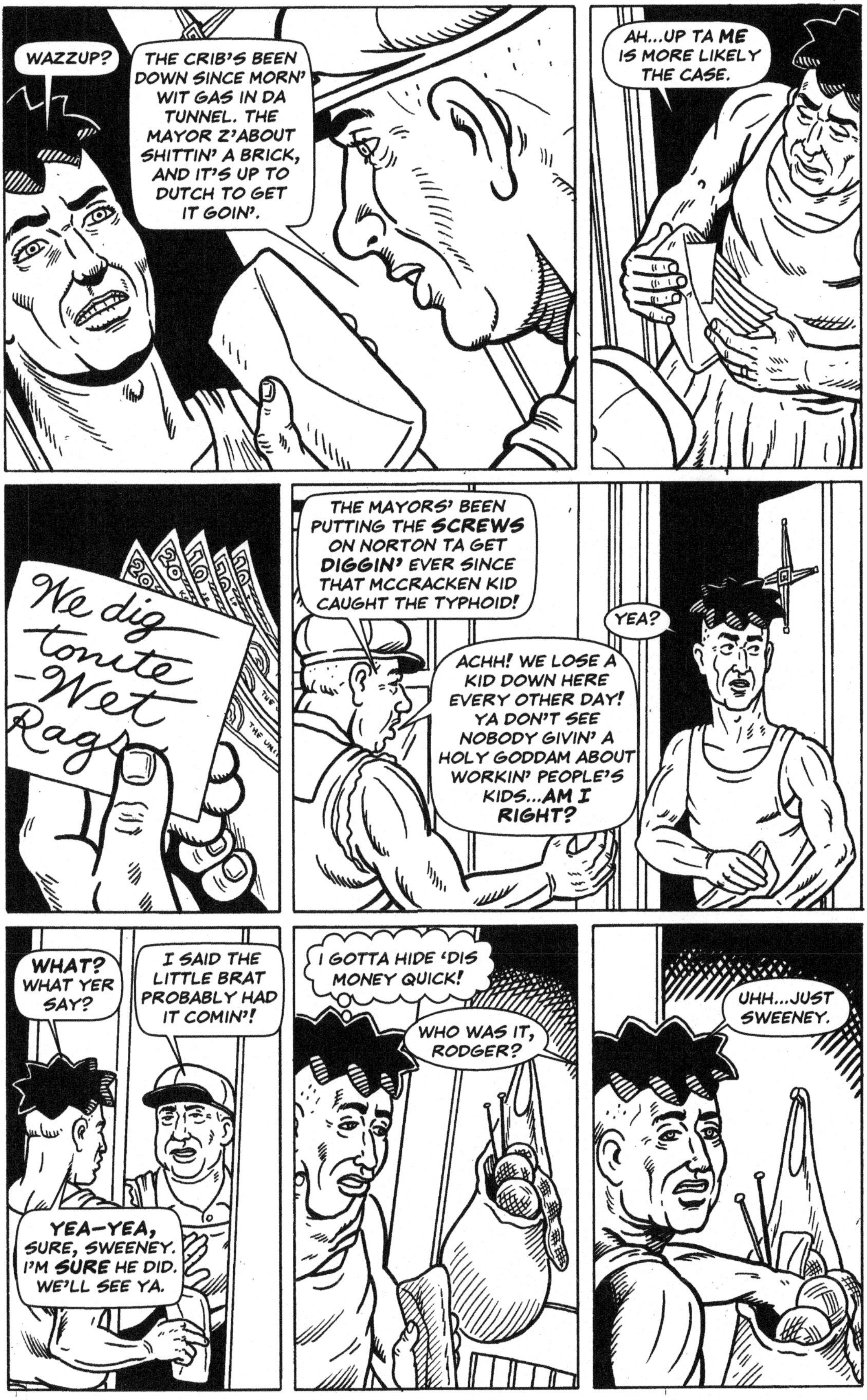
WAZZUP?
THE CRIB'S BEEN DOWN SINCE MORN' WIT GAS IN DA TUNNEL. THE MAYOR Z'ABOUT SHITTIN' A BRICK, AND IT'S UP TO DUTCH TO GET IT GOIN'.
AH...UP TA ME IS MORE LIKELY THE CASE.
We dig tonite -Wet Rags
THE MAYORS' BEEN PUTTING THE SCREWS ON NORTON TA GET DIGGIN' EVER SINCE THAT MCCRACKEN KID CAUGHT THE TYPHOID!
YEA?
ACHH! WE LOSE A KID DOWN HERE EVERY OTHER DAY! YA DON'T SEE NOBODY GIVIN' A HOLY GODDAM ABOUT WORKIN' PEOPLE'S KIDS...AM I RIGHT?
WHAT? WHAT YER SAY?
I SAID THE LITTLE BRAT PROBABLY HAD IT COMIN'!
YEA-YEA, SURE, SWEENEY. I'M SURE HE DID. WE'LL SEE YA.
I GOTTA HIDE 'DIS MONEY QUICK!
WHO WAS IT, RODGER?
UHH...JUST SWEENEY.

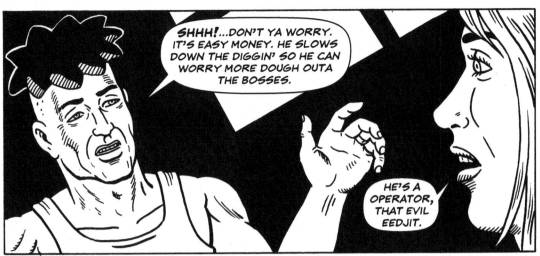

SHHH!...DON'T YA WORRY. IT'S EASY MONEY. HE SLOWS DOWN THE DIGGIN' SO HE CAN WORRY MORE DOUGH OUTA THE BOSSES.

HE'S A OPERATOR, THAT EVIL EEDJIT.

AHH...YOU WATCH. WE'LL PROBABLY BE PAID FER PLAYIN' CARDS ALL NIGHT!!

WHAT ELSE DOES HE KEEP IN THE MONEYBELT B'SIDES MONEY?

HE SQUARRELS AWAY EVERYTHING IMAGINABLE—I THINK HE EVEN KEEPS HIS FALSE TEETH IN IT.

HEE HEE!

AHH! NOW THERE'S YER BEAUTIFUL SMILE GOIN' THERE.

AYE—I'M A LUCKY MAN TA HAVE TWO BEAUTIFUL WOMEN TA LOOK AFTER ME!

I NEED A CUP 'O SOMETHIN' BEFORE I GO. HOW 'BOUT SOME TEA?

TEA IT IS! YOUNG LIL AND I WILL SET SOME WATER TA BOIL!

29

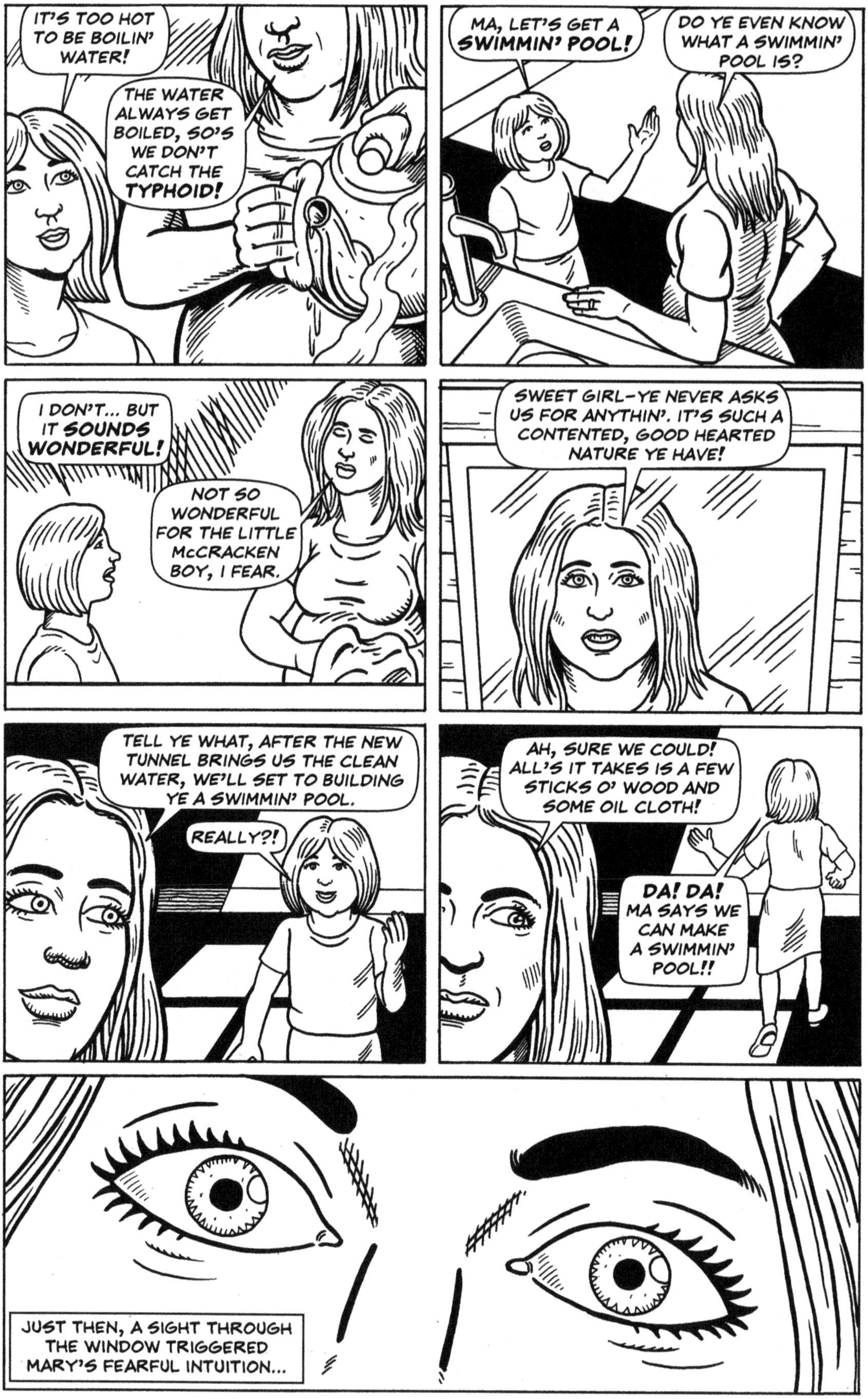
IT'S TOO HOT TO BE BOILIN' WATER!
THE WATER ALWAYS GET BOILED, SO'S WE DON'T CATCH THE TYPHOID!
MA, LET'S GET A SWIMMIN' POOL!
DO YE EVEN KNOW WHAT A SWIMMIN' POOL IS?
I DON'T... BUT IT SOUNDS WONDERFUL!
NOT SO WONDERFUL FOR THE LITTLE McCRACKEN BOY, I FEAR.
SWEET GIRL-YE NEVER ASKS US FOR ANYTHIN'. IT'S SUCH A CONTENTED, GOOD HEARTED NATURE YE HAVE!
TELL YE WHAT, AFTER THE NEW TUNNEL BRINGS US THE CLEAN WATER, WE'LL SET TO BUILDING YE A SWIMMIN' POOL.
REALLY?!
AH, SURE WE COULD! ALL'S IT TAKES IS A FEW STICKS O' WOOD AND SOME OIL CLOTH!
DA! DA! MA SAYS WE CAN MAKE A SWIMMIN' POOL!!
JUST THEN, A SIGHT THROUGH THE WINDOW TRIGGERED MARY'S FEARFUL INTUITION...

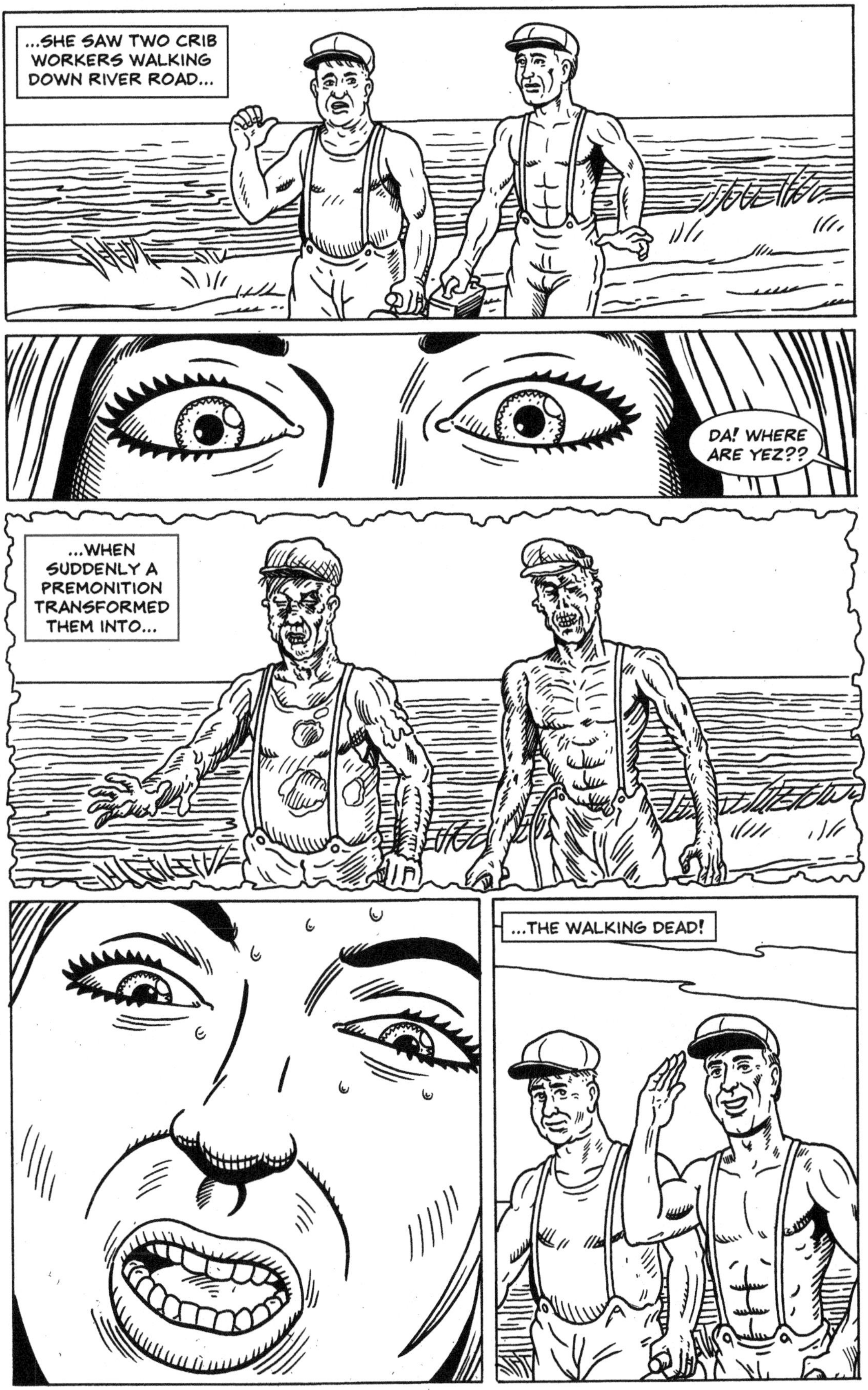
...SHE SAW TWO CRIB WORKERS WALKING DOWN RIVER ROAD...
DA! WHERE ARE YEZ??
...WHEN SUDDENLY A PREMONITION TRANSFORMED THEM INTO...
...THE WALKING DEAD!

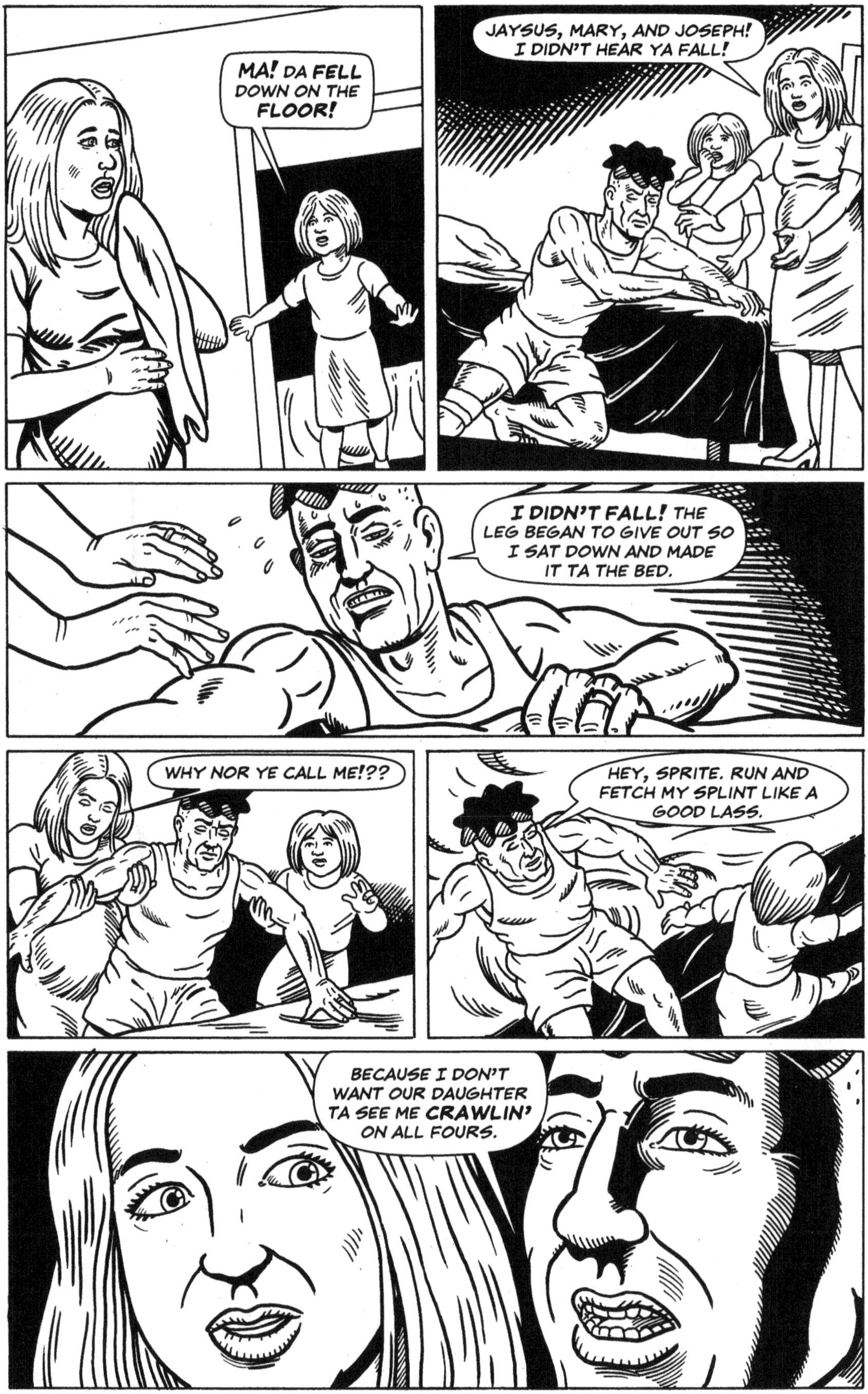
MA! DA FELL DOWN ON THE FLOOR!
JAYSUS, MARY, AND JOSEPH! I DIDN'T HEAR YA FALL!
I DIDN'T FALL! THE LEG BEGAN TO GIVE OUT SO I SAT DOWN AND MADE IT TA THE BED.
WHY NOR YE CALL ME!??
HEY, SPRITE. RUN AND FETCH MY SPLINT LIKE A GOOD LASS.
BECAUSE I DON'T WANT OUR DAUGHTER TA SEE ME CRAWLIN' ON ALL FOURS.

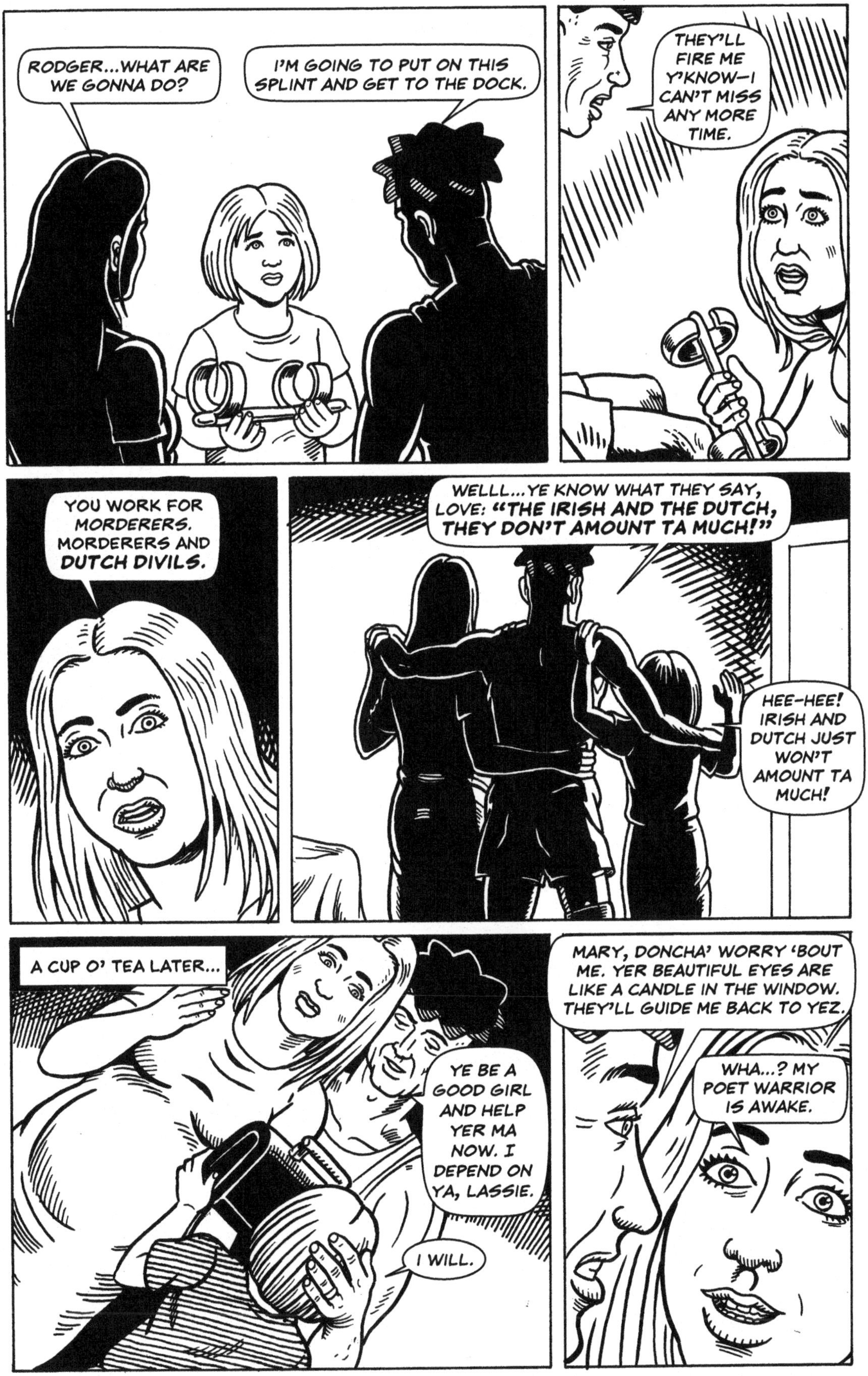
RODGER...WHAT ARE WE GONNA DO?
I'M GOING TO PUT ON THIS SPLINT AND GET TO THE DOCK.
THEY'LL FIRE ME Y'KNOW—I CAN'T MISS ANY MORE TIME.
YOU WORK FOR MORDERERS. MORDERERS AND DUTCH DIVILS.
WELLL...YE KNOW WHAT THEY SAY, LOVE: "THE IRISH AND THE DUTCH, THEY DON'T AMOUNT TA MUCH!"
HEE-HEE! IRISH AND DUTCH JUST WON'T AMOUNT TA MUCH!
A CUP O' TEA LATER...
YE BE A GOOD GIRL AND HELP YER MA NOW. I DEPEND ON YA, LASSIE.
I WILL.
MARY, DONCHA' WORRY 'BOUT ME. YER BEAUTIFUL EYES ARE LIKE A CANDLE IN THE WINDOW. THEY'LL GUIDE ME BACK TO YEZ.
WHA...? MY POET WARRIOR IS AWAKE.

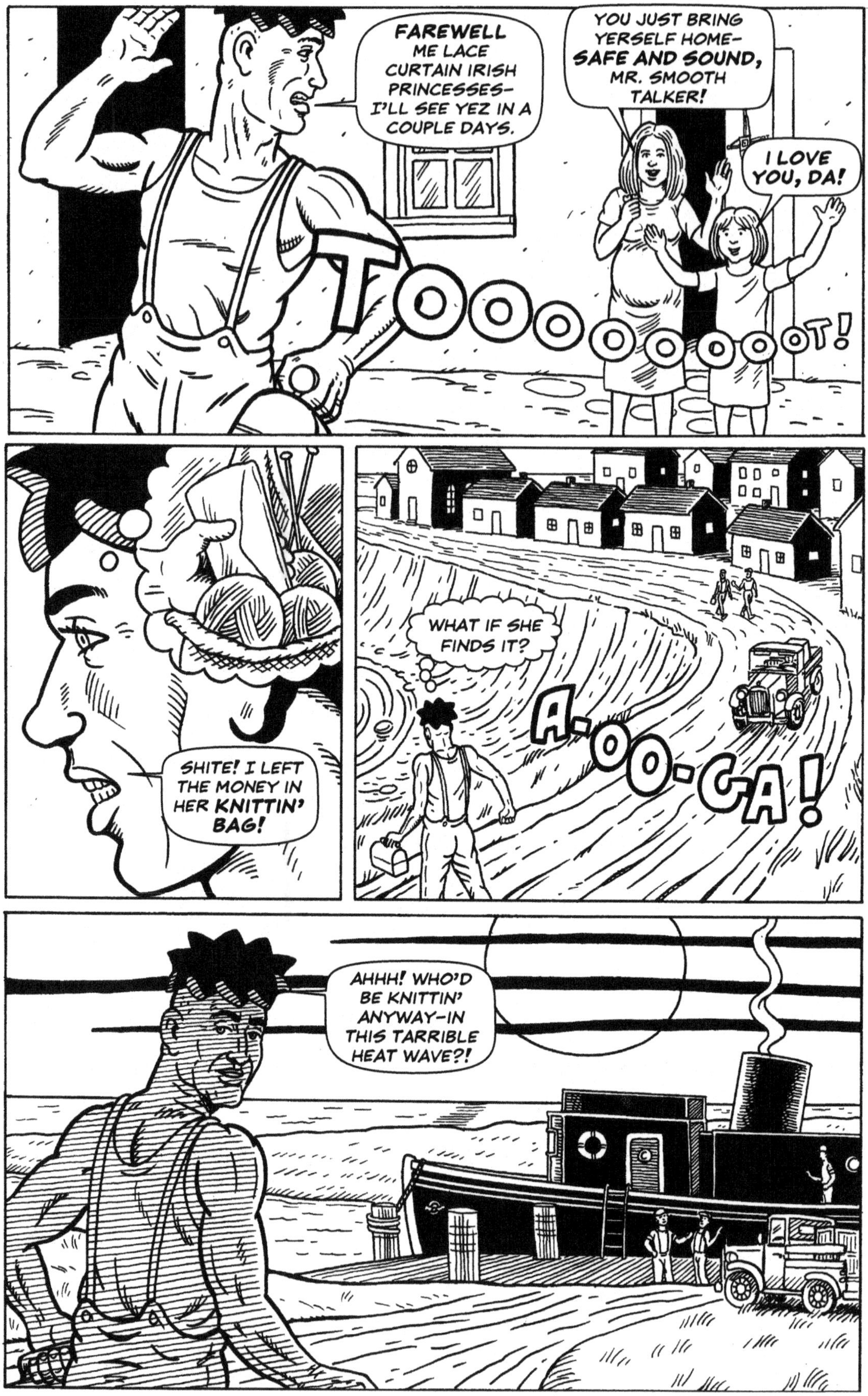
FAREWELL ME LACE CURTAIN IRISH PRINCESSES- I'LL SEE YEZ IN A COUPLE DAYS.
YOU JUST BRING YERSELF HOME- SAFE AND SOUND, MR. SMOOTH TALKER!
I LOVE YOU, DA!
TOOOOOOOOT!
SHITE! I LEFT THE MONEY IN HER KNITTIN' BAG!
WHAT IF SHE FINDS IT?
A-OO-GA!
AHHH! WHO'D BE KNITTIN' ANYWAY-IN THIS TARRIBLE HEAT WAVE?!

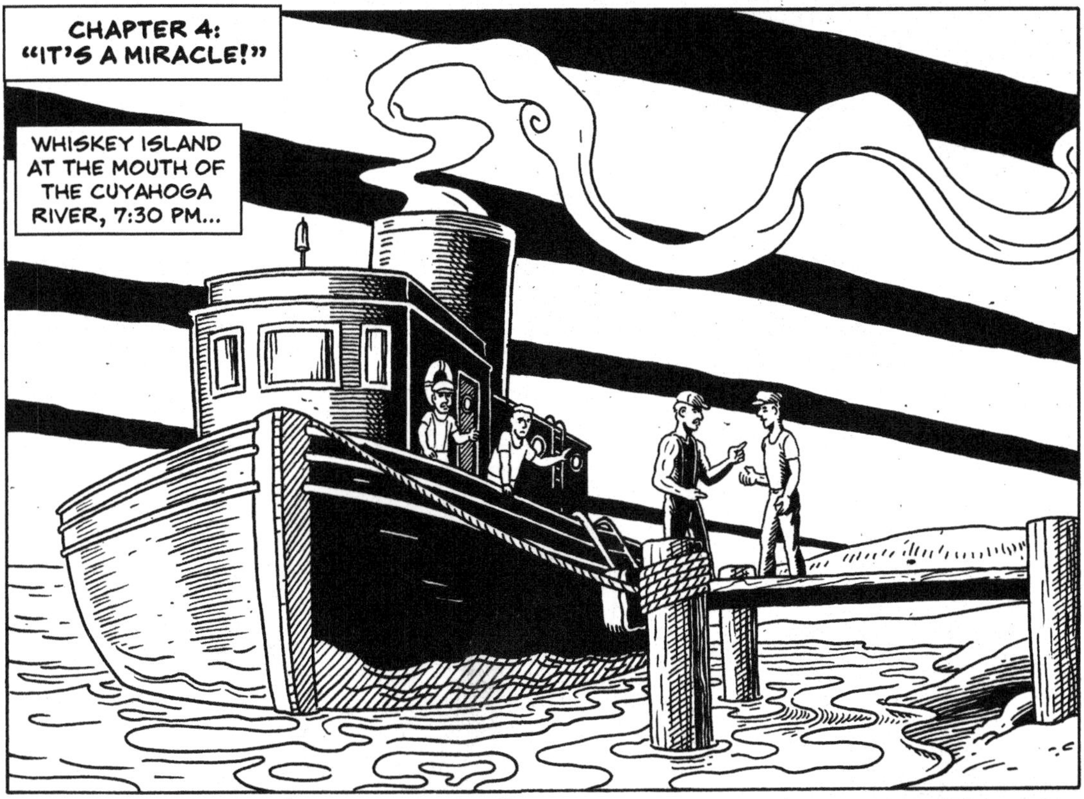
CHAPTER 4:
"IT'S A MIRACLE!"
WHISKEY ISLAND AT THE MOUTH OF THE CUYAHOGA RIVER, 7:30 PM...

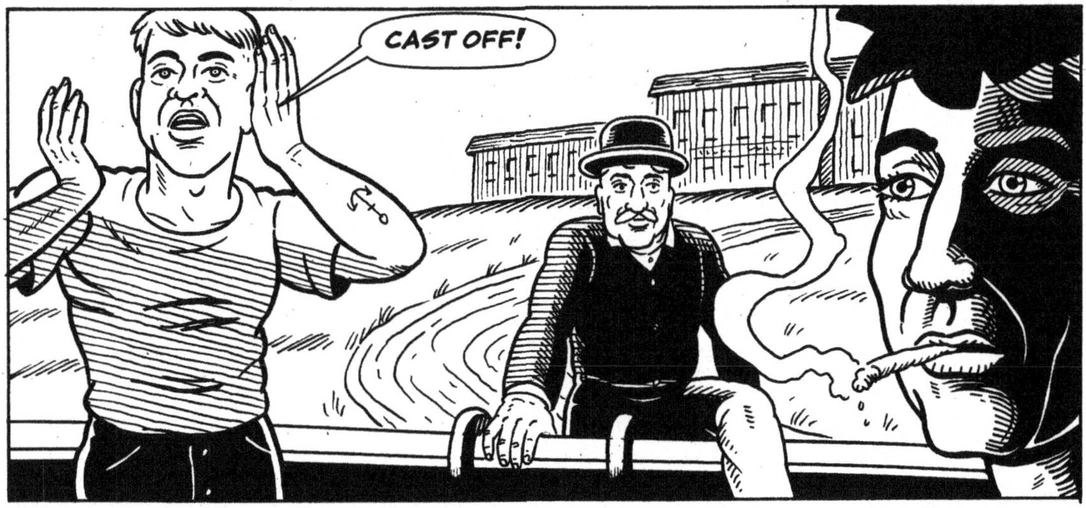
CAST OFF!

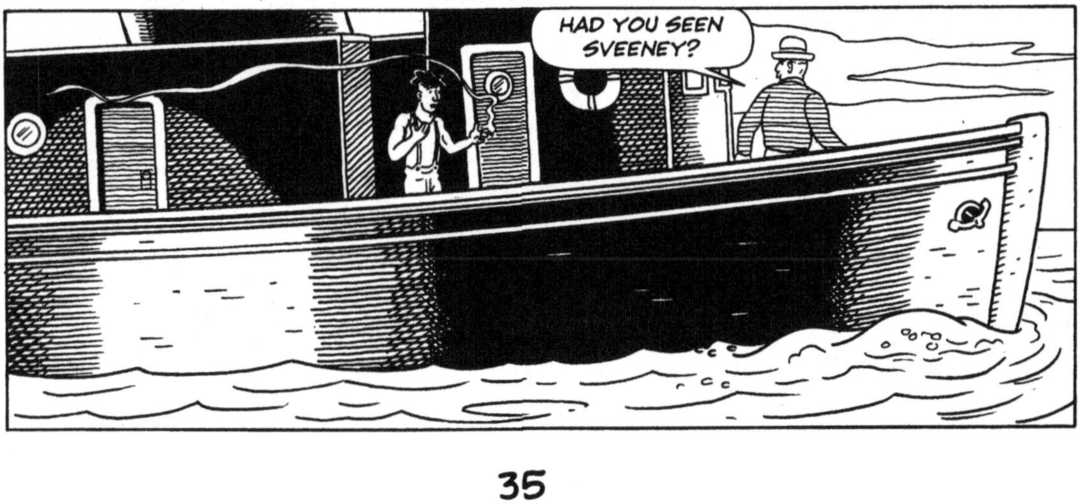
HAD YOU SEEN SVEENEY?

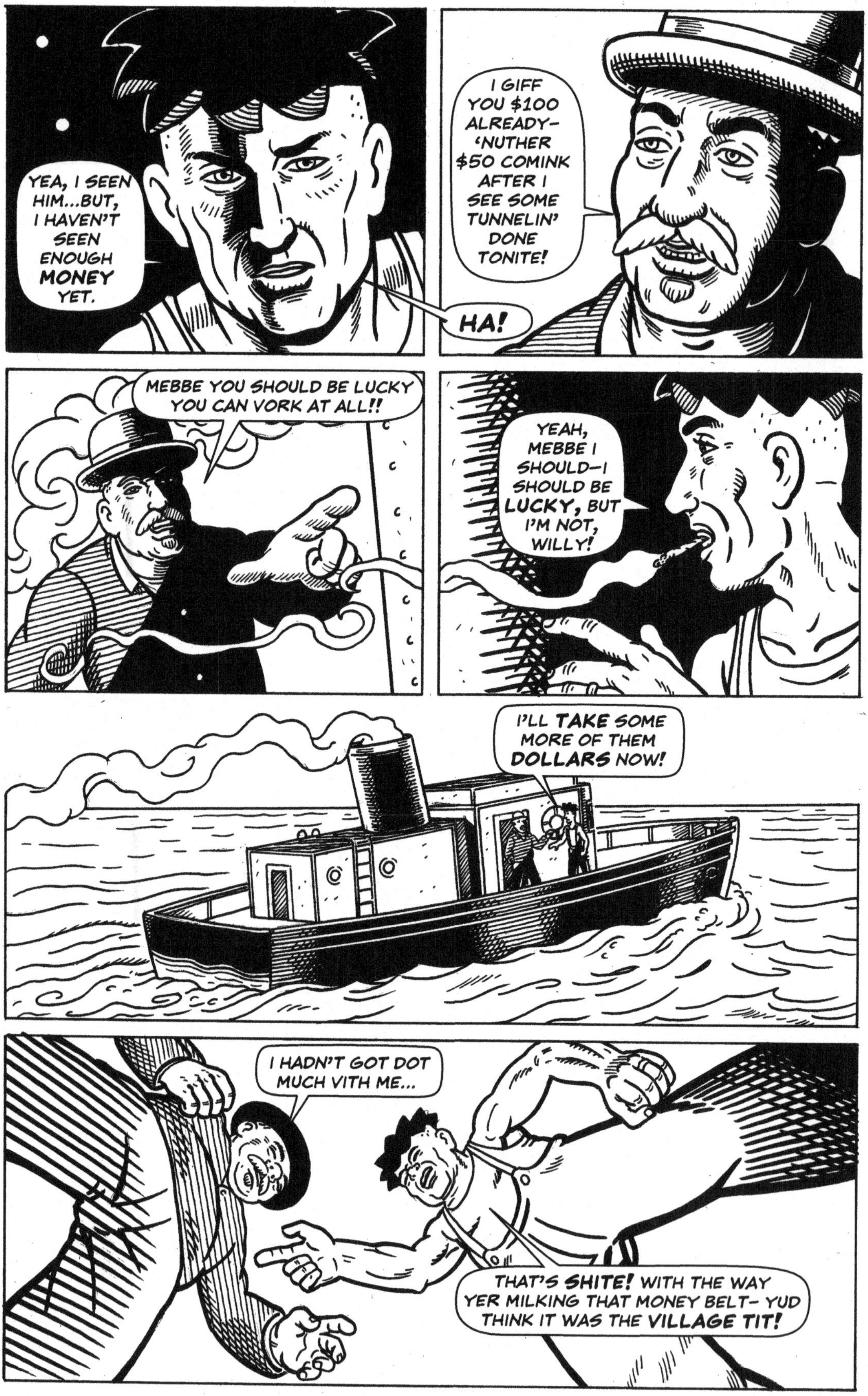
YEA, I SEEN HIM...BUT, I HAVEN'T SEEN ENOUGH MONEY YET.
I GIFF YOU $100 ALREADY- 'NUTHER $50 COMINK AFTER I SEE SOME TUNNELIN' DONE TONITE!
HA!
MEBBE YOU SHOULD BE LUCKY YOU CAN VORK AT ALL!!
YEAH, MEBBE I SHOULD-I SHOULD BE LUCKY, BUT I'M NOT, WILLY!
I'LL TAKE SOME MORE OF THEM DOLLARS NOW!
I HADN'T GOT DOT MUCH VITH ME...
THAT'S SHITE! WITH THE WAY YER MILKING THAT MONEY BELT- YUD THINK IT WAS THE VILLAGE TIT!

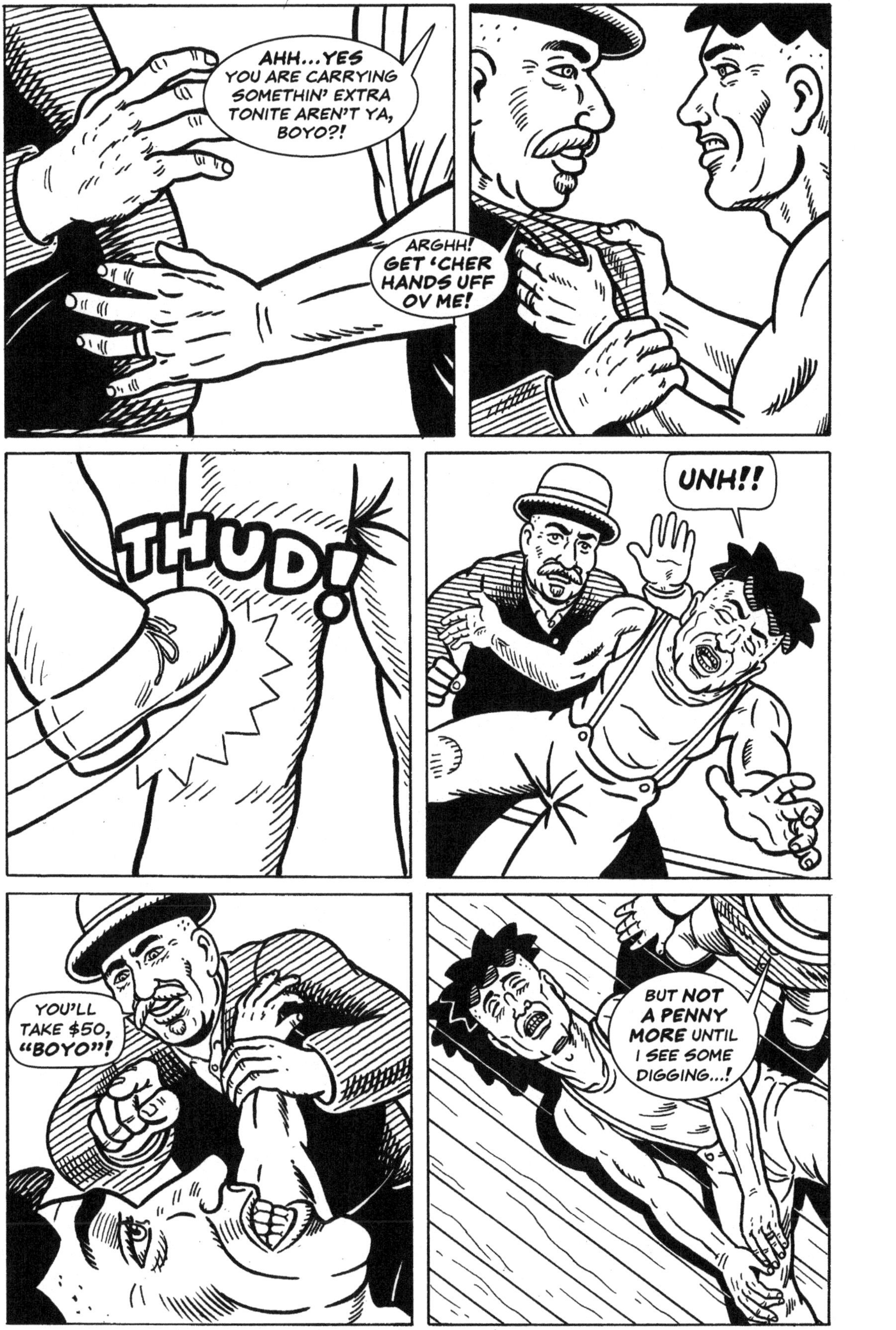
AHH...YES YOU ARE CARRYING SOMETHIN' EXTRA TONITE AREN'T YA, BOYO?!
ARGHH! GET 'CHER HANDS UFF OV ME!
THUD!
UNH!!
YOU'LL TAKE $50, "BOYO"!
BUT NOT A PENNY MORE UNTIL I SEE SOME DIGGING...!

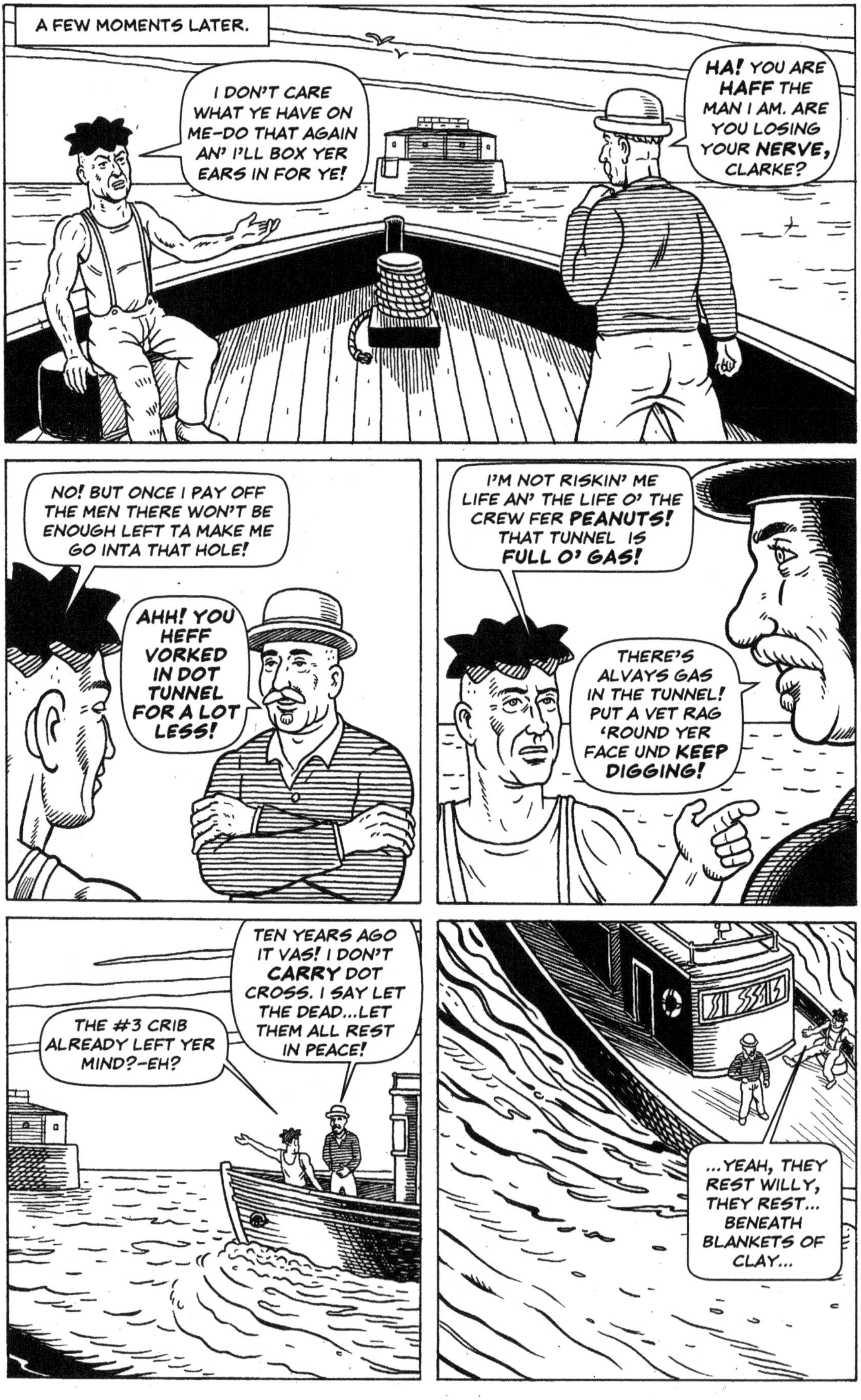
A FEW MOMENTS LATER.
I DON'T CARE WHAT YE HAVE ON ME-DO THAT AGAIN AN' I'LL BOX YER EARS IN FOR YE!
HA! YOU ARE HAFF THE MAN I AM. ARE YOU LOSING YOUR NERVE, CLARKE?
NO! BUT ONCE I PAY OFF THE MEN THERE WON'T BE ENOUGH LEFT TA MAKE ME GO INTA THAT HOLE!
AHH! YOU HEFF VORKED IN DOT TUNNEL FOR A LOT LESS!
I'M NOT RISKIN' ME LIFE AN' THE LIFE O' THE CREW FER PEANUTS! THAT TUNNEL IS FULL O' GAS!
THERE'S ALVAYS GAS IN THE TUNNEL! PUT A VET RAG 'ROUND YER FACE UND KEEP DIGGING!
THE #3 CRIB ALREADY LEFT YER MIND?-EH?
TEN YEARS AGO IT VAS! I DON'T CARRY DOT CROSS. I SAY LET THE DEAD...LET THEM ALL REST IN PEACE!
...YEAH, THEY REST WILLY, THEY REST... BENEATH BLANKETS OF CLAY...

TELL ME, WILLY... HOW D'YA DO IT? HOW D'YA *FORGET* CRIB #3?

I WANT YE TO TEACH *ME*...

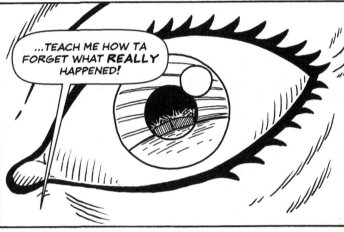

...TEACH ME HOW TA FORGET WHAT *REALLY* HAPPENED!

RETURNING TO A TIME *10 YEARS EARLIER* WHEN CLARKE AND A TEAM OF SANDHOGS BEGAN THEIR FATEFUL SHIFT ON THE CRIB #3...

MR. GALLAGHER! WHO CARRIES THE BIRDS?

RINI CARRIES 'EM. HE AND LAVELLE WILL GO ON AHEAD.

WHAT IF... UH, THE GAS GETS 'EM?

YER A GREAT ONE FER THE "WHAT IFS", LADDIE.

THERE ARE NO "WHAT IFS" IN THE TUNNEL TRADES... CERTAINLY NOT THIS TUNNEL!

AWWW—SHITE! LOOKS LIKE WE GOT THE DUTCHMAN ON THE AIRLOCK TODAY, LADS.

THE MAN'S A GOBSHITE! TRUST HIM LIKE A 10 CENT WATCH!

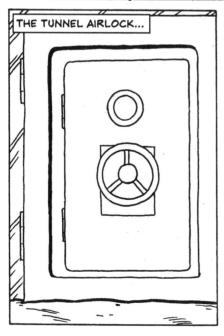

THE TUNNEL AIRLOCK...

THE TUNNELS WERE PRESSURIZED AND AIR REFRESHED BY A STEAM ENGINE COMPRESSOR LOCATED ON THE CRIB'S TOP DECK. TOO MUCH PRESSURE MEANT THE BENDS ONCE YOU ASCENDED UP THE MAIN SHAFT. TOO LITTLE OR LOSS OF PRESSURE COULD CAUSE THE TUNNEL TO COLLAPSE OR FILL WITH METHANE GAS AND WATER.

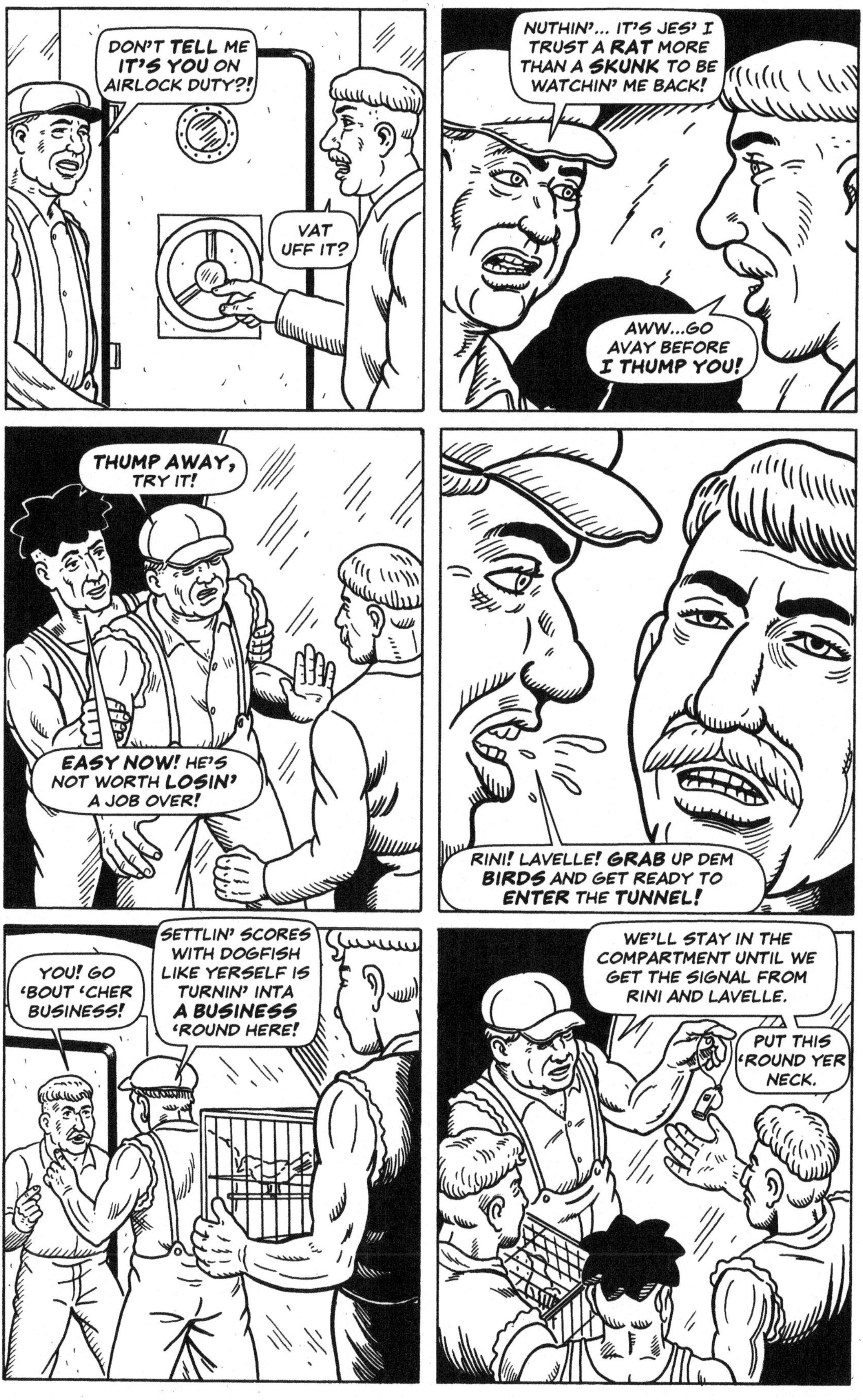
DON'T TELL ME IT'S YOU ON AIRLOCK DUTY?!
VAT UFF IT?
NUTHIN'... IT'S JES' I TRUST A RAT MORE THAN A SKUNK TO BE WATCHIN' ME BACK!
AWW...GO AVAY BEFORE I THUMP YOU!
THUMP AWAY, TRY IT!
EASY NOW! HE'S NOT WORTH LOSIN' A JOB OVER!
RINI! LAVELLE! GRAB UP DEM BIRDS AND GET READY TO ENTER THE TUNNEL!
YOU! GO 'BOUT 'CHER BUSINESS!
SETTLIN' SCORES WITH DOGFISH LIKE YERSELF IS TURNIN' INTA A BUSINESS 'ROUND HERE!
WE'LL STAY IN THE COMPARTMENT UNTIL WE GET THE SIGNAL FROM RINI AND LAVELLE.
PUT THIS 'ROUND YER NECK.

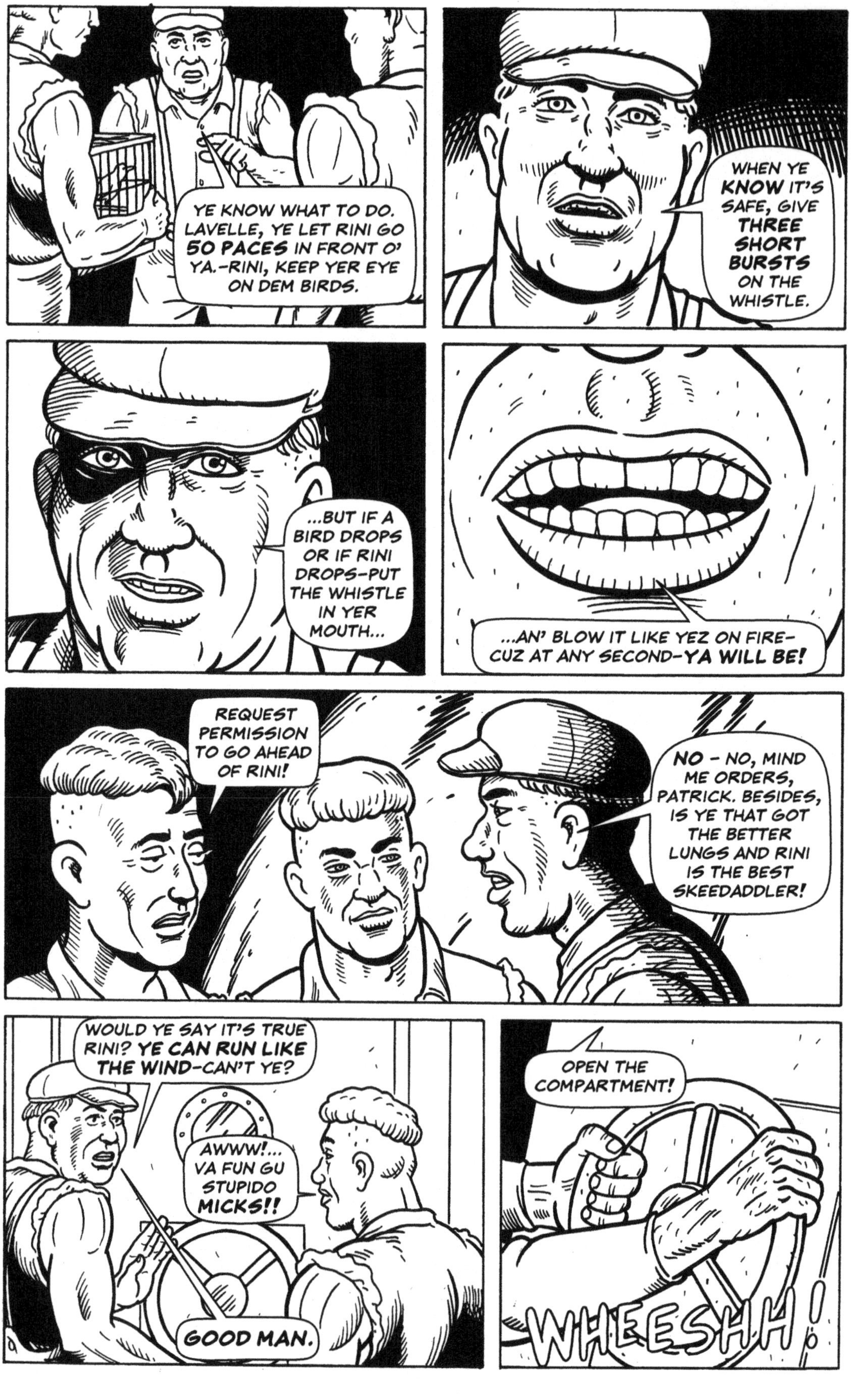

YE KNOW WHAT TO DO. LAVELLE, YE LET RINI GO 50 PACES IN FRONT O' YA.-RINI, KEEP YER EYE ON DEM BIRDS.
WHEN YE KNOW IT'S SAFE, GIVE THREE SHORT BURSTS ON THE WHISTLE.
...BUT IF A BIRD DROPS OR IF RINI DROPS-PUT THE WHISTLE IN YER MOUTH...
...AN' BLOW IT LIKE YEZ ON FIRE-CUZ AT ANY SECOND-YA WILL BE!
REQUEST PERMISSION TO GO AHEAD OF RINI!
NO - NO, MIND ME ORDERS, PATRICK. BESIDES, IS YE THAT GOT THE BETTER LUNGS AND RINI IS THE BEST SKEEDADDLER!
WOULD YE SAY IT'S TRUE RINI? YE CAN RUN LIKE THE WIND-CAN'T YE?
AWWW!... VA FUN GU STUPIDO MICKS!!
GOOD MAN.
OPEN THE COMPARTMENT!
WHEESHH!

REMEMBER! IF ALL'S CLEAR GIMME THREE BURSTS OF THE WHISTLE AND WE'LL VENTURE IN BEHIND YEZ.

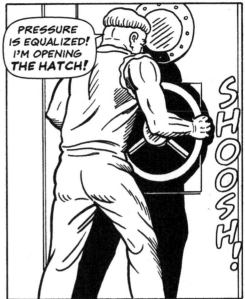

PRESSURE IS EQUALIZED! I'M OPENING THE HATCH!

SHOOSH!

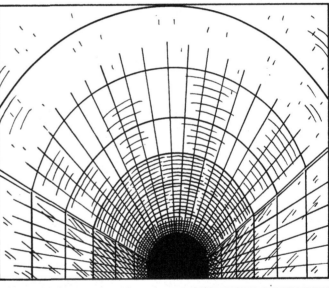

ENTERING THE TUNNEL, MR. GALLAGHER!

WE'LL **WAIT** FOR YOUR SIGNAL.

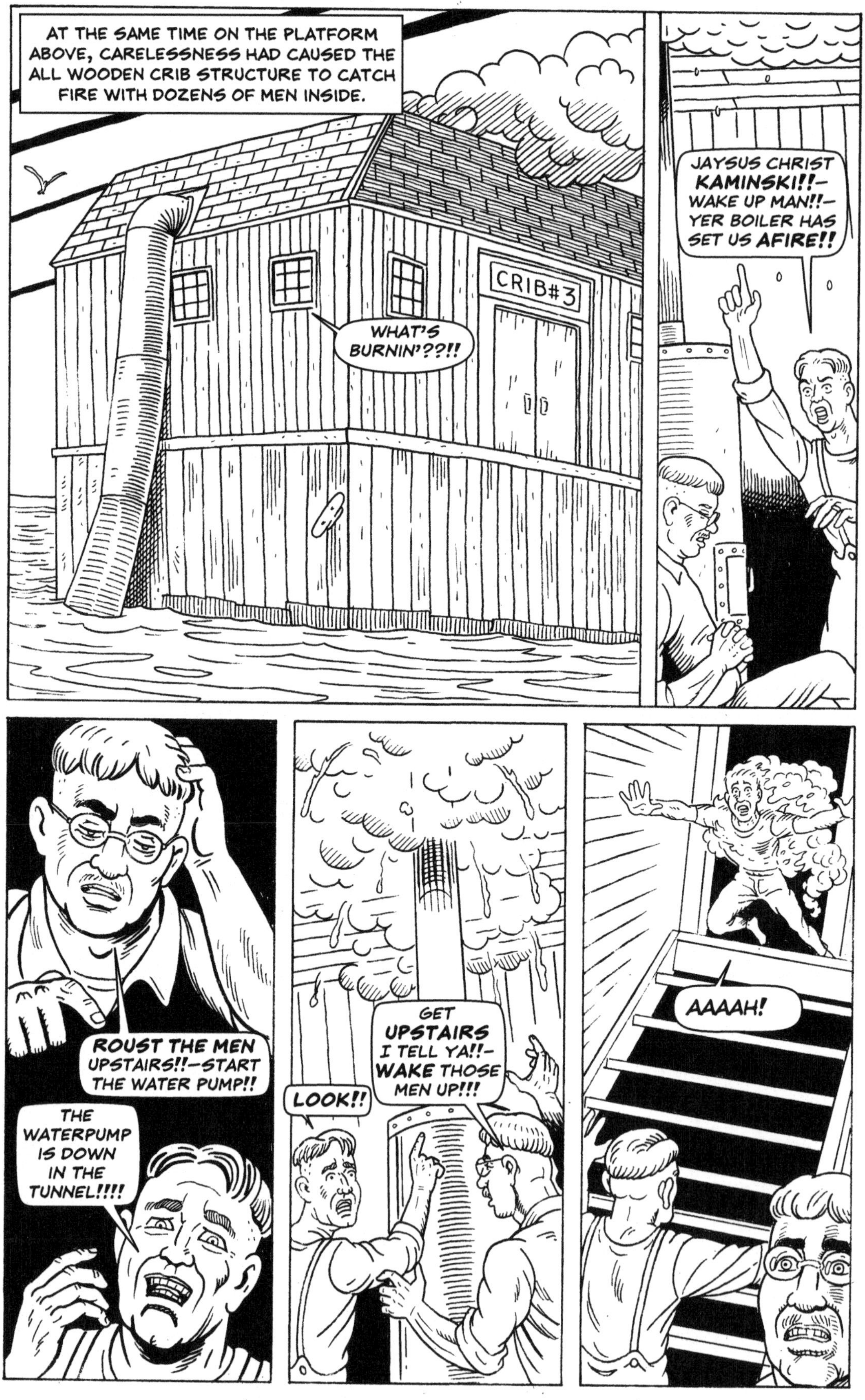
AT THE SAME TIME ON THE PLATFORM ABOVE, CARELESSNESS HAD CAUSED THE ALL WOODEN CRIB STRUCTURE TO CATCH FIRE WITH DOZENS OF MEN INSIDE.
CRIB#3
WHAT'S BURNIN'??!!
JAYSUS CHRIST KAMINSKI!!– WAKE UP MAN!!– YER BOILER HAS SET US AFIRE!!
ROUST THE MEN UPSTAIRS!!–START THE WATER PUMP!!
THE WATERPUMP IS DOWN IN THE TUNNEL!!!!
GET UPSTAIRS I TELL YA!!– WAKE THOSE MEN UP!!!
LOOK!!
AAAAH!

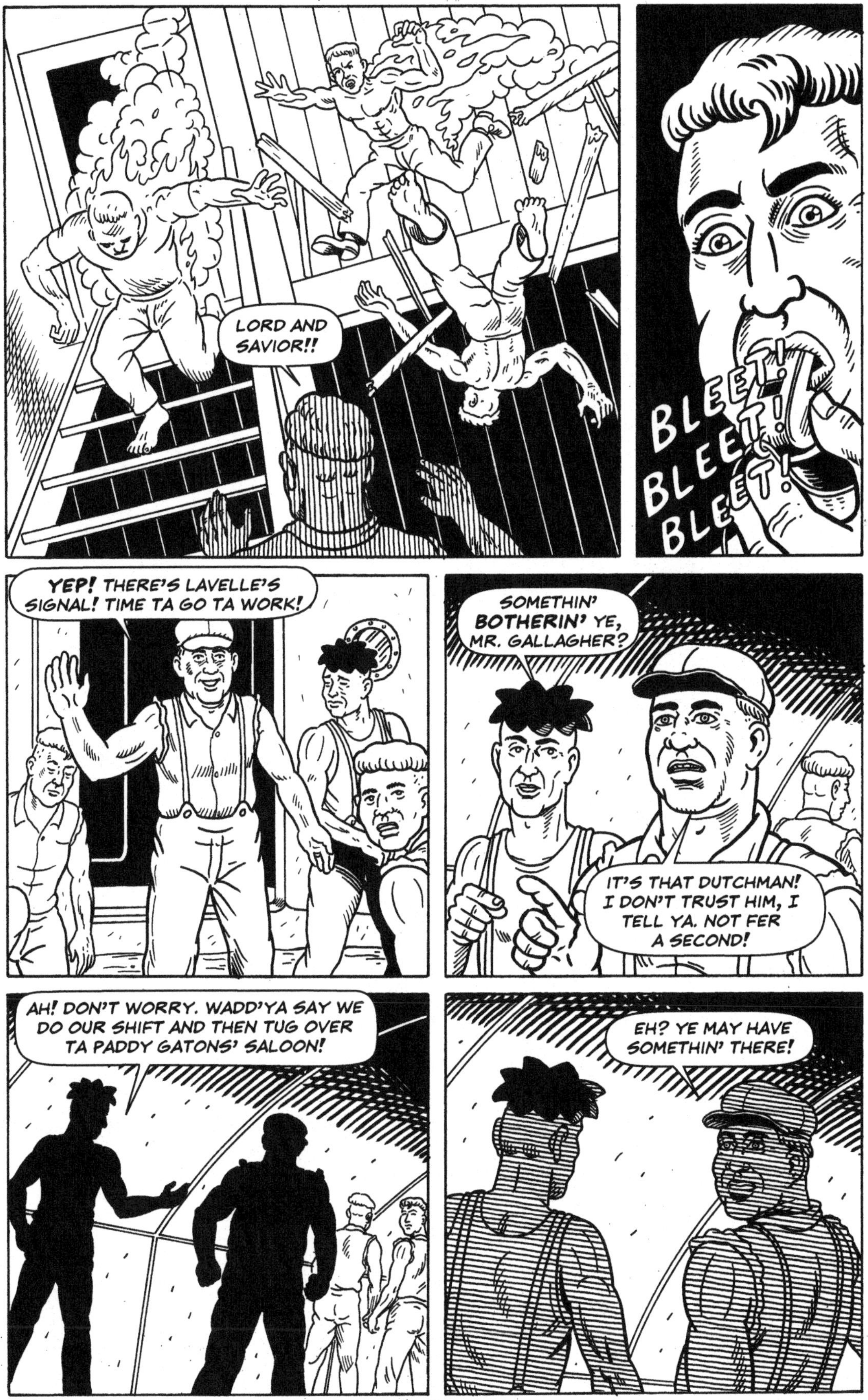
LORD AND SAVIOR!!
BLEET! BLEET! BLEET!
YEP! THERE'S LAVELLE'S SIGNAL! TIME TA GO TA WORK!
SOMETHIN' BOTHERIN' YE, MR. GALLAGHER?
IT'S THAT DUTCHMAN! I DON'T TRUST HIM, I TELL YA. NOT FER A SECOND!
AH! DON'T WORRY. WADD'YA SAY WE DO OUR SHIFT AND THEN TUG OVER TA PADDY GATONS' SALOON!
EH? YE MAY HAVE SOMETHIN' THERE!

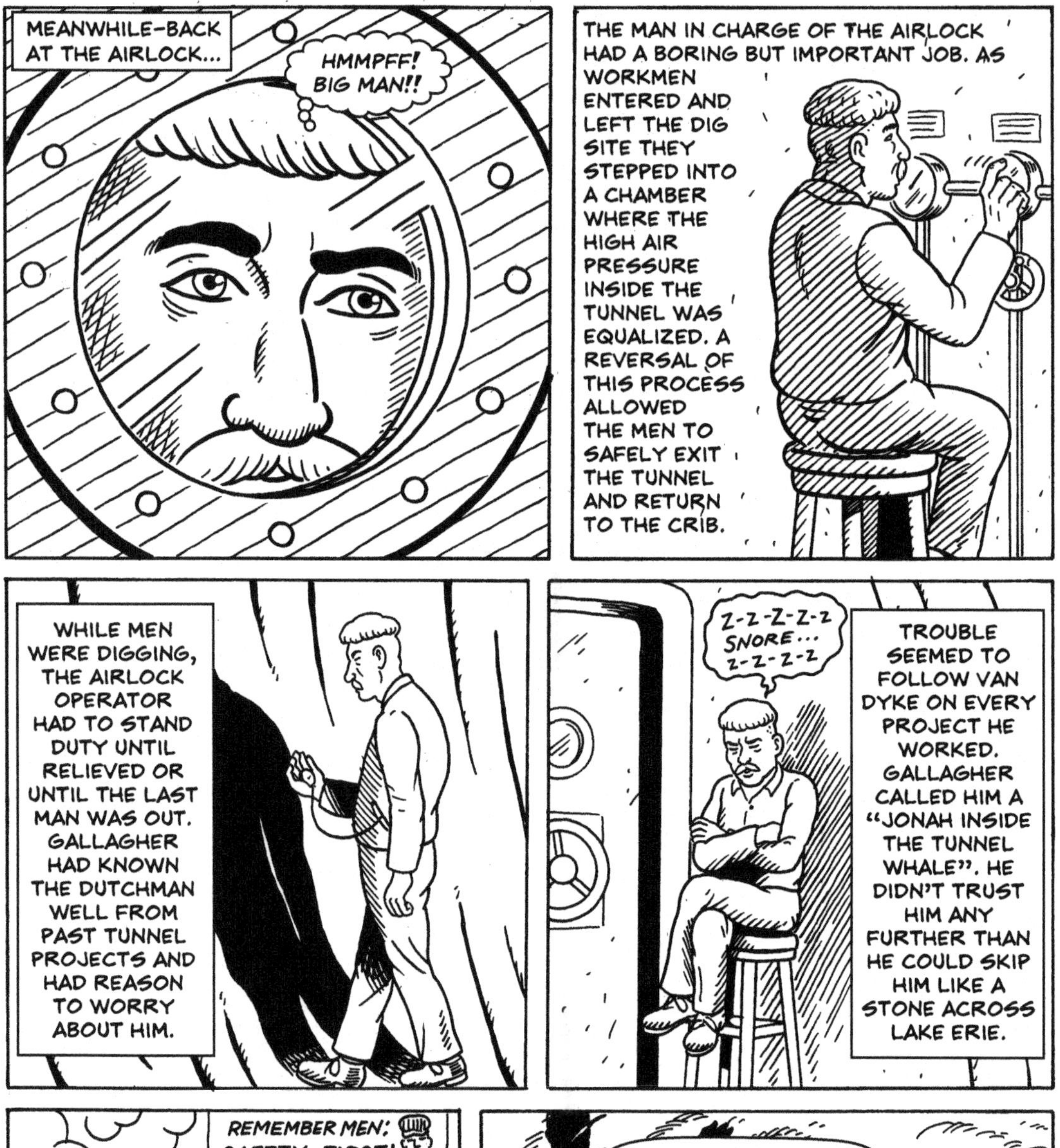
MEANWHILE–BACK AT THE AIRLOCK...
HMMPFF! BIG MAN!!
THE MAN IN CHARGE OF THE AIRLOCK HAD A BORING BUT IMPORTANT JOB. AS WORKMEN ENTERED AND LEFT THE DIG SITE THEY STEPPED INTO A CHAMBER WHERE THE HIGH AIR PRESSURE INSIDE THE TUNNEL WAS EQUALIZED. A REVERSAL OF THIS PROCESS ALLOWED THE MEN TO SAFELY EXIT THE TUNNEL AND RETURN TO THE CRIB.
WHILE MEN WERE DIGGING, THE AIRLOCK OPERATOR HAD TO STAND DUTY UNTIL RELIEVED OR UNTIL THE LAST MAN WAS OUT. GALLAGHER HAD KNOWN THE DUTCHMAN WELL FROM PAST TUNNEL PROJECTS AND HAD REASON TO WORRY ABOUT HIM.
Z-Z-Z-Z-Z SNORE... Z-Z-Z-Z
TROUBLE SEEMED TO FOLLOW VAN DYKE ON EVERY PROJECT HE WORKED. GALLAGHER CALLED HIM A "JONAH INSIDE THE TUNNEL WHALE". HE DIDN'T TRUST HIM ANY FURTHER THAN HE COULD SKIP HIM LIKE A STONE ACROSS LAKE ERIE.
REMEMBER MEN: SAFETY FIRST!
ZZZZZZZ
HERE WE ARE, BOYOS! AND...THE WORK SHE BE WAITIN' FOR US!
MR. GALLAGHER ...OVER HERE!

WHAT 'AVE WE?

ONE O' THE MULES DIED! STIFF AS A BOARD. THE OTHERS LOOK FIT. D'YA TINK IT WAS GAS?

NAWW! JES' HER TIME TA GO! HAVE LAVELLE TAKE HER TO THE AIRLOCK. WE'LL TAKE 'ER UP WIT US LATER.

LEAVE THE DEAD MULE AT THE AIRLOCK!...TELL VAN DYKE HE'S LOST ANOTHER RELATIVE!

MEANWHILE–AT THE AIRLOCK...

SNAAAK..COUGH! SNIK.. COUGH! COUGH!..VASS? HEY... VAT THE...?!

...VAT IS DOT?

AAAK! OWW! GOEDE HEMEL! DER CRIB IS ON FIRE!!

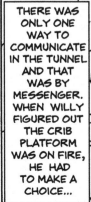

THERE WAS ONLY ONE WAY TO COMMUNICATE IN THE TUNNEL AND THAT WAS BY MESSENGER. WHEN WILLY FIGURED OUT THE CRIB PLATFORM WAS ON FIRE, HE HAD TO MAKE A CHOICE...

IN CASE OF FIRE BREAK GLASS

...HE COULD EITHER RUN DOWN THE TUNNEL TO WARN THE MEN AND RISK GETTING TRAPPED WITH THEM, OR HE COULD ABANDON HIS POST AND GET OUT BEFORE IT WAS TOO LATE!

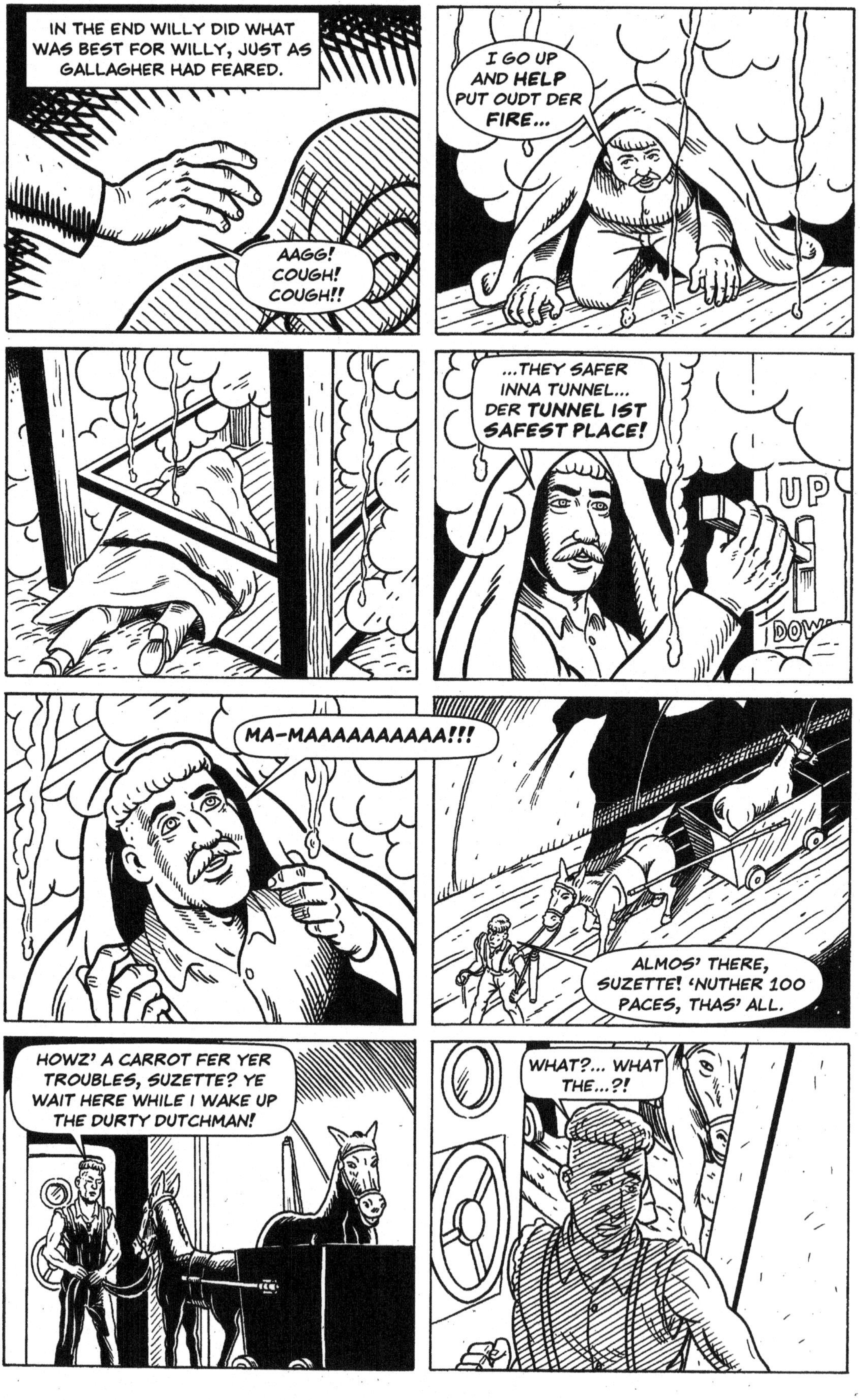
IN THE END WILLY DID WHAT WAS BEST FOR WILLY, JUST AS GALLAGHER HAD FEARED.
AAGG! COUGH! COUGH!!
I GO UP AND HELP PUT OUDT DER FIRE...
...THEY SAFER INNA TUNNEL... DER TUNNEL IST SAFEST PLACE!
UP
MA-MAAAAAAAAAA!!!
ALMOS' THERE, SUZETTE! 'NUTHER 100 PACES, THAS' ALL.
HOWZ' A CARROT FER YER TROUBLES, SUZETTE? YE WAIT HERE WHILE I WAKE UP THE DURTY DUTCHMAN!
WHAT?... WHAT THE...?!

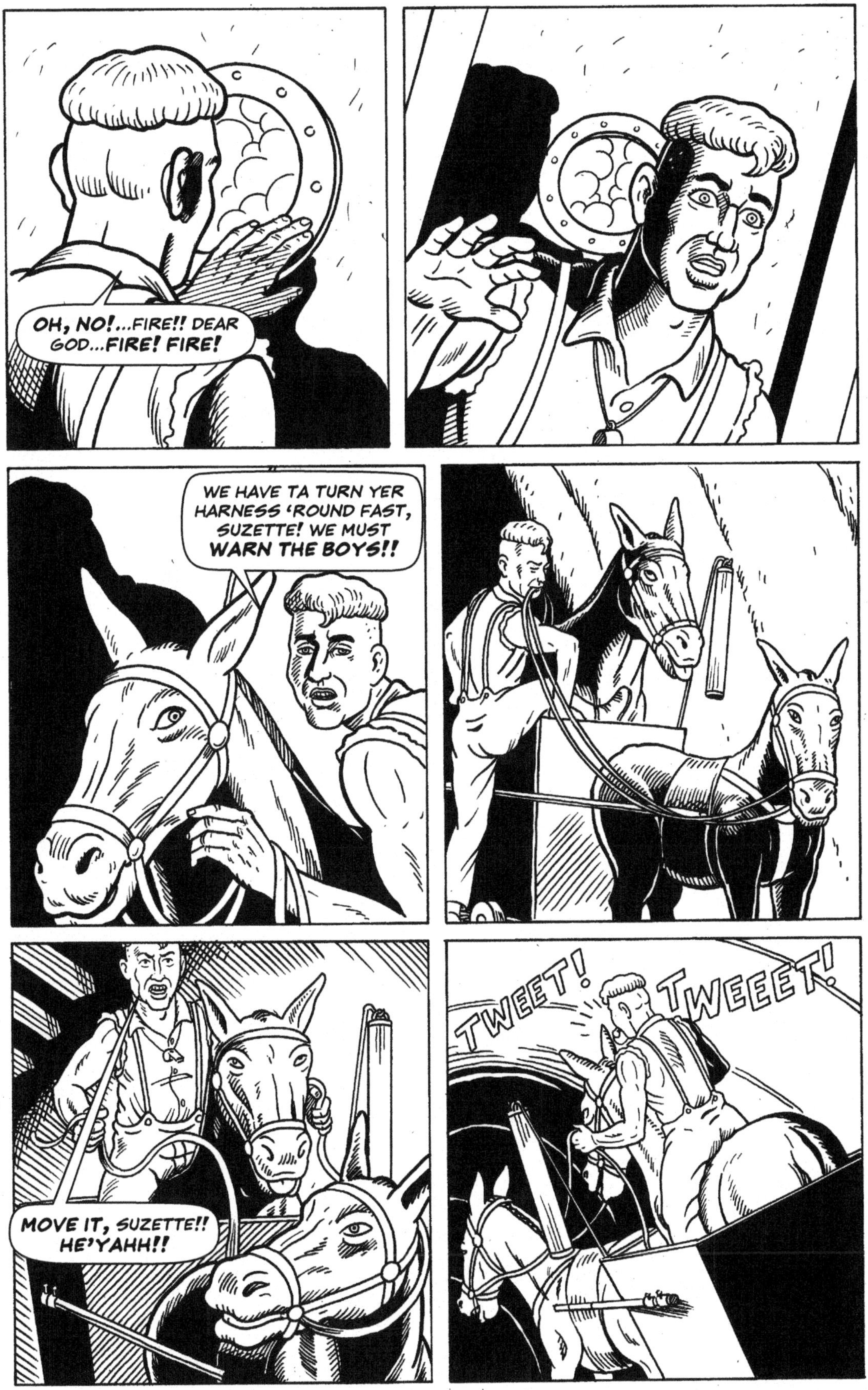
OH, NO!...FIRE!! DEAR GOD...FIRE! FIRE!
WE HAVE TA TURN YER HARNESS 'ROUND FAST, SUZETTE! WE MUST WARN THE BOYS!!
MOVE IT, SUZETTE!! HE'YAHH!!
TWEET!
TWEEET!

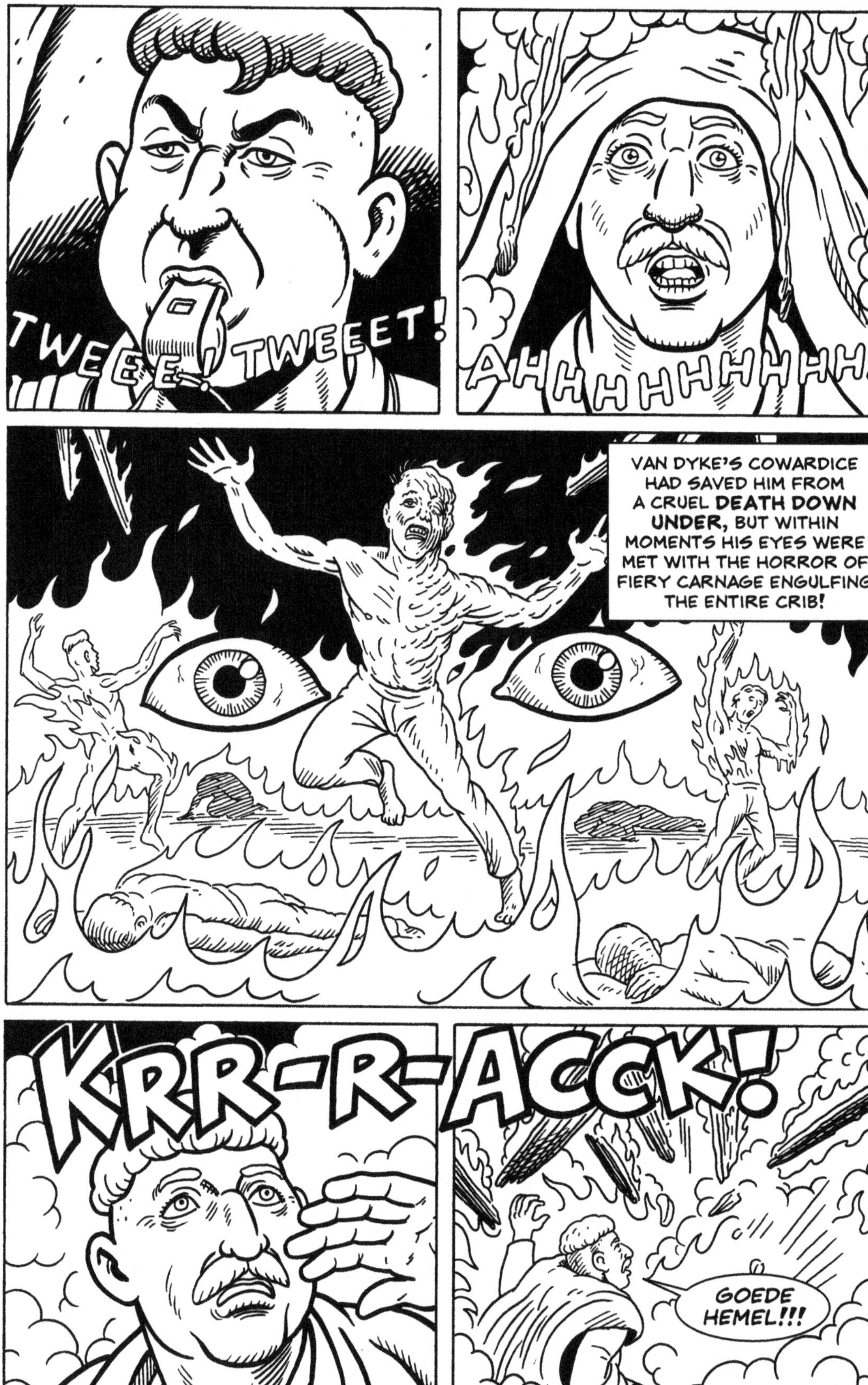
TWEEE! TWEEET!
AHHHHHHHHHH!
VAN DYKE'S COWARDICE HAD SAVED HIM FROM A CRUEL **DEATH DOWN UNDER**, BUT WITHIN MOMENTS HIS EYES WERE MET WITH THE HORROR OF FIERY CARNAGE ENGULFING THE ENTIRE CRIB!
KRR-R-ACCK!
GOEDE HEMEL!!!

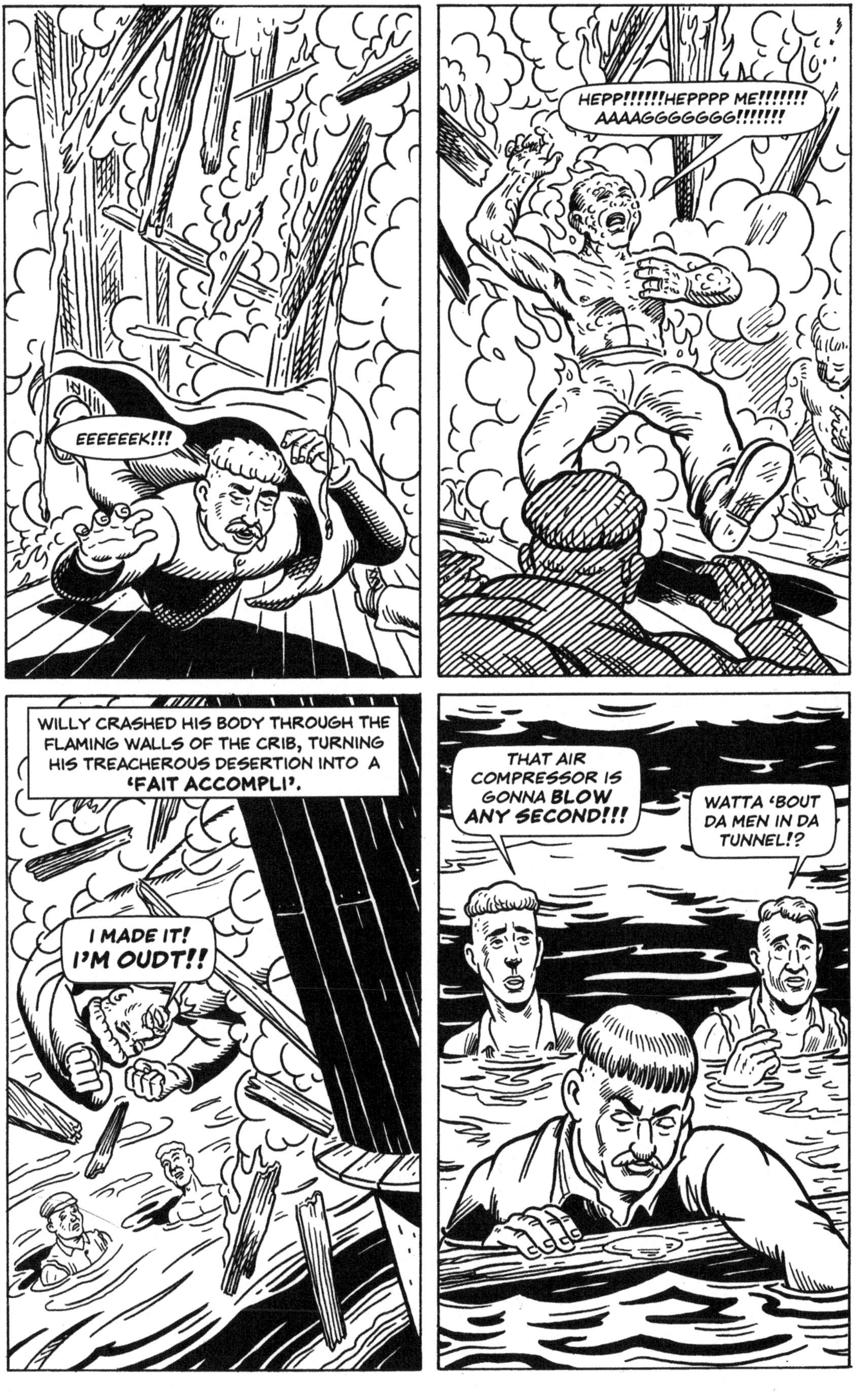
EEEEEEK!!!
HEPP!!!!!!HEPPPP ME!!!!!!!
AAAAGGGGGGG!!!!!!!
WILLY CRASHED HIS BODY THROUGH THE FLAMING WALLS OF THE CRIB, TURNING HIS TREACHEROUS DESERTION INTO A 'FAIT ACCOMPLI'.
I MADE IT! I'M OUDT!!
THAT AIR COMPRESSOR IS GONNA BLOW ANY SECOND!!!
WATTA 'BOUT DA MEN IN DA TUNNEL!?

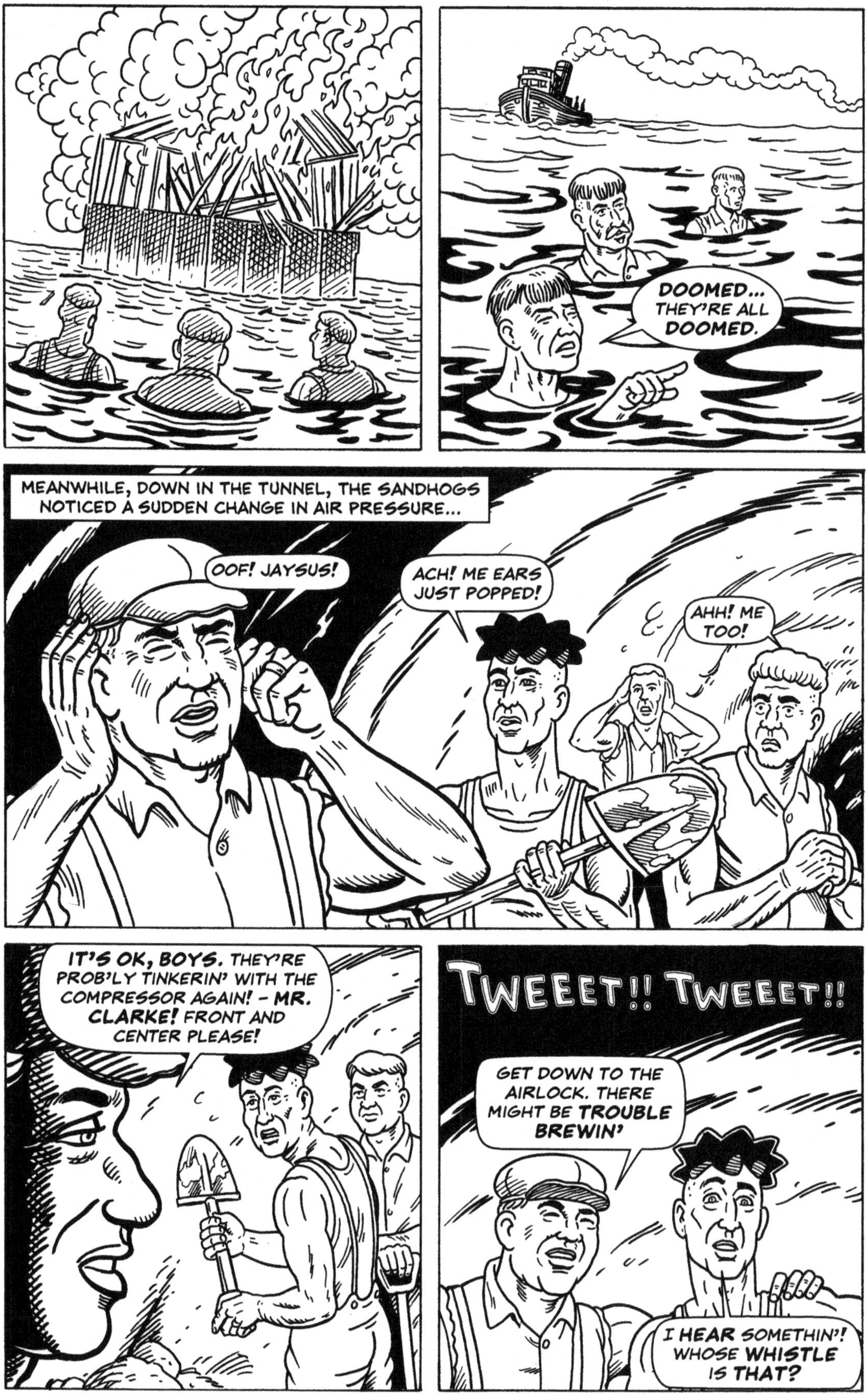
DOOMED... THEY'RE ALL DOOMED.
MEANWHILE, DOWN IN THE TUNNEL, THE SANDHOGS NOTICED A SUDDEN CHANGE IN AIR PRESSURE...
OOF! JAYSUS!
ACH! ME EARS JUST POPPED!
AHH! ME TOO!
IT'S OK, BOYS. THEY'RE PROB'LY TINKERIN' WITH THE COMPRESSOR AGAIN! – MR. CLARKE! FRONT AND CENTER PLEASE!
TWEEET!! TWEEET!!
GET DOWN TO THE AIRLOCK. THERE MIGHT BE TROUBLE BREWIN'
I HEAR SOMETHIN'! WHOSE WHISTLE IS THAT?

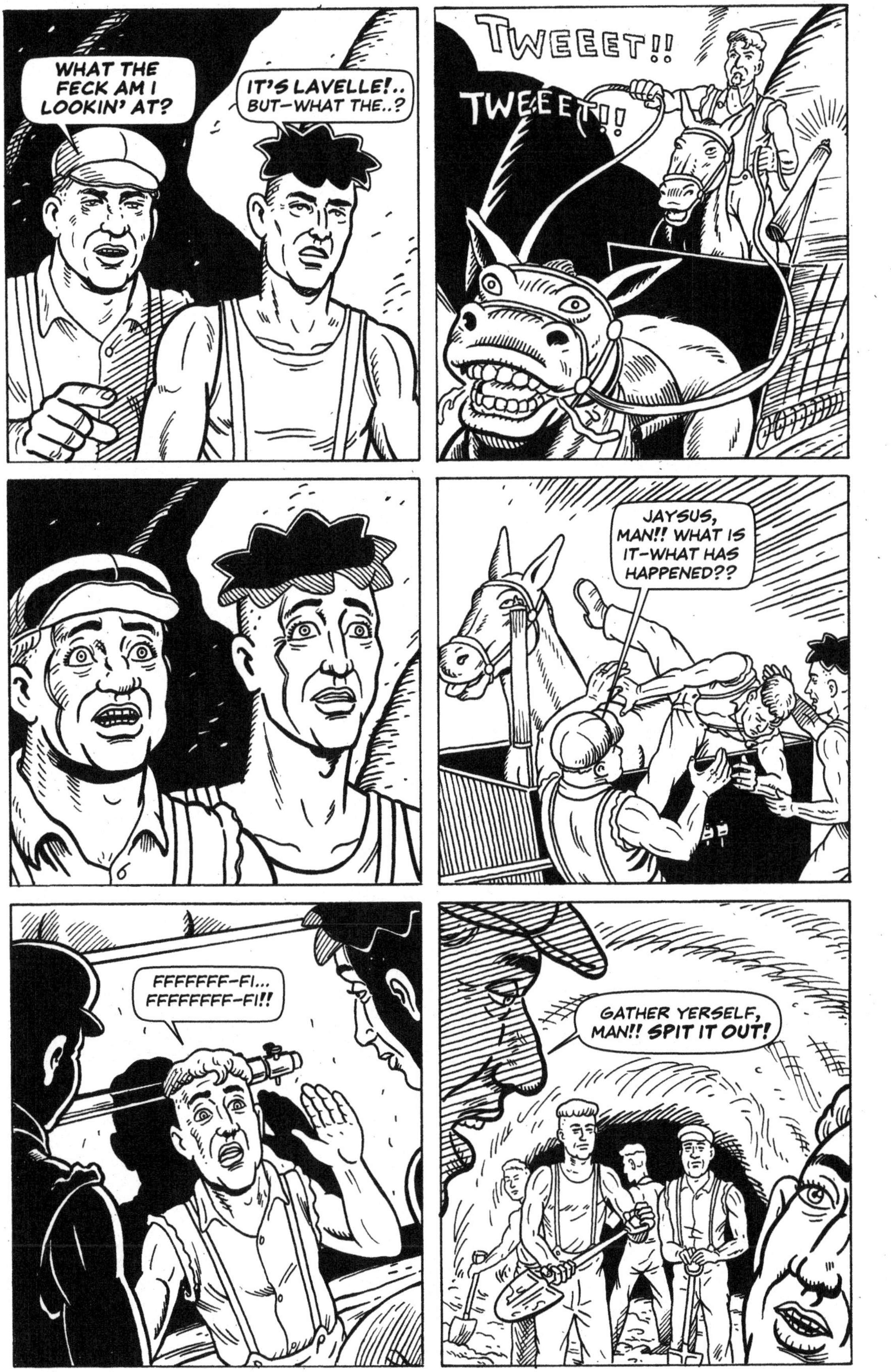
WHAT THE FECK AM I LOOKIN' AT?
IT'S LAVELLE!.. BUT—WHAT THE..?
TWEEET!!
TWEEET!!
JAYSUS, MAN!! WHAT IS IT—WHAT HAS HAPPENED??
FFFFFFF-FI... FFFFFFFF-FI!!
GATHER YERSELF, MAN!! SPIT IT OUT!

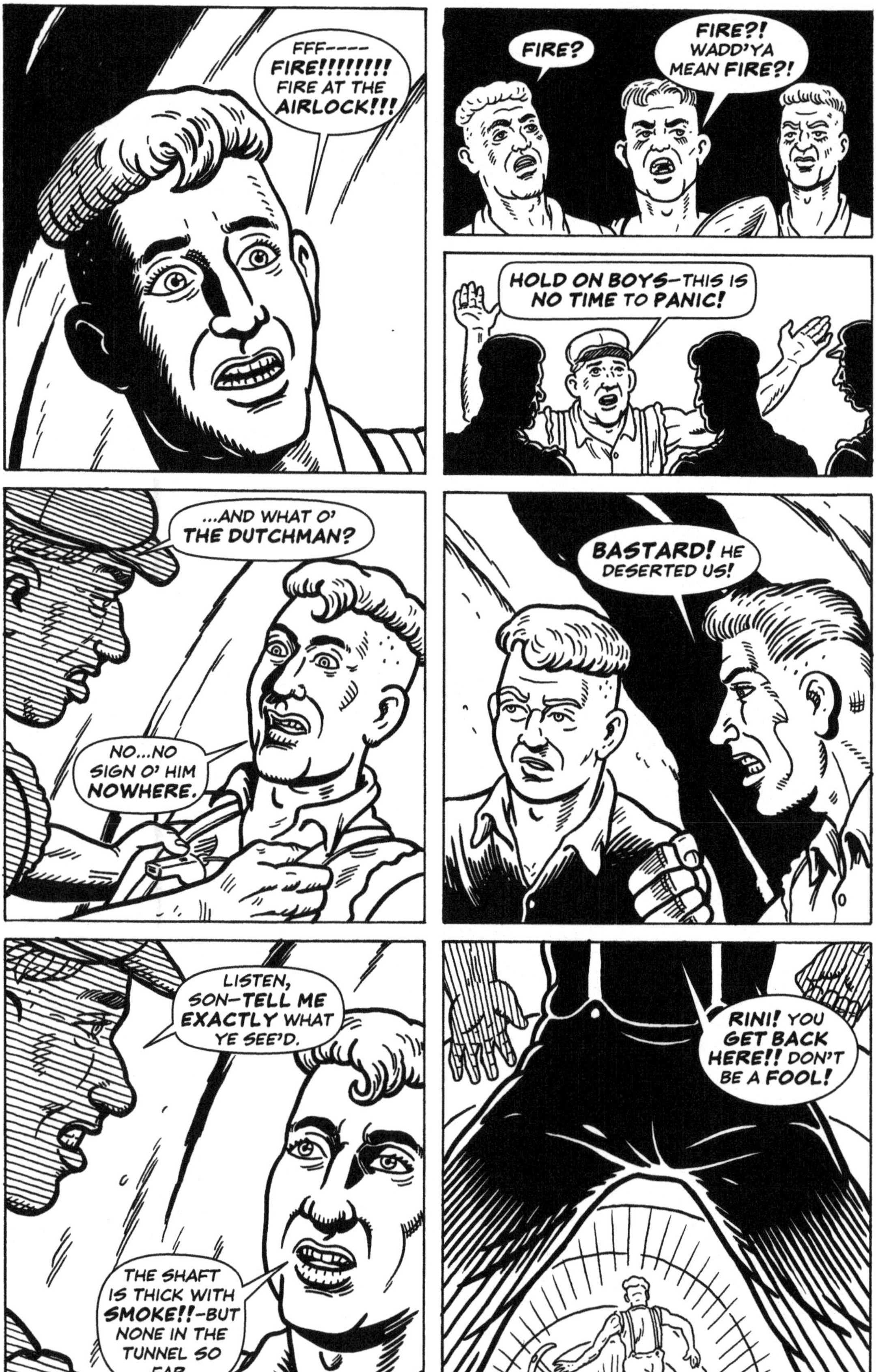
FFF---- FIRE!!!!!!!! FIRE AT THE AIRLOCK!!!
FIRE?
FIRE?! WADD'YA MEAN FIRE?!
HOLD ON BOYS—THIS IS NO TIME TO PANIC!
...AND WHAT O' THE DUTCHMAN?
NO...NO SIGN O' HIM NOWHERE.
BASTARD! HE DESERTED US!
LISTEN, SON—TELL ME EXACTLY WHAT YE SEE'D.
THE SHAFT IS THICK WITH SMOKE!!—BUT NONE IN THE TUNNEL SO FAR.
RINI! YOU GET BACK HERE!! DON'T BE A FOOL!

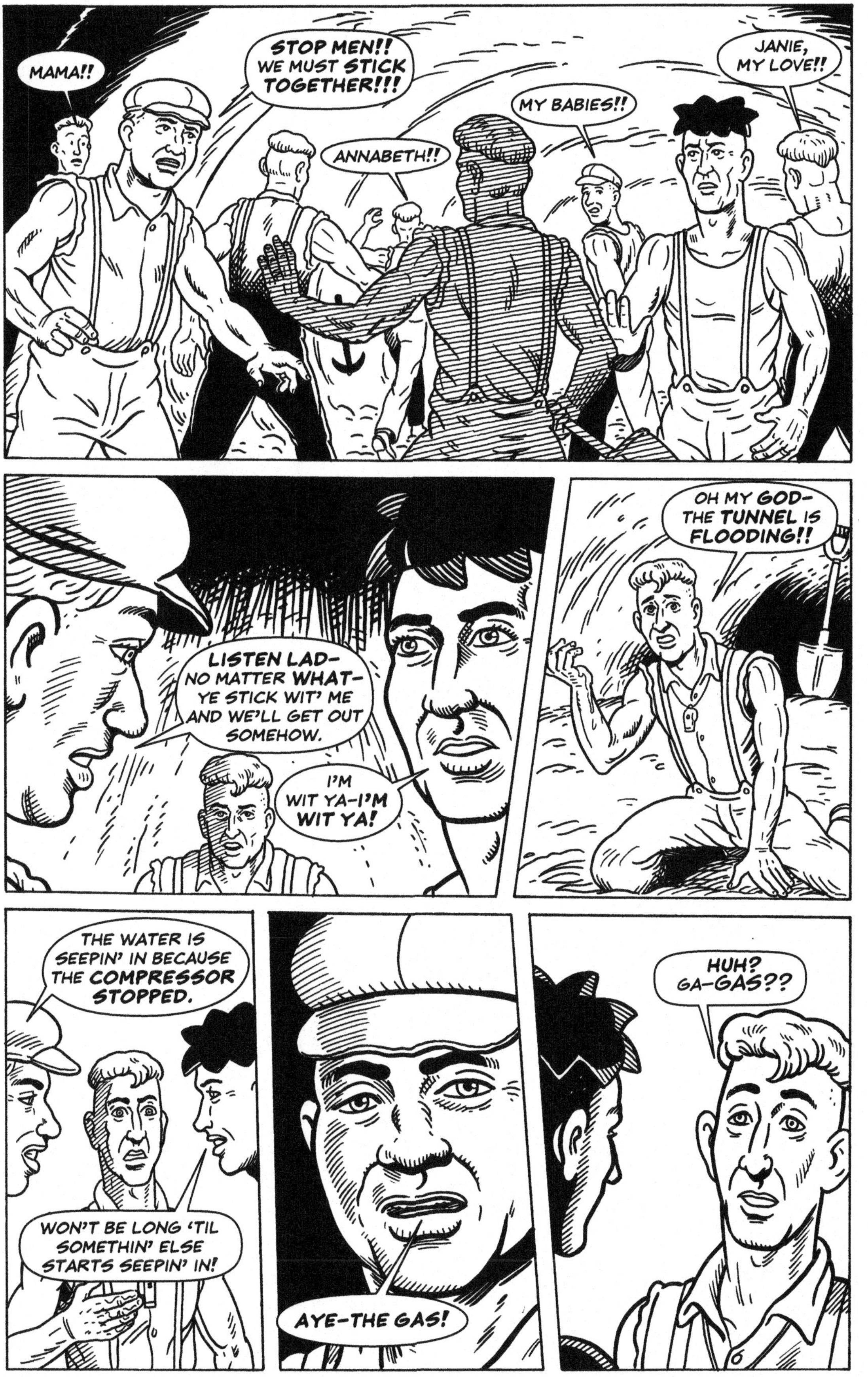
MAMA!!
STOP MEN!! WE MUST STICK TOGETHER!!!
ANNABETH!!
MY BABIES!!
JANIE, MY LOVE!!
LISTEN LAD- NO MATTER WHAT- YE STICK WIT' ME AND WE'LL GET OUT SOMEHOW.
I'M WIT YA-I'M WIT YA!
OH MY GOD- THE TUNNEL IS FLOODING!!
THE WATER IS SEEPIN' IN BECAUSE THE COMPRESSOR STOPPED.
WON'T BE LONG 'TIL SOMETHIN' ELSE STARTS SEEPIN' IN!
AYE-THE GAS!
HUH? GA-GAS??

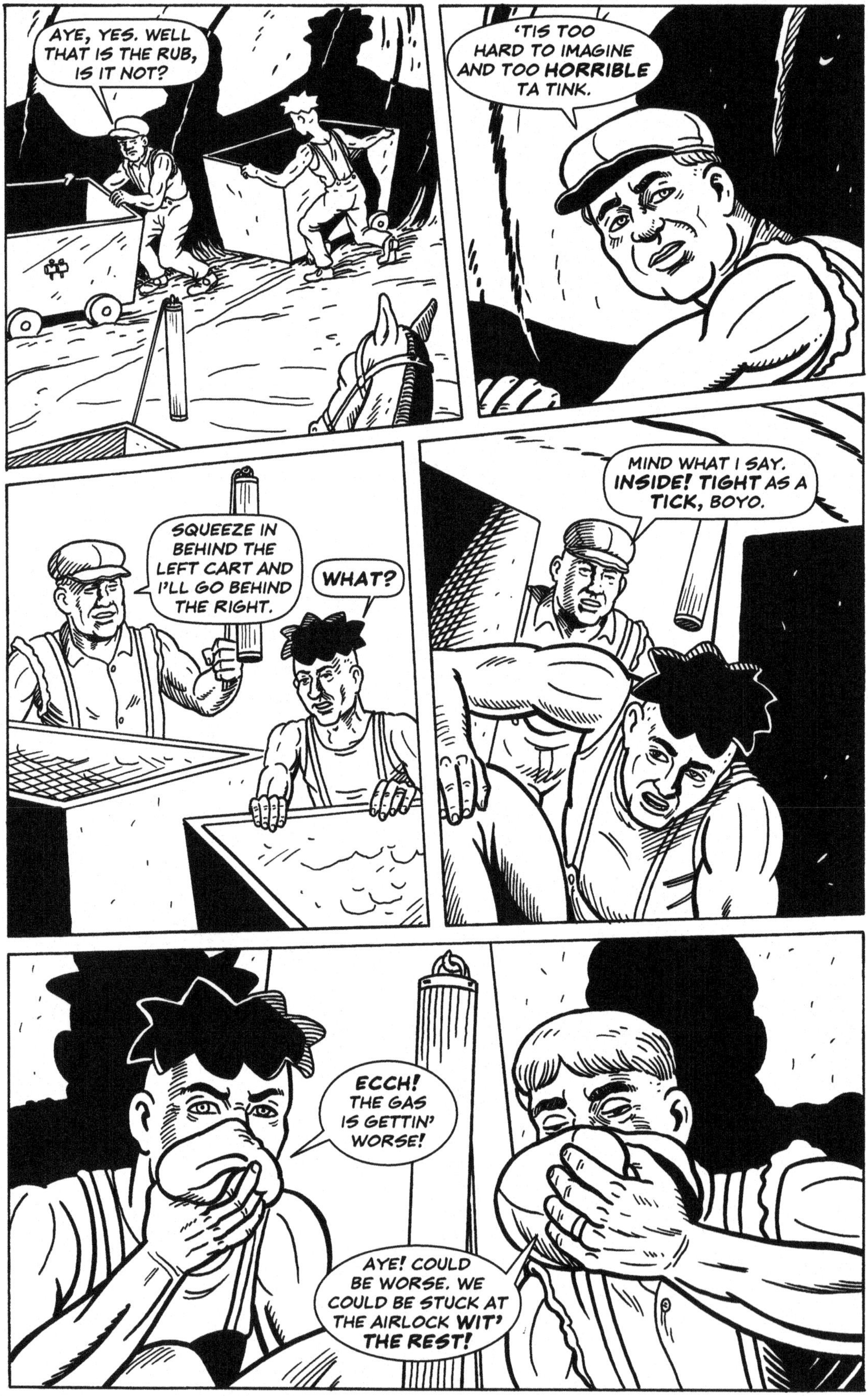
AYE, YES. WELL THAT IS THE RUB, IS IT NOT?
'TIS TOO HARD TO IMAGINE AND TOO **HORRIBLE** TA TINK.
SQUEEZE IN BEHIND THE LEFT CART AND I'LL GO BEHIND THE RIGHT.
WHAT?
MIND WHAT I SAY. **INSIDE! TIGHT** AS A **TICK,** BOYO.
ECCH! THE GAS IS GETTIN' WORSE!
AYE! COULD BE WORSE. WE COULD BE STUCK AT THE AIRLOCK **WIT' THE REST!**

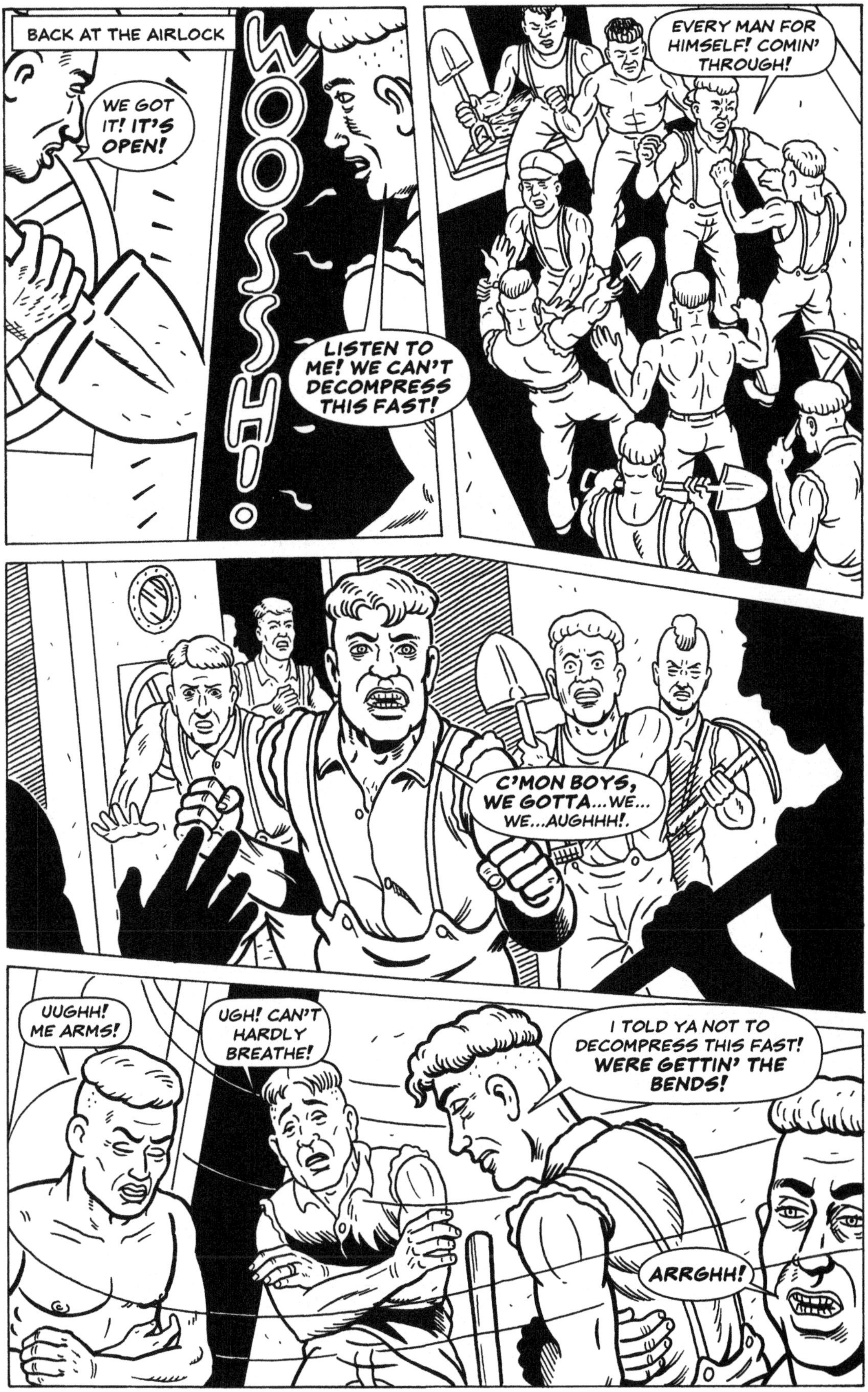
BACK AT THE AIRLOCK
WE GOT IT! IT'S OPEN!
WOOSHH!
LISTEN TO ME! WE CAN'T DECOMPRESS THIS FAST!
EVERY MAN FOR HIMSELF! COMIN' THROUGH!
C'MON BOYS, WE GOTTA...WE... WE...AUGHHH!.
UUGHH! ME ARMS!
UGH! CAN'T HARDLY BREATHE!
I TOLD YA NOT TO DECOMPRESS THIS FAST! WERE GETTIN' THE BENDS!
ARRGHH!

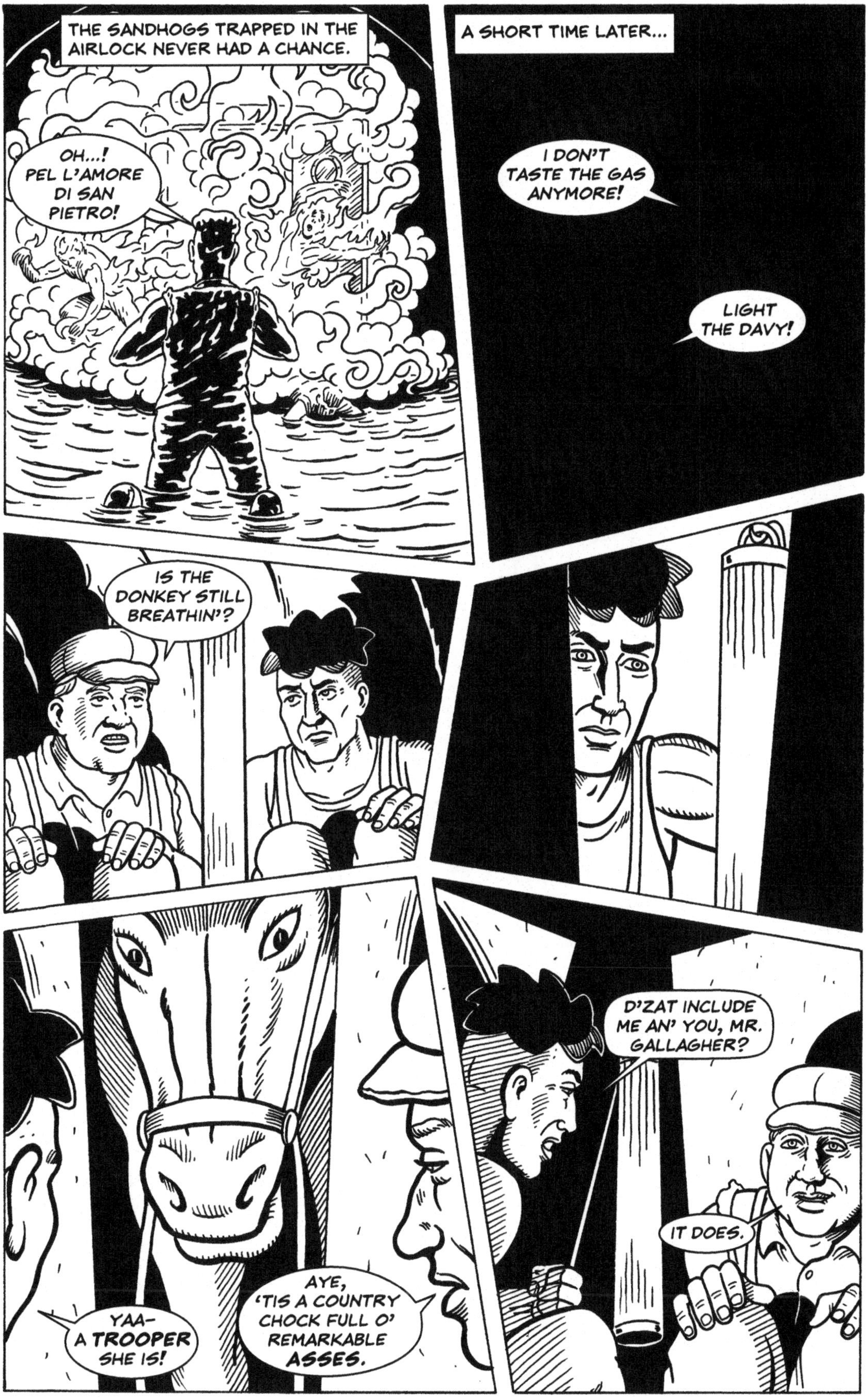

THE SANDHOGS TRAPPED IN THE AIRLOCK NEVER HAD A CHANCE.
OH...! PEL L'AMORE DI SAN PIETRO!
A SHORT TIME LATER...
I DON'T TASTE THE GAS ANYMORE!
LIGHT THE DAVY!
IS THE DONKEY STILL BREATHIN'?
YAA- A **TROOPER** SHE IS!
AYE, 'TIS A COUNTRY CHOCK FULL O' REMARKABLE **ASSES.**
D'ZAT INCLUDE ME AN' YOU, MR. GALLAGHER?
IT DOES.

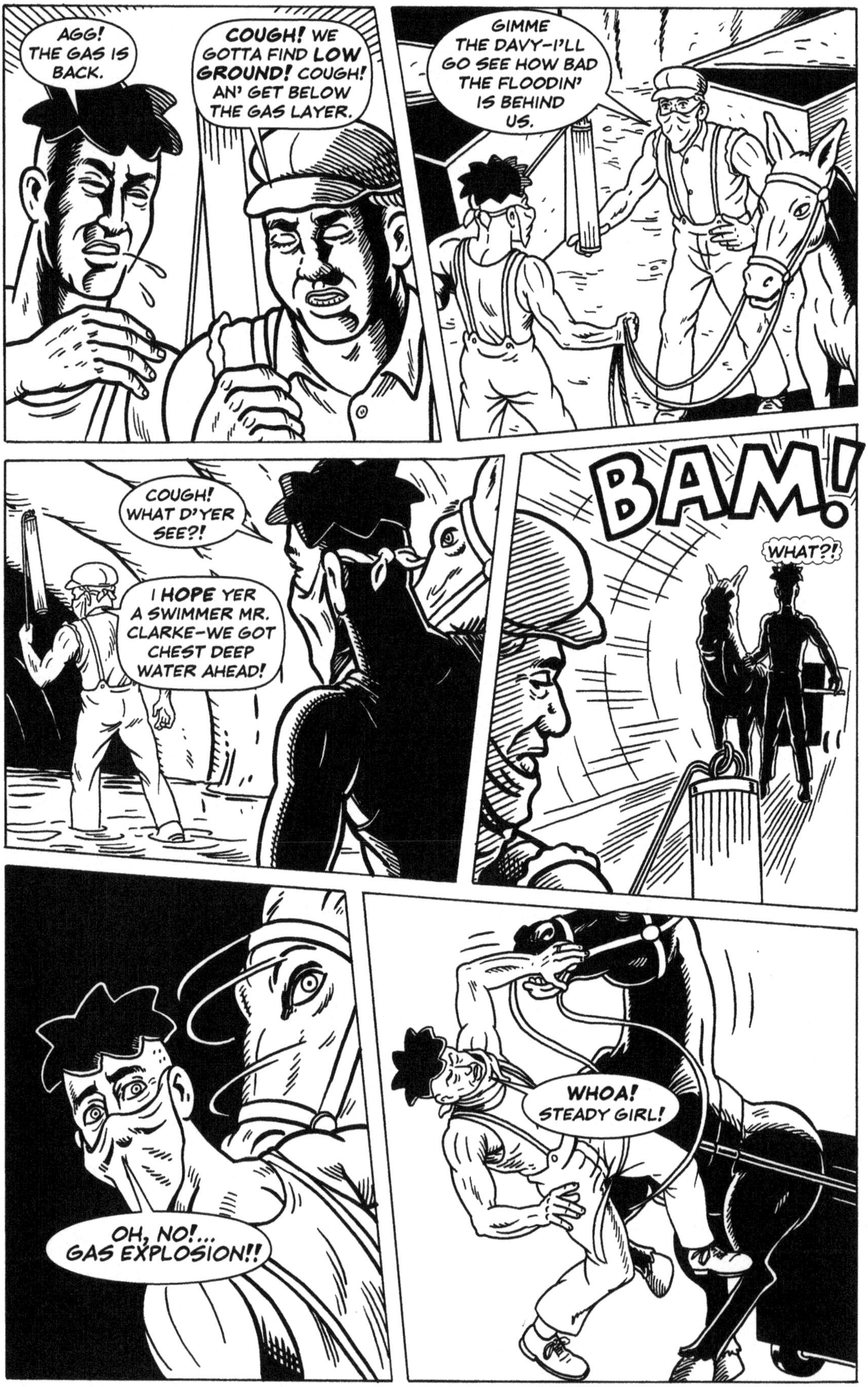
AGG! THE GAS IS BACK.
COUGH! WE GOTTA FIND LOW GROUND! COUGH! AN' GET BELOW THE GAS LAYER.
GIMME THE DAVY–I'LL GO SEE HOW BAD THE FLOODIN' IS BEHIND US.
COUGH! WHAT D'YER SEE?!
I HOPE YER A SWIMMER MR. CLARKE–WE GOT CHEST DEEP WATER AHEAD!
BAM!
WHAT?!
OH, NO!... GAS EXPLOSION!!
WHOA! STEADY GIRL!

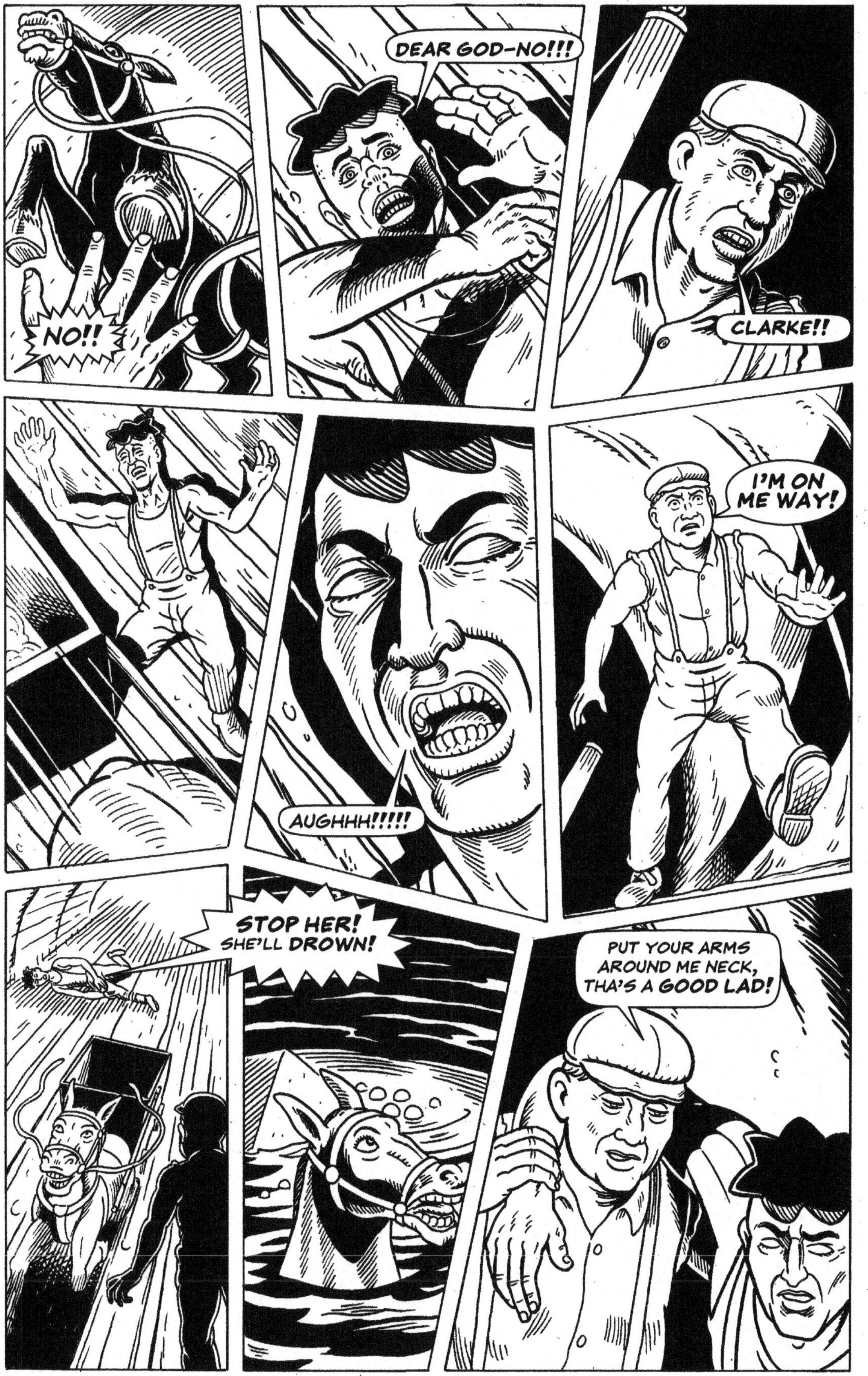
NO!!
DEAR GOD–NO!!!
CLARKE!!
AUGHHH!!!!!
I'M ON ME WAY!
STOP HER! SHE'LL DROWN!
PUT YOUR ARMS AROUND ME NECK, THA'S A GOOD LAD!

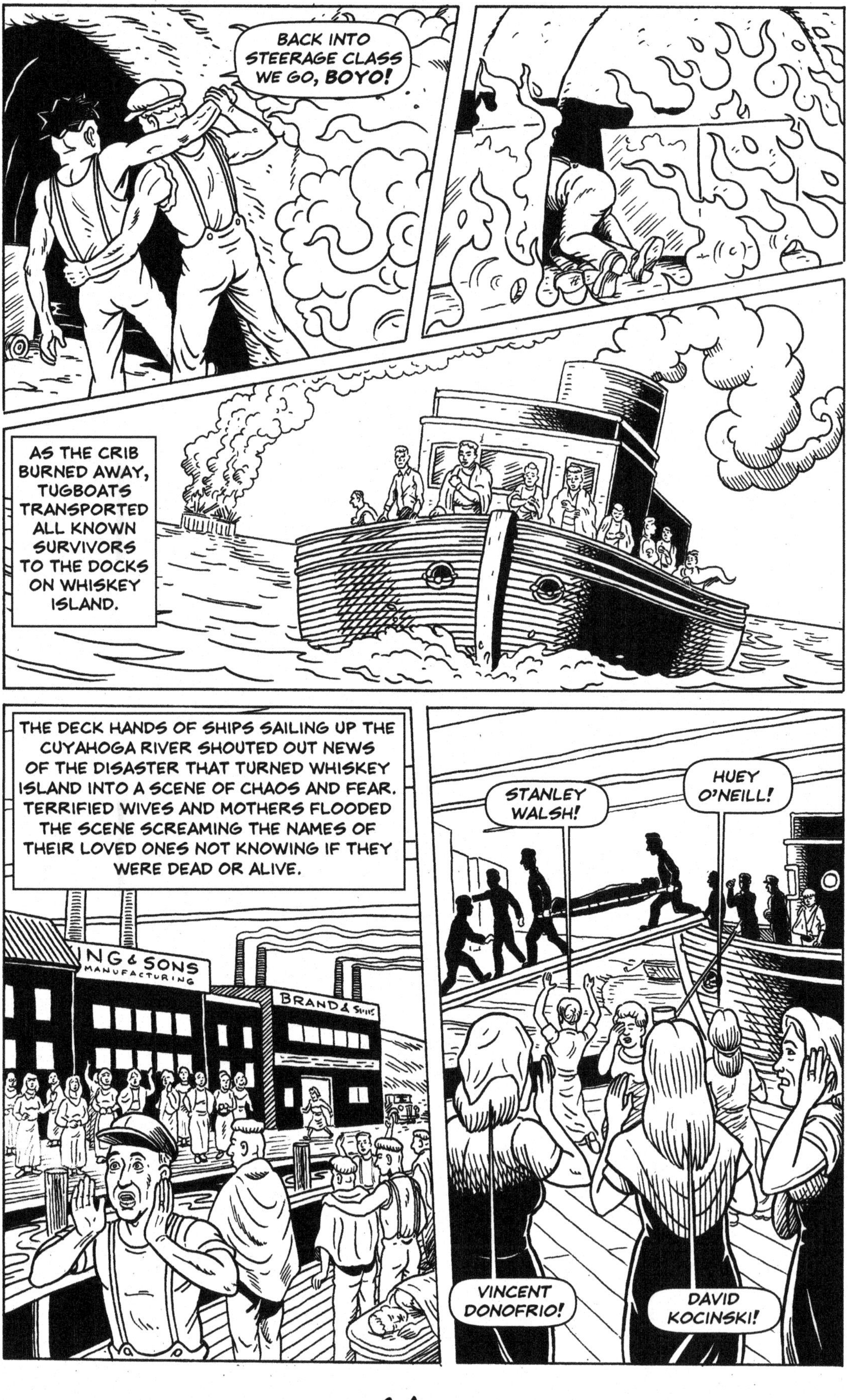
BACK INTO STEERAGE CLASS WE GO, BOYO!
AS THE CRIB BURNED AWAY, TUGBOATS TRANSPORTED ALL KNOWN SURVIVORS TO THE DOCKS ON WHISKEY ISLAND.
THE DECK HANDS OF SHIPS SAILING UP THE CUYAHOGA RIVER SHOUTED OUT NEWS OF THE DISASTER THAT TURNED WHISKEY ISLAND INTO A SCENE OF CHAOS AND FEAR. TERRIFIED WIVES AND MOTHERS FLOODED THE SCENE SCREAMING THE NAMES OF THEIR LOVED ONES NOT KNOWING IF THEY WERE DEAD OR ALIVE.
ING & SONS
MANUFACTURING
STANLEY WALSH!
HUEY O'NEILL!
VINCENT DONOFRIO!
DAVID KOCINSKI!

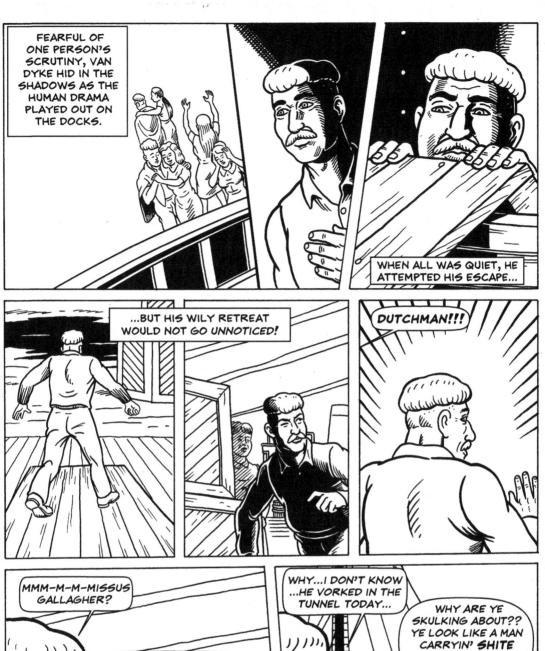

FEARFUL OF ONE PERSON'S SCRUTINY, VAN DYKE HID IN THE SHADOWS AS THE HUMAN DRAMA PLAYED OUT ON THE DOCKS.

WHEN ALL WAS QUIET, HE ATTEMPTED HIS ESCAPE...

...BUT HIS WILY RETREAT WOULD NOT GO UNNOTICED!

DUTCHMAN!!!

MMM—M—M—MISSUS GALLAGHER?

WHERE BE OUR HUSBANDS?! WHERE'S JOHNNY GALLAGHER?!!

WHY...I DON'T KNOW ...HE VORKED IN THE TUNNEL TODAY...

WHY ARE YE SKULKING ABOUT?? YE LOOK LIKE A MAN CARRYIN' SHITE AROUND IN HIS UNDERCLOTHES!

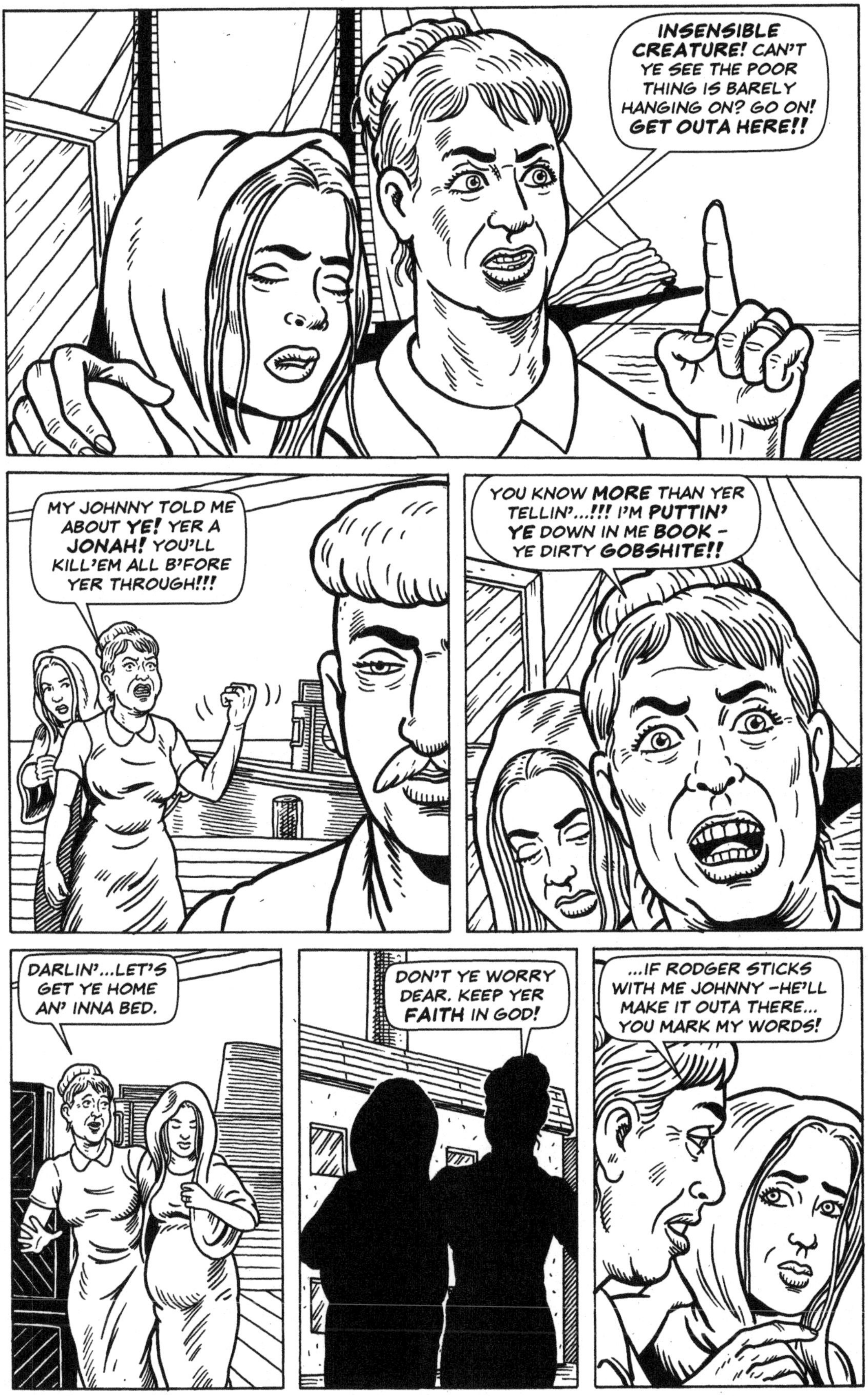
INSENSIBLE CREATURE! CAN'T YE SEE THE POOR THING IS BARELY HANGING ON? GO ON! GET OUTA HERE!!
MY JOHNNY TOLD ME ABOUT YE! YER A JONAH! YOU'LL KILL'EM ALL B'FORE YER THROUGH!!!
YOU KNOW MORE THAN YER TELLIN'...!!! I'M PUTTIN' YE DOWN IN ME BOOK - YE DIRTY GOBSHITE!!
DARLIN'...LET'S GET YE HOME AN' INNA BED.
DON'T YE WORRY DEAR. KEEP YER FAITH IN GOD!
...IF RODGER STICKS WITH ME JOHNNY -HE'LL MAKE IT OUTA THERE... YOU MARK MY WORDS!

68

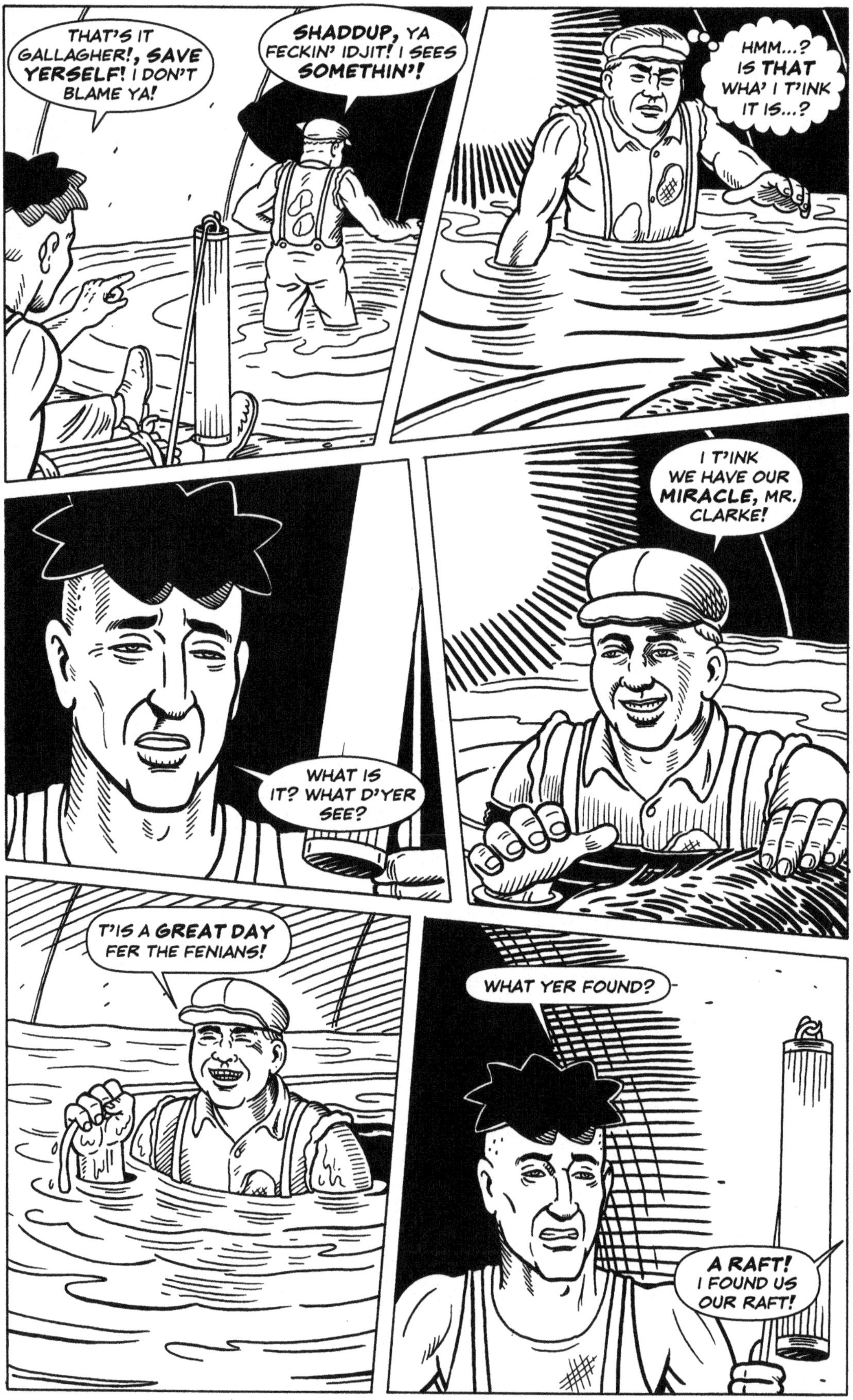
THAT'S IT GALLAGHER!, SAVE YERSELF! I DON'T BLAME YA!
SHADDUP, YA FECKIN' IDJIT! I SEES SOMETHIN'!
HMM...? IS THAT WHA' I T'INK IT IS...?
WHAT IS IT? WHAT D'YER SEE?
I T'INK WE HAVE OUR MIRACLE, MR. CLARKE!
T'IS A GREAT DAY FER THE FENIANS!
WHAT YER FOUND?
A RAFT! I FOUND US OUR RAFT!

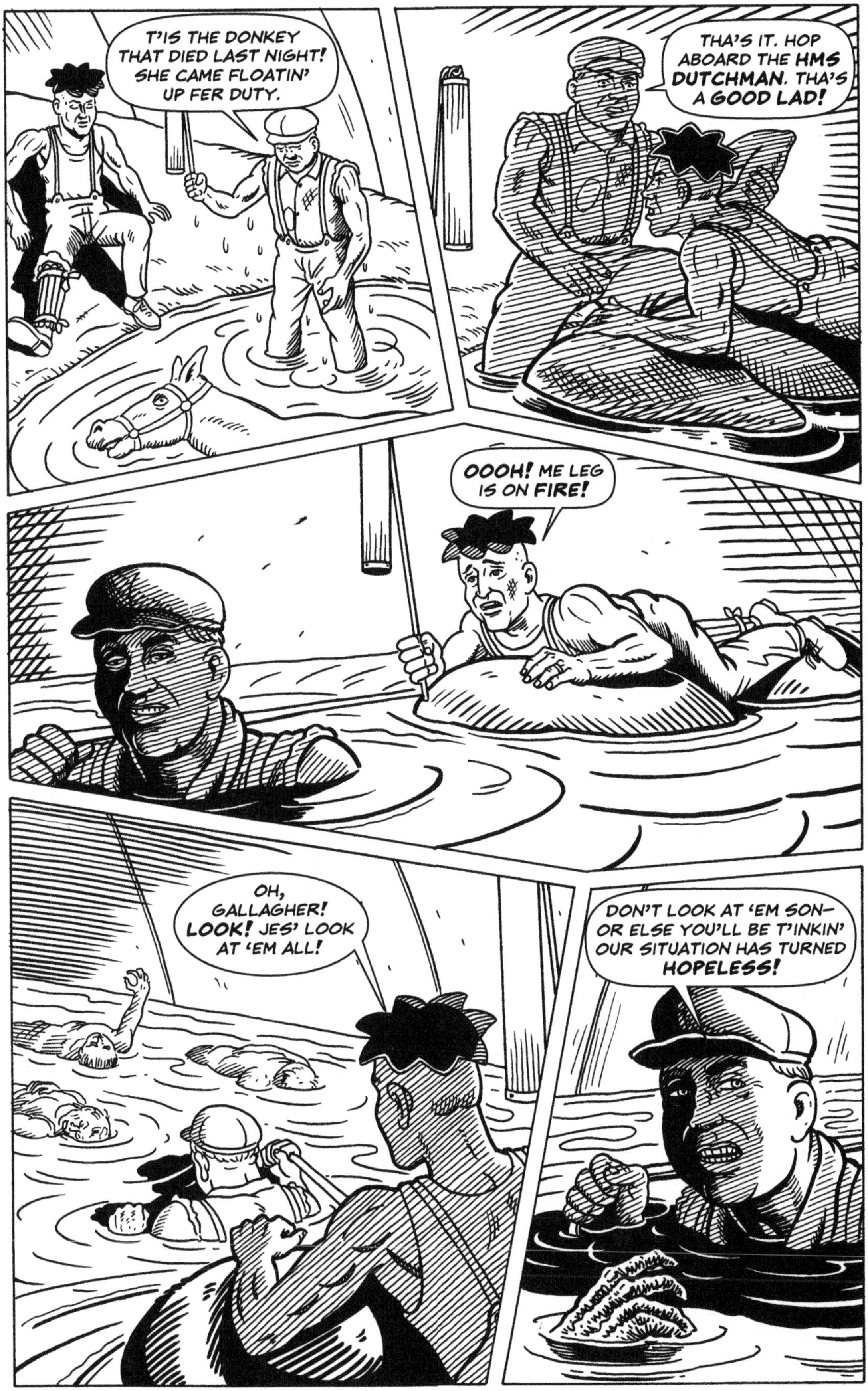
T'IS THE DONKEY THAT DIED LAST NIGHT! SHE CAME FLOATIN' UP FER DUTY.
THA'S IT. HOP ABOARD THE HMS DUTCHMAN. THA'S A GOOD LAD!
OOOH! ME LEG IS ON FIRE!
OH, GALLAGHER! LOOK! JES' LOOK AT 'EM ALL!
DON'T LOOK AT 'EM SON– OR ELSE YOU'LL BE T'INKIN' OUR SITUATION HAS TURNED HOPELESS!

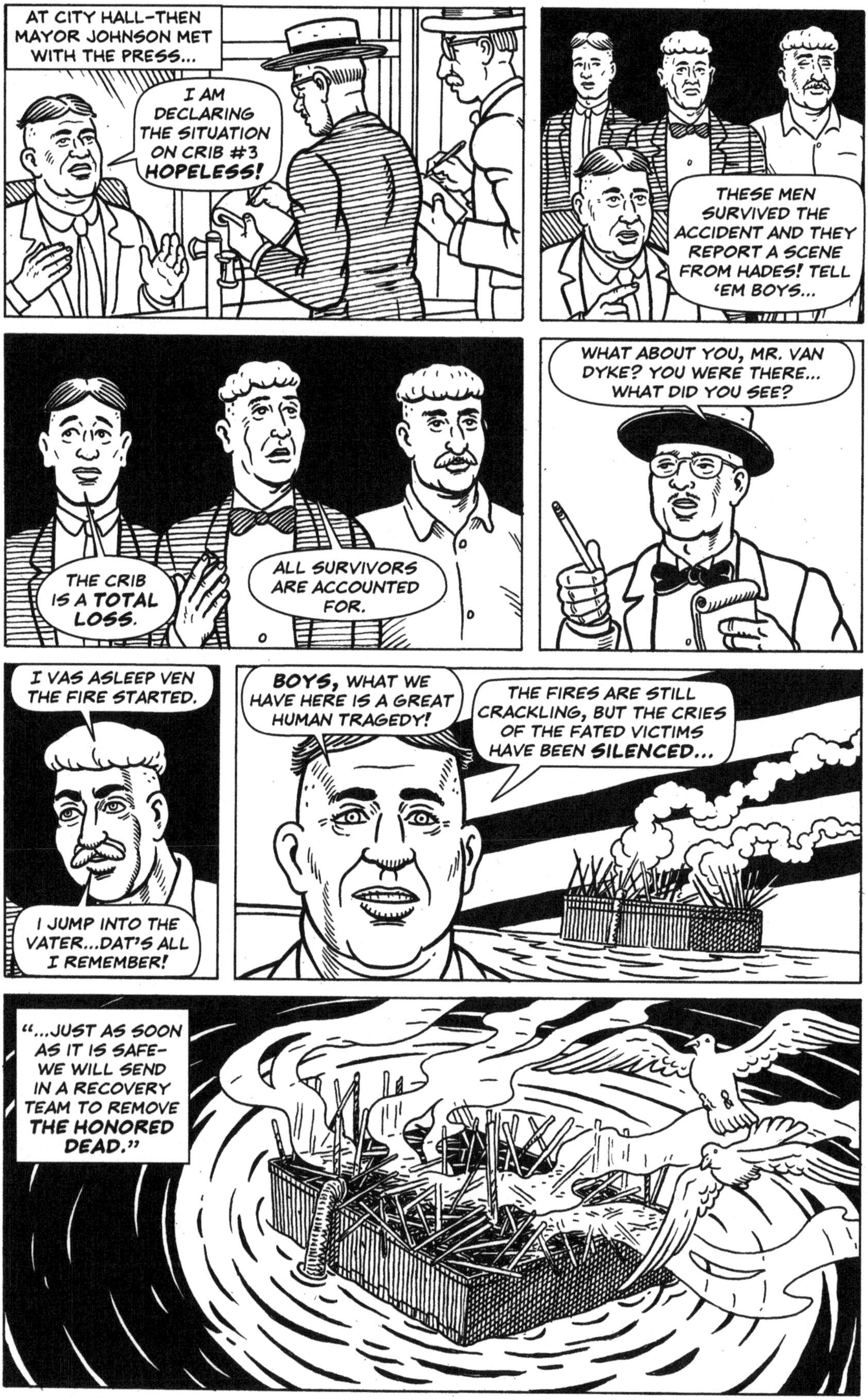
AT CITY HALL–THEN MAYOR JOHNSON MET WITH THE PRESS...
I AM DECLARING THE SITUATION ON CRIB #3 HOPELESS!
THESE MEN SURVIVED THE ACCIDENT AND THEY REPORT A SCENE FROM HADES! TELL 'EM BOYS...
THE CRIB IS A TOTAL LOSS.
ALL SURVIVORS ARE ACCOUNTED FOR.
WHAT ABOUT YOU, MR. VAN DYKE? YOU WERE THERE... WHAT DID YOU SEE?
I VAS ASLEEP VEN THE FIRE STARTED.
I JUMP INTO THE VATER...DAT'S ALL I REMEMBER!
BOYS, WHAT WE HAVE HERE IS A GREAT HUMAN TRAGEDY!
THE FIRES ARE STILL CRACKLING, BUT THE CRIES OF THE FATED VICTIMS HAVE BEEN SILENCED...
"...JUST AS SOON AS IT IS SAFE– WE WILL SEND IN A RECOVERY TEAM TO REMOVE THE HONORED DEAD."

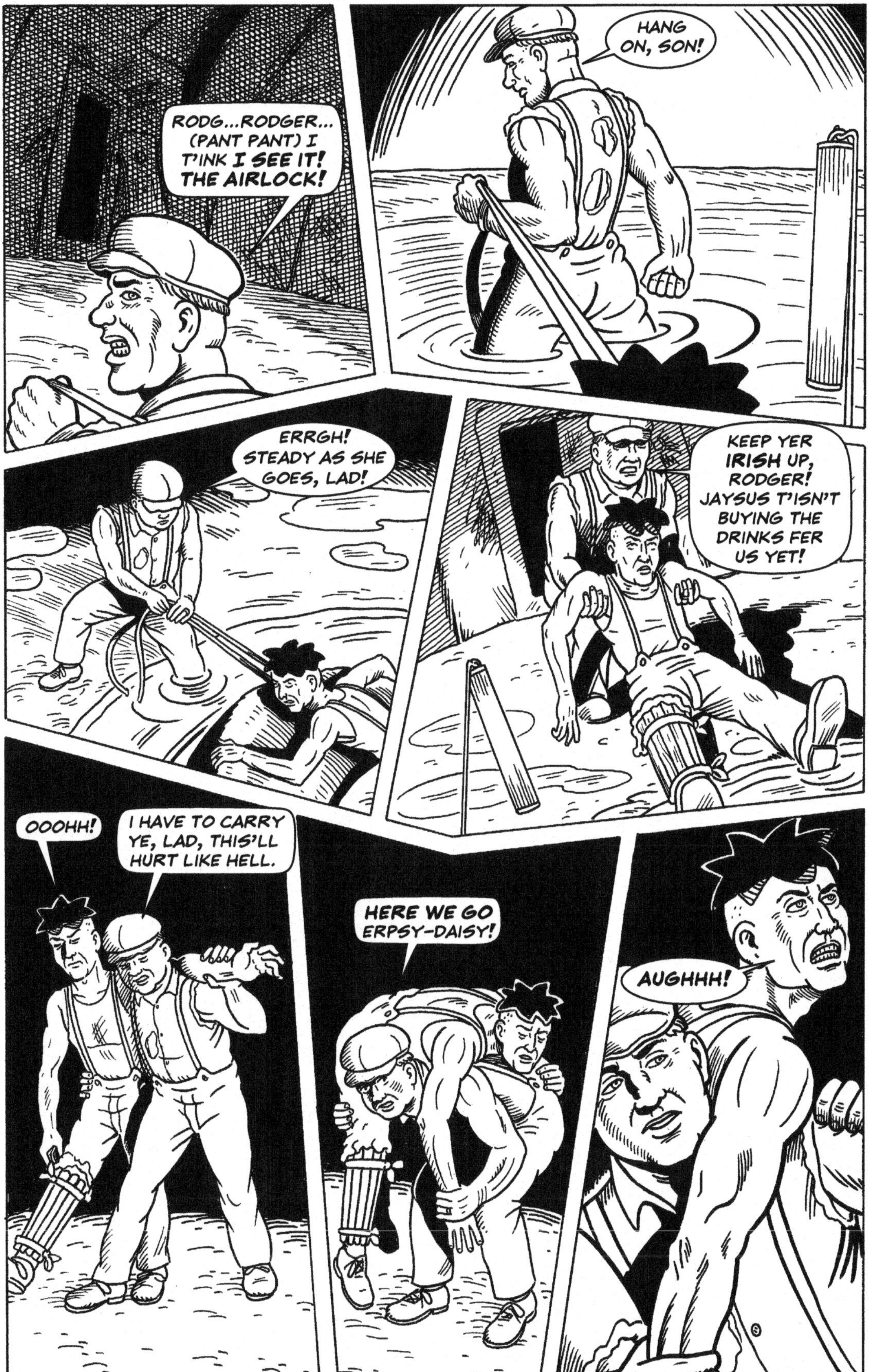
RODG...RODGER... (PANT PANT) I T'INK I SEE IT! THE AIRLOCK!
HANG ON, SON!
ERRGH! STEADY AS SHE GOES, LAD!
KEEP YER IRISH UP, RODGER! JAYSUS T'ISN'T BUYING THE DRINKS FER US YET!
OOOHH!
I HAVE TO CARRY YE, LAD, THIS'LL HURT LIKE HELL.
HERE WE GO ERPSY-DAISY!
AUGHHH!

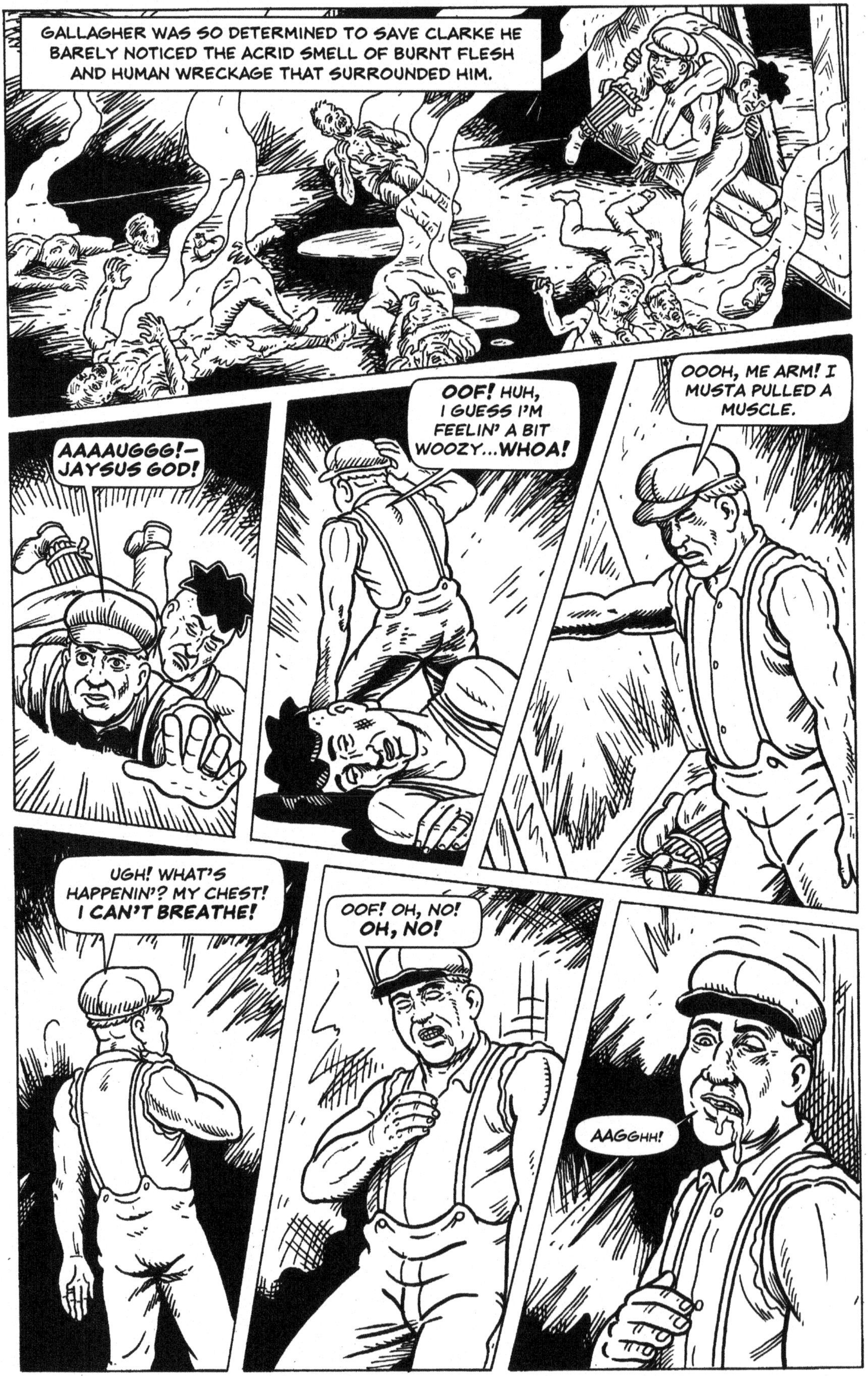
GALLAGHER WAS SO DETERMINED TO SAVE CLARKE HE BARELY NOTICED THE ACRID SMELL OF BURNT FLESH AND HUMAN WRECKAGE THAT SURROUNDED HIM.
AAAAUGGG!— JAYSUS GOD!
OOF! HUH, I GUESS I'M FEELIN' A BIT WOOZY...WHOA!
OOOH, ME ARM! I MUSTA PULLED A MUSCLE.
UGH! WHAT'S HAPPENIN'? MY CHEST! I CAN'T BREATHE!
OOF! OH, NO! OH, NO!
AAGGHH!

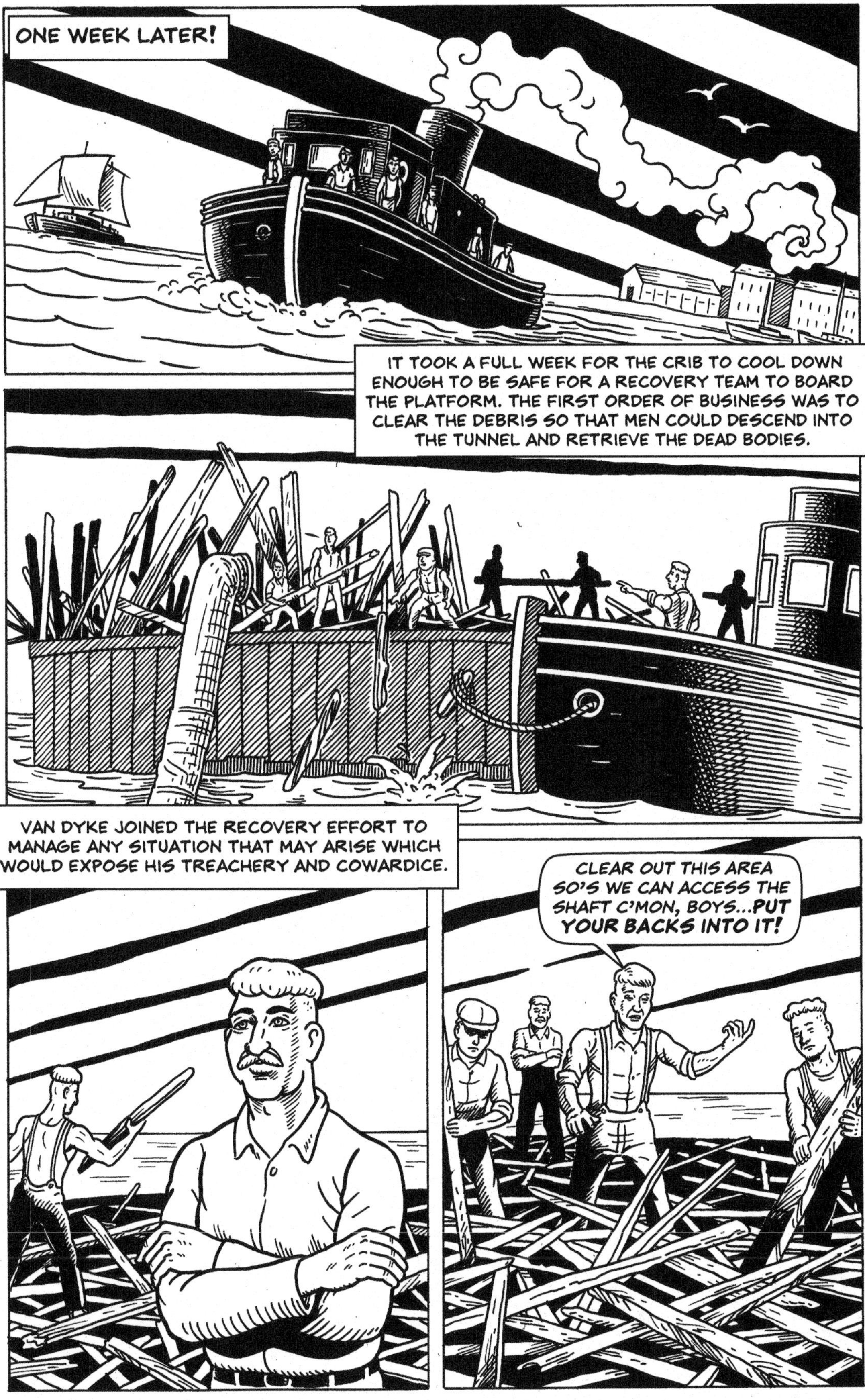
ONE WEEK LATER!
IT TOOK A FULL WEEK FOR THE CRIB TO COOL DOWN ENOUGH TO BE SAFE FOR A RECOVERY TEAM TO BOARD THE PLATFORM. THE FIRST ORDER OF BUSINESS WAS TO CLEAR THE DEBRIS SO THAT MEN COULD DESCEND INTO THE TUNNEL AND RETRIEVE THE DEAD BODIES.
VAN DYKE JOINED THE RECOVERY EFFORT TO MANAGE ANY SITUATION THAT MAY ARISE WHICH WOULD EXPOSE HIS TREACHERY AND COWARDICE.
CLEAR OUT THIS AREA SO'S WE CAN ACCESS THE SHAFT C'MON, BOYS...PUT YOUR BACKS INTO IT!

TWO HOURS LATER...

THAT'LL DO IT! HAND ME THAT BLOCK O' WOOD THERE!

LISTEN CLOSELY, BOYS! IF SHE **SPLASHES** WE'LL KNOW THE TUNNEL **IS FLOODED!**

ANY O' YOUSE HEAR A SPLASH?

BING! BANG! CLUNK!

SOUNDED LIKE IT HIT DRY LAND TO ME!

TRY IT AGAIN.

OK, LISTEN WITH **ALL YOUR EARS** THIS TIME—READY?

BANG! BANG!

HEY! I DIDN'T EVEN DROP IT YET.

MEBBE THE FIRST PIECE IS **STILL FALLING !**

WHAT'S ALL THE RUMPUS?

NOISES, SIR! NOISES IN THE SHAFT!

O'MALLEY! HAND ME THAT HOOK SPANNER!

AHH! MOST LIKELY YOU HEAR **DEBRIS** FALLING IN THE SHAFT.

BANG! BANG! BANG!

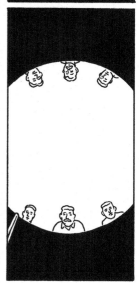

76

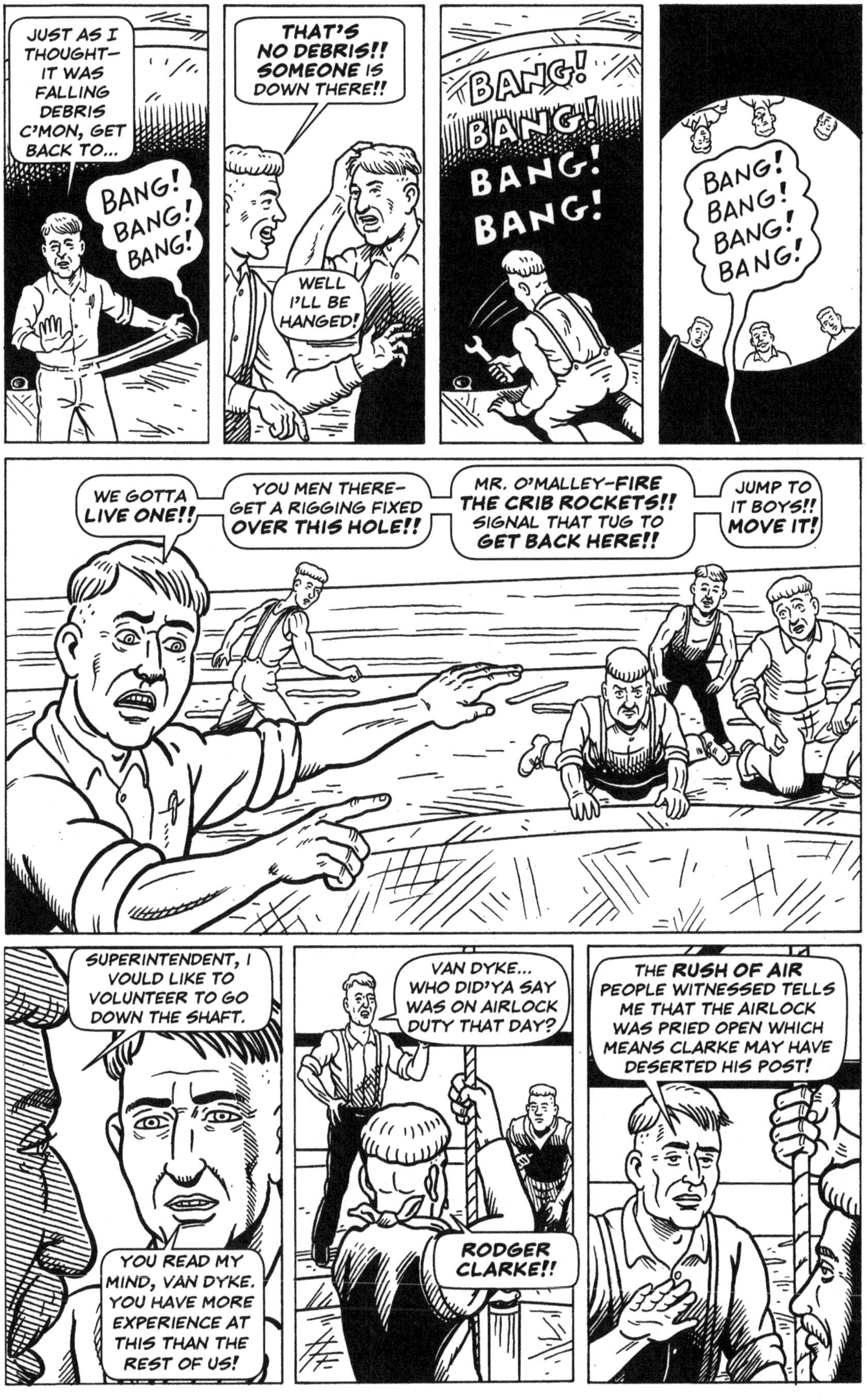
JUST AS I THOUGHT— IT WAS FALLING DEBRIS C'MON, GET BACK TO...
BANG! BANG! BANG!
THAT'S NO DEBRIS!! SOMEONE IS DOWN THERE!!
WELL I'LL BE HANGED!
BANG! BANG! BANG! BANG!
BANG! BANG! BANG! BANG!
WE GOTTA LIVE ONE!!
YOU MEN THERE— GET A RIGGING FIXED OVER THIS HOLE!!
MR. O'MALLEY—FIRE THE CRIB ROCKETS!! SIGNAL THAT TUG TO GET BACK HERE!!
JUMP TO IT BOYS!! MOVE IT!
SUPERINTENDENT, I VOULD LIKE TO VOLUNTEER TO GO DOWN THE SHAFT.
YOU READ MY MIND, VAN DYKE. YOU HAVE MORE EXPERIENCE AT THIS THAN THE REST OF US!
VAN DYKE... WHO DID'YA SAY WAS ON AIRLOCK DUTY THAT DAY?
RODGER CLARKE!!
THE RUSH OF AIR PEOPLE WITNESSED TELLS ME THAT THE AIRLOCK WAS PRIED OPEN WHICH MEANS CLARKE MAY HAVE DESERTED HIS POST!

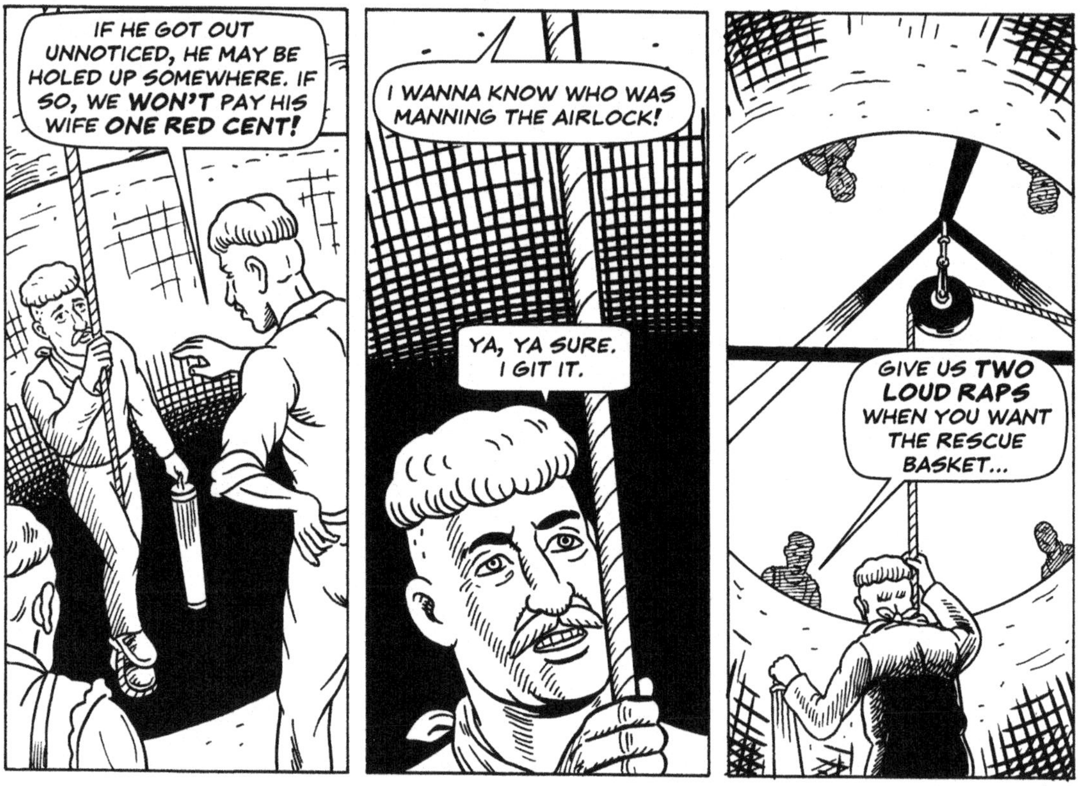
IF HE GOT OUT UNNOTICED, HE MAY BE HOLED UP SOMEWHERE. IF SO, WE **WON'T** PAY HIS WIFE **ONE RED CENT!**
I WANNA KNOW WHO WAS MANNING THE AIRLOCK!
YA, YA SURE. I GIT IT.
GIVE US **TWO LOUD RAPS** WHEN YOU WANT THE RESCUE BASKET...

THE SHAFT WAS APPROXIMATELY 200 FEET LONG, WHICH PLACED ITS BASE 75 FEET BELOW THE LAKE BED. VAN DYKE WRAPPED A WET TOWEL AROUND HIS FACE TO HELP PROTECT HIM FROM THE METHANE GAS, BUT NO TOWEL OR MASK COULD EVER FILTER OUT THE ***HORRIFIC*** SIGHTS AND SMELLS THAT AWAITED HIM IN THE TUNNEL.

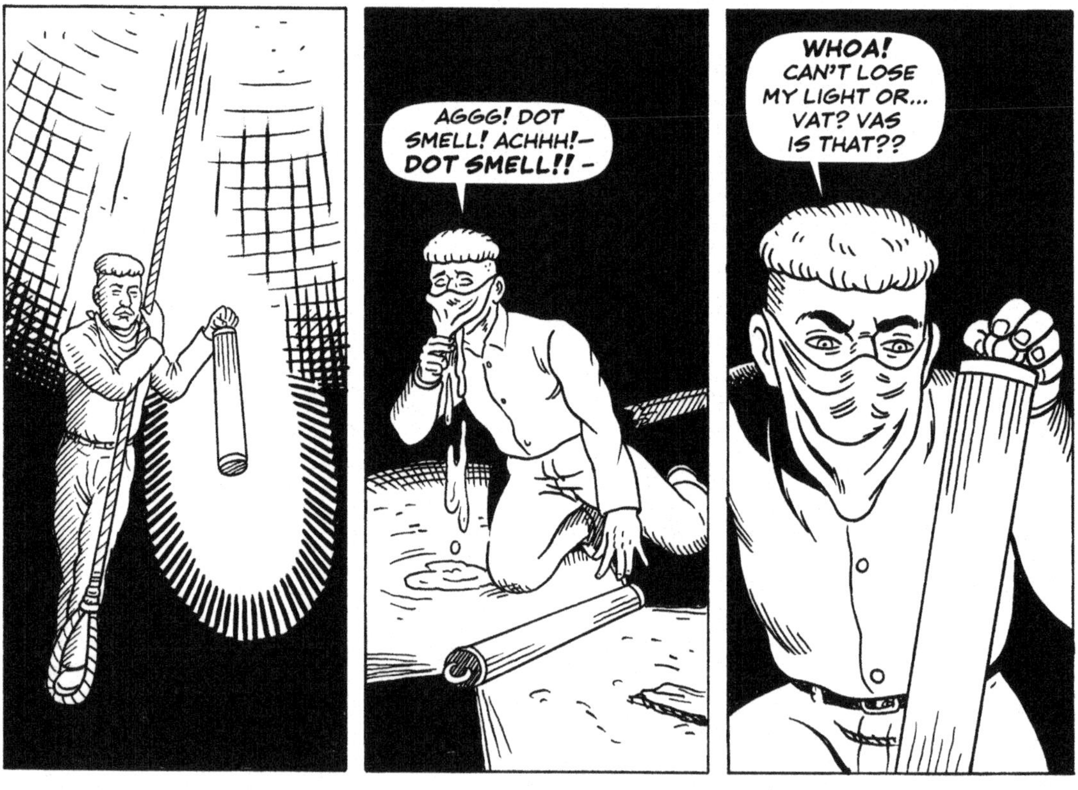
AGGG! DOT SMELL! ACHHH!– **DOT SMELL!!** –
WHOA! CAN'T LOSE MY LIGHT OR... VAT? VAS IS THAT??

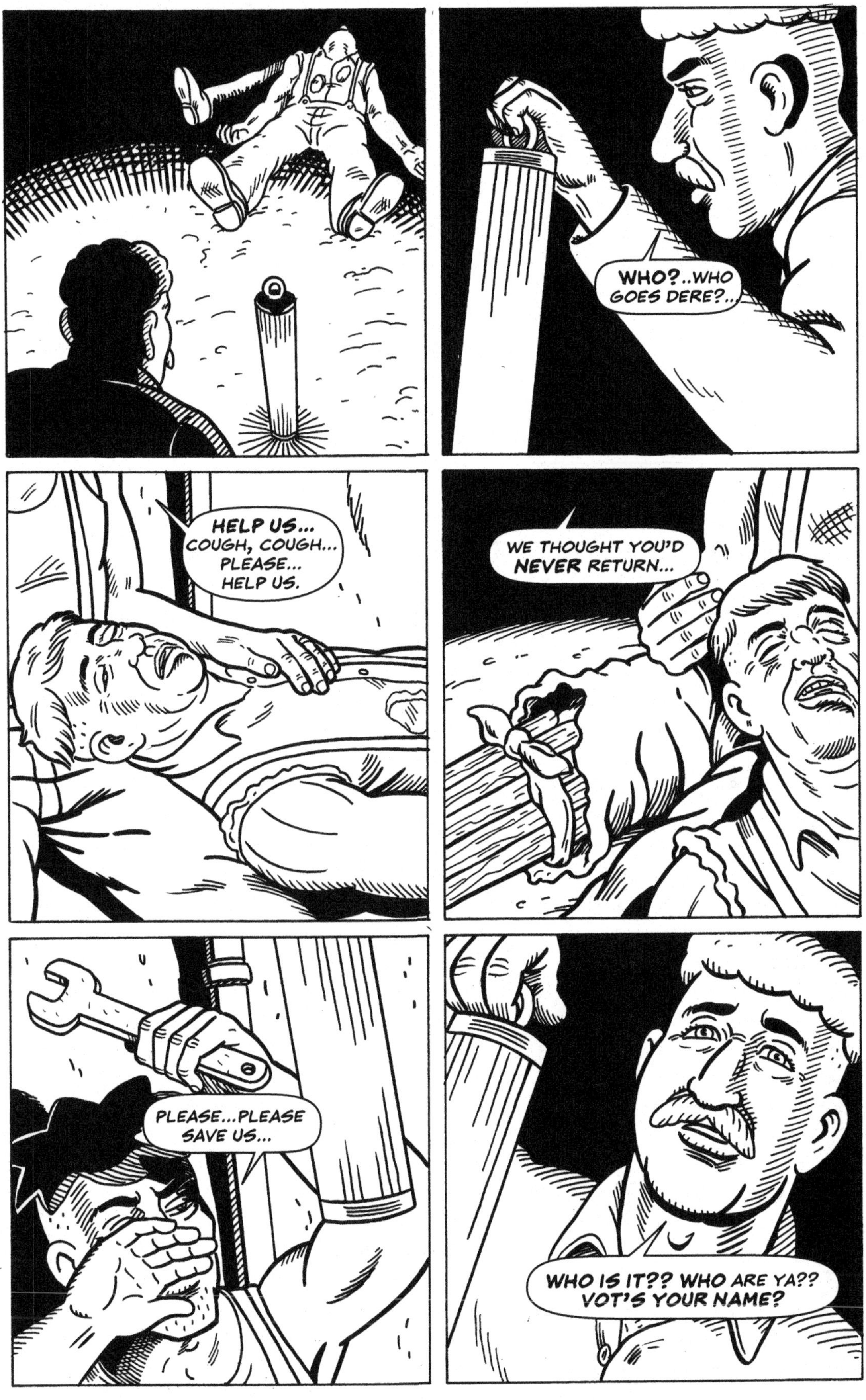
WHO?..WHO GOES DERE?..
HELP US... COUGH, COUGH... PLEASE... HELP US.
WE THOUGHT YOU'D NEVER RETURN...
PLEASE...PLEASE SAVE US...
WHO IS IT?? WHO ARE YA?? VOT'S YOUR NAME?

CLARKE...MY NAME IS CLARKE...AND THIS IS...JOHNNY... JOHNNY GALLAGHER.

ISS HE DEAD?

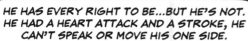

HE HAS EVERY RIGHT TO BE...BUT HE'S NOT. HE HAD A HEART ATTACK AND A STROKE, HE CAN'T SPEAK OR MOVE HIS ONE SIDE.

UND YOU CLARKE— VOT OF YOU? VOT HAPPENED TO YOUR LEG?

RUN OVER BY A MUCK CART! 'T'WAS JOHNNY...JOHNNY WHO SAVED ME. I BEEN BANGIN' ON THE PIPE FOR WEEK? WHAT THE HELL KEPT YE?

HOW DID YOU GEDT DIS FAR VITH HIM ON A BROKEN LEG?

81

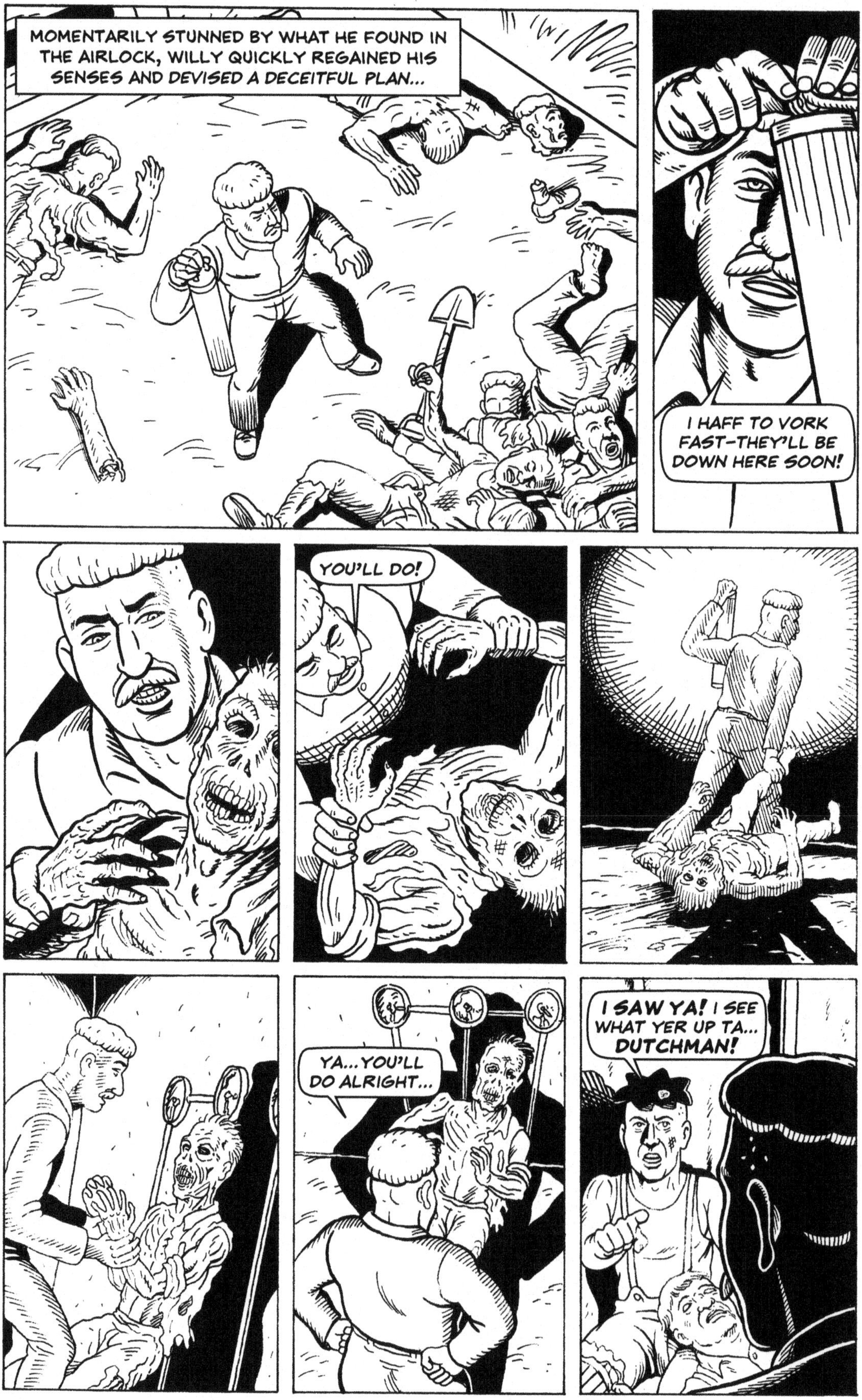
MOMENTARILY STUNNED BY WHAT HE FOUND IN THE AIRLOCK, WILLY QUICKLY REGAINED HIS SENSES AND DEVISED A DECEITFUL PLAN...
I HAFF TO VORK FAST–THEY'LL BE DOWN HERE SOON!
YOU'LL DO!
YA...YOU'LL DO ALRIGHT...
I SAW YA! I SEE WHAT YER UP TA... DUTCHMAN!

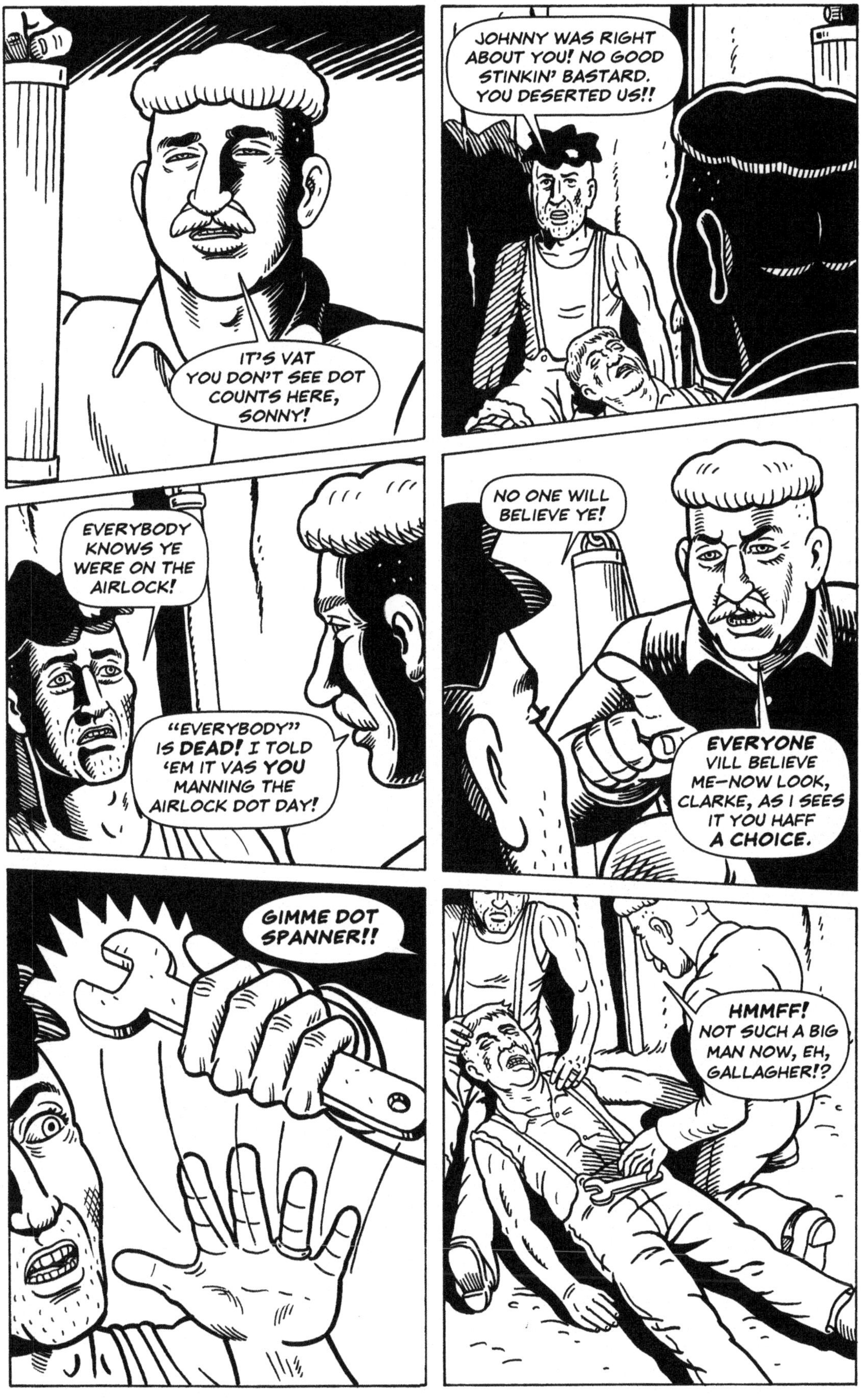
IT'S VAT YOU DON'T SEE DOT COUNTS HERE, SONNY!
JOHNNY WAS RIGHT ABOUT YOU! NO GOOD STINKIN' BASTARD. YOU DESERTED US!!
EVERYBODY KNOWS YE WERE ON THE AIRLOCK!
"EVERYBODY" IS DEAD! I TOLD 'EM IT VAS YOU MANNING THE AIRLOCK DOT DAY!
NO ONE WILL BELIEVE YE!
EVERYONE VILL BELIEVE ME—NOW LOOK, CLARKE, AS I SEES IT YOU HAFF A CHOICE.
GIMME DOT SPANNER!!
HMMFF! NOT SUCH A BIG MAN NOW, EH, GALLAGHER!?

84

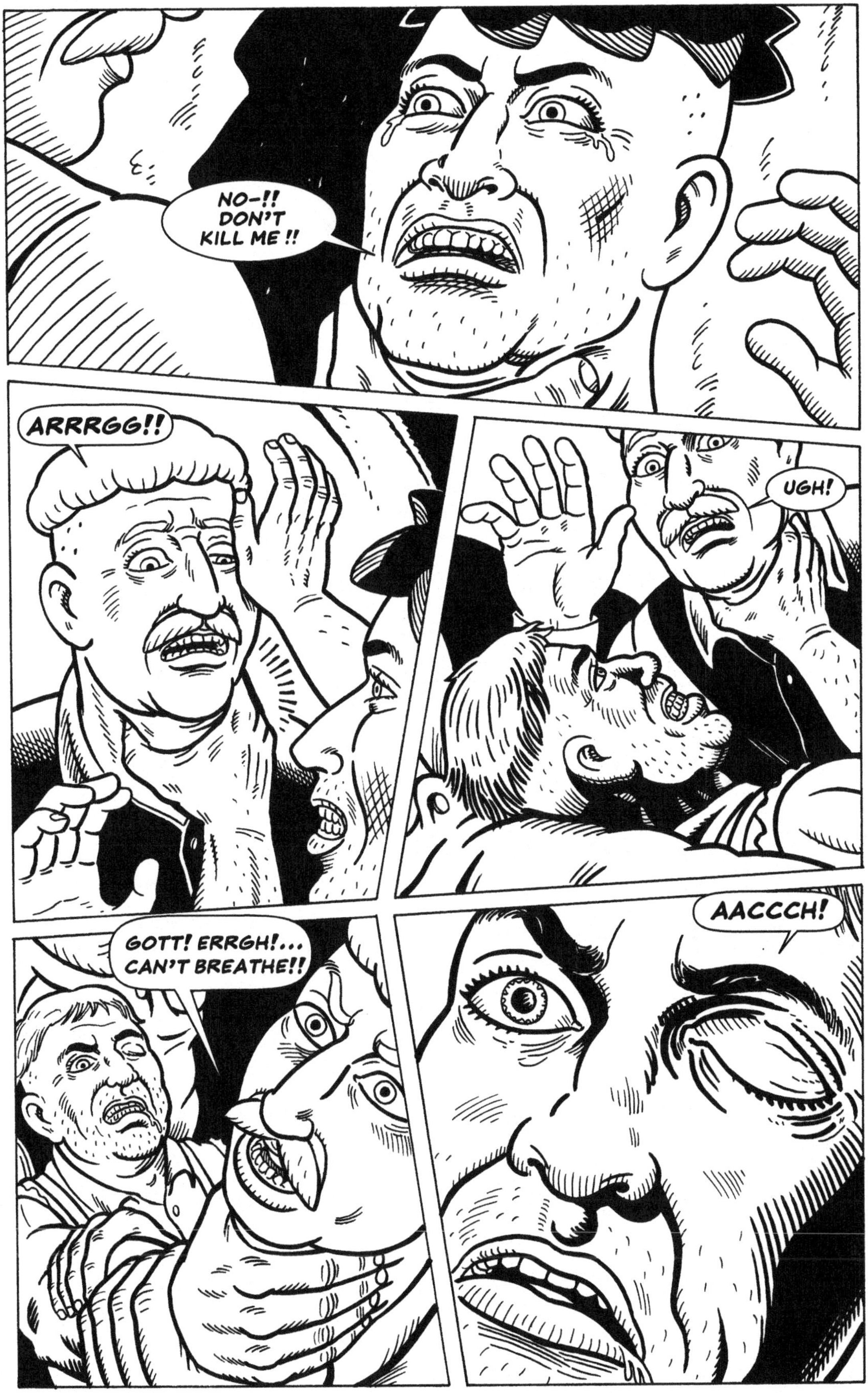
NO-!! DON'T KILL ME !!
ARRRGG!!
UGH!
GOTT! ERRGH!... CAN'T BREATHE!!
AACCCH!

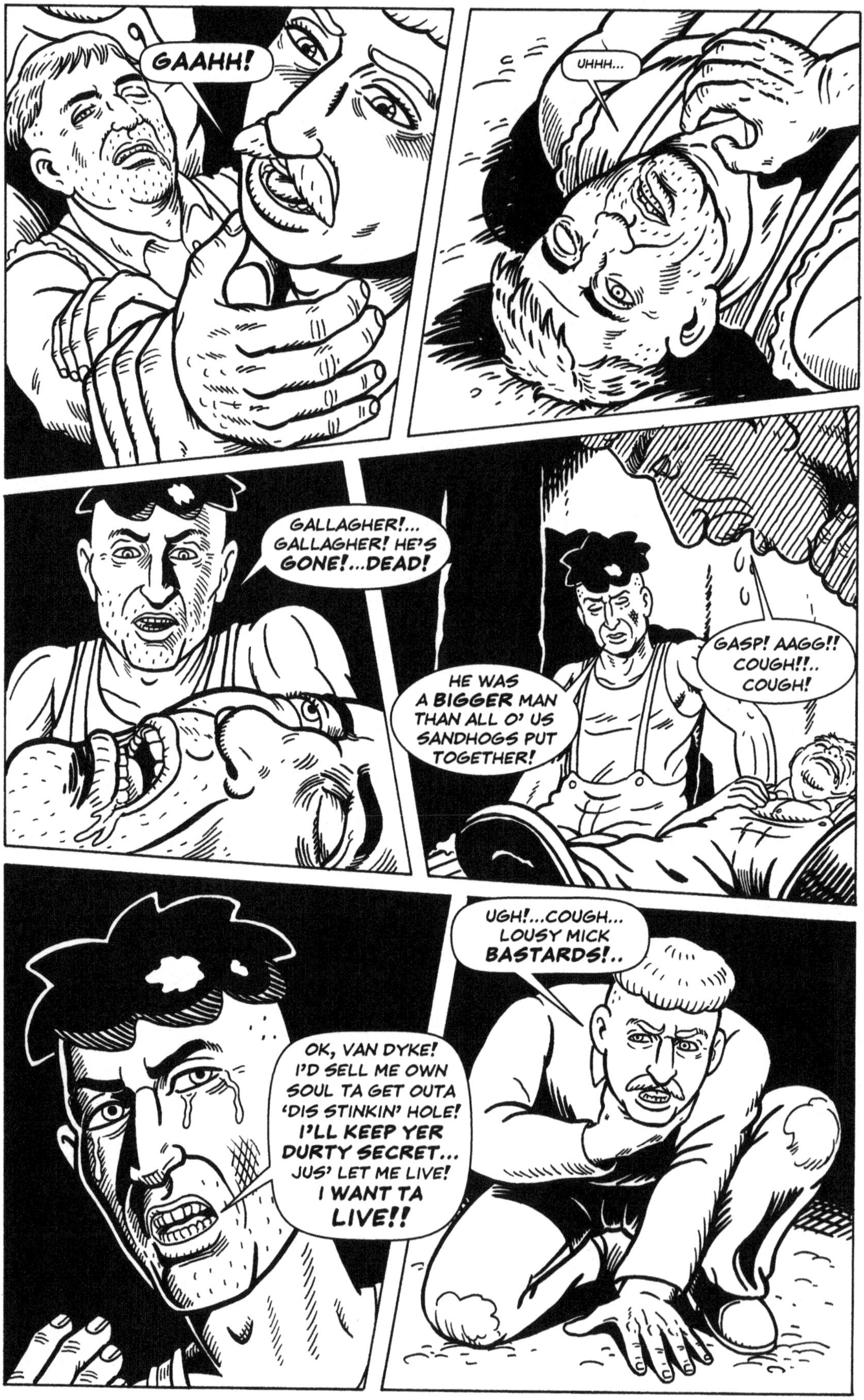
GAAHH!
UHHH...
GALLAGHER!... GALLAGHER! HE'S GONE!...DEAD!
HE WAS A BIGGER MAN THAN ALL O' US SANDHOGS PUT TOGETHER!
GASP! AAGG!! COUGH!!.. COUGH!
OK, VAN DYKE! I'D SELL ME OWN SOUL TA GET OUTA 'DIS STINKIN' HOLE! I'LL KEEP YER DURTY SECRET... JUS' LET ME LIVE! I WANT TA LIVE!!
UGH!...COUGH... LOUSY MICK BASTARDS!..

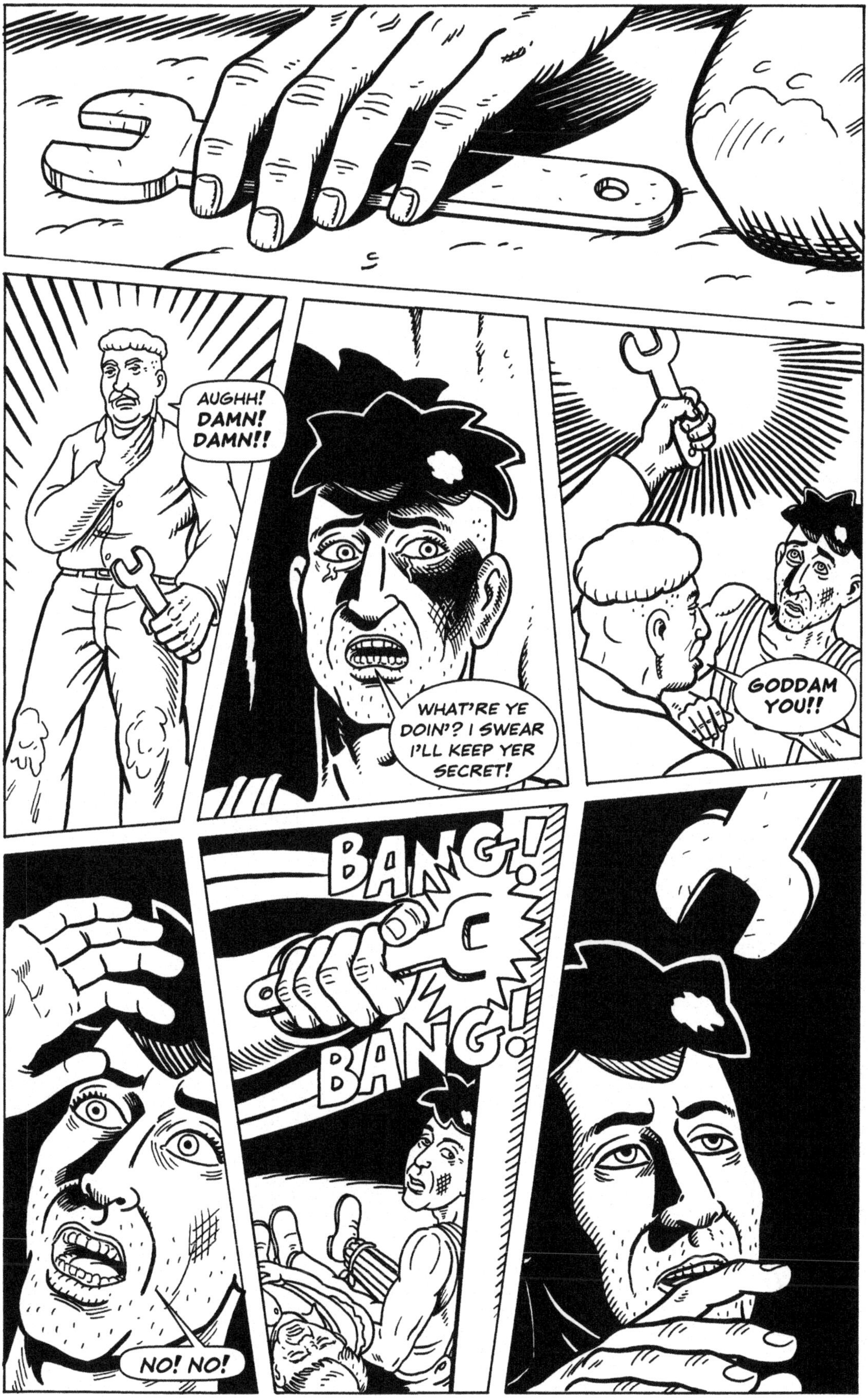
AUGHH! DAMN! DAMN!!
WHAT'RE YE DOIN'? I SWEAR I'LL KEEP YER SECRET!
GODDAM YOU!!
NO! NO!
BANG!
BANG!

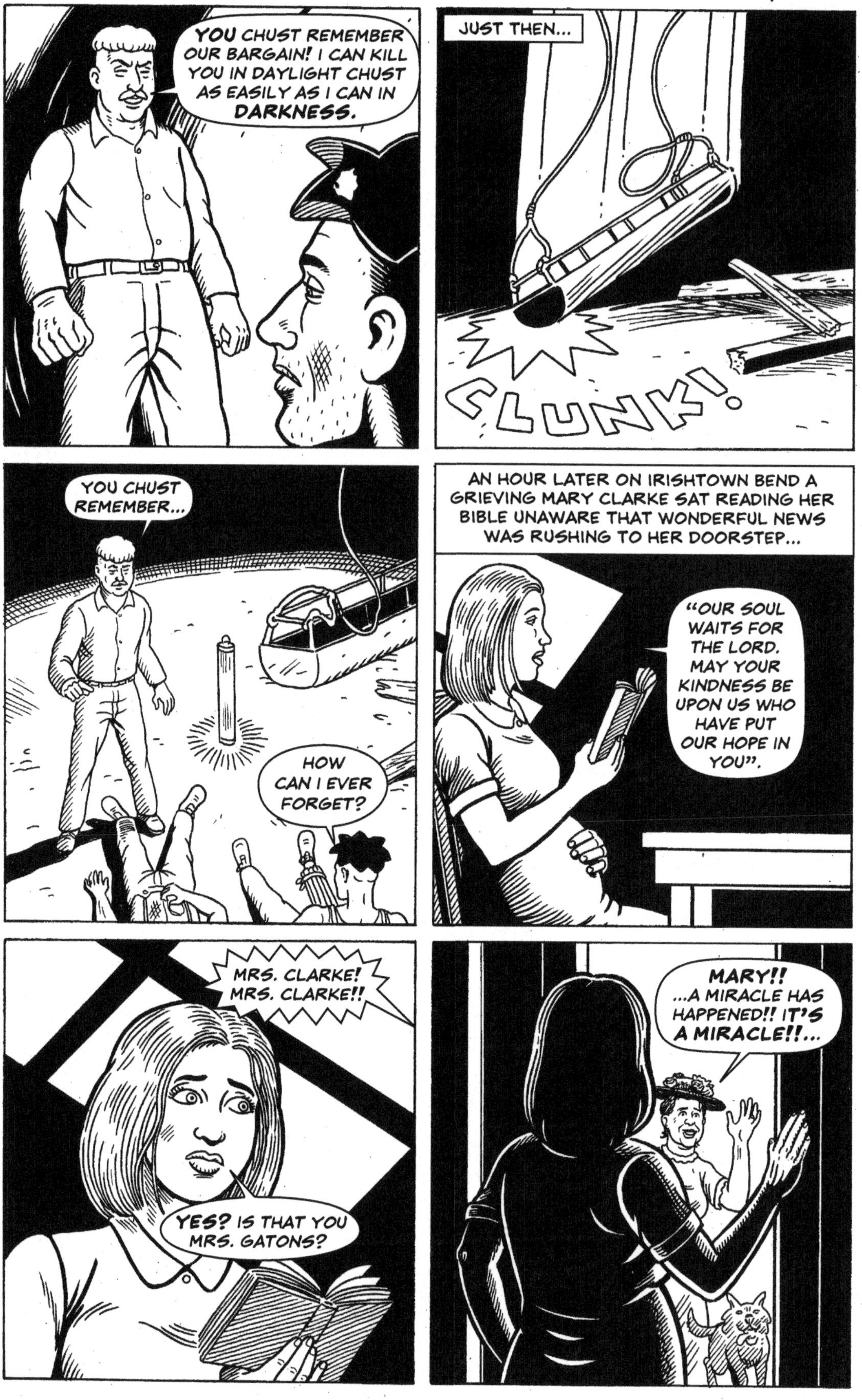
YOU CHUST REMEMBER OUR BARGAIN! I CAN KILL YOU IN DAYLIGHT CHUST AS EASILY AS I CAN IN DARKNESS.
JUST THEN...
CLUNK!
YOU CHUST REMEMBER...
HOW CAN I EVER FORGET?
AN HOUR LATER ON IRISHTOWN BEND A GRIEVING MARY CLARKE SAT READING HER BIBLE UNAWARE THAT WONDERFUL NEWS WAS RUSHING TO HER DOORSTEP...
"OUR SOUL WAITS FOR THE LORD. MAY YOUR KINDNESS BE UPON US WHO HAVE PUT OUR HOPE IN YOU".
MRS. CLARKE! MRS. CLARKE!!
YES? IS THAT YOU MRS. GATONS?
MARY!! ...A MIRACLE HAS HAPPENED!! IT'S A MIRACLE!!...

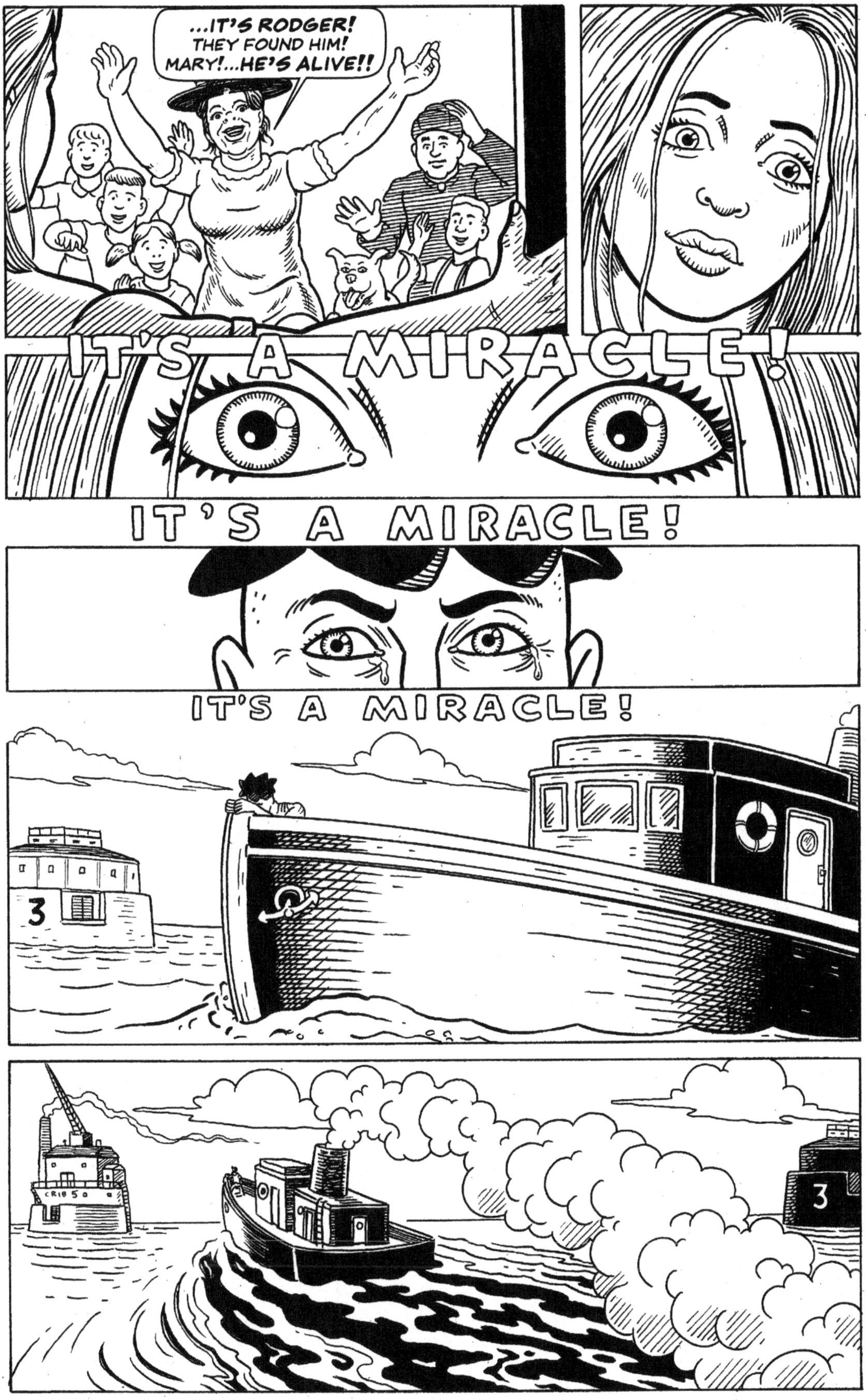
...IT'S RODGER! THEY FOUND HIM! MARY!...HE'S ALIVE!!
IT'S A MIRACLE!
IT'S A MIRACLE!
IT'S A MIRACLE!
3
CRIB 5
3

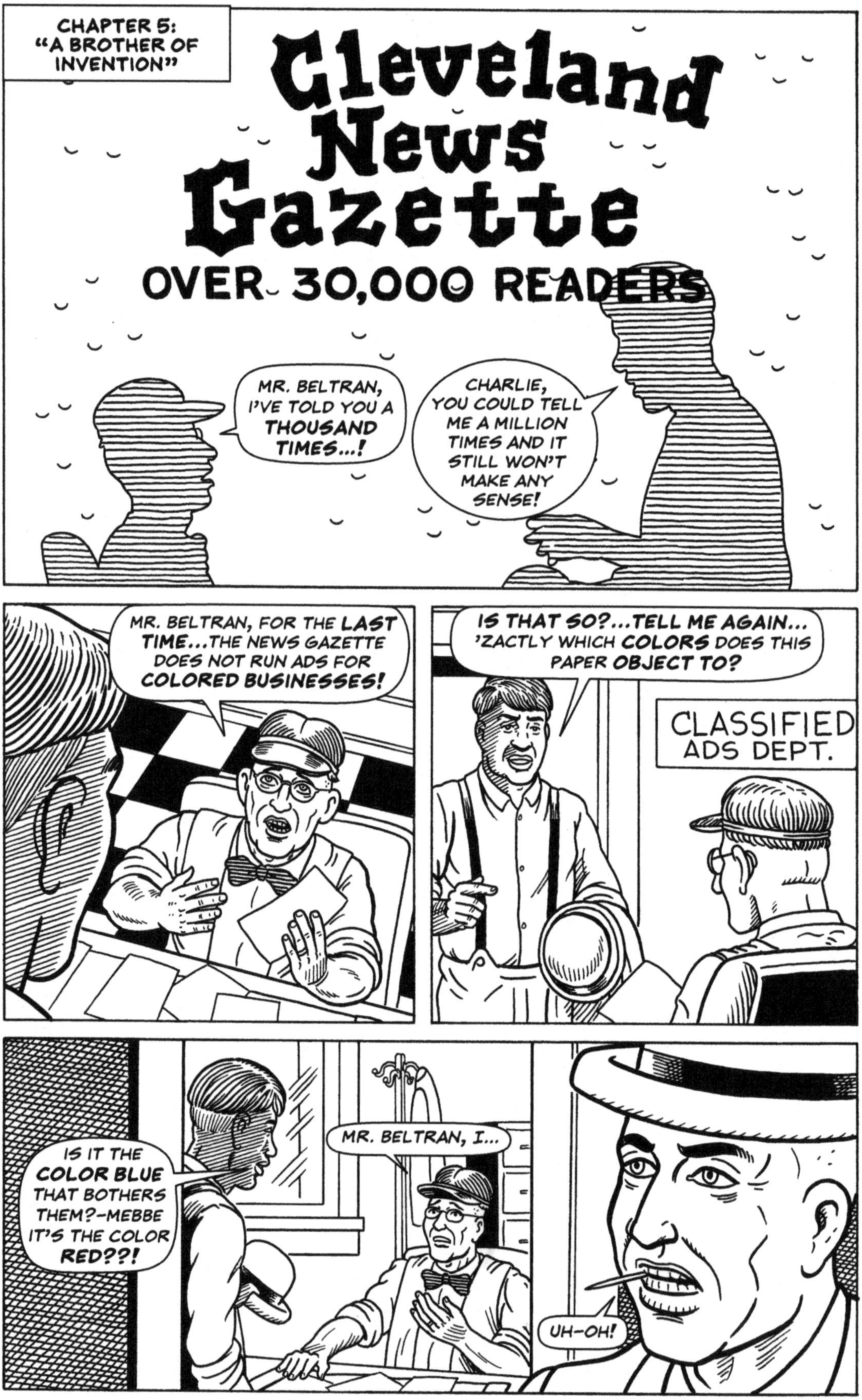
CHAPTER 5: "A BROTHER OF INVENTION"
Cleveland News Gazette
OVER 30,000 READERS
MR. BELTRAN, I'VE TOLD YOU A THOUSAND TIMES...!
CHARLIE, YOU COULD TELL ME A MILLION TIMES AND IT STILL WON'T MAKE ANY SENSE!
MR. BELTRAN, FOR THE LAST TIME...THE NEWS GAZETTE DOES NOT RUN ADS FOR COLORED BUSINESSES!
IS THAT SO?...TELL ME AGAIN... 'ZACTLY WHICH COLORS DOES THIS PAPER OBJECT TO?
CLASSIFIED ADS DEPT.
IS IT THE COLOR BLUE THAT BOTHERS THEM?-MEBBE IT'S THE COLOR RED??!
MR. BELTRAN, I...
UH-OH!

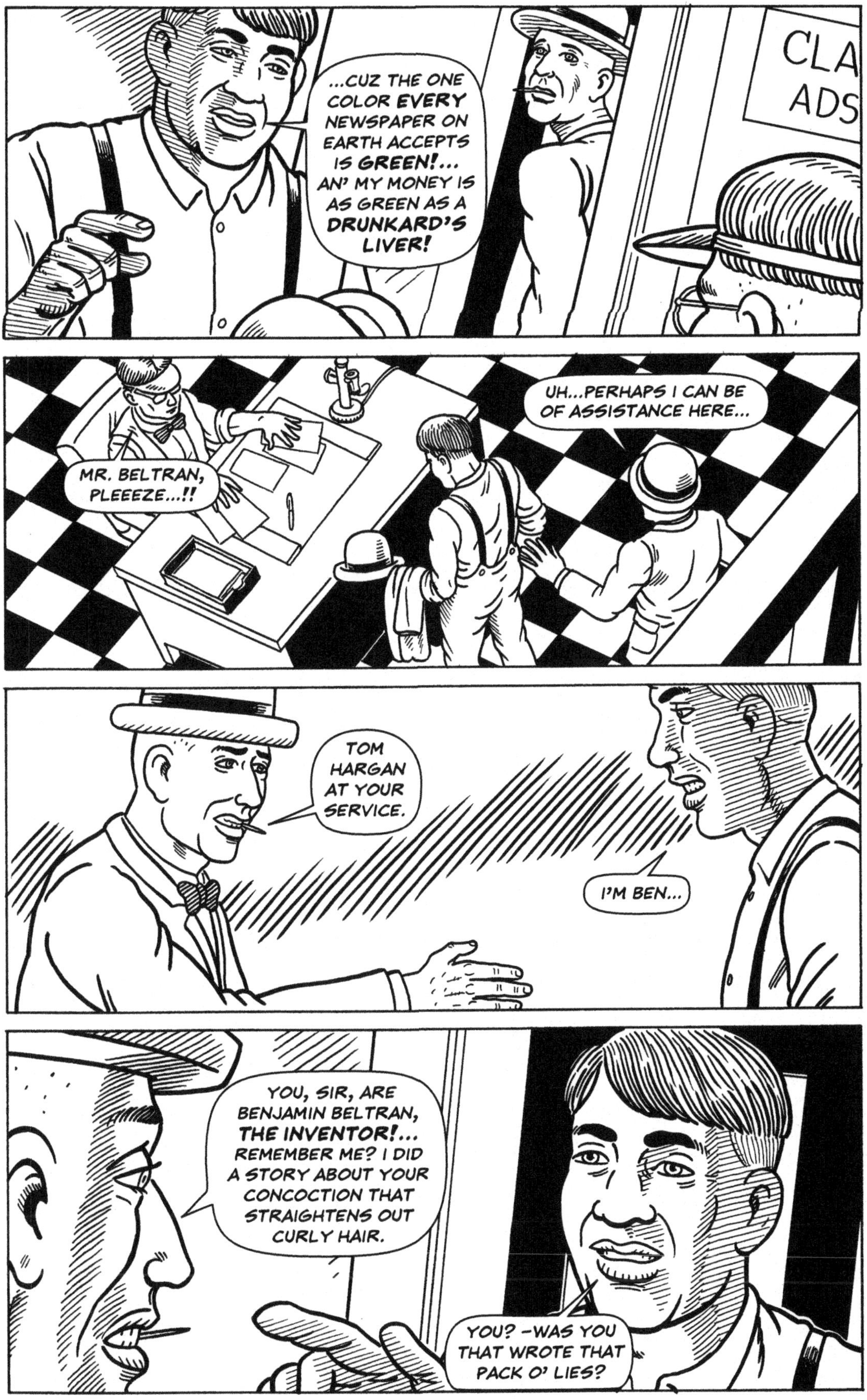
CLA
ADS
...CUZ THE ONE COLOR EVERY NEWSPAPER ON EARTH ACCEPTS IS GREEN!... AN' MY MONEY IS AS GREEN AS A DRUNKARD'S LIVER!
UH...PERHAPS I CAN BE OF ASSISTANCE HERE...
MR. BELTRAN, PLEEEZE...!!
TOM HARGAN AT YOUR SERVICE.
I'M BEN...
YOU, SIR, ARE BENJAMIN BELTRAN, THE INVENTOR!... REMEMBER ME? I DID A STORY ABOUT YOUR CONCOCTION THAT STRAIGHTENS OUT CURLY HAIR.
YOU? -WAS YOU THAT WROTE THAT PACK O' LIES?

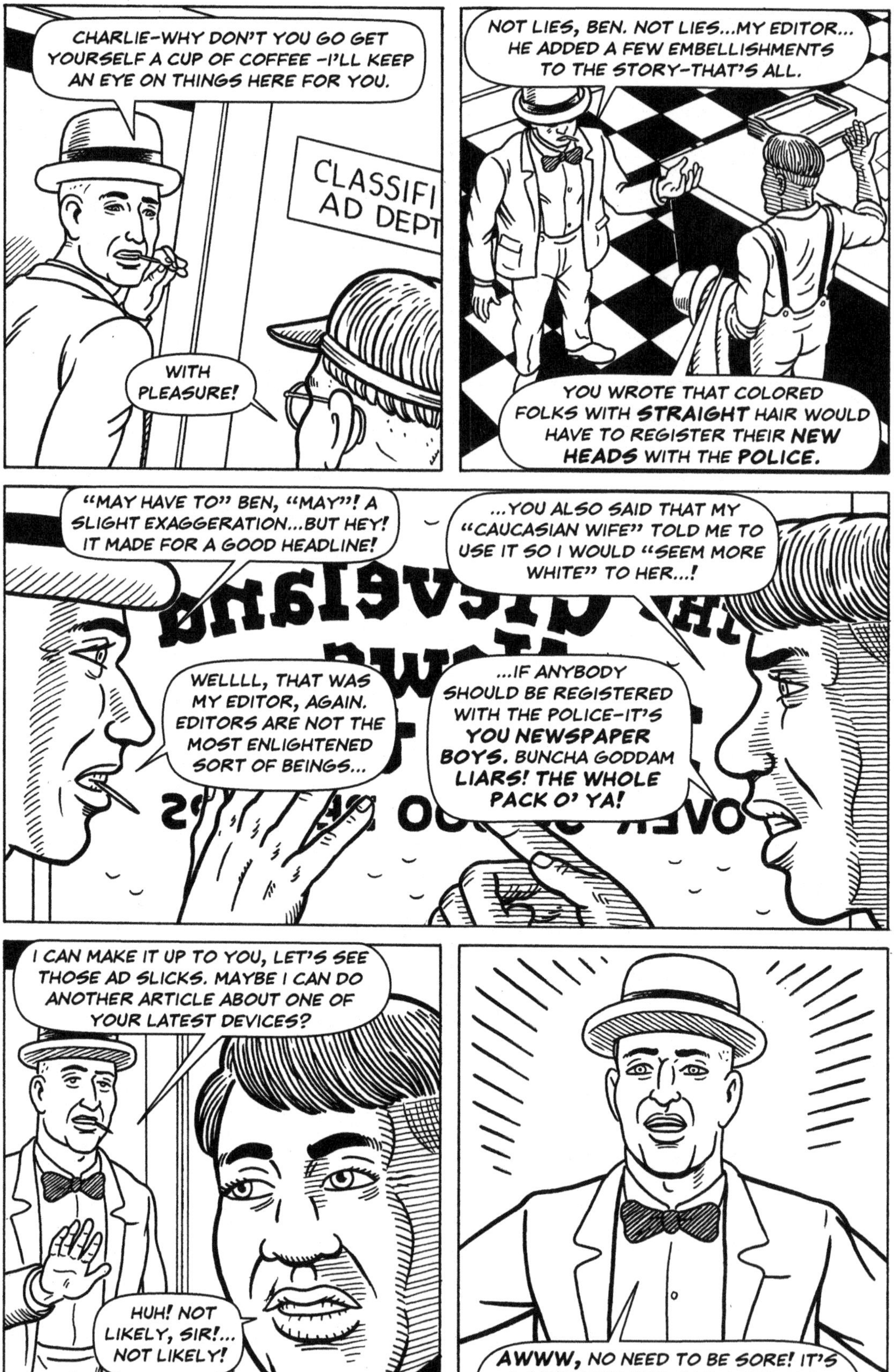
CHARLIE–WHY DON'T YOU GO GET YOURSELF A CUP OF COFFEE –I'LL KEEP AN EYE ON THINGS HERE FOR YOU.
CLASSIFI
AD DEPT
WITH PLEASURE!
NOT LIES, BEN. NOT LIES...MY EDITOR... HE ADDED A FEW EMBELLISHMENTS TO THE STORY–THAT'S ALL.
YOU WROTE THAT COLORED FOLKS WITH STRAIGHT HAIR WOULD HAVE TO REGISTER THEIR NEW HEADS WITH THE POLICE.
"MAY HAVE TO" BEN, "MAY"! A SLIGHT EXAGGERATION...BUT HEY! IT MADE FOR A GOOD HEADLINE!
...YOU ALSO SAID THAT MY "CAUCASIAN WIFE" TOLD ME TO USE IT SO I WOULD "SEEM MORE WHITE" TO HER...!
WELLLL, THAT WAS MY EDITOR, AGAIN. EDITORS ARE NOT THE MOST ENLIGHTENED SORT OF BEINGS...
...IF ANYBODY SHOULD BE REGISTERED WITH THE POLICE–IT'S YOU NEWSPAPER BOYS. BUNCHA GODDAM LIARS! THE WHOLE PACK O' YA!
I CAN MAKE IT UP TO YOU, LET'S SEE THOSE AD SLICKS. MAYBE I CAN DO ANOTHER ARTICLE ABOUT ONE OF YOUR LATEST DEVICES?
HUH! NOT LIKELY, SIR!... NOT LIKELY!
AWWW, NO NEED TO BE SORE! IT'S A GREAT WAY TO SHOW OFF YOUR INVENTIONS IN THE NEWSPAPERS...NOT TO MENTION THE ONLY WAY!

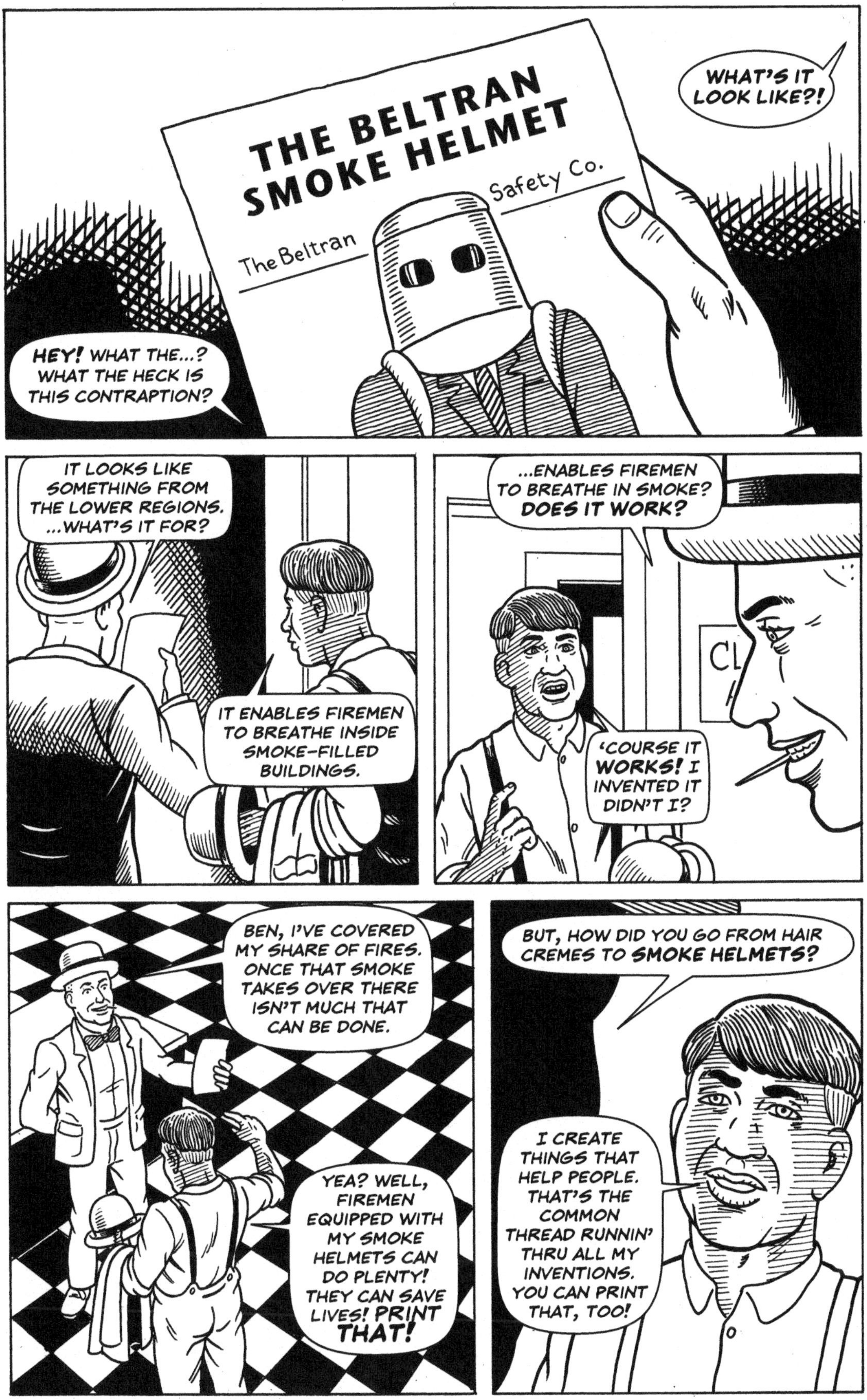
THE BELTRAN SMOKE HELMET
The Beltran
Safety Co.
WHAT'S IT LOOK LIKE?!
HEY! WHAT THE...? WHAT THE HECK IS THIS CONTRAPTION?
IT LOOKS LIKE SOMETHING FROM THE LOWER REGIONS. ...WHAT'S IT FOR?
IT ENABLES FIREMEN TO BREATHE INSIDE SMOKE-FILLED BUILDINGS.
...ENABLES FIREMEN TO BREATHE IN SMOKE? DOES IT WORK?
'COURSE IT WORKS! I INVENTED IT DIDN'T I?
BEN, I'VE COVERED MY SHARE OF FIRES. ONCE THAT SMOKE TAKES OVER THERE ISN'T MUCH THAT CAN BE DONE.
YEA? WELL, FIREMEN EQUIPPED WITH MY SMOKE HELMETS CAN DO PLENTY! THEY CAN SAVE LIVES! PRINT THAT!
BUT, HOW DID YOU GO FROM HAIR CREMES TO SMOKE HELMETS?
I CREATE THINGS THAT HELP PEOPLE. THAT'S THE COMMON THREAD RUNNIN' THRU ALL MY INVENTIONS. YOU CAN PRINT THAT, TOO!

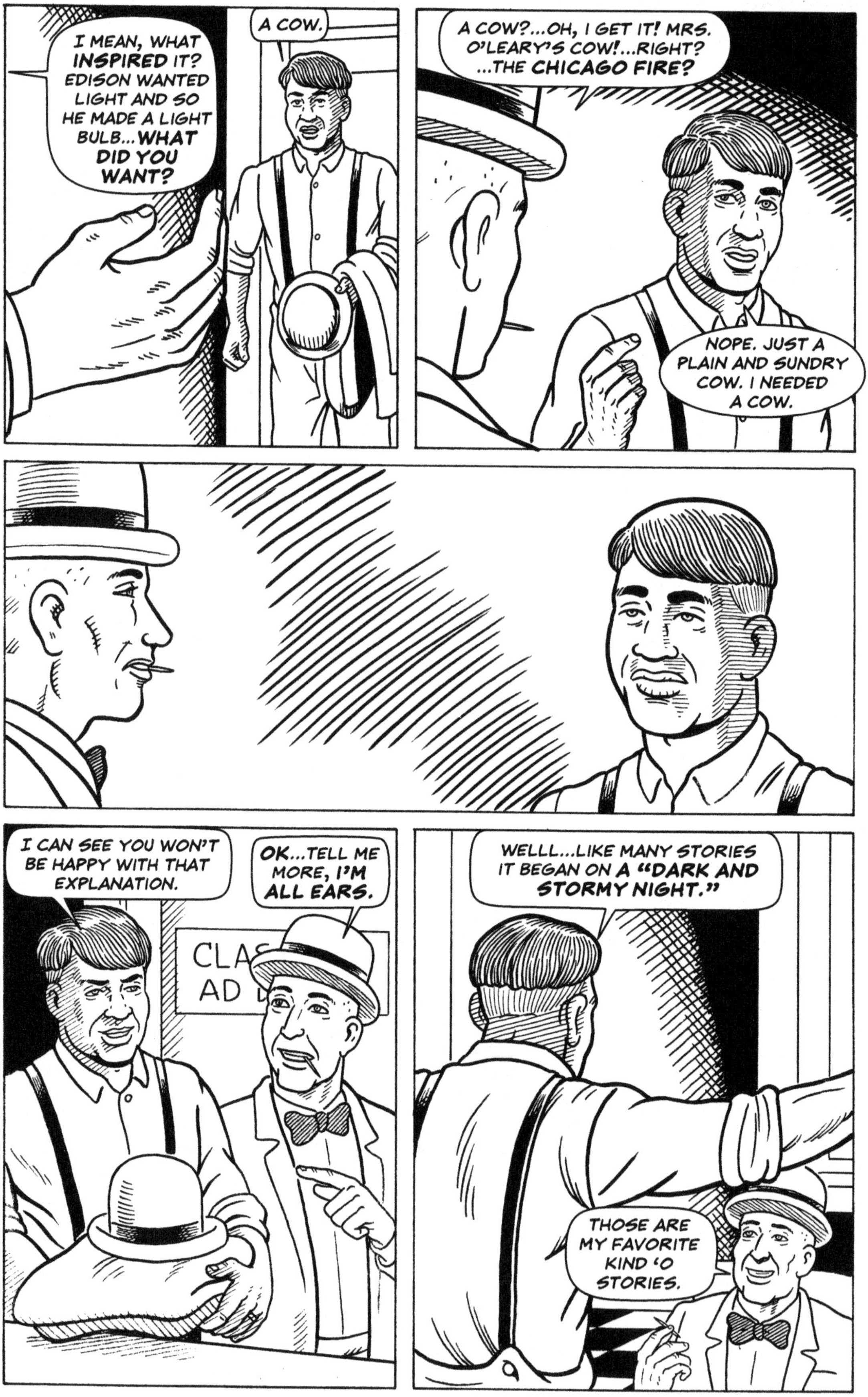
I MEAN, WHAT INSPIRED IT? EDISON WANTED LIGHT AND SO HE MADE A LIGHT BULB...WHAT DID YOU WANT?
A COW.
A COW?...OH, I GET IT! MRS. O'LEARY'S COW!...RIGHT? ...THE CHICAGO FIRE?
NOPE. JUST A PLAIN AND SUNDRY COW. I NEEDED A COW.
I CAN SEE YOU WON'T BE HAPPY WITH THAT EXPLANATION.
OK...TELL ME MORE, I'M ALL EARS.
WELLL...LIKE MANY STORIES IT BEGAN ON A "DARK AND STORMY NIGHT."
THOSE ARE MY FAVORITE KIND 'O STORIES.

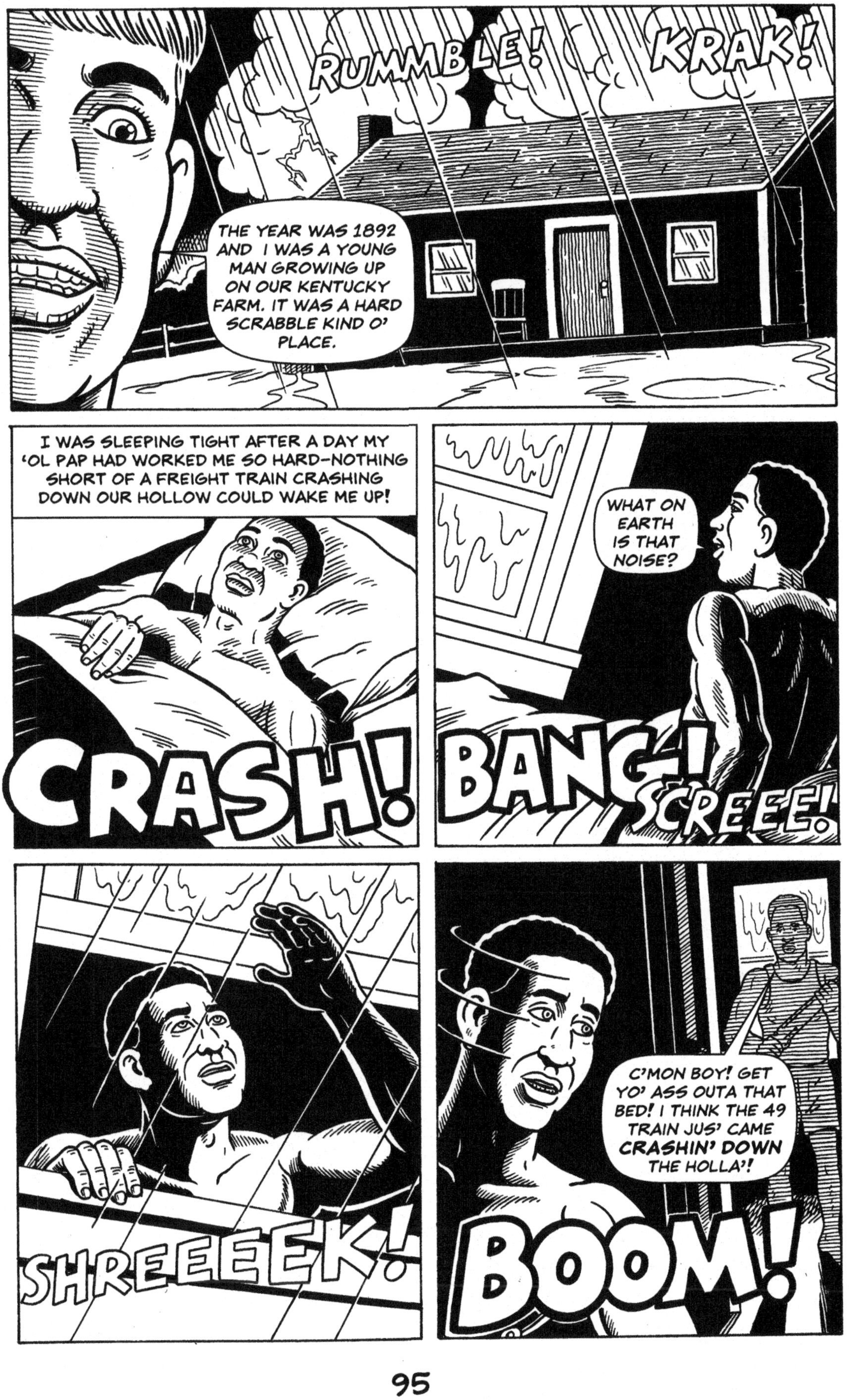
RUMMBLE!
KRAK!
THE YEAR WAS 1892 AND I WAS A YOUNG MAN GROWING UP ON OUR KENTUCKY FARM. IT WAS A HARD SCRABBLE KIND O' PLACE.
I WAS SLEEPING TIGHT AFTER A DAY MY 'OL PAP HAD WORKED ME SO HARD—NOTHING SHORT OF A FREIGHT TRAIN CRASHING DOWN OUR HOLLOW COULD WAKE ME UP!
CRASH!
WHAT ON EARTH IS THAT NOISE?
BANG!
SCREEE!
SHREEEEEK!
C'MON BOY! GET YO' ASS OUTA THAT BED! I THINK THE 49 TRAIN JUS' CAME CRASHIN' DOWN THE HOLLA'!
BOOM!

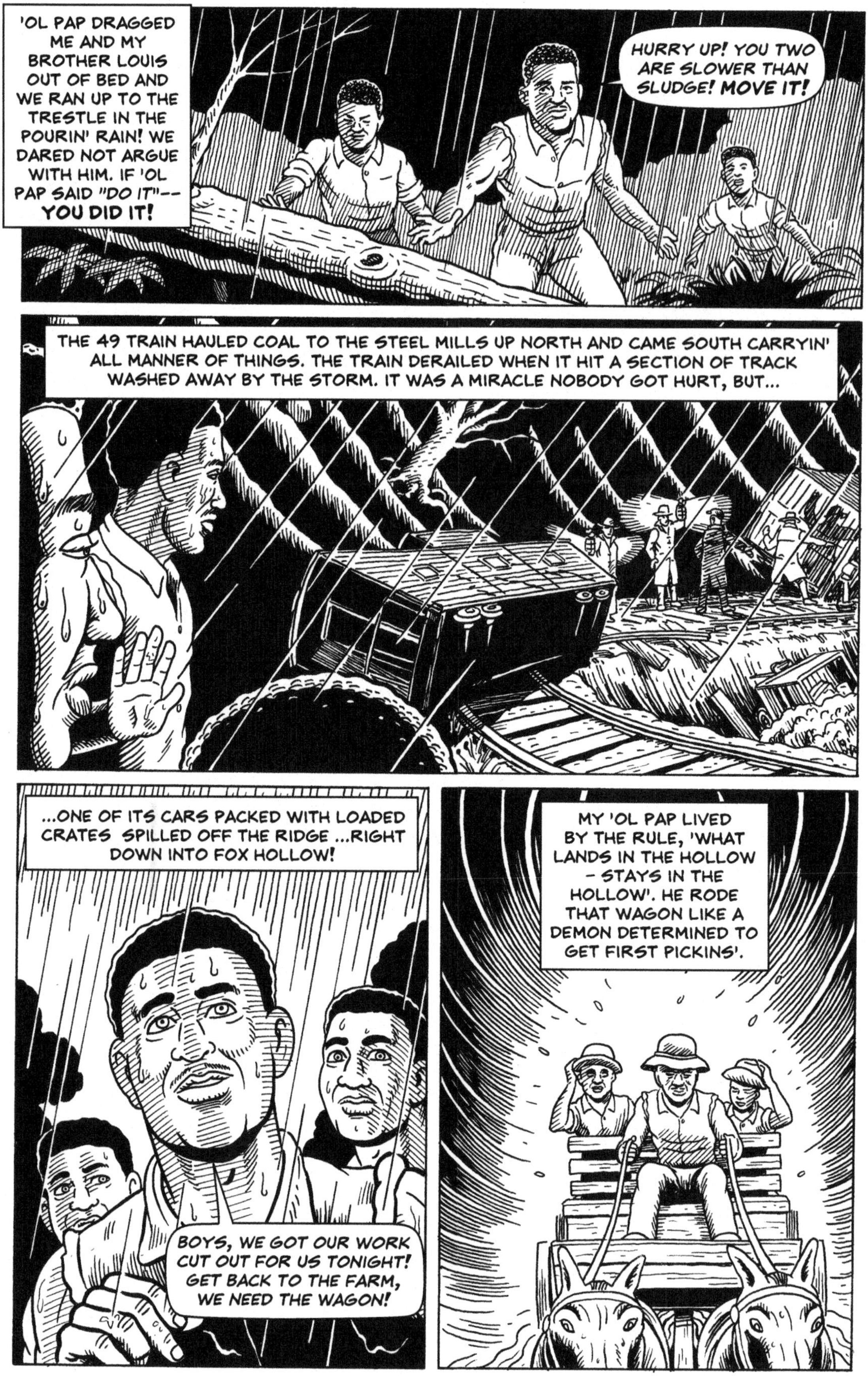
'OL PAP DRAGGED ME AND MY BROTHER LOUIS OUT OF BED AND WE RAN UP TO THE TRESTLE IN THE POURIN' RAIN! WE DARED NOT ARGUE WITH HIM. IF 'OL PAP SAID "DO IT"-- YOU DID IT!
HURRY UP! YOU TWO ARE SLOWER THAN SLUDGE! MOVE IT!
THE 49 TRAIN HAULED COAL TO THE STEEL MILLS UP NORTH AND CAME SOUTH CARRYIN' ALL MANNER OF THINGS. THE TRAIN DERAILED WHEN IT HIT A SECTION OF TRACK WASHED AWAY BY THE STORM. IT WAS A MIRACLE NOBODY GOT HURT, BUT...
...ONE OF ITS CARS PACKED WITH LOADED CRATES SPILLED OFF THE RIDGE ...RIGHT DOWN INTO FOX HOLLOW!
BOYS, WE GOT OUR WORK CUT OUT FOR US TONIGHT! GET BACK TO THE FARM, WE NEED THE WAGON!
MY 'OL PAP LIVED BY THE RULE, 'WHAT LANDS IN THE HOLLOW - STAYS IN THE HOLLOW'. HE RODE THAT WAGON LIKE A DEMON DETERMINED TO GET FIRST PICKINS'.

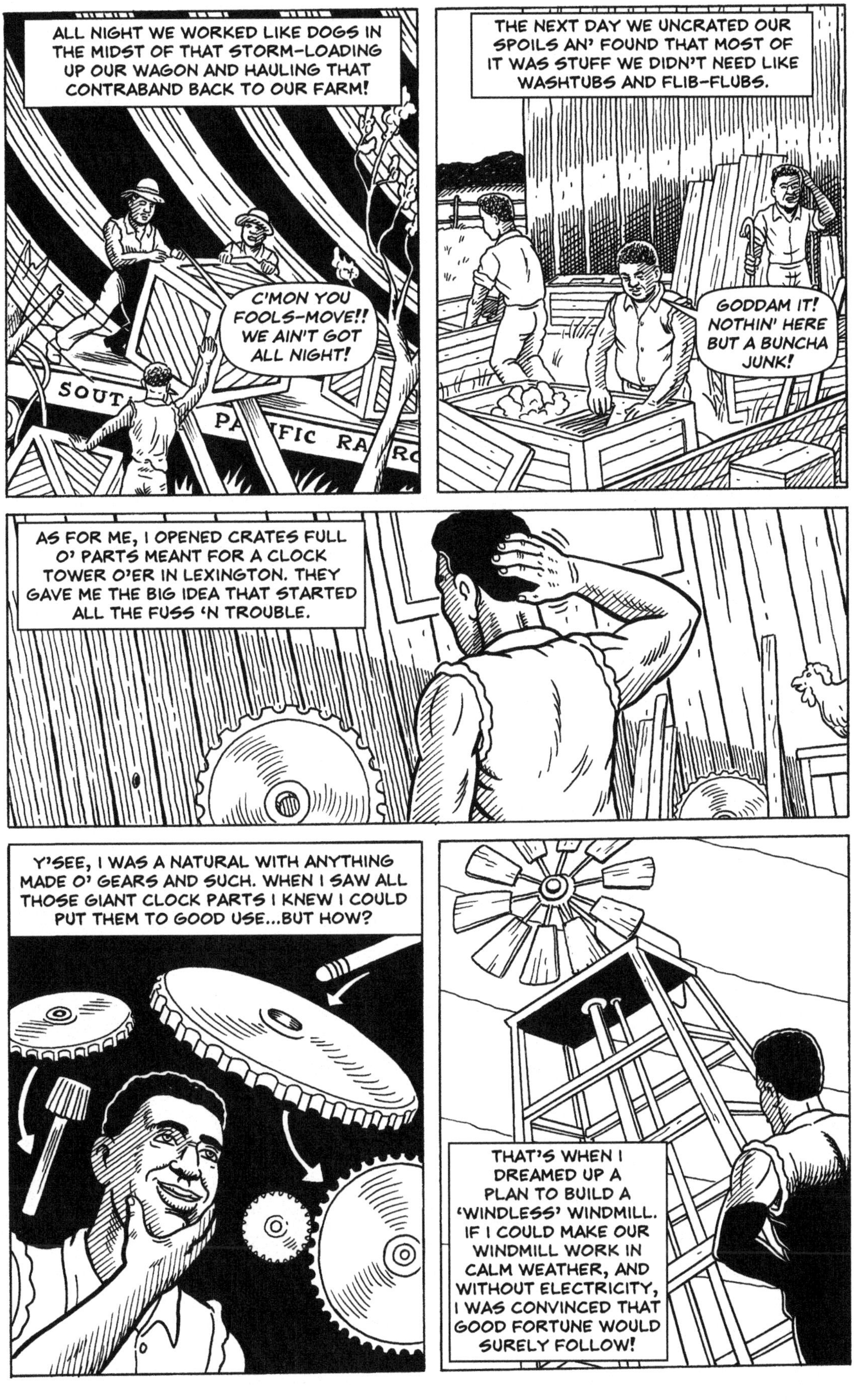
ALL NIGHT WE WORKED LIKE DOGS IN THE MIDST OF THAT STORM–LOADING UP OUR WAGON AND HAULING THAT CONTRABAND BACK TO OUR FARM!
C'MON YOU FOOLS–MOVE!! WE AIN'T GOT ALL NIGHT!
THE NEXT DAY WE UNCRATED OUR SPOILS AN' FOUND THAT MOST OF IT WAS STUFF WE DIDN'T NEED LIKE WASHTUBS AND FLIB–FLUBS.
GODDAM IT! NOTHIN' HERE BUT A BUNCHA JUNK!
AS FOR ME, I OPENED CRATES FULL O' PARTS MEANT FOR A CLOCK TOWER O'ER IN LEXINGTON. THEY GAVE ME THE BIG IDEA THAT STARTED ALL THE FUSS 'N TROUBLE.
Y'SEE, I WAS A NATURAL WITH ANYTHING MADE O' GEARS AND SUCH. WHEN I SAW ALL THOSE GIANT CLOCK PARTS I KNEW I COULD PUT THEM TO GOOD USE...BUT HOW?
THAT'S WHEN I DREAMED UP A PLAN TO BUILD A 'WINDLESS' WINDMILL. IF I COULD MAKE OUR WINDMILL WORK IN CALM WEATHER, AND WITHOUT ELECTRICITY, I WAS CONVINCED THAT GOOD FORTUNE WOULD SURELY FOLLOW!

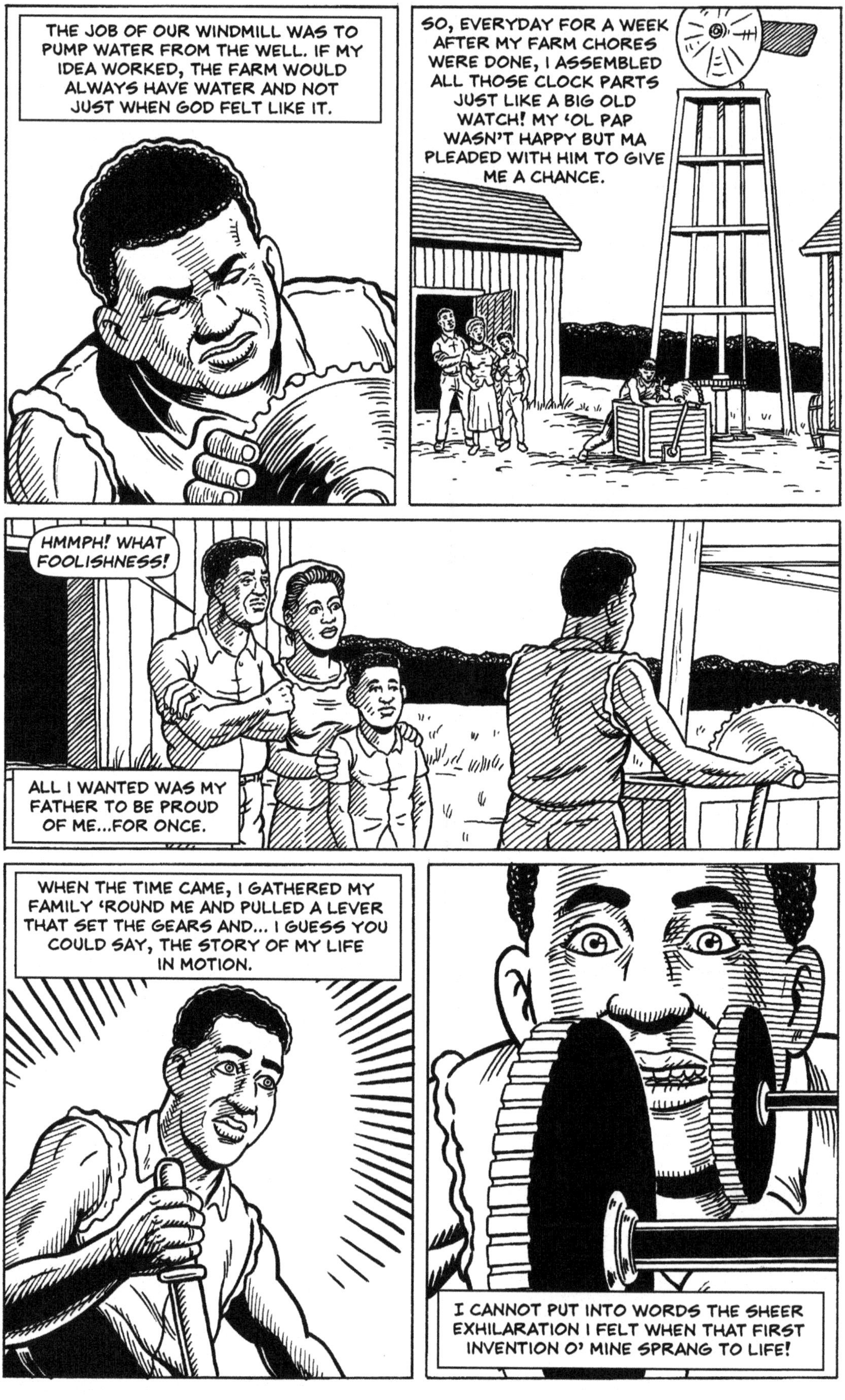
THE JOB OF OUR WINDMILL WAS TO PUMP WATER FROM THE WELL. IF MY IDEA WORKED, THE FARM WOULD ALWAYS HAVE WATER AND NOT JUST WHEN GOD FELT LIKE IT.
SO, EVERYDAY FOR A WEEK AFTER MY FARM CHORES WERE DONE, I ASSEMBLED ALL THOSE CLOCK PARTS JUST LIKE A BIG OLD WATCH! MY 'OL PAP WASN'T HAPPY BUT MA PLEADED WITH HIM TO GIVE ME A CHANCE.
HMMPH! WHAT FOOLISHNESS!
ALL I WANTED WAS MY FATHER TO BE PROUD OF ME...FOR ONCE.
WHEN THE TIME CAME, I GATHERED MY FAMILY 'ROUND ME AND PULLED A LEVER THAT SET THE GEARS AND... I GUESS YOU COULD SAY, THE STORY OF MY LIFE IN MOTION.
I CANNOT PUT INTO WORDS THE SHEER EXHILARATION I FELT WHEN THAT FIRST INVENTION O' MINE SPRANG TO LIFE!

BUT MY JOY WAS SHORT-LIVED 'CUZ I HAD LEFT OUT ONE IMPORTANT DETAIL FROM THE DESIGN.

SLOW IT DOWN, YOU FOOL! IT AIN'T BUILT TO SPIN THAT FAST!

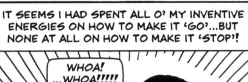

IT SEEMS I HAD SPENT ALL O' MY INVENTIVE ENERGIES ON HOW TO MAKE IT 'GO'...BUT NONE AT ALL ON HOW TO MAKE IT 'STOP'!

WHOA! ...WHOA!!!!!

KRIK!

STOP IT, BOY! STOP IT!! IT'S COMIN' APART!!

KRAK!

I CAN'T STOP IT, PAP! IT'S GOT A MIND OF ITS OWN!!!

KRISH!

WHIZZ! THWIP! HONK! HONK!

99

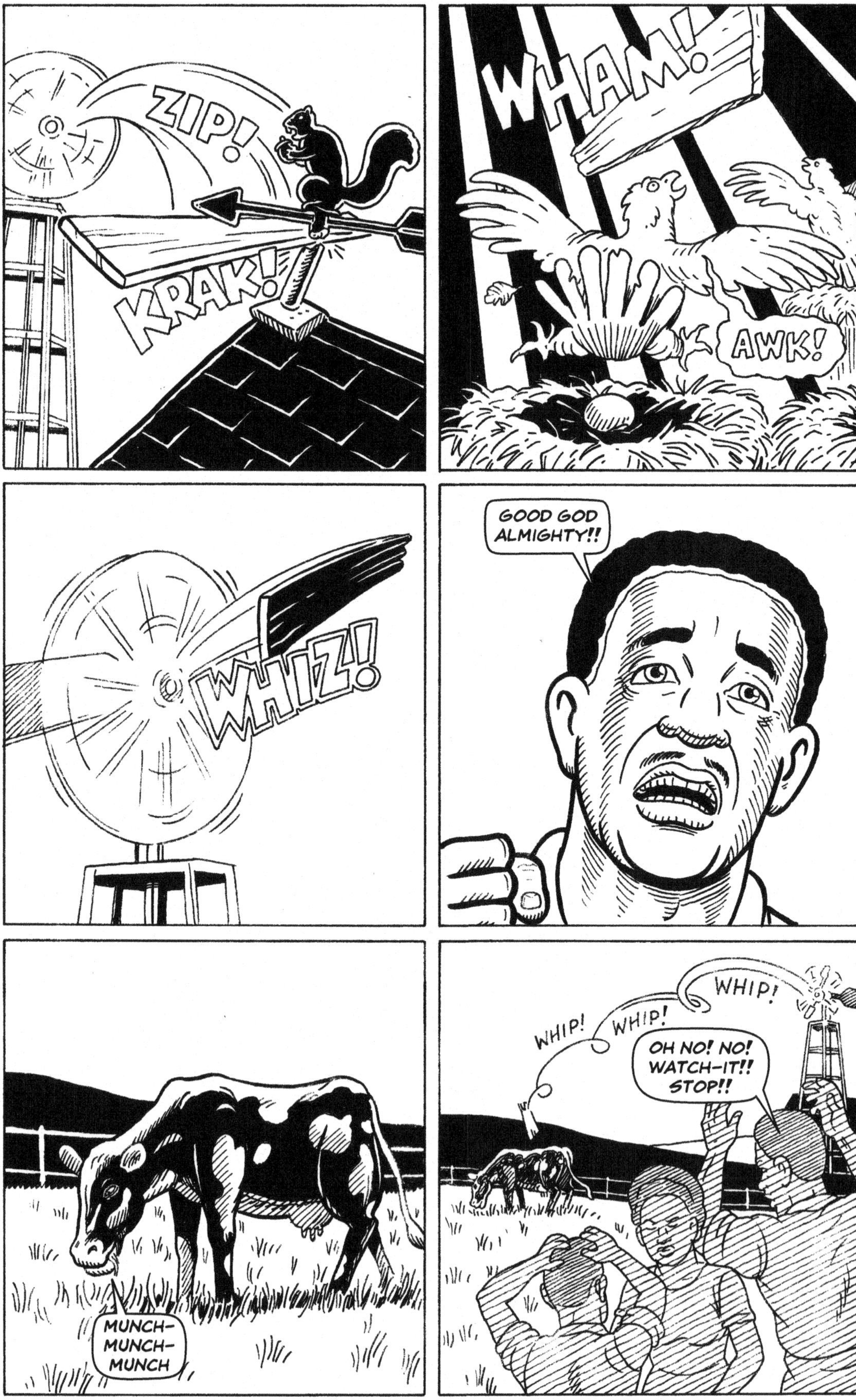

ZIP!
KRAK!
WHAM!
AWK!
WHIZ!
GOOD GOD ALMIGHTY!!
MUNCH-MUNCH-MUNCH
WHIP!
WHIP!
WHIP!
OH NO! NO! WATCH-IT!! STOP!!

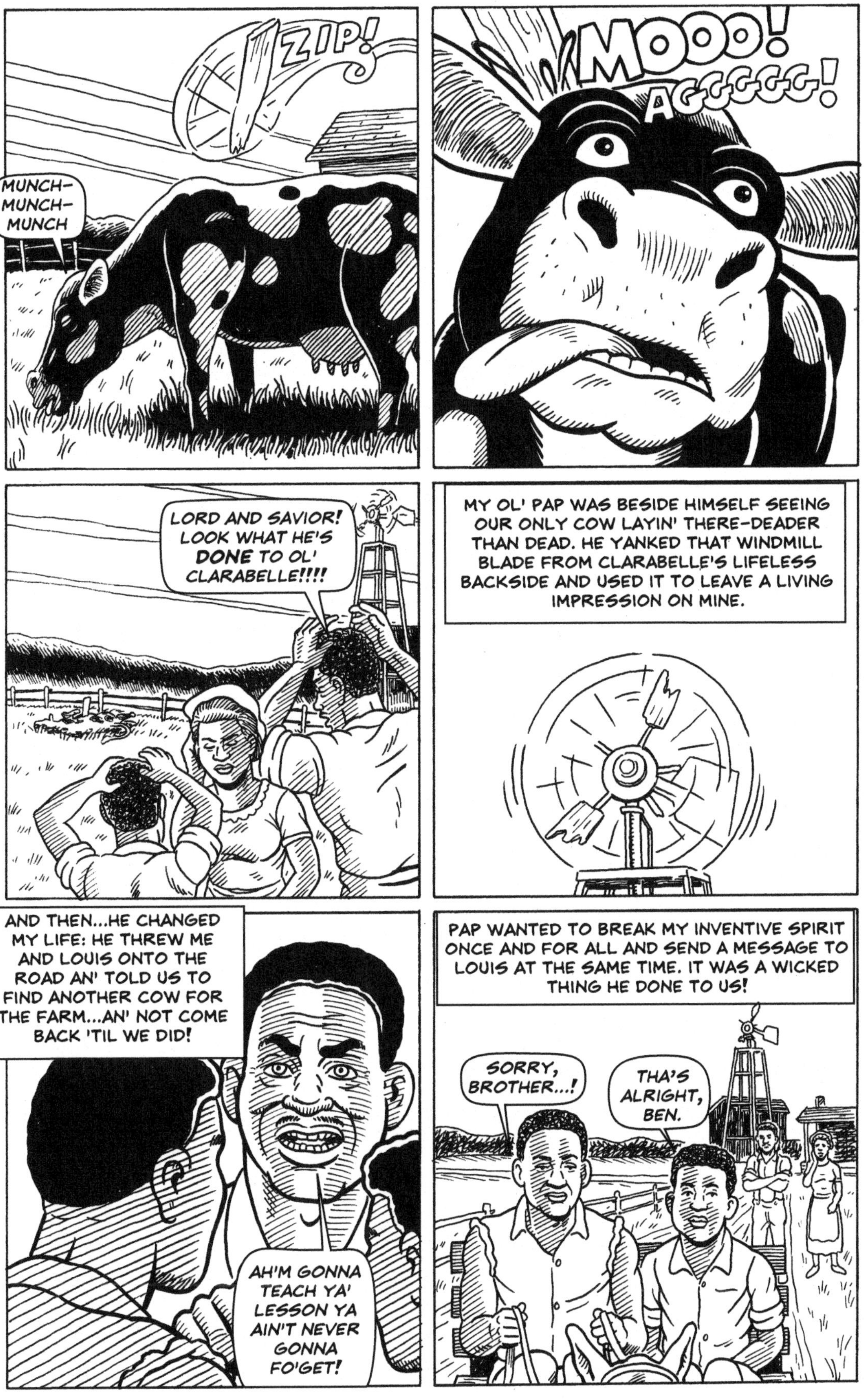
ZIP!
MUNCH-MUNCH-MUNCH
MOOO! AGGGGG!
LORD AND SAVIOR! LOOK WHAT HE'S DONE TO OL' CLARABELLE!!!!
MY OL' PAP WAS BESIDE HIMSELF SEEING OUR ONLY COW LAYIN' THERE-DEADER THAN DEAD. HE YANKED THAT WINDMILL BLADE FROM CLARABELLE'S LIFELESS BACKSIDE AND USED IT TO LEAVE A LIVING IMPRESSION ON MINE.
AND THEN...HE CHANGED MY LIFE: HE THREW ME AND LOUIS ONTO THE ROAD AN' TOLD US TO FIND ANOTHER COW FOR THE FARM...AN' NOT COME BACK 'TIL WE DID!
AH'M GONNA TEACH YA' LESSON YA AIN'T NEVER GONNA FO'GET!
PAP WANTED TO BREAK MY INVENTIVE SPIRIT ONCE AND FOR ALL AND SEND A MESSAGE TO LOUIS AT THE SAME TIME. IT WAS A WICKED THING HE DONE TO US!
SORRY, BROTHER...!
THA'S ALRIGHT, BEN.

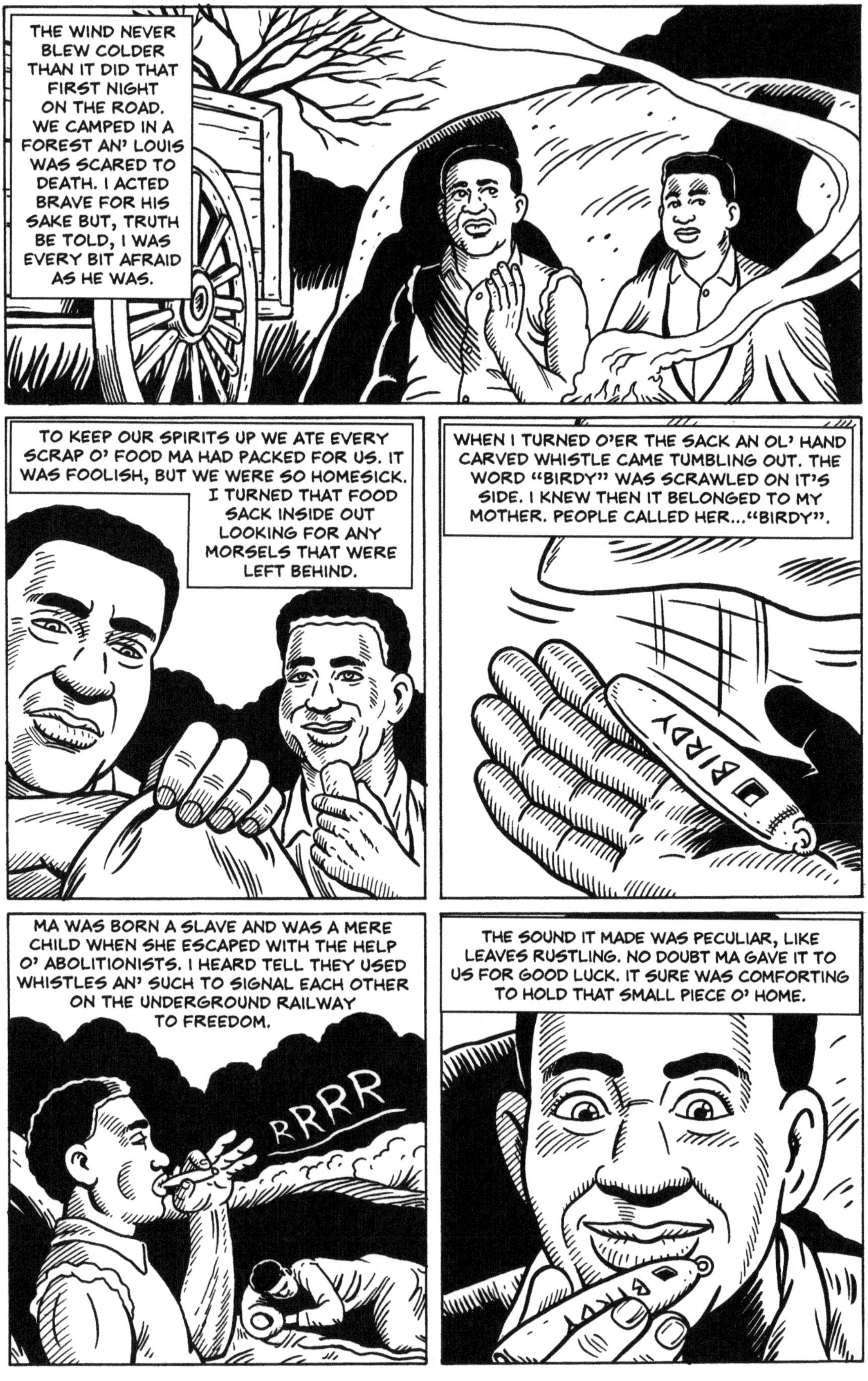
THE WIND NEVER BLEW COLDER THAN IT DID THAT FIRST NIGHT ON THE ROAD. WE CAMPED IN A FOREST AN' LOUIS WAS SCARED TO DEATH. I ACTED BRAVE FOR HIS SAKE BUT, TRUTH BE TOLD, I WAS EVERY BIT AFRAID AS HE WAS.
TO KEEP OUR SPIRITS UP WE ATE EVERY SCRAP O' FOOD MA HAD PACKED FOR US. IT WAS FOOLISH, BUT WE WERE SO HOMESICK.
I TURNED THAT FOOD SACK INSIDE OUT LOOKING FOR ANY MORSELS THAT WERE LEFT BEHIND.
WHEN I TURNED O'ER THE SACK AN OL' HAND CARVED WHISTLE CAME TUMBLING OUT. THE WORD "BIRDY" WAS SCRAWLED ON IT'S SIDE. I KNEW THEN IT BELONGED TO MY MOTHER. PEOPLE CALLED HER..."BIRDY".
BIRDY
MA WAS BORN A SLAVE AND WAS A MERE CHILD WHEN SHE ESCAPED WITH THE HELP O' ABOLITIONISTS. I HEARD TELL THEY USED WHISTLES AN' SUCH TO SIGNAL EACH OTHER ON THE UNDERGROUND RAILWAY TO FREEDOM.
RRRR
THE SOUND IT MADE WAS PECULIAR, LIKE LEAVES RUSTLING. NO DOUBT MA GAVE IT TO US FOR GOOD LUCK. IT SURE WAS COMFORTING TO HOLD THAT SMALL PIECE O' HOME.

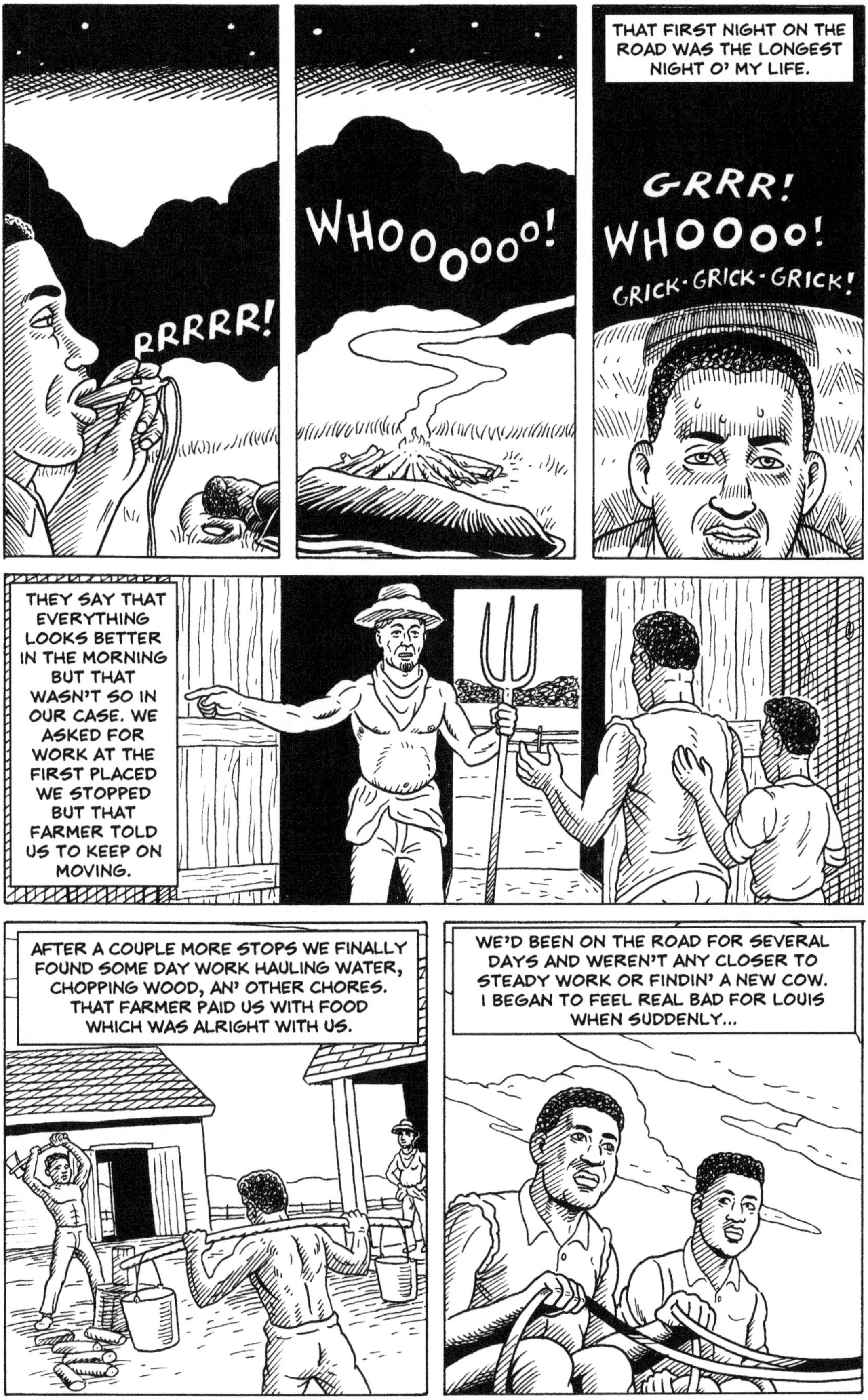
RRRRR!
WHOOOOOO!
THAT FIRST NIGHT ON THE ROAD WAS THE LONGEST NIGHT O' MY LIFE.
GRRR!
WHOOOOO!
GRICK-GRICK-GRICK!
THEY SAY THAT EVERYTHING LOOKS BETTER IN THE MORNING BUT THAT WASN'T SO IN OUR CASE. WE ASKED FOR WORK AT THE FIRST PLACED WE STOPPED BUT THAT FARMER TOLD US TO KEEP ON MOVING.
AFTER A COUPLE MORE STOPS WE FINALLY FOUND SOME DAY WORK HAULING WATER, CHOPPING WOOD, AN' OTHER CHORES. THAT FARMER PAID US WITH FOOD WHICH WAS ALRIGHT WITH US.
WE'D BEEN ON THE ROAD FOR SEVERAL DAYS AND WEREN'T ANY CLOSER TO STEADY WORK OR FINDIN' A NEW COW. I BEGAN TO FEEL REAL BAD FOR LOUIS WHEN SUDDENLY...

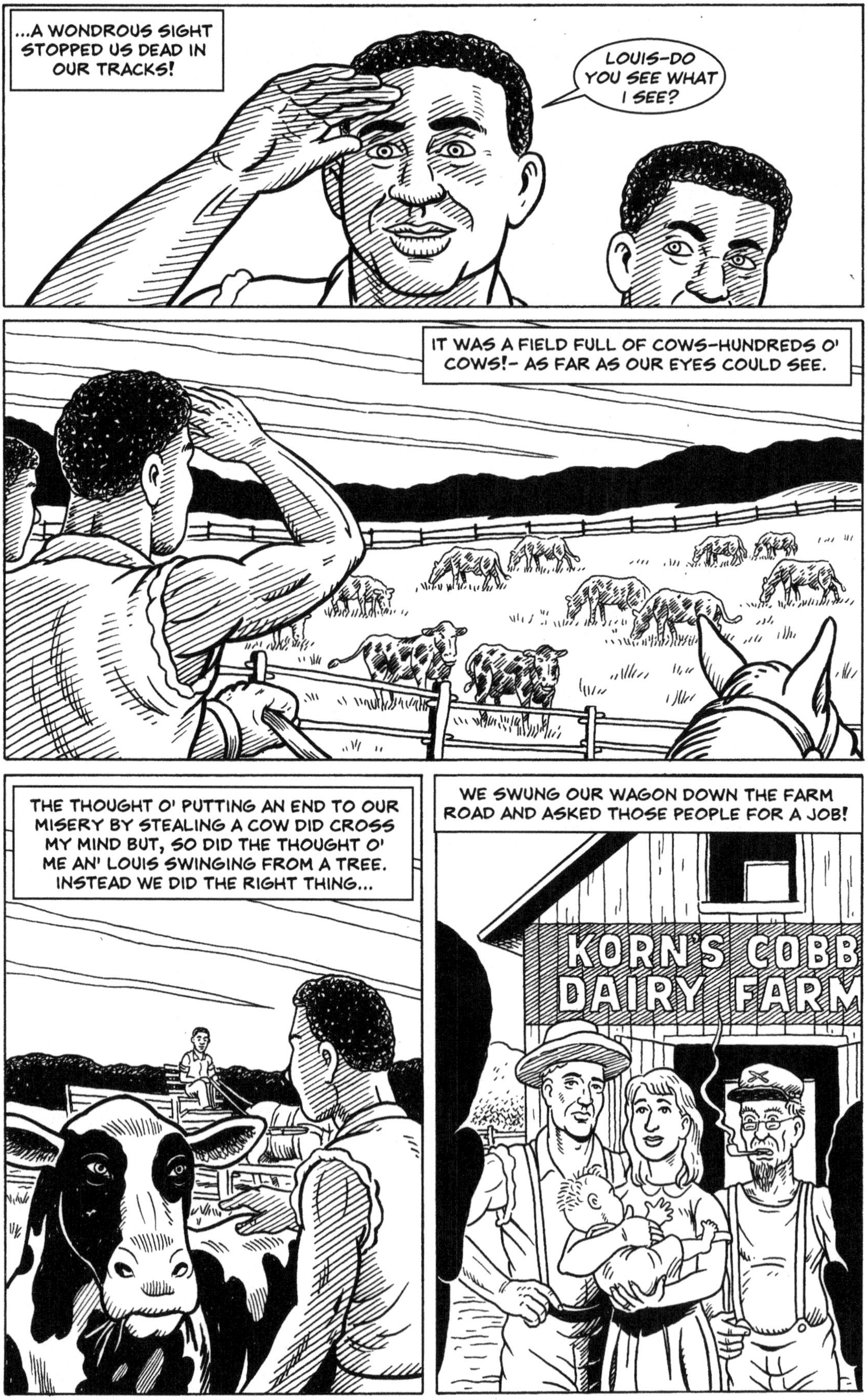
...A WONDROUS SIGHT STOPPED US DEAD IN OUR TRACKS!
LOUIS-DO YOU SEE WHAT I SEE?
IT WAS A FIELD FULL OF COWS-HUNDREDS O' COWS!- AS FAR AS OUR EYES COULD SEE.
THE THOUGHT O' PUTTING AN END TO OUR MISERY BY STEALING A COW DID CROSS MY MIND BUT, SO DID THE THOUGHT O' ME AN' LOUIS SWINGING FROM A TREE. INSTEAD WE DID THE RIGHT THING...
WE SWUNG OUR WAGON DOWN THE FARM ROAD AND ASKED THOSE PEOPLE FOR A JOB!
KORN'S COBB
DAIRY FARM

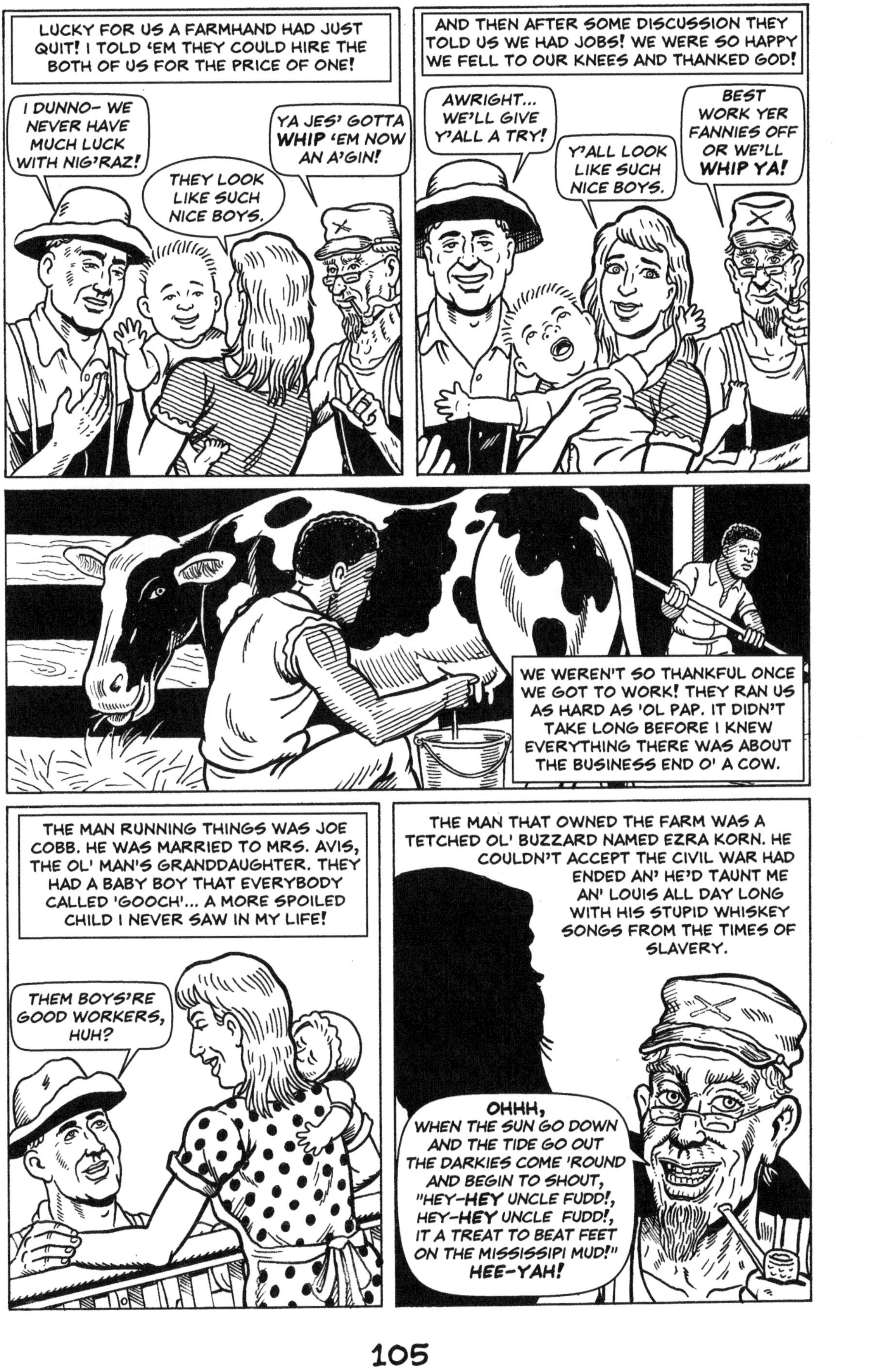
LUCKY FOR US A FARMHAND HAD JUST QUIT! I TOLD 'EM THEY COULD HIRE THE BOTH OF US FOR THE PRICE OF ONE!
I DUNNO– WE NEVER HAVE MUCH LUCK WITH NIG'RAZ!
THEY LOOK LIKE SUCH NICE BOYS.
YA JES' GOTTA WHIP 'EM NOW AN A'GIN!
AND THEN AFTER SOME DISCUSSION THEY TOLD US WE HAD JOBS! WE WERE SO HAPPY WE FELL TO OUR KNEES AND THANKED GOD!
AWRIGHT... WE'LL GIVE Y'ALL A TRY!
Y'ALL LOOK LIKE SUCH NICE BOYS.
BEST WORK YER FANNIES OFF OR WE'LL WHIP YA!
WE WEREN'T SO THANKFUL ONCE WE GOT TO WORK! THEY RAN US AS HARD AS 'OL PAP. IT DIDN'T TAKE LONG BEFORE I KNEW EVERYTHING THERE WAS ABOUT THE BUSINESS END O' A COW.
THE MAN RUNNING THINGS WAS JOE COBB. HE WAS MARRIED TO MRS. AVIS, THE OL' MAN'S GRANDDAUGHTER. THEY HAD A BABY BOY THAT EVERYBODY CALLED 'GOOCH'... A MORE SPOILED CHILD I NEVER SAW IN MY LIFE!
THEM BOYS'RE GOOD WORKERS, HUH?
THE MAN THAT OWNED THE FARM WAS A TETCHED OL' BUZZARD NAMED EZRA KORN. HE COULDN'T ACCEPT THE CIVIL WAR HAD ENDED AN' HE'D TAUNT ME AN' LOUIS ALL DAY LONG WITH HIS STUPID WHISKEY SONGS FROM THE TIMES OF SLAVERY.
OHHH, WHEN THE SUN GO DOWN AND THE TIDE GO OUT THE DARKIES COME 'ROUND AND BEGIN TO SHOUT, "HEY-HEY UNCLE FUDD!, HEY-HEY UNCLE FUDD!, IT A TREAT TO BEAT FEET ON THE MISSISSIPI MUD!" HEE-YAH!

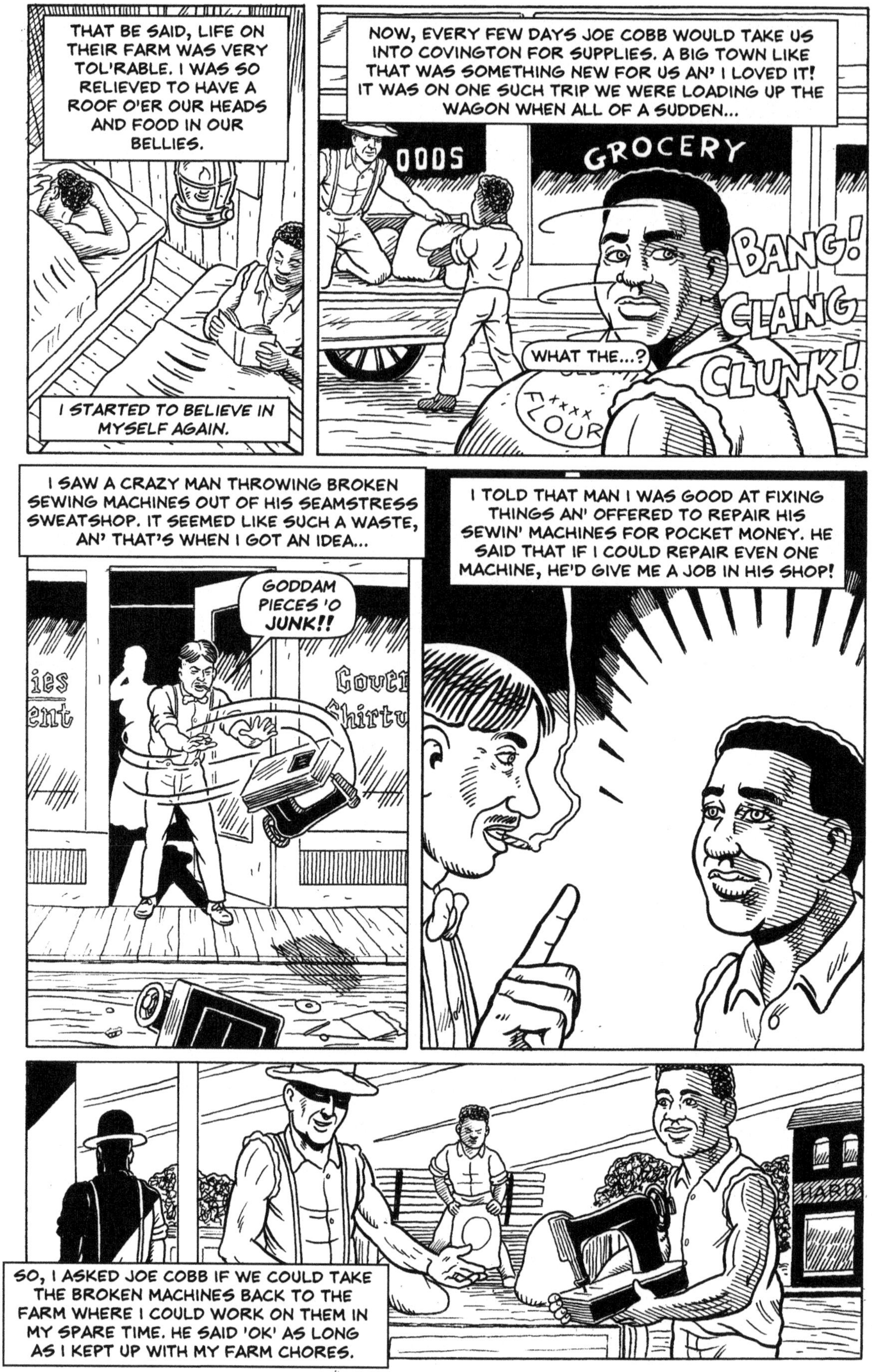
THAT BE SAID, LIFE ON THEIR FARM WAS VERY TOL'RABLE. I WAS SO RELIEVED TO HAVE A ROOF O'ER OUR HEADS AND FOOD IN OUR BELLIES.
I STARTED TO BELIEVE IN MYSELF AGAIN.
NOW, EVERY FEW DAYS JOE COBB WOULD TAKE US INTO COVINGTON FOR SUPPLIES. A BIG TOWN LIKE THAT WAS SOMETHING NEW FOR US AN' I LOVED IT! IT WAS ON ONE SUCH TRIP WE WERE LOADING UP THE WAGON WHEN ALL OF A SUDDEN...
OODS
GROCERY
BANG!
CLANG
CLUNK!
WHAT THE...?
FLOUR
I SAW A CRAZY MAN THROWING BROKEN SEWING MACHINES OUT OF HIS SEAMSTRESS SWEATSHOP. IT SEEMED LIKE SUCH A WASTE, AN' THAT'S WHEN I GOT AN IDEA...
GODDAM PIECES 'O JUNK!!
I TOLD THAT MAN I WAS GOOD AT FIXING THINGS AN' OFFERED TO REPAIR HIS SEWIN' MACHINES FOR POCKET MONEY. HE SAID THAT IF I COULD REPAIR EVEN ONE MACHINE, HE'D GIVE ME A JOB IN HIS SHOP!
SO, I ASKED JOE COBB IF WE COULD TAKE THE BROKEN MACHINES BACK TO THE FARM WHERE I COULD WORK ON THEM IN MY SPARE TIME. HE SAID 'OK' AS LONG AS I KEPT UP WITH MY FARM CHORES.

WORKING NIGHTS I WAS ABLE TO FIX THREE SEWING MACHINES FROM PARTS I SCAVENGED FROM TWO OTHERS. I HAD TO TEST THEM BACK AT THE SWEATSHOP, BUT I KNEW THEY'D WORK AGAIN.

SURE ENOUGH, WHEN ME AND LOUIS RETURNED TO THE SHOP AND HOOKED THEM UP, THEY PURRED LIKE KITTENS. THAT MAN OFFERED ME A JOB ON THE SPOT AT $2 PER WEEK AN' I ACCEPTED WITHOUT BATTIN' AN EYE!!

WE LEFT COVINGTON AND HEADED BACK TO THE FARM. WE WERE JUST A HALF MILE AWAY WHEN TROUBLE APPEARED ON THE HORIZON!

LOUIS! THE FARMHOUSE!! IT'S ON FIRE!

ONE THING I KNOW...THE TROUBLE WITH TROUBLE IS THAT IT USUALLY SHOWS UP WEARIN' A FAMILIAR FACE.

I HEARD MRS. AVIS SAY MANY TIMES, "GRAMPA, SMOKIN' WILL BE YOUR DEATH!", BUT HE NEVER LISTENED. I GUESS HE WAS TOO BUSY BEING HIMSELF.

Z-Z-Z-Z-Z

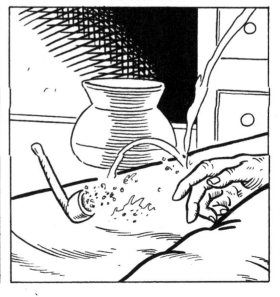

IN THE END, SHE WAS RIGHT! THE OL' GEEZER HAD MADE HIS PLAY FOR THE AFTERLIFE, AND IT APPEARED HE WOULD TAKE SOMEBODY WITH HIM!

LOUIS AND I ARRIVED UPON A SCENE OF TOTAL CHAOS! WE DIDN'T UNDERSTAND HOW BAD IT WAS UNTIL SOMEBODY SAID...

THERE'S A BABY IN THERE!!

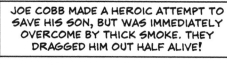

JOE COBB MADE A HEROIC ATTEMPT TO SAVE HIS SON, BUT WAS IMMEDIATELY OVERCOME BY THICK SMOKE. THEY DRAGGED HIM OUT HALF ALIVE!

LET ME GO! LET ME GO!

MAH BABY! SOMEONE SAVE MAH BABY!!

IT WAS FORTUNATE THE CHILD HAD INSTINCTS TO SAVE HIS OWN SELF. SOMETHIN' HE MUSTA SEEN HAD INSPIRED HIS FIRST GOOD IDEA...

...'CUZ 'OL BABY GOOCH CLIMBED RIGHT OUT O' THAT CRIB AN' DROPPED HIS LITTLE FANNY ONTO THE FLOOR!

AND FROM THERE HE FOUND THE PLACE WHERE CHILDREN, DOGS, AND DRUNKS GO TO HIDE WHEN TROUBLE IS IN THE HOUSE!

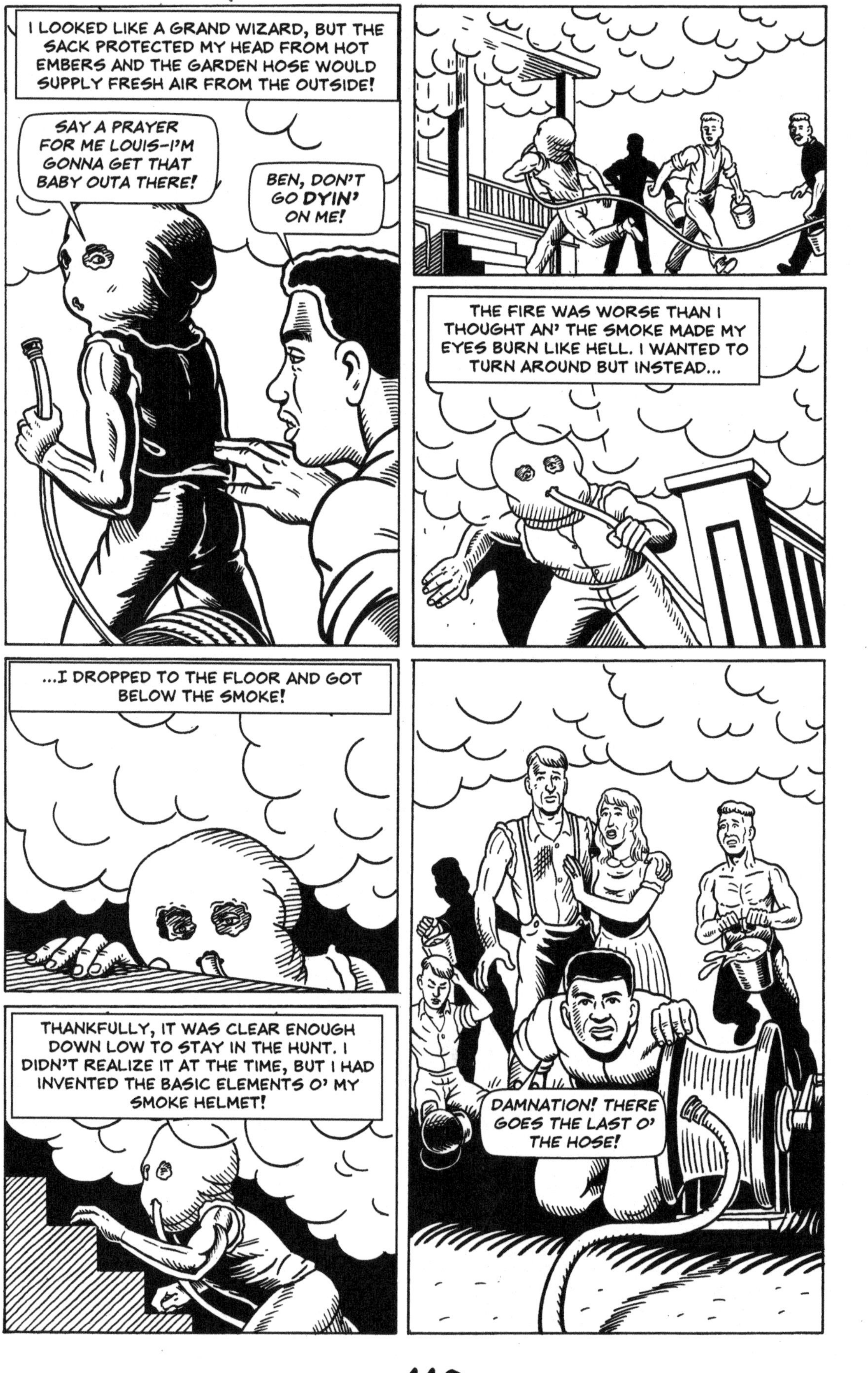
I LOOKED LIKE A GRAND WIZARD, BUT THE SACK PROTECTED MY HEAD FROM HOT EMBERS AND THE GARDEN HOSE WOULD SUPPLY FRESH AIR FROM THE OUTSIDE!
SAY A PRAYER FOR ME LOUIS—I'M GONNA GET THAT BABY OUTA THERE!
BEN, DON'T GO DYIN' ON ME!
THE FIRE WAS WORSE THAN I THOUGHT AN' THE SMOKE MADE MY EYES BURN LIKE HELL. I WANTED TO TURN AROUND BUT INSTEAD...
...I DROPPED TO THE FLOOR AND GOT BELOW THE SMOKE!
THANKFULLY, IT WAS CLEAR ENOUGH DOWN LOW TO STAY IN THE HUNT. I DIDN'T REALIZE IT AT THE TIME, BUT I HAD INVENTED THE BASIC ELEMENTS O' MY SMOKE HELMET!
DAMNATION! THERE GOES THE LAST O' THE HOSE!

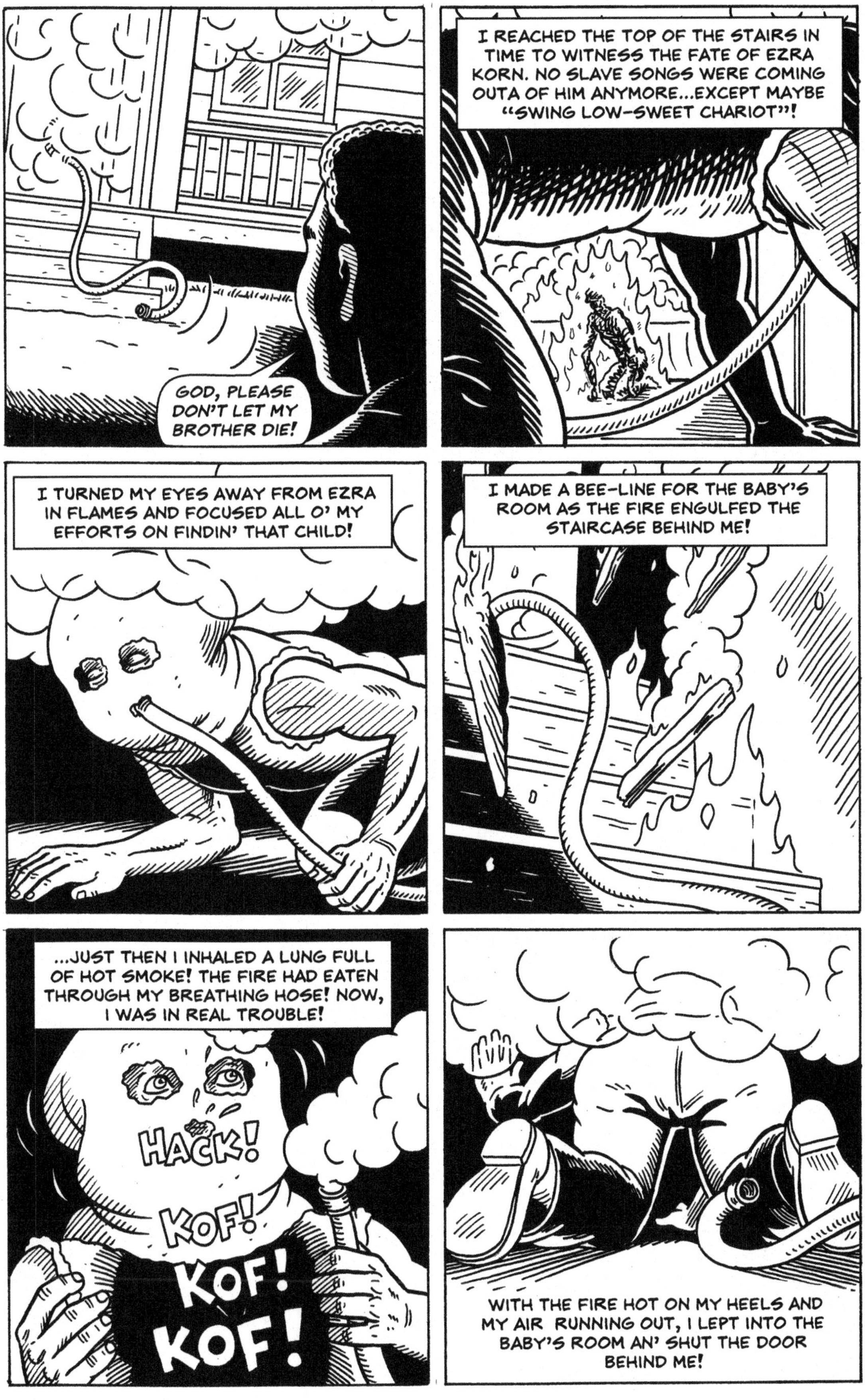
GOD, PLEASE DON'T LET MY BROTHER DIE!
I REACHED THE TOP OF THE STAIRS IN TIME TO WITNESS THE FATE OF EZRA KORN. NO SLAVE SONGS WERE COMING OUTA OF HIM ANYMORE...EXCEPT MAYBE "SWING LOW-SWEET CHARIOT"!
I TURNED MY EYES AWAY FROM EZRA IN FLAMES AND FOCUSED ALL O' MY EFFORTS ON FINDIN' THAT CHILD!
I MADE A BEE-LINE FOR THE BABY'S ROOM AS THE FIRE ENGULFED THE STAIRCASE BEHIND ME!
...JUST THEN I INHALED A LUNG FULL OF HOT SMOKE! THE FIRE HAD EATEN THROUGH MY BREATHING HOSE! NOW, I WAS IN REAL TROUBLE!
HACK!
KOF!
KOF!
KOF!
WITH THE FIRE HOT ON MY HEELS AND MY AIR RUNNING OUT, I LEPT INTO THE BABY'S ROOM AN' SHUT THE DOOR BEHIND ME!

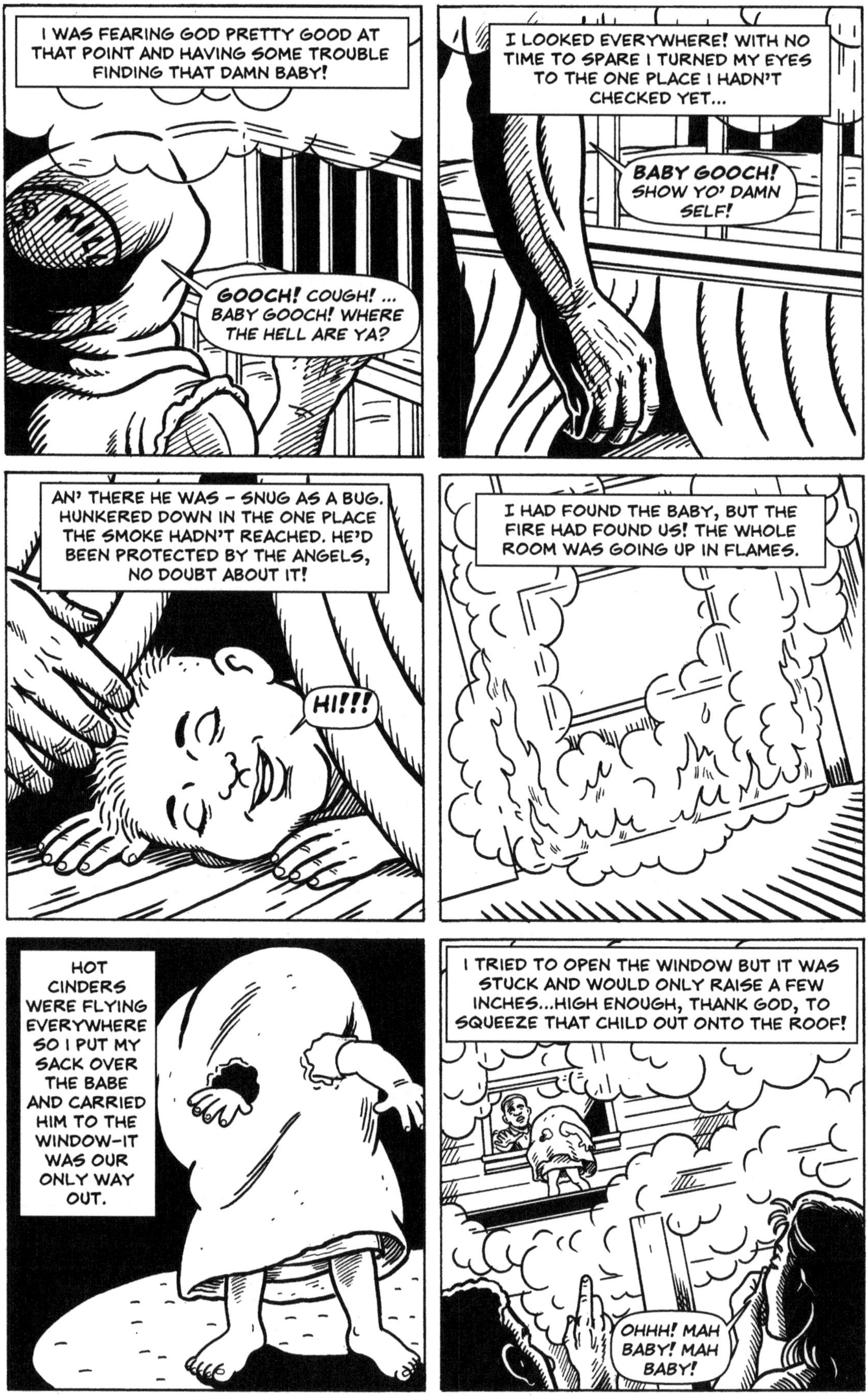
I WAS FEARING GOD PRETTY GOOD AT THAT POINT AND HAVING SOME TROUBLE FINDING THAT DAMN BABY!
GOOCH! COUGH! ... BABY GOOCH! WHERE THE HELL ARE YA?
I LOOKED EVERYWHERE! WITH NO TIME TO SPARE I TURNED MY EYES TO THE ONE PLACE I HADN'T CHECKED YET...
BABY GOOCH! SHOW YO' DAMN SELF!
AN' THERE HE WAS - SNUG AS A BUG. HUNKERED DOWN IN THE ONE PLACE THE SMOKE HADN'T REACHED. HE'D BEEN PROTECTED BY THE ANGELS, NO DOUBT ABOUT IT!
HI!!!
I HAD FOUND THE BABY, BUT THE FIRE HAD FOUND US! THE WHOLE ROOM WAS GOING UP IN FLAMES.
HOT CINDERS WERE FLYING EVERYWHERE SO I PUT MY SACK OVER THE BABE AND CARRIED HIM TO THE WINDOW–IT WAS OUR ONLY WAY OUT.
I TRIED TO OPEN THE WINDOW BUT IT WAS STUCK AND WOULD ONLY RAISE A FEW INCHES...HIGH ENOUGH, THANK GOD, TO SQUEEZE THAT CHILD OUT ONTO THE ROOF!
OHHH! MAH BABY! MAH BABY!

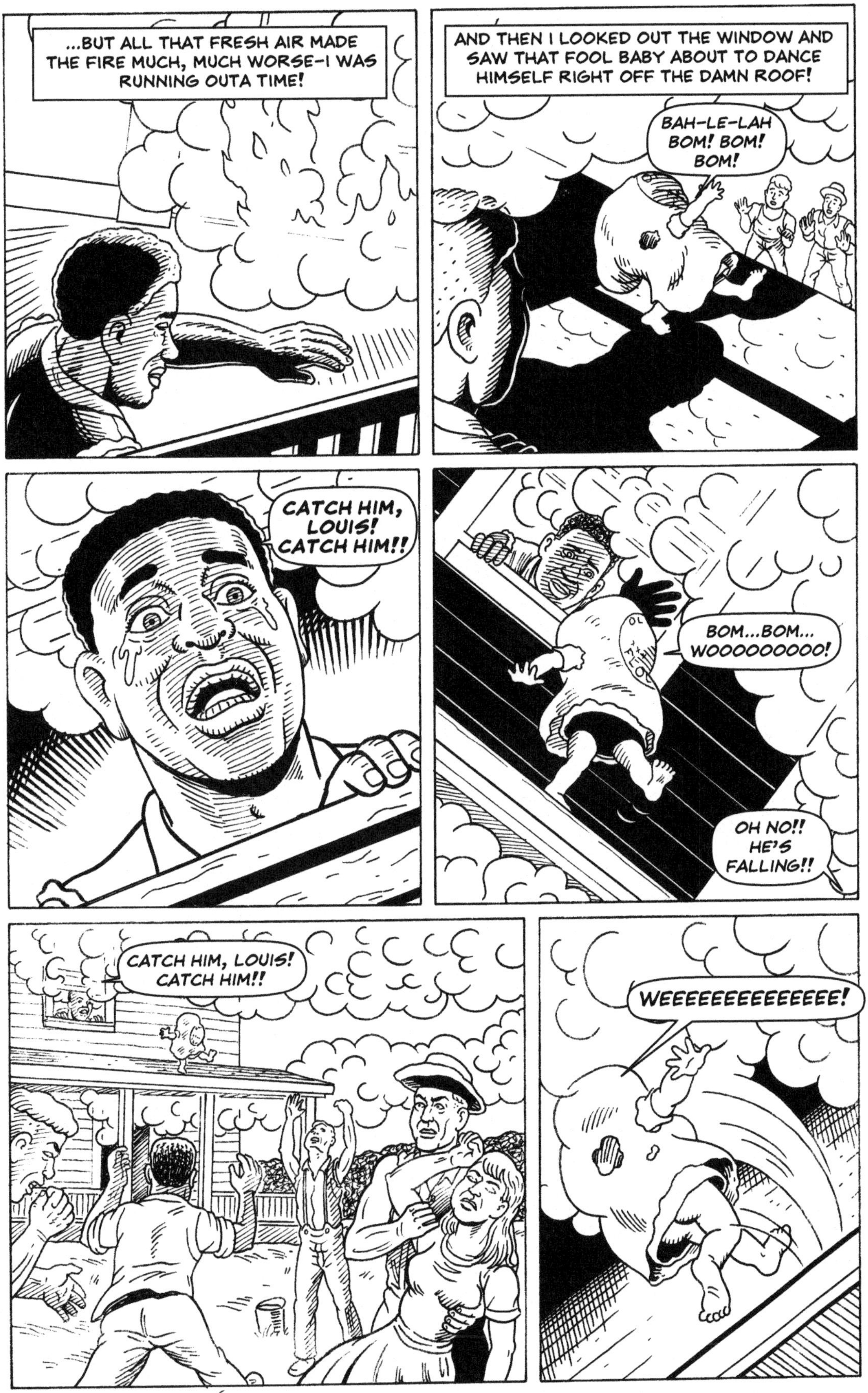
...BUT ALL THAT FRESH AIR MADE THE FIRE MUCH, MUCH WORSE—I WAS RUNNING OUTA TIME!
AND THEN I LOOKED OUT THE WINDOW AND SAW THAT FOOL BABY ABOUT TO DANCE HIMSELF RIGHT OFF THE DAMN ROOF!
BAH-LE-LAH BOM! BOM! BOM!
CATCH HIM, LOUIS! CATCH HIM!!
BOM...BOM... WOOOOOOOOO!
OH NO!! HE'S FALLING!!
CATCH HIM, LOUIS! CATCH HIM!!
WEEEEEEEEEEEEE!

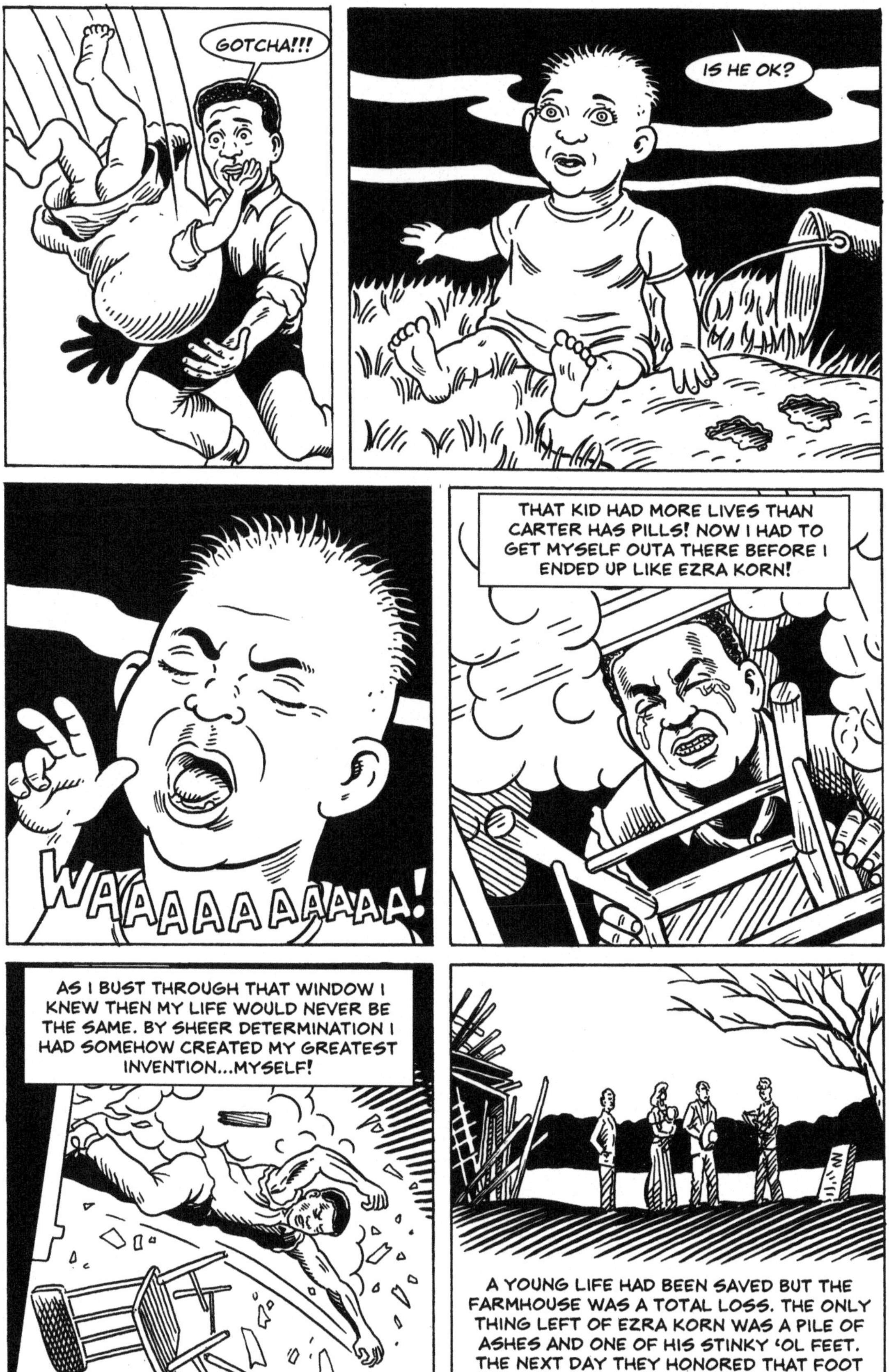
GOTCHA!!!
IS HE OK?
WAAAAAAAAAAA!
THAT KID HAD MORE LIVES THAN CARTER HAS PILLS! NOW I HAD TO GET MYSELF OUTA THERE BEFORE I ENDED UP LIKE EZRA KORN!
AS I BUST THROUGH THAT WINDOW I KNEW THEN MY LIFE WOULD NEVER BE THE SAME. BY SHEER DETERMINATION I HAD SOMEHOW CREATED MY GREATEST INVENTION...MYSELF!
A YOUNG LIFE HAD BEEN SAVED BUT THE FARMHOUSE WAS A TOTAL LOSS. THE ONLY THING LEFT OF EZRA KORN WAS A PILE OF ASHES AND ONE OF HIS STINKY 'OL FEET. THE NEXT DAY THEY HONORED THAT FOOT WITH A FULL CHRISTIAN BURIAL AND A CHICKEN LUNCH.

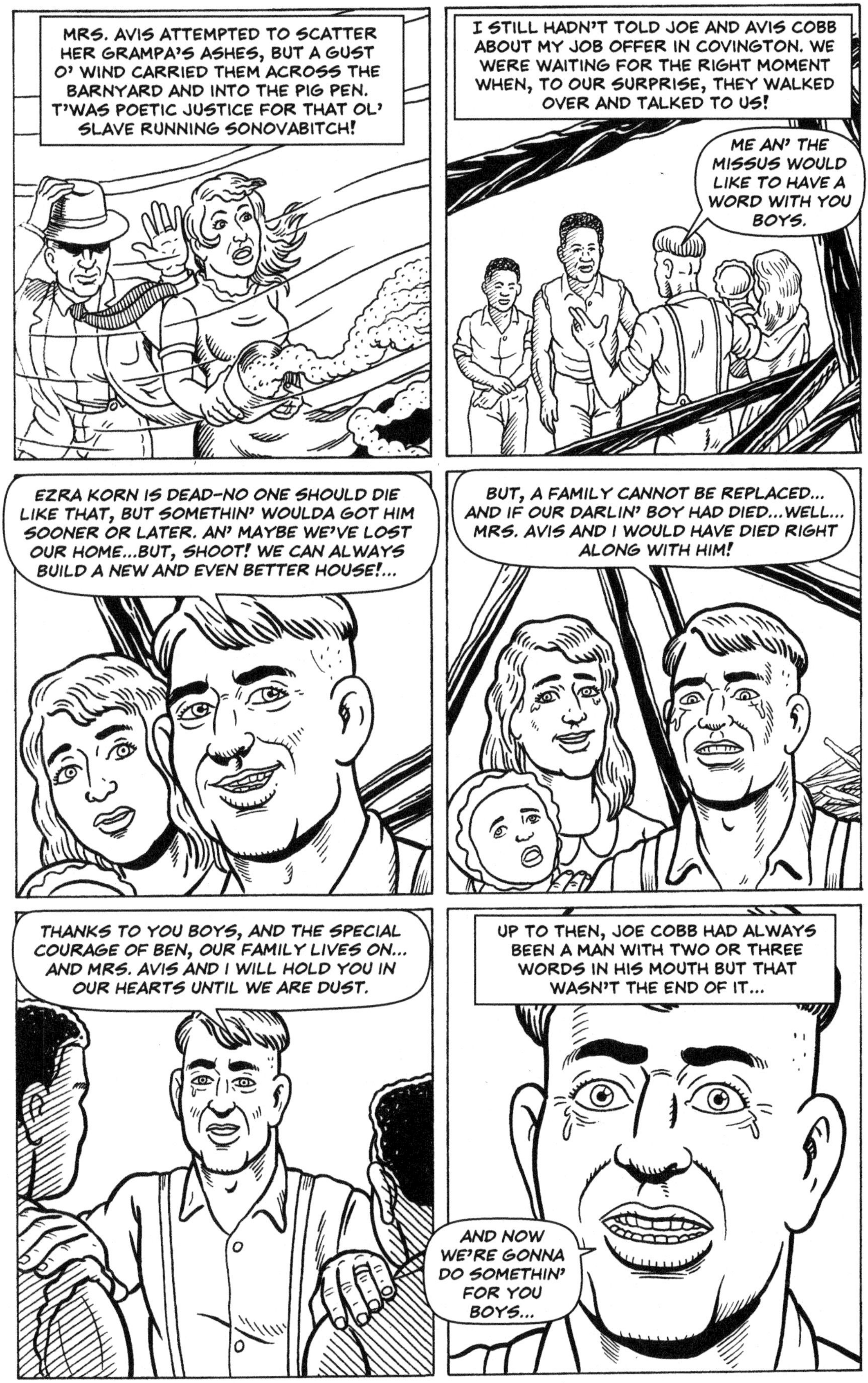

MRS. AVIS ATTEMPTED TO SCATTER HER GRAMPA'S ASHES, BUT A GUST O' WIND CARRIED THEM ACROSS THE BARNYARD AND INTO THE PIG PEN. T'WAS POETIC JUSTICE FOR THAT OL' SLAVE RUNNING SONOVABITCH!
I STILL HADN'T TOLD JOE AND AVIS COBB ABOUT MY JOB OFFER IN COVINGTON. WE WERE WAITING FOR THE RIGHT MOMENT WHEN, TO OUR SURPRISE, THEY WALKED OVER AND TALKED TO US!
ME AN' THE MISSUS WOULD LIKE TO HAVE A WORD WITH YOU BOYS.
EZRA KORN IS DEAD—NO ONE SHOULD DIE LIKE THAT, BUT SOMETHIN' WOULDA GOT HIM SOONER OR LATER. AN' MAYBE WE'VE LOST OUR HOME...BUT, SHOOT! WE CAN ALWAYS BUILD A NEW AND EVEN BETTER HOUSE!...
BUT, A FAMILY CANNOT BE REPLACED... AND IF OUR DARLIN' BOY HAD DIED...WELL... MRS. AVIS AND I WOULD HAVE DIED RIGHT ALONG WITH HIM!
THANKS TO YOU BOYS, AND THE SPECIAL COURAGE OF BEN, OUR FAMILY LIVES ON... AND MRS. AVIS AND I WILL HOLD YOU IN OUR HEARTS UNTIL WE ARE DUST.
UP TO THEN, JOE COBB HAD ALWAYS BEEN A MAN WITH TWO OR THREE WORDS IN HIS MOUTH BUT THAT WASN'T THE END OF IT...
AND NOW WE'RE GONNA DO SOMETHIN' FOR YOU BOYS...

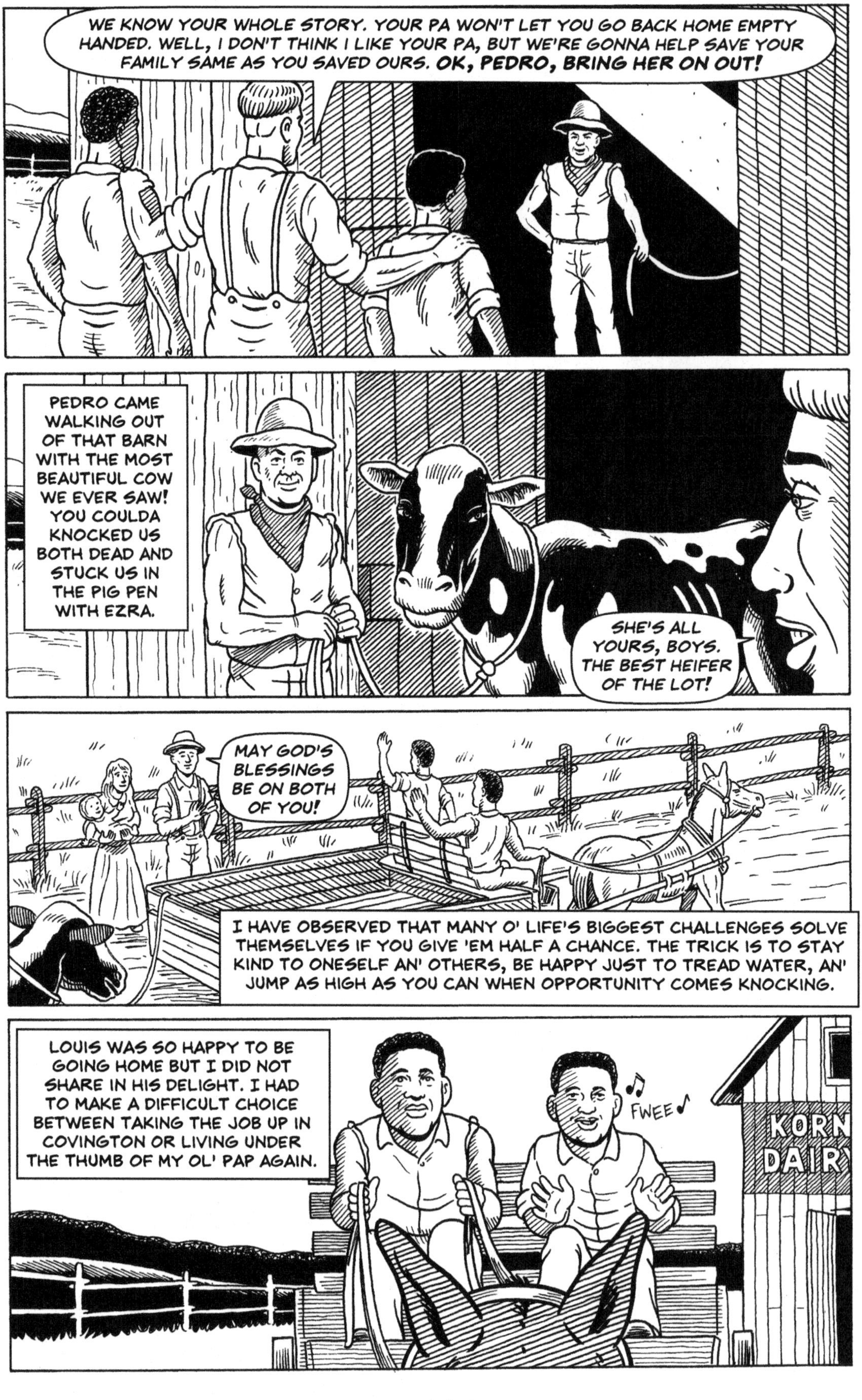
WE KNOW YOUR WHOLE STORY. YOUR PA WON'T LET YOU GO BACK HOME EMPTY HANDED. WELL, I DON'T THINK I LIKE YOUR PA, BUT WE'RE GONNA HELP SAVE YOUR FAMILY SAME AS YOU SAVED OURS. OK, PEDRO, BRING HER ON OUT!
PEDRO CAME WALKING OUT OF THAT BARN WITH THE MOST BEAUTIFUL COW WE EVER SAW! YOU COULDA KNOCKED US BOTH DEAD AND STUCK US IN THE PIG PEN WITH EZRA.
SHE'S ALL YOURS, BOYS. THE BEST HEIFER OF THE LOT!
MAY GOD'S BLESSINGS BE ON BOTH OF YOU!
I HAVE OBSERVED THAT MANY O' LIFE'S BIGGEST CHALLENGES SOLVE THEMSELVES IF YOU GIVE 'EM HALF A CHANCE. THE TRICK IS TO STAY KIND TO ONESELF AN' OTHERS, BE HAPPY JUST TO TREAD WATER, AN' JUMP AS HIGH AS YOU CAN WHEN OPPORTUNITY COMES KNOCKING.
LOUIS WAS SO HAPPY TO BE GOING HOME BUT I DID NOT SHARE IN HIS DELIGHT. I HAD TO MAKE A DIFFICULT CHOICE BETWEEN TAKING THE JOB UP IN COVINGTON OR LIVING UNDER THE THUMB OF MY OL' PAP AGAIN.
FWEE
KORN
DAIRY

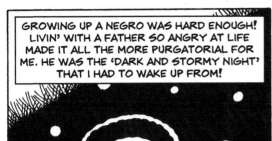

GROWING UP A NEGRO WAS HARD ENOUGH! LIVIN' WITH A FATHER SO ANGRY AT LIFE MADE IT ALL THE MORE PURGATORIAL FOR ME. HE WAS THE 'DARK AND STORMY NIGHT' THAT I HAD TO WAKE UP FROM!

BEN!...WAKE UP! WAKE UP, BEN!

LOOK, BEN! WE'S HOME! THERE'S MA AND PAP!

HERE YA GO, BROTHER. SHOW 'EM YOU CAN TAKE IT IN THE REST O' THE WAY.

LOUIS, I HAVE A CHANCE FOR A BETTER LIFE THAN WHAT OL' PAP HAS IN STORE FOR ME DOWN THERE. IF I DON'T TAKE IT NOW, I MAY NEVER GET OUTA HERE.

I KNOW YOUR MIND, BEN. I FIGGERED THIS MIGHT HAPPEN. DON'T WORRY, I'LL FIX THINGS WITH MA. SHE'LL UNDERSTAND.

YOU'RE A GOOD BROTHER, LOUIS... AN' THE BEST FRIEND I'LL EVER HAVE.

SO, I MADE MY CHOICE TO JOURNEY DOWN THE UNCERTAIN ROADS IN SEARCH OF A BETTER FUTURE.

UPON REACHING THE CREST O' THE HILL ABOVE THE FARM, I REMEMBERED SOMETHING I'D BEEN CARRYING AROUND MY NECK FOR WEEKS.

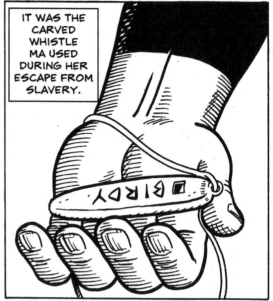

IT WAS THE CARVED WHISTLE MA USED DURING HER ESCAPE FROM SLAVERY.

I WAVED AN' SAID 'FARE THEE WELL' TO MY FAMILY AND GAVE THAT WHISTLE A GOOD BLOW.

IT MADE THE STRANGE, PITIFUL SOUND THAT SEEMED FITTING FOR THE UNJUST WORLD IT CAME FROM...

RRRR

...AN' OFF I WENT. WITH THE MONEY EARNED IN COVINGTON AN' OTHER PLACES, I PAID MY WAY THROUGH SCHOOL. EVENTUALLY, MY JOURNEY BROUGHT ME HERE, TO CLEVELAND, WHERE I CHOSE TO LAY DOWN MY ROOTS.

AN' THAT SIR, IS HOW A LOWLY COW INSPIRED ONE O' MY FINEST INVENTIONS —THE BELTRAN SMOKE HELMET.

WELL, THAT'S QUITE A STORY, BELTRAN, QUITE A STORY, BUT...

...BUT WHAT?

BUT...MY EDITOR WILL NEVER PRINT IT. HE AND OUR READERS WOULD FIND IT...WELL..., 'UNACCEPTABLE'.

WHAT WON'T THEY ACCEPT? THAT A NEGRO HAS THE INTELLIGENCE TO INVENT SUCH A DEVICE?

NO, IT'S NOT THAT. IT'S JUST THAT OUR READERS WILL NEVER ACCEPT A NEGRO AS THE "HERO" OF A STORY.

HMMPH! SPOKEN LIKE A TRUE GATEKEEPER OF THE EVERLASTING LIE!

GODDAM IT! JUST WHO ARE THESE "READERS" ANYWAYS? AREN'T I A "READER", TOO?

THE Clevel News Gazett OVER 30,000 REAL

MA—THERE'S STILL PEOPLE IN THE WORLD THAT CAN HEAR THE CALL O' YOUR OL' WHISTLE ...

BIRDY

...(SIGH)...AN' I GUESS I'M ONE OF 'EM.

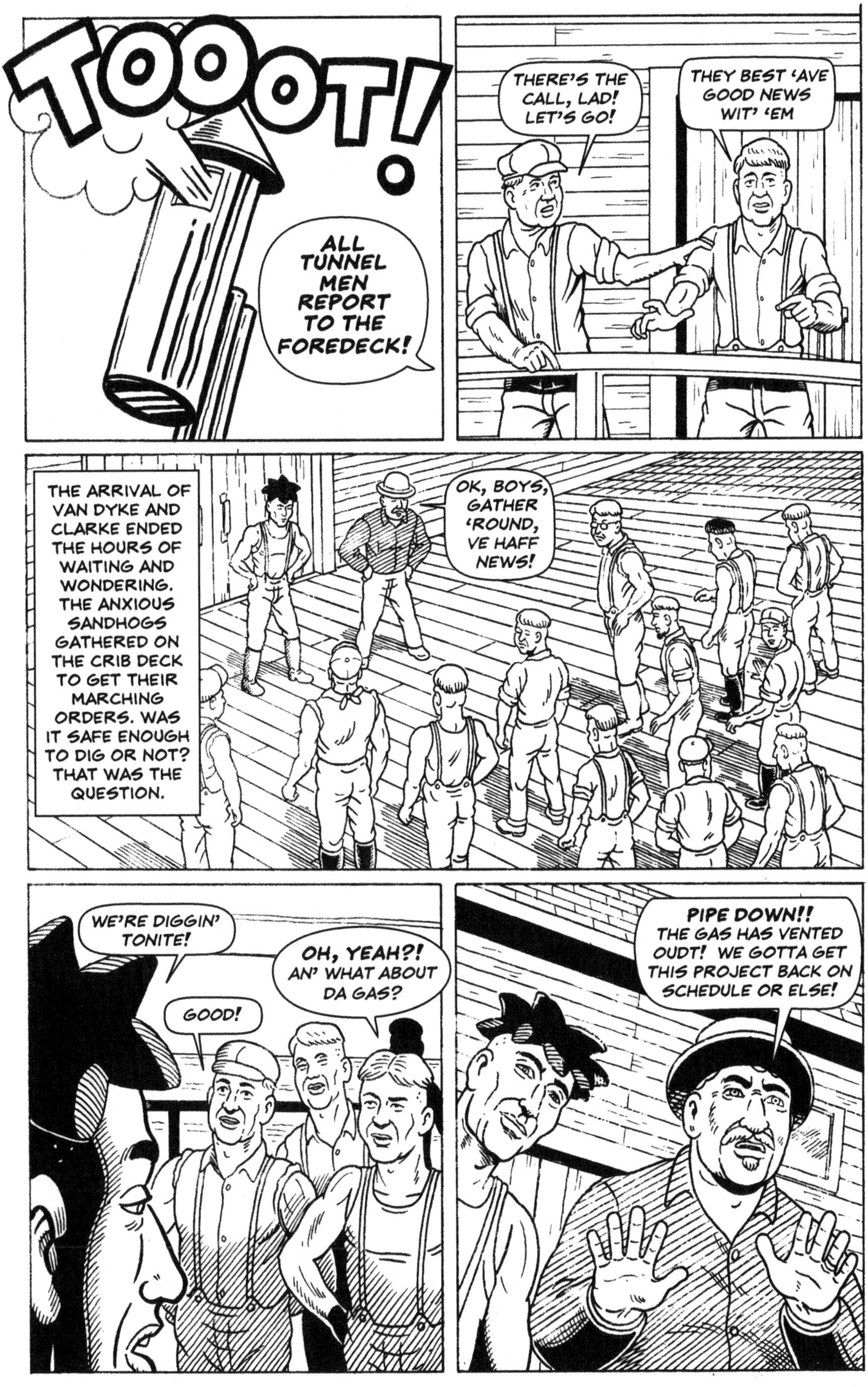
TOOOT!
ALL TUNNEL MEN REPORT TO THE FOREDECK!
THERE'S THE CALL, LAD! LET'S GO!
THEY BEST 'AVE GOOD NEWS WIT' 'EM
THE ARRIVAL OF VAN DYKE AND CLARKE ENDED THE HOURS OF WAITING AND WONDERING. THE ANXIOUS SANDHOGS GATHERED ON THE CRIB DECK TO GET THEIR MARCHING ORDERS. WAS IT SAFE ENOUGH TO DIG OR NOT? THAT WAS THE QUESTION.
OK, BOYS, GATHER 'ROUND, VE HAFF NEWS!
WE'RE DIGGIN' TONITE!
GOOD!
OH, YEAH?! AN' WHAT ABOUT DA GAS?
PIPE DOWN!! THE GAS HAS VENTED OUDT! WE GOTTA GET THIS PROJECT BACK ON SCHEDULE OR ELSE!

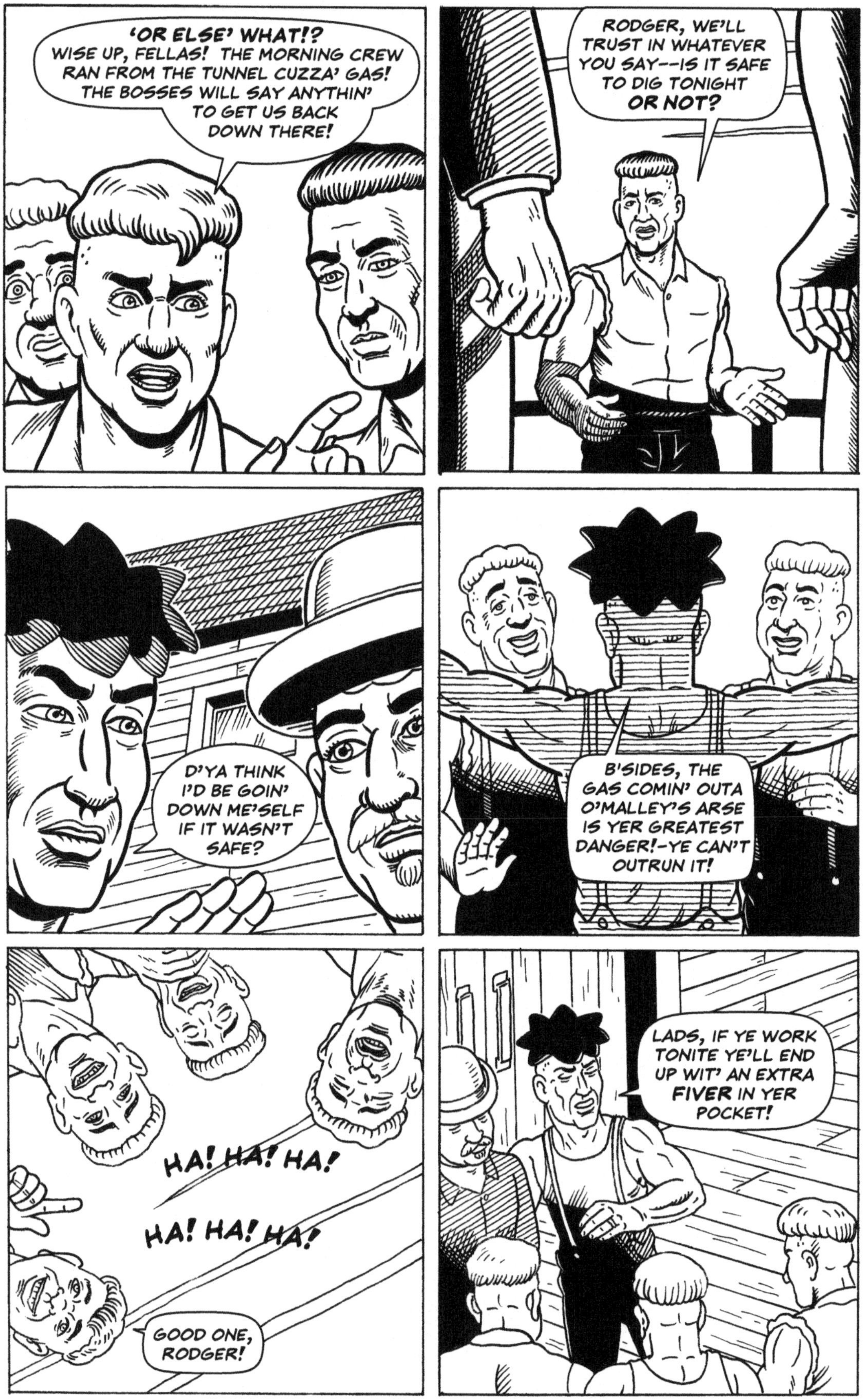
'OR ELSE' WHAT!? WISE UP, FELLAS! THE MORNING CREW RAN FROM THE TUNNEL CUZZA' GAS! THE BOSSES WILL SAY ANYTHIN' TO GET US BACK DOWN THERE!
RODGER, WE'LL TRUST IN WHATEVER YOU SAY--IS IT SAFE TO DIG TONIGHT OR NOT?
D'YA THINK I'D BE GOIN' DOWN ME'SELF IF IT WASN'T SAFE?
B'SIDES, THE GAS COMIN' OUTA O'MALLEY'S ARSE IS YER GREATEST DANGER!-YE CAN'T OUTRUN IT!
HA! HA! HA!
HA! HA! HA!
GOOD ONE, RODGER!
LADS, IF YE WORK TONITE YE'LL END UP WIT' AN EXTRA FIVER IN YER POCKET!

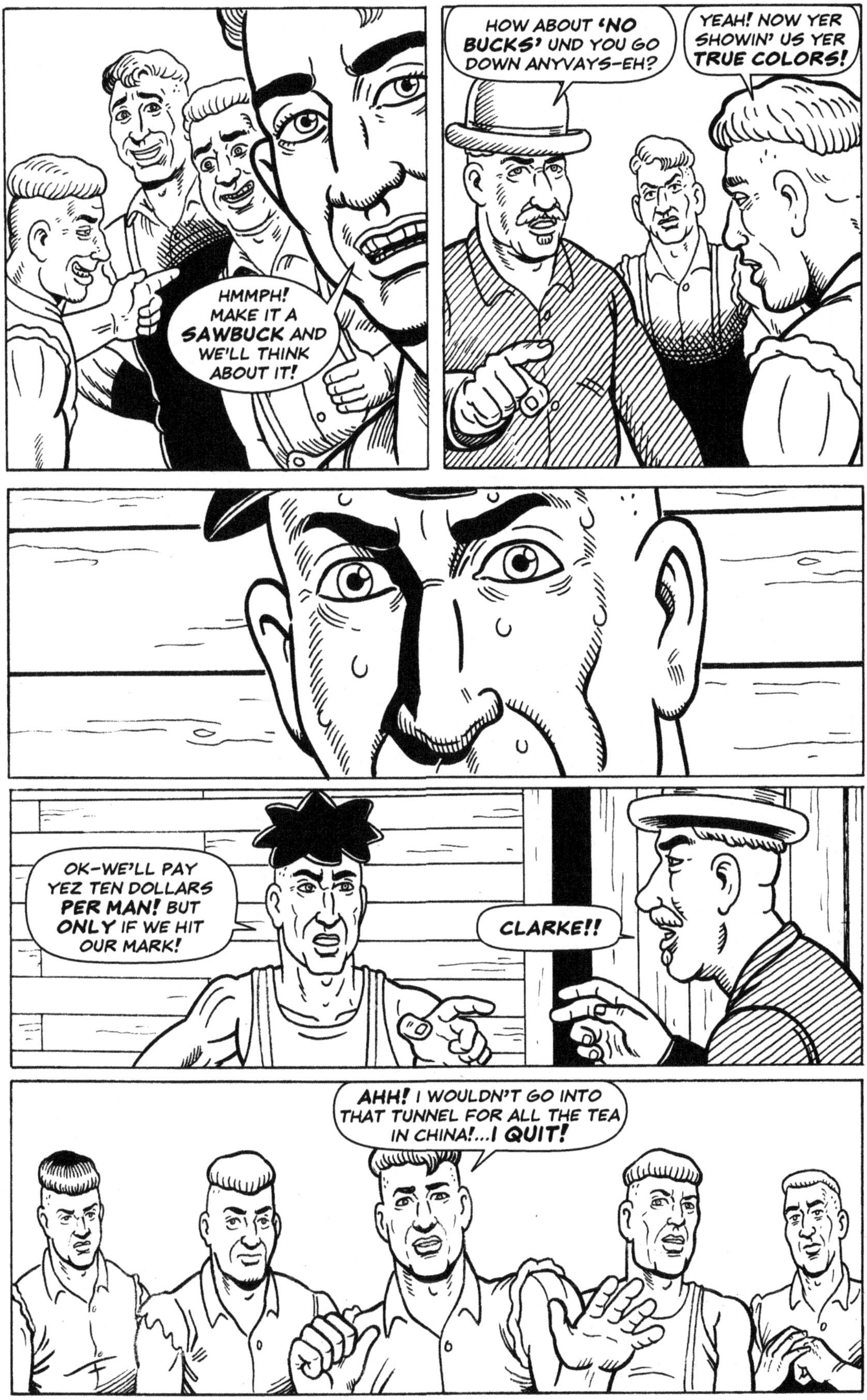
HMMPH! MAKE IT A SAWBUCK AND WE'LL THINK ABOUT IT!
HOW ABOUT 'NO BUCKS' UND YOU GO DOWN ANYVAYS-EH?
YEAH! NOW YER SHOWIN' US YER TRUE COLORS!
OK-WE'LL PAY YEZ TEN DOLLARS PER MAN! BUT ONLY IF WE HIT OUR MARK!
CLARKE!!
AHH! I WOULDN'T GO INTO THAT TUNNEL FOR ALL THE TEA IN CHINA!...I QUIT!

124

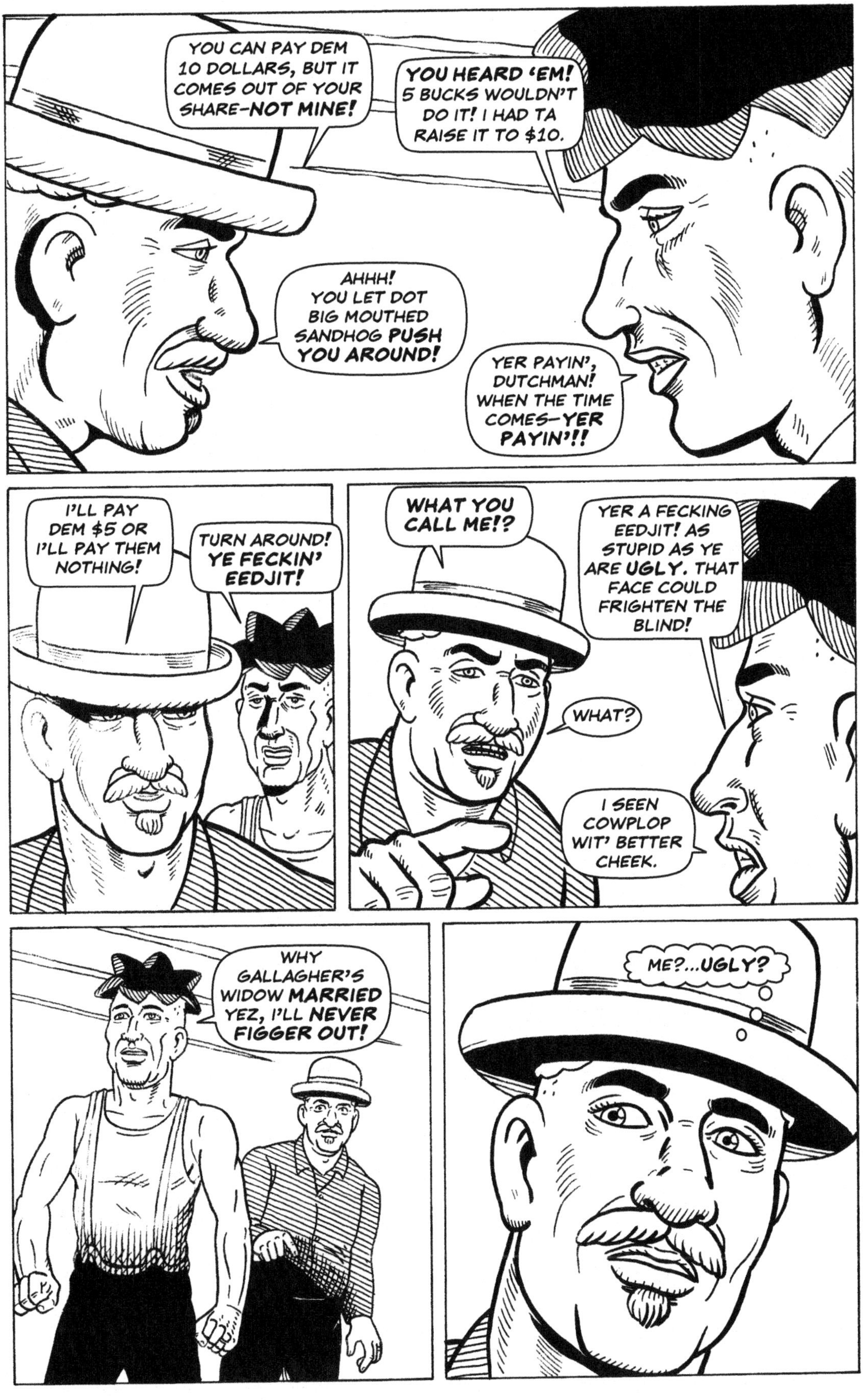
YOU CAN PAY DEM 10 DOLLARS, BUT IT COMES OUT OF YOUR SHARE–NOT MINE!
YOU HEARD 'EM! 5 BUCKS WOULDN'T DO IT! I HAD TA RAISE IT TO $10.
AHHH! YOU LET DOT BIG MOUTHED SANDHOG PUSH YOU AROUND!
YER PAYIN', DUTCHMAN! WHEN THE TIME COMES–YER PAYIN'!!
I'LL PAY DEM $5 OR I'LL PAY THEM NOTHING!
TURN AROUND! YE FECKIN' EEDJIT!
WHAT YOU CALL ME!?
YER A FECKING EEDJIT! AS STUPID AS YE ARE UGLY. THAT FACE COULD FRIGHTEN THE BLIND!
WHAT?
I SEEN COWPLOP WIT' BETTER CHEEK.
WHY GALLAGHER'S WIDOW MARRIED YEZ, I'LL NEVER FIGGER OUT!
ME?...UGLY?

THE SANDHOG WHO QUIT LEFT CLARKE HAUNTED WITH A SENSE OF DOUBT AND DREAD. 'WHAT GOOD IS MONEY', CLARKE PONDERED, 'IF YOU'RE TOO **DEAD** TO SPEND IT'?

'...AND WHAT OF MY OWN FAMILY— WHO WILL PROVIDE FOR THEM?'

'AWW, STOP YER WORRYIN', THEY'RE **TOO BEAUTIFUL** FER TRAGEDY...'

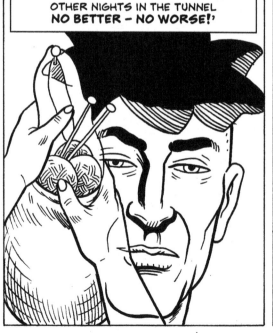

'...THIS NIGHT WILL BE LIKE A *THOUSAND* OTHER NIGHTS IN THE TUNNEL **NO BETTER – NO WORSE!**'

HEY! CLARKE!!

126

127

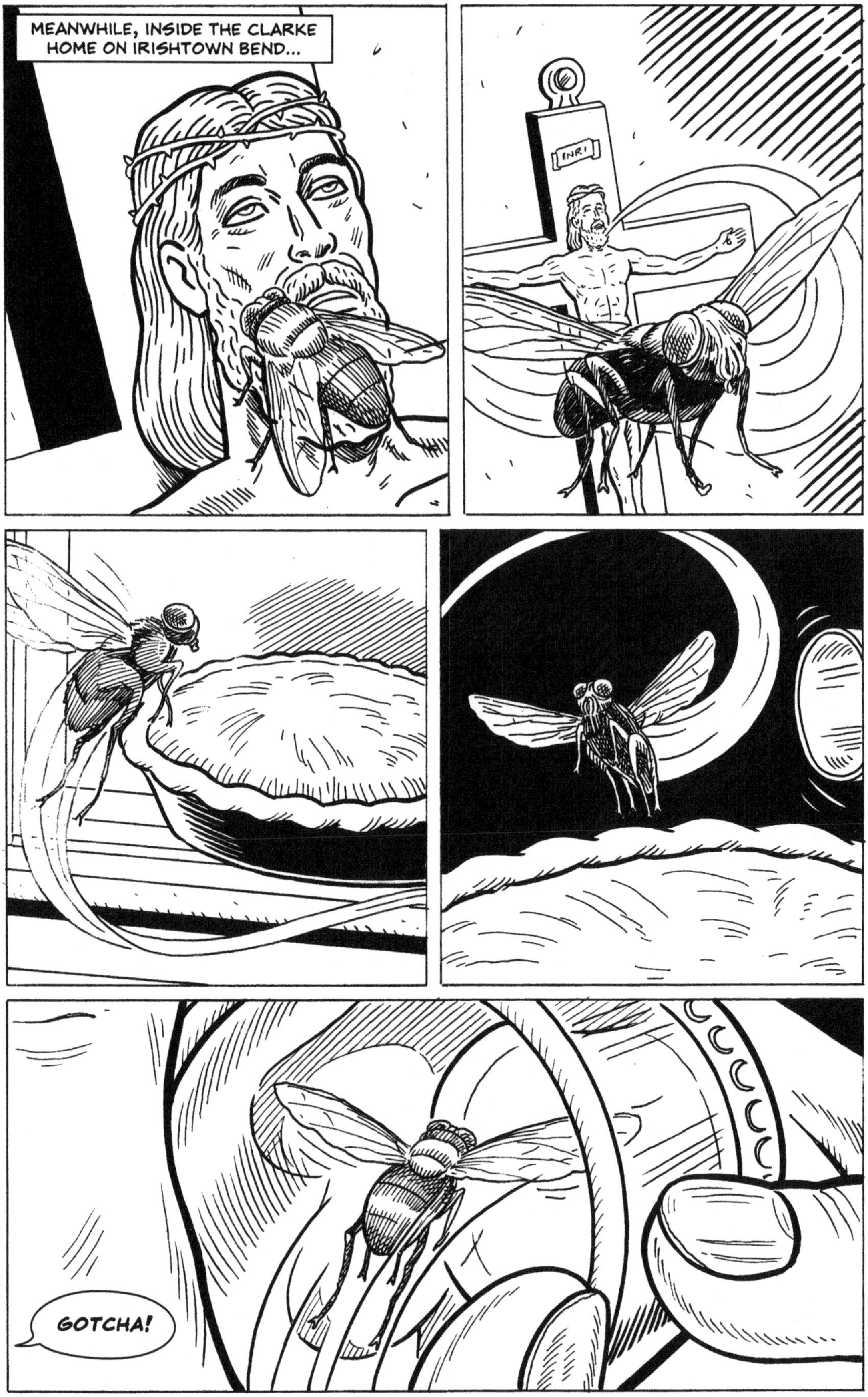
MEANWHILE, INSIDE THE CLARKE HOME ON IRISHTOWN BEND...
INRI
GOTCHA!

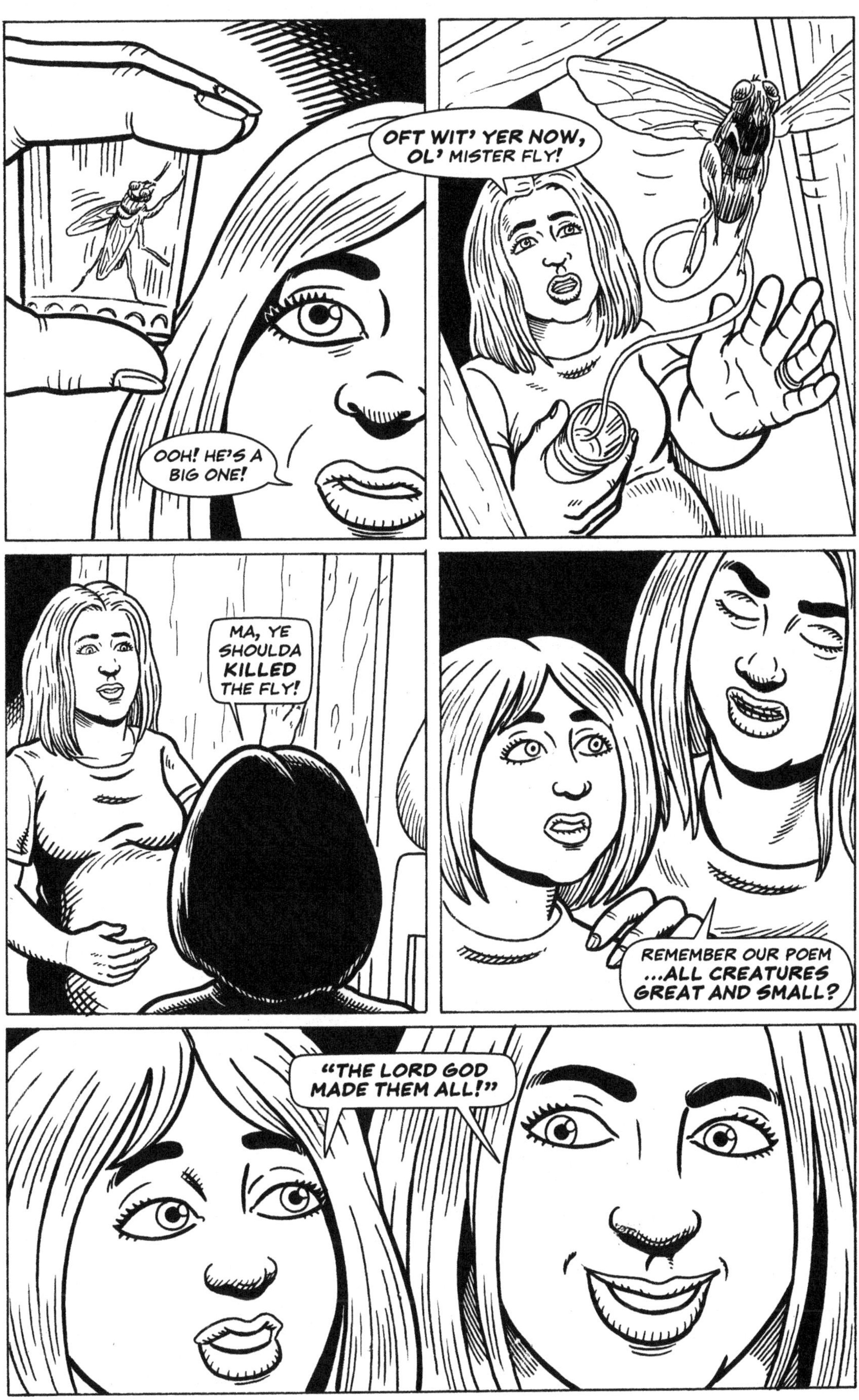
OOH! HE'S A BIG ONE!
OFT WIT' YER NOW, OL' MISTER FLY!
MA, YE SHOULDA **KILLED** THE FLY!
REMEMBER OUR POEM ...ALL CREATURES GREAT AND SMALL?
"THE LORD GOD MADE THEM ALL!"

EVEN A WEE FLY DESERVES A FIGHTIN' CHANCE IN THIS WORLD.

I'LL KNIT AWHILE AND THEN IT'S OFF TA BED WITH YA!

WHAT'S 'DIS, NOW?

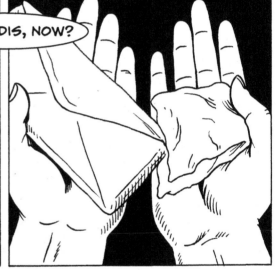

SWEENEY!!

I'LL BE BACK IN A JIFF, SWEET GIRL!...I HAVE TO TALK TO MRS. SWEENEY.

ALRIGHT!

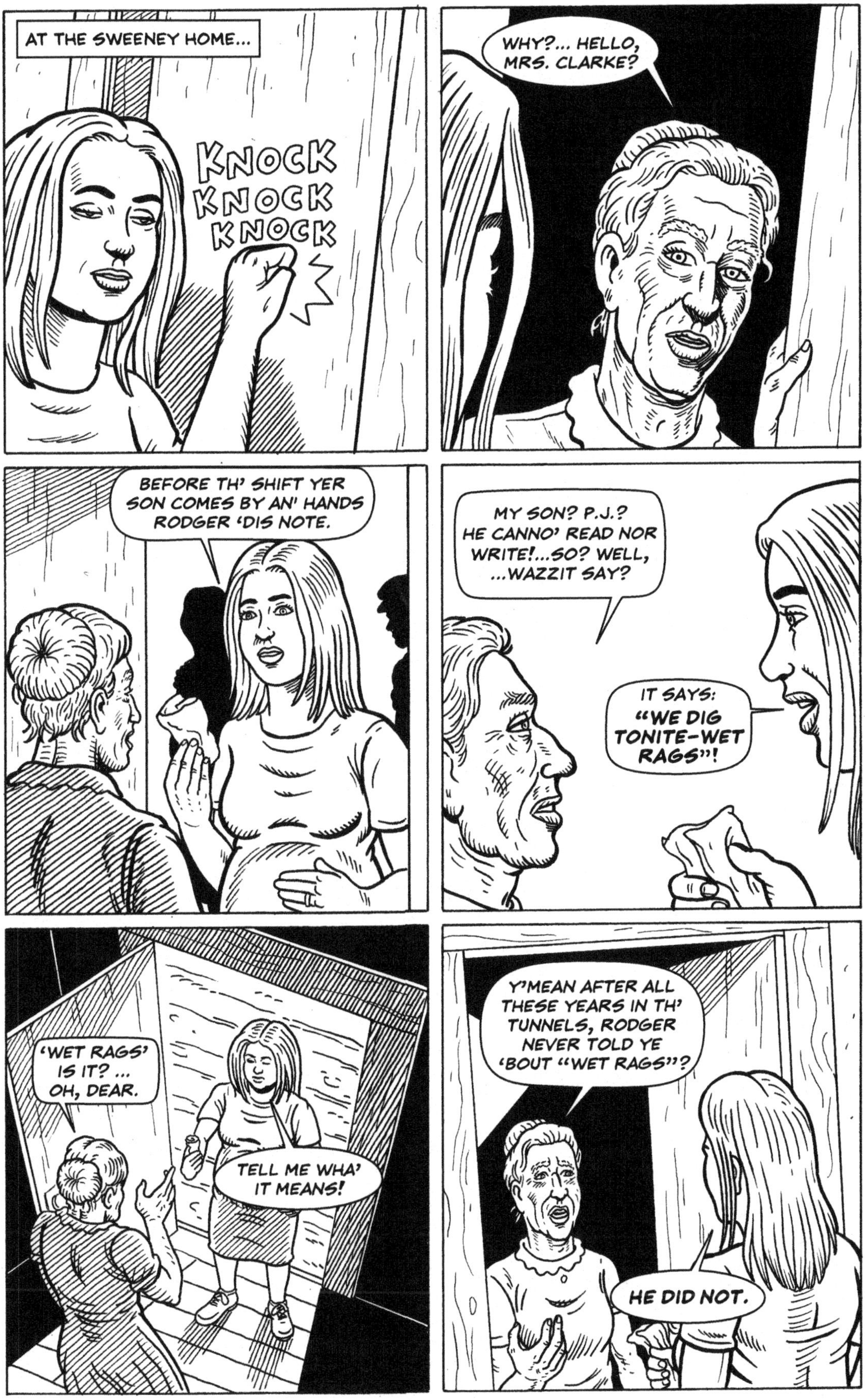
AT THE SWEENEY HOME...
KNOCK KNOCK KNOCK
WHY?... HELLO, MRS. CLARKE?
BEFORE TH' SHIFT YER SON COMES BY AN' HANDS RODGER 'DIS NOTE.
MY SON? P.J.? HE CANNO' READ NOR WRITE!...SO? WELL, ...WAZZIT SAY?
IT SAYS: "WE DIG TONITE-WET RAGS"!
'WET RAGS' IS IT? ... OH, DEAR.
TELL ME WHA' IT MEANS!
Y'MEAN AFTER ALL THESE YEARS IN TH' TUNNELS, RODGER NEVER TOLD YE 'BOUT "WET RAGS"?
HE DID NOT.

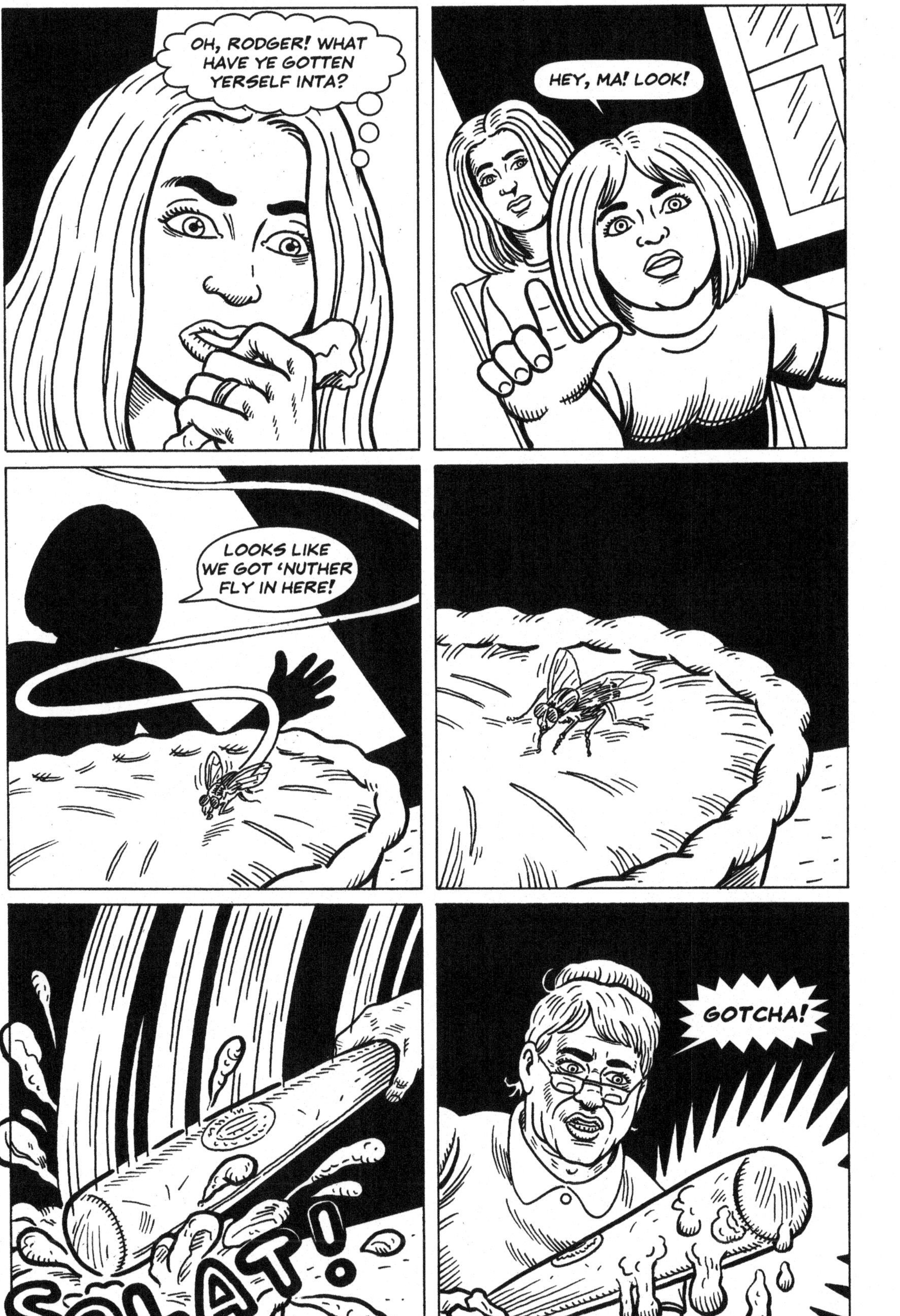
OH, RODGER! WHAT HAVE YE GOTTEN YERSELF INTA?
HEY, MA! LOOK!
LOOKS LIKE WE GOT 'NUTHER FLY IN HERE!
SPLAT!
GOTCHA!

134

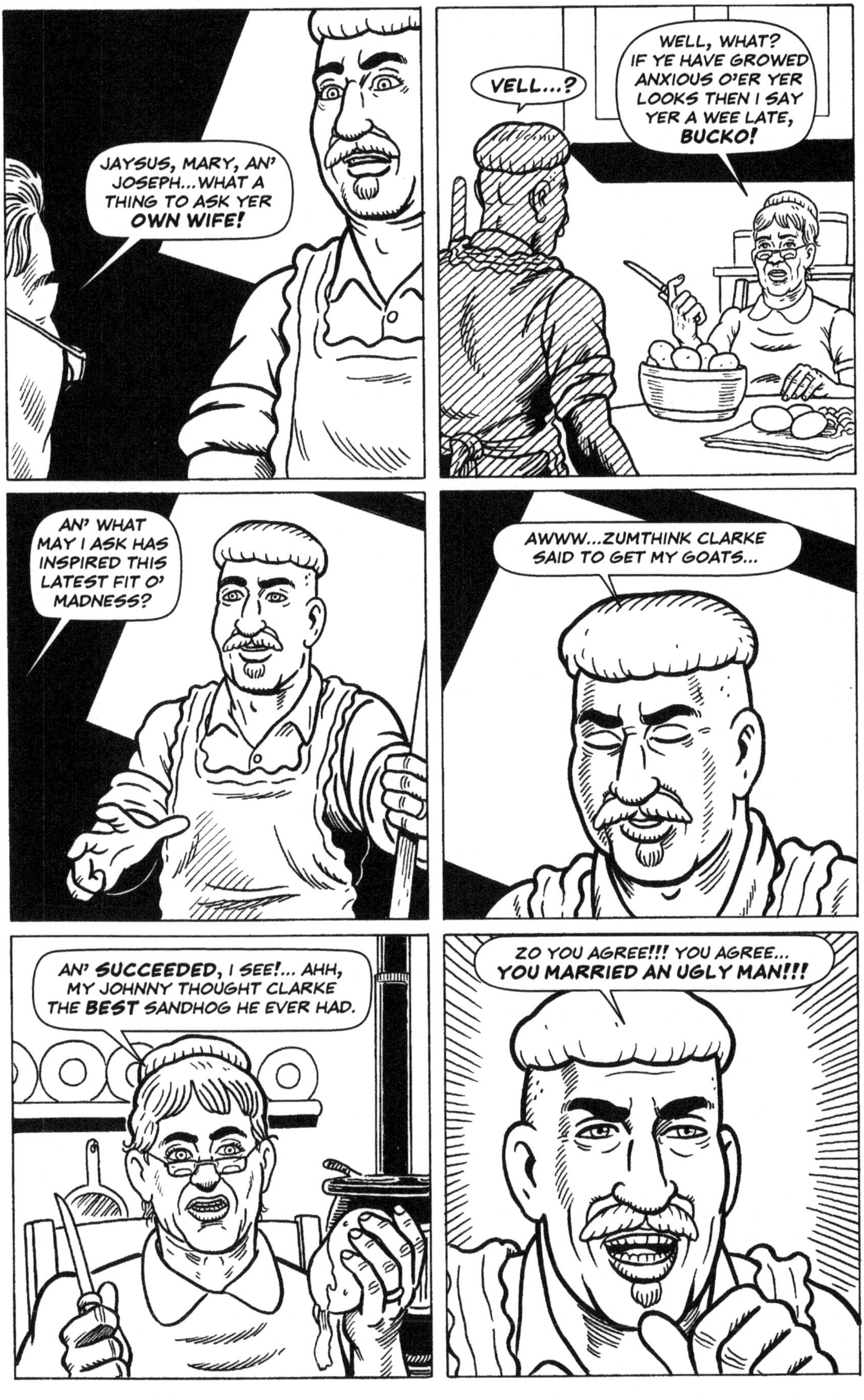
JAYSUS, MARY, AN' JOSEPH...WHAT A THING TO ASK YER OWN WIFE!
VELL...?
WELL, WHAT? IF YE HAVE GROWED ANXIOUS O'ER YER LOOKS THEN I SAY YER A WEE LATE, BUCKO!
AN' WHAT MAY I ASK HAS INSPIRED THIS LATEST FIT O' MADNESS?
AWWW...ZUMTHINK CLARKE SAID TO GET MY GOATS...
AN' SUCCEEDED, I SEE!... AHH, MY JOHNNY THOUGHT CLARKE THE BEST SANDHOG HE EVER HAD.
ZO YOU AGREE!!! YOU AGREE... YOU MARRIED AN UGLY MAN!!!

YES, IT'S TRUE, BUT A WOMAN IN MY POSITION CANNO' BE TOO PARTICULAR!!

WHEN JOHNNY DIED I NEEDED THE SECURITY OF A STEADY MAN...AND YE HAVE BROUGHT ME THAT, WILLY.

OOH...SOB... SOB...SOB!

...AN' BESIDES YE BECAME A FINE FATHER FIGURE FER ME TOMMY-BOY!

TOMMY!... SOB!... TOMMY BOY!

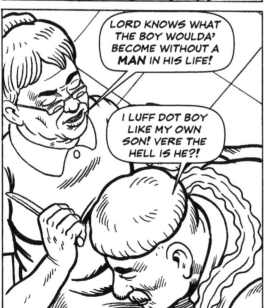

LORD KNOWS WHAT THE BOY WOULDA' BECOME WITHOUT A **MAN** IN HIS LIFE!

I LUFF DOT BOY LIKE MY OWN SON! VERE THE HELL IS HE?!

HE'S WORKIN' A DOUBLE SHIFT AT THE TAXI STAND— WORKIN' **LIKE A SLAVE!**

I TAUGHT HIM TO BE CHUST LIKE ME!

136

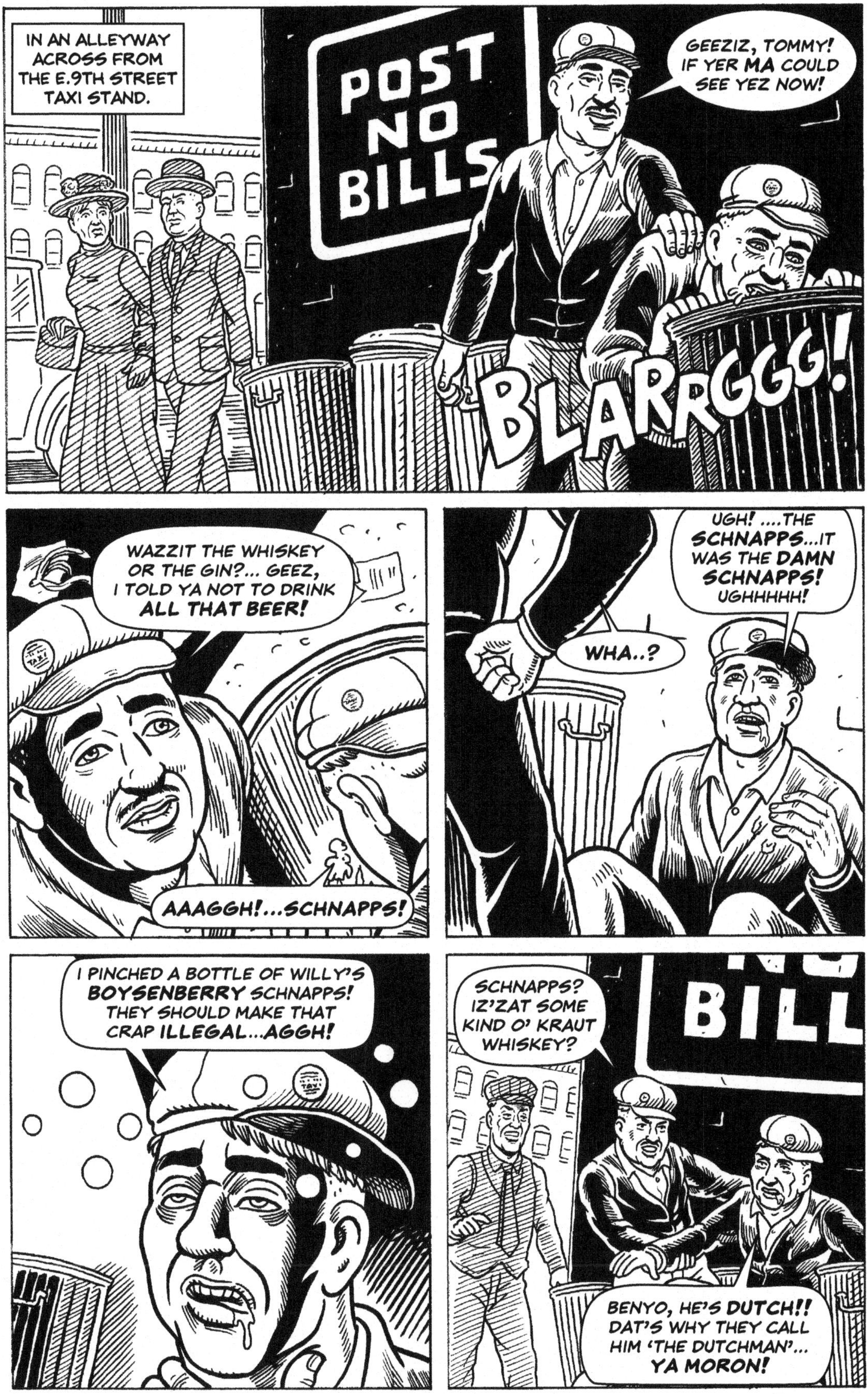
IN AN ALLEYWAY ACROSS FROM THE E.9TH STREET TAXI STAND.
POST NO BILLS
GEEZIZ, TOMMY! IF YER MA COULD SEE YEZ NOW!
BLARRGGG!
WAZZIT THE WHISKEY OR THE GIN?... GEEZ, I TOLD YA NOT TO DRINK ALL THAT BEER!
AAAGGH!...SCHNAPPS!
WHA..?
UGH! ....THE SCHNAPPS...IT WAS THE DAMN SCHNAPPS! UGHHHHH!
I PINCHED A BOTTLE OF WILLY'S BOYSENBERRY SCHNAPPS! THEY SHOULD MAKE THAT CRAP ILLEGAL...AGGH!
SCHNAPPS? IZ'ZAT SOME KIND O' KRAUT WHISKEY?
BENYO, HE'S DUTCH!! DAT'S WHY THEY CALL HIM 'THE DUTCHMAN'... YA MORON!

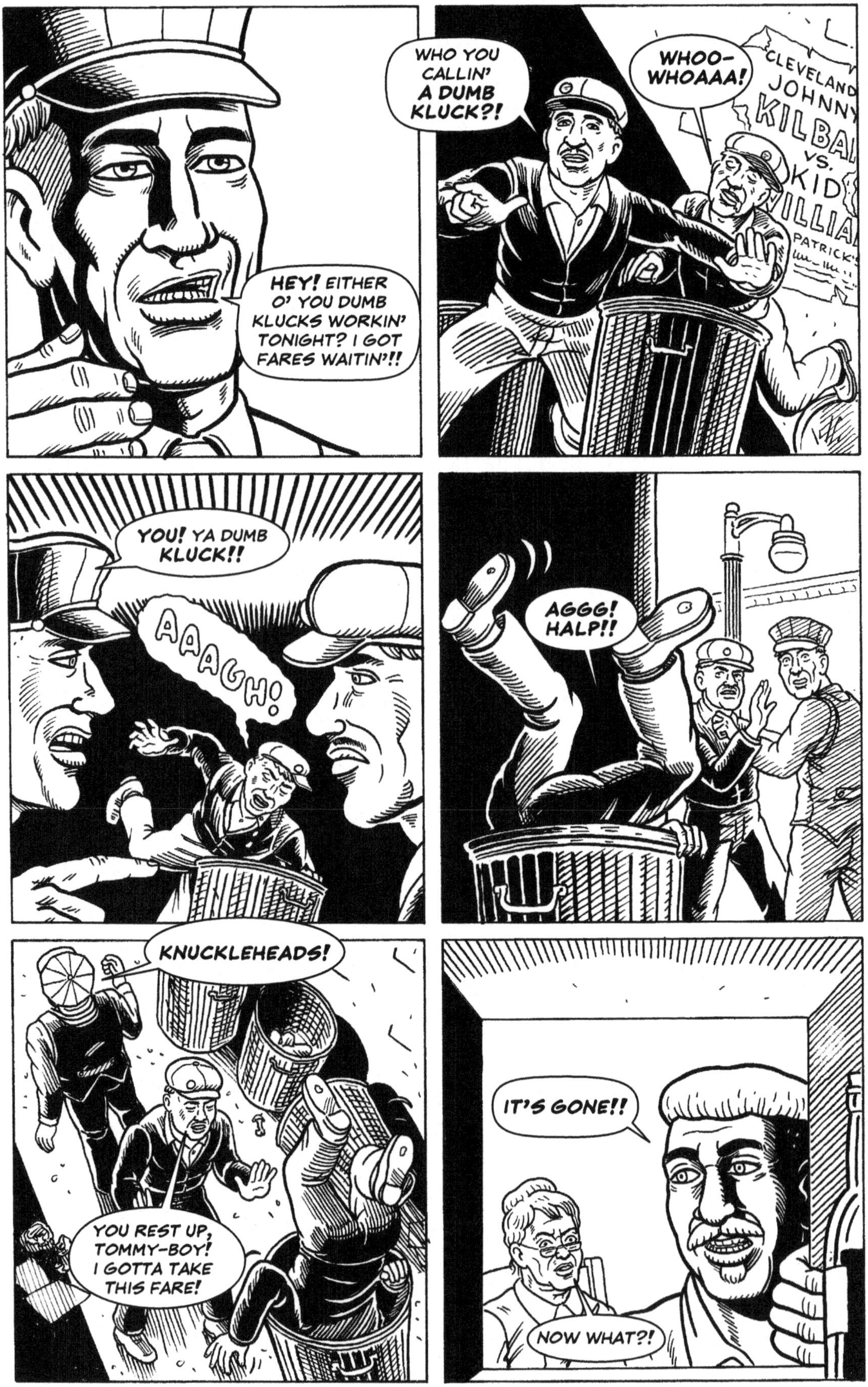
HEY! EITHER O' YOU DUMB KLUCKS WORKIN' TONIGHT? I GOT FARES WAITIN'!!
WHO YOU CALLIN' A DUMB KLUCK?!
WHOO-WHOAAA!
CLEVELAND JOHNNY KILBA VS. KID WILLIA
PATRICK'S
YOU! YA DUMB KLUCK!!
AAAGH!
AGGG! HALP!!
KNUCKLEHEADS!
YOU REST UP, TOMMY-BOY! I GOTTA TAKE THIS FARE!
IT'S GONE!!
NOW WHAT?!

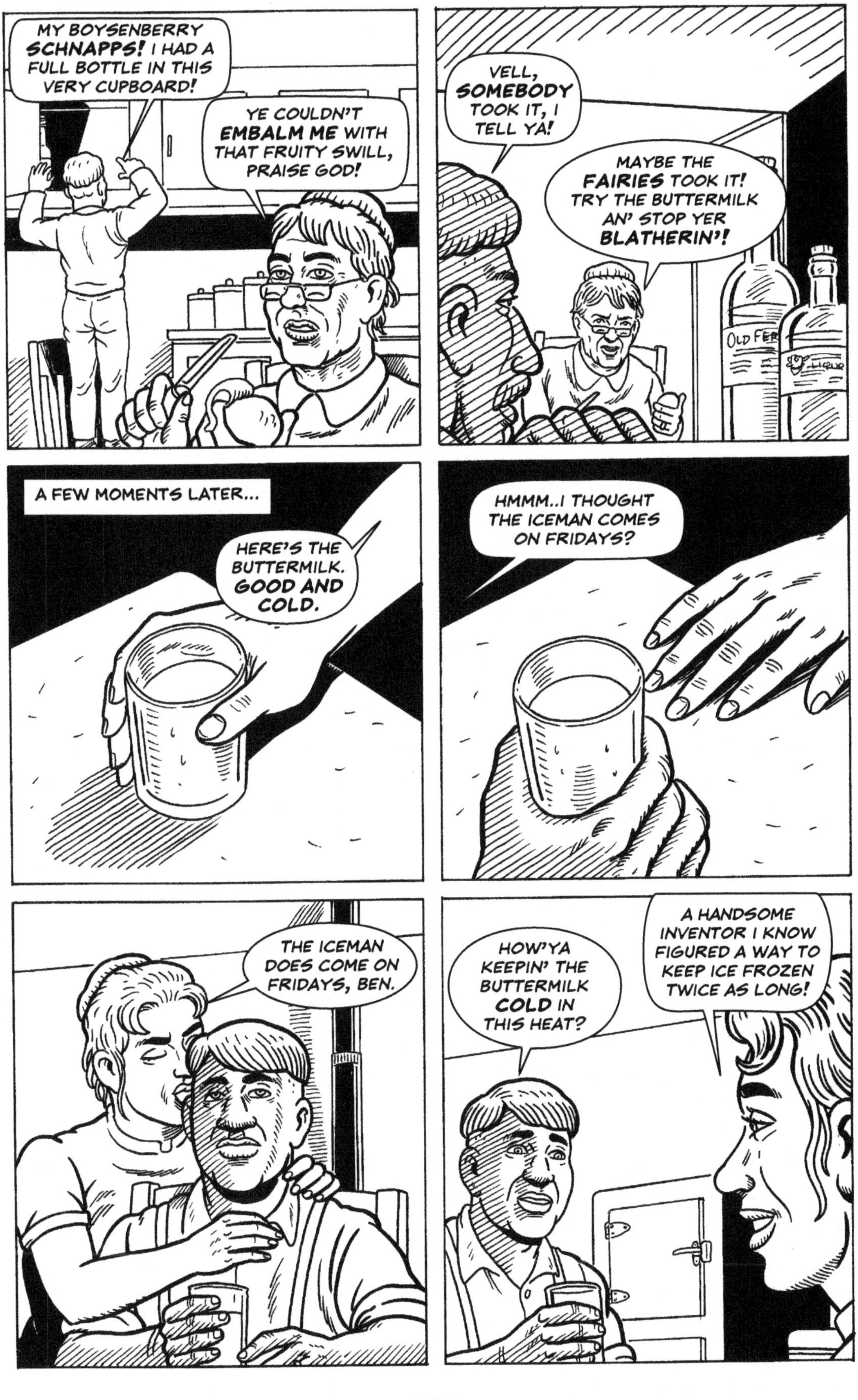
MY BOYSENBERRY SCHNAPPS! I HAD A FULL BOTTLE IN THIS VERY CUPBOARD!
YE COULDN'T EMBALM ME WITH THAT FRUITY SWILL, PRAISE GOD!
VELL, SOMEBODY TOOK IT, I TELL YA!
MAYBE THE FAIRIES TOOK IT! TRY THE BUTTERMILK AN' STOP YER BLATHERIN'!
A FEW MOMENTS LATER...
HERE'S THE BUTTERMILK. GOOD AND COLD.
HMMM..I THOUGHT THE ICEMAN COMES ON FRIDAYS?
THE ICEMAN DOES COME ON FRIDAYS, BEN.
HOW'YA KEEPIN' THE BUTTERMILK COLD IN THIS HEAT?
A HANDSOME INVENTOR I KNOW FIGURED A WAY TO KEEP ICE FROZEN TWICE AS LONG!

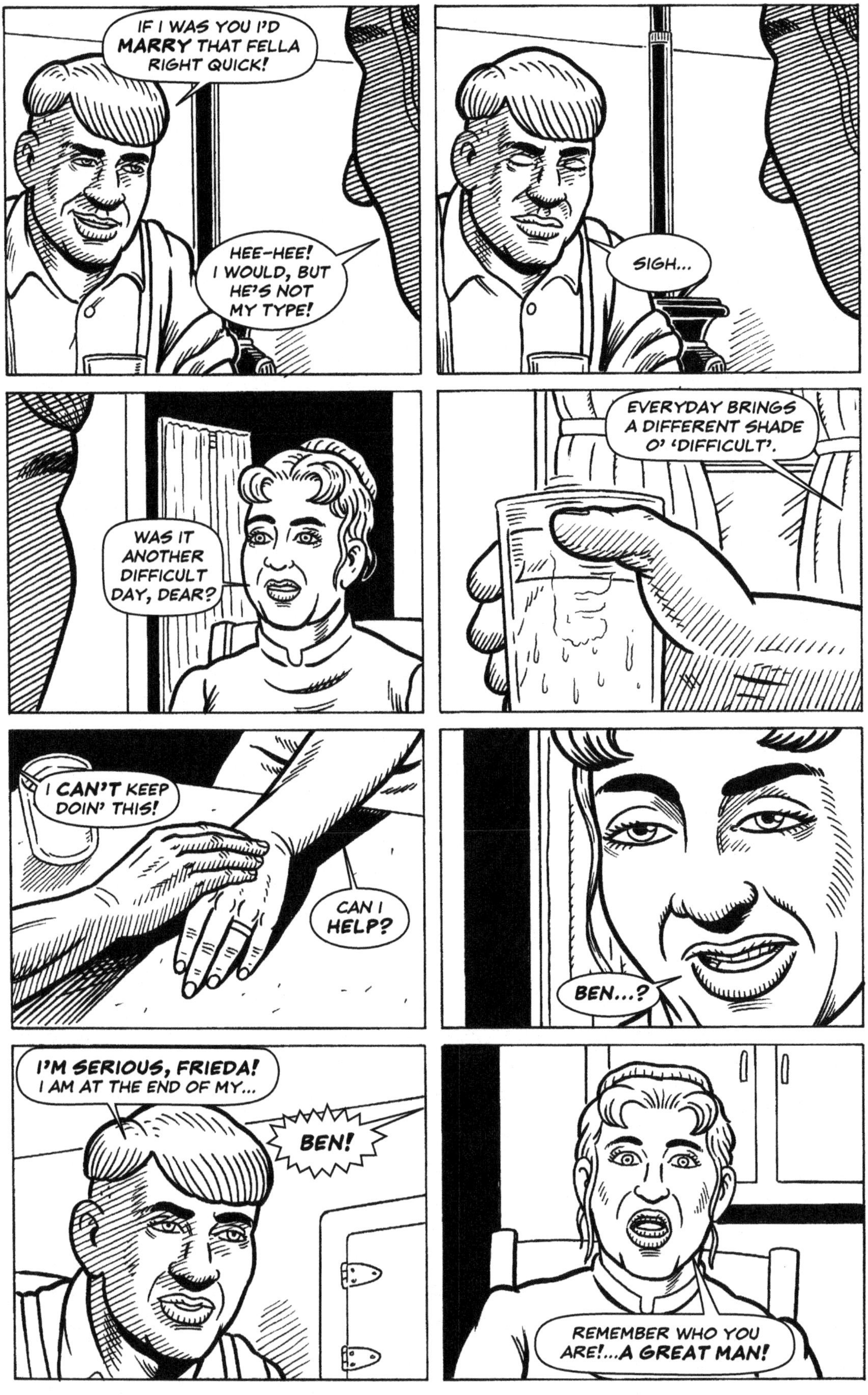
IF I WAS YOU I'D MARRY THAT FELLA RIGHT QUICK!
HEE-HEE! I WOULD, BUT HE'S NOT MY TYPE!
SIGH...
WAS IT ANOTHER DIFFICULT DAY, DEAR?
EVERYDAY BRINGS A DIFFERENT SHADE O' 'DIFFICULT'.
I CAN'T KEEP DOIN' THIS!
CAN I HELP?
BEN...?
I'M SERIOUS, FRIEDA! I AM AT THE END OF MY...
BEN!
REMEMBER WHO YOU ARE!...A GREAT MAN!

I AM **NOT** A GREAT MAN...

WELL...I'LL LEAVE YOU TO WALLOW IN YOUR BUTTERMILK...

HOLD ON...HOLD ON, GIRL. LET'S CONVERSE AWHILE.

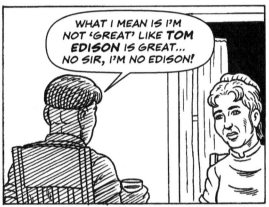

WHAT I MEAN IS I'M NOT 'GREAT' LIKE **TOM EDISON** IS GREAT... NO SIR, I'M NO EDISON!

TOM EDISON IS A STINKY OLD MAN WHO PUTS HIS NAME ON THE SWEAT AND TOIL OF OTHERS...AND LOOK AT WHAT HE DID TO **TESLA!**

TESLA? THAT MAN IS AS MAD AS A MARCH HARE. I'LL TAKE STINKY O'ER CRAZY ANY OL' DAY!

I'M JUST SAYING THAT THE SMOKE HELMET IS GOING TO SAVE LIVES AND SOON THE WORLD WILL KNOW THAT YOU ARE A GREAT MAN, TOO!

I'M A GREAT MAN WHO DRAGS HIMSELF ALL O'ER CREATION DRESSED LIKE AN INDIAN. IT'S NUTHIN' BUT PURE HUMILIATION...!

IT'S CALLED PROVIDING AND PUTTING A ROOF OVER OUR HEADS! YOU'RE A GREAT MAN, BEN–IT'S NOT YOUR FAULT!

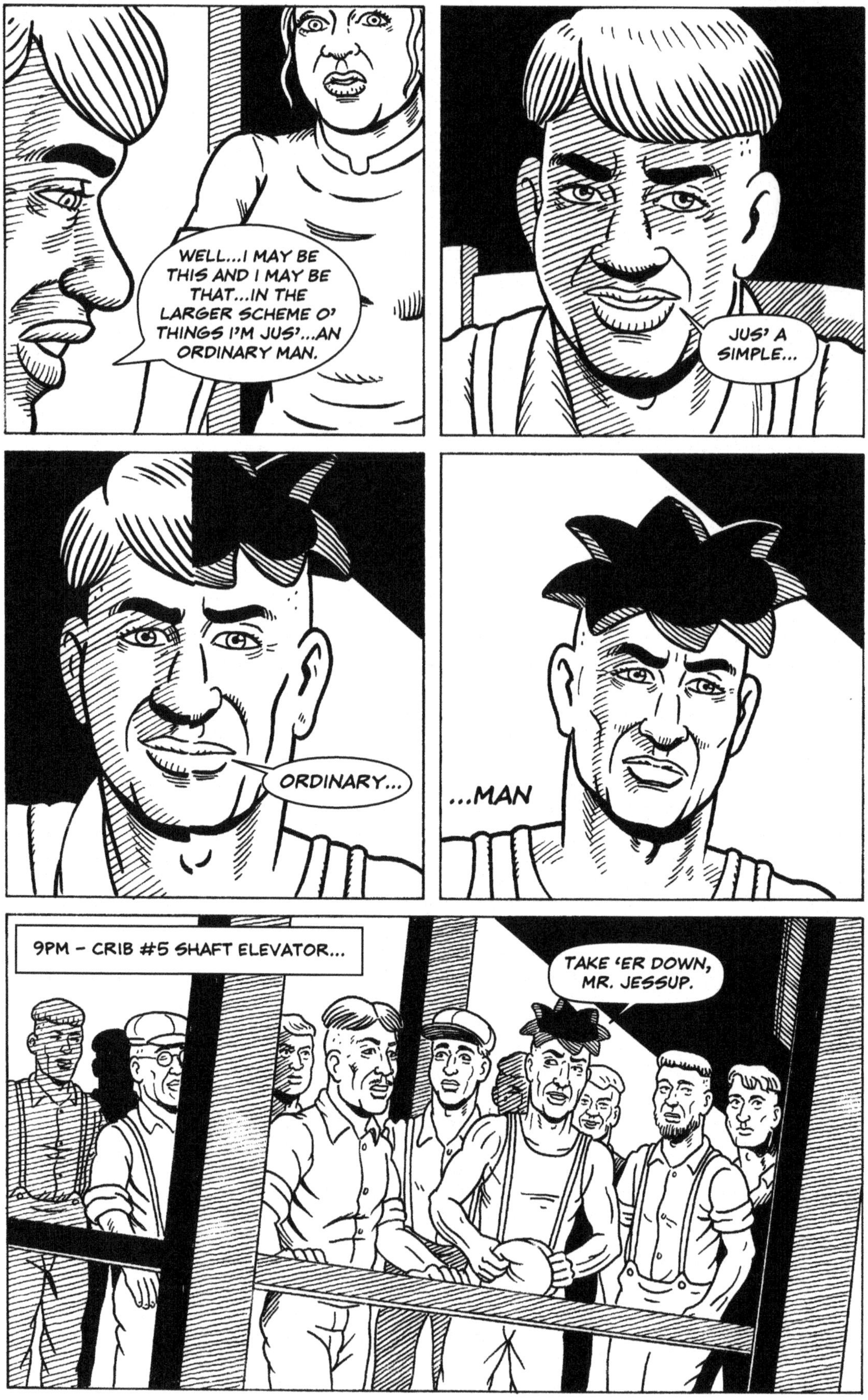
WELL...I MAY BE THIS AND I MAY BE THAT...IN THE LARGER SCHEME O' THINGS I'M JUS'...AN ORDINARY MAN.
JUS' A SIMPLE...
ORDINARY...
...MAN
9PM – CRIB #5 SHAFT ELEVATOR...
TAKE 'ER DOWN, MR. JESSUP.

143

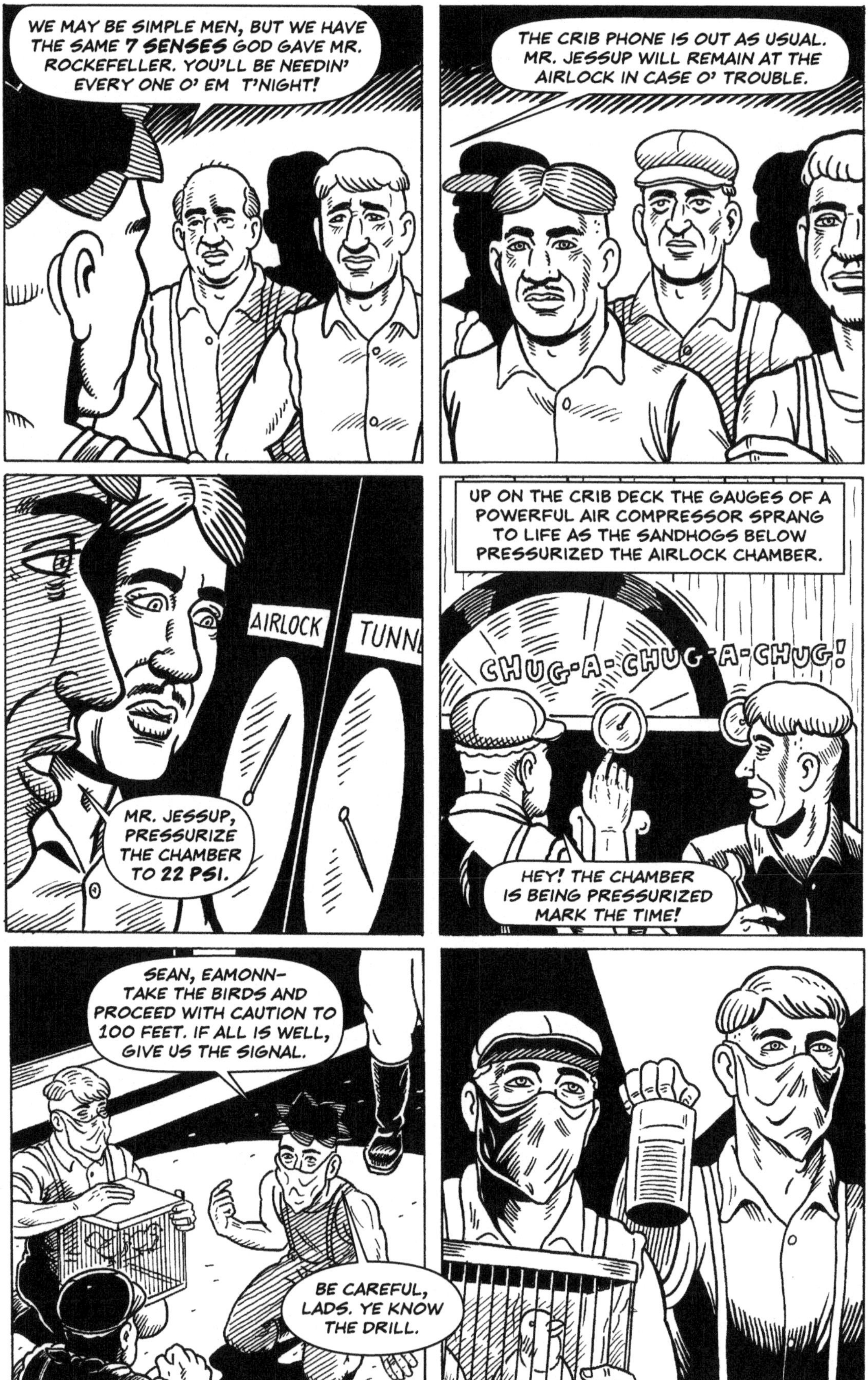
WE MAY BE SIMPLE MEN, BUT WE HAVE THE SAME 7 SENSES GOD GAVE MR. ROCKEFELLER. YOU'LL BE NEEDIN' EVERY ONE O' EM T'NIGHT!
THE CRIB PHONE IS OUT AS USUAL. MR. JESSUP WILL REMAIN AT THE AIRLOCK IN CASE O' TROUBLE.
AIRLOCK
TUNN
MR. JESSUP, PRESSURIZE THE CHAMBER TO 22 PSI.
UP ON THE CRIB DECK THE GAUGES OF A POWERFUL AIR COMPRESSOR SPRANG TO LIFE AS THE SANDHOGS BELOW PRESSURIZED THE AIRLOCK CHAMBER.
CHUG-A-CHUG-A-CHUG!
HEY! THE CHAMBER IS BEING PRESSURIZED MARK THE TIME!
SEAN, EAMONN- TAKE THE BIRDS AND PROCEED WITH CAUTION TO 100 FEET. IF ALL IS WELL, GIVE US THE SIGNAL.
BE CAREFUL, LADS. YE KNOW THE DRILL.

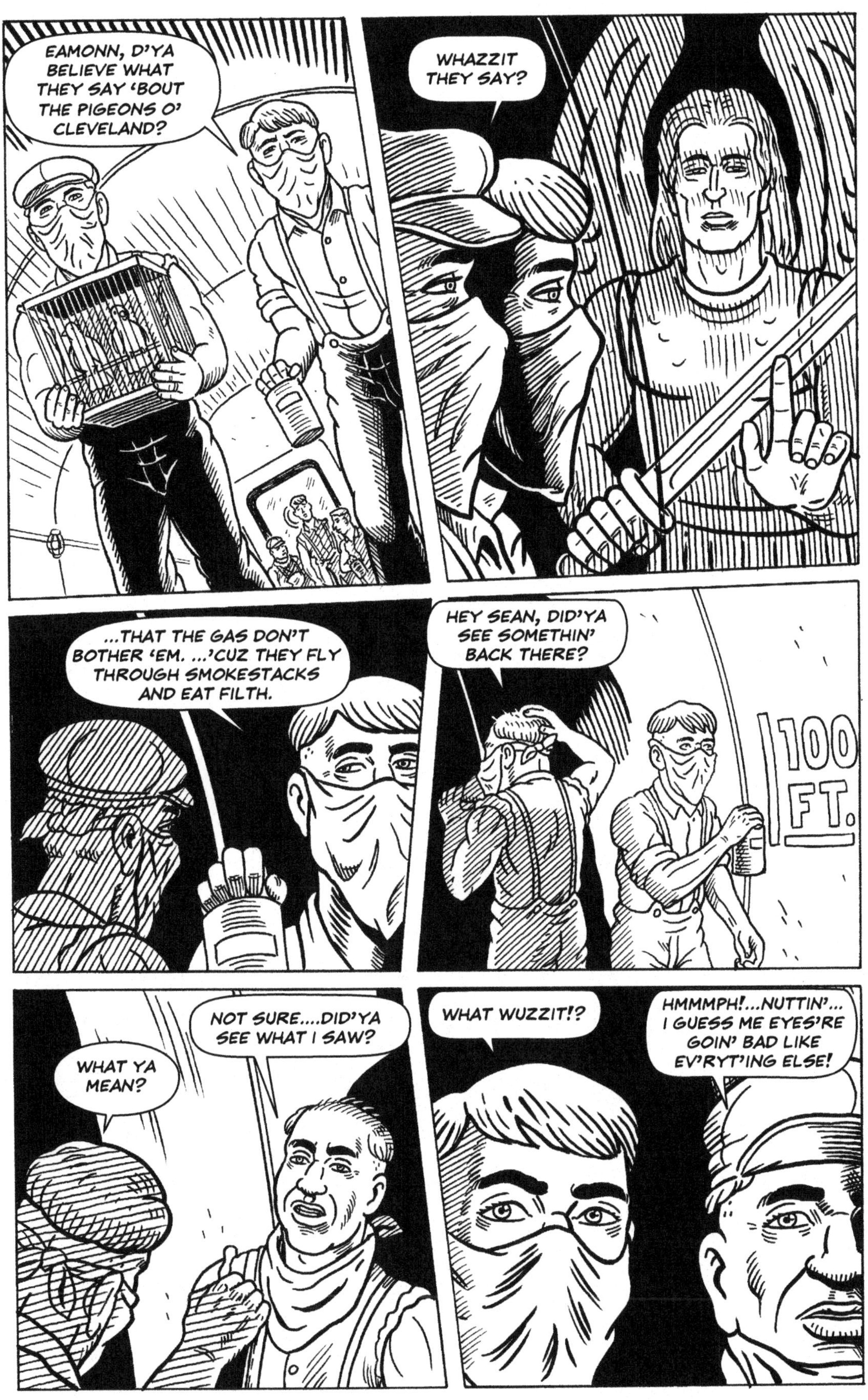
EAMONN, D'YA BELIEVE WHAT THEY SAY 'BOUT THE PIGEONS O' CLEVELAND?
WHAZZIT THEY SAY?
...THAT THE GAS DON'T BOTHER 'EM. ...'CUZ THEY FLY THROUGH SMOKESTACKS AND EAT FILTH.
HEY SEAN, DID'YA SEE SOMETHIN' BACK THERE?
100 FT.
WHAT YA MEAN?
NOT SURE....DID'YA SEE WHAT I SAW?
WHAT WUZZIT!?
HMMMPH!...NUTTIN'... I GUESS ME EYES'RE GOIN' BAD LIKE EV'RYT'ING ELSE!

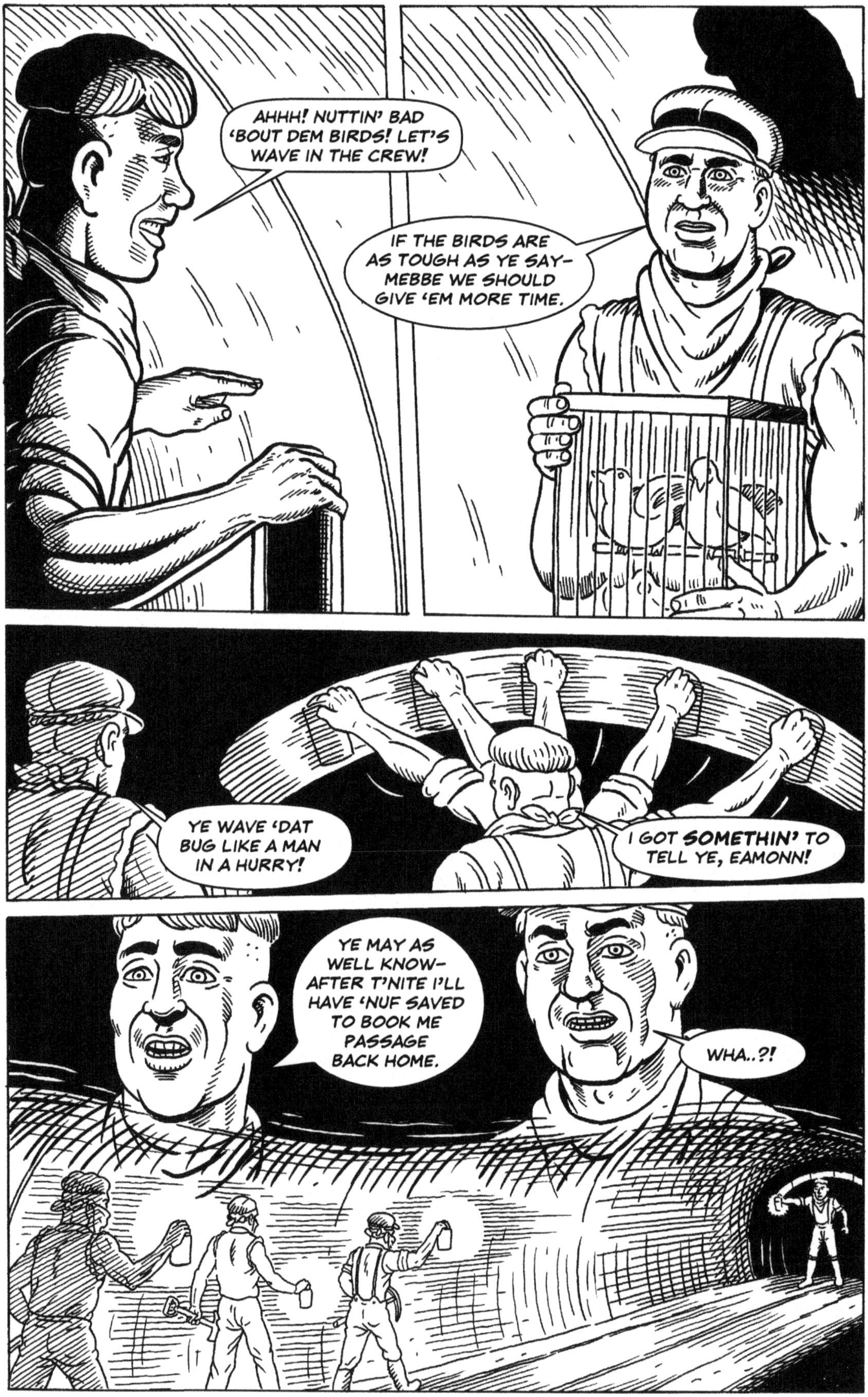
AHHH! NUTTIN' BAD 'BOUT DEM BIRDS! LET'S WAVE IN THE CREW!
IF THE BIRDS ARE AS TOUGH AS YE SAY-MEBBE WE SHOULD GIVE 'EM MORE TIME.
YE WAVE 'DAT BUG LIKE A MAN IN A HURRY!
I GOT SOMETHIN' TO TELL YE, EAMONN!
YE MAY AS WELL KNOW-AFTER T'NITE I'LL HAVE 'NUF SAVED TO BOOK ME PASSAGE BACK HOME.
WHA..?!

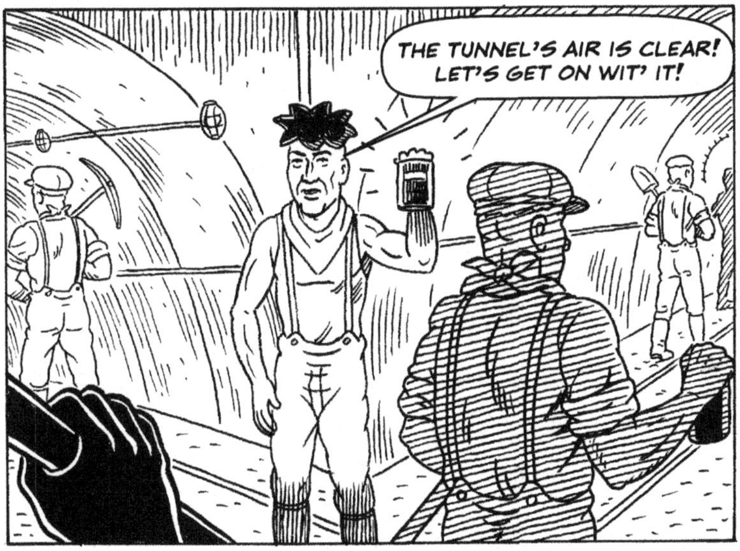
THE TUNNEL'S AIR IS CLEAR! LET'S GET ON WIT' IT!

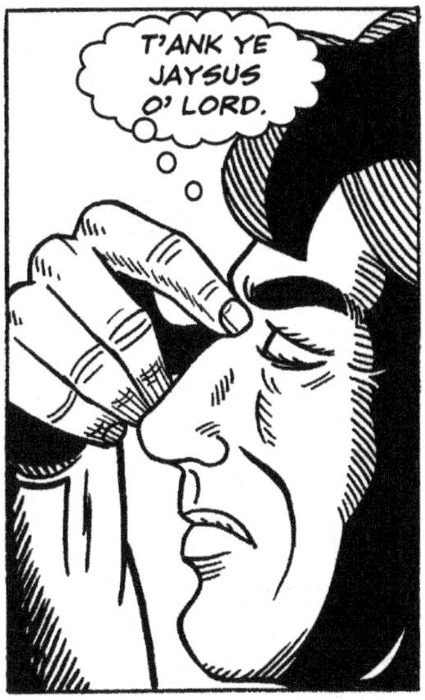
T'ANK YE JAYSUS O' LORD.

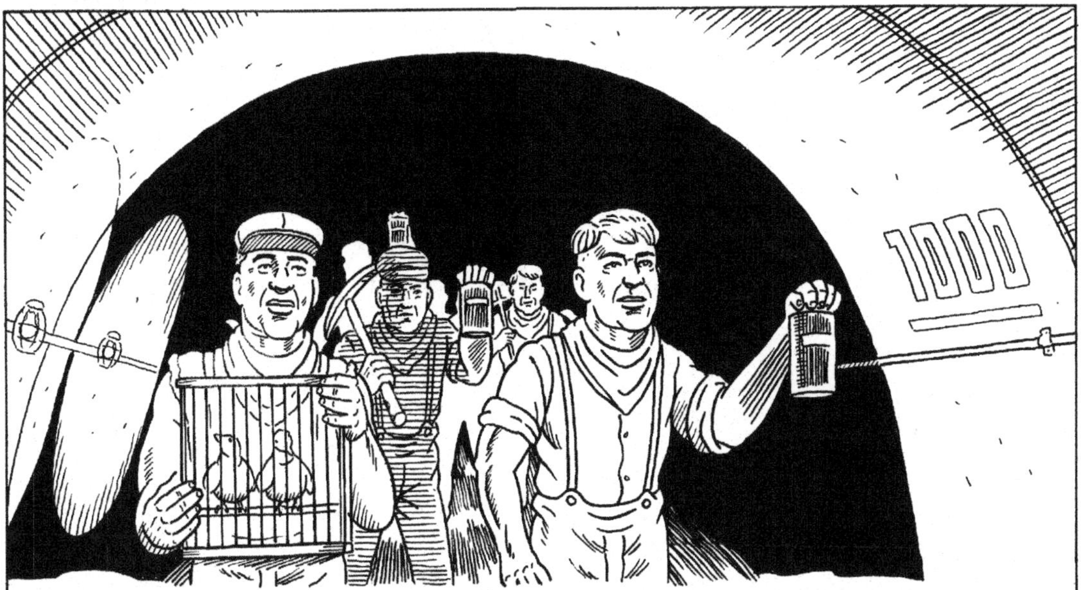
1000

THE SANDHOG'S FATEFUL DESCENT INTO THE BOWELS OF CRIB #5 HAD TAKEN PLACE ON A HOT JULY NIGHT IN 1916 THAT FOLLOWED A DAY WHERE LITTLE HAD GONE RIGHT IN CLEVELAND. THE CITY WAS COPING WITH A KILLER HEAT WAVE AND A LARGE WAREHOUSE FIRE IN BIG ITALY. THE LATTER REQUIRED ALL OF THE FIREFIGHTING AND RESCUE RESOURCES THAT THE CITY COULD MUSTER. IRONICALLY, WHILE PEOPLE SLEPT OUTSIDE OF THEIR STIFLING TENEMENTS AND FIREMEN LABORED IN HELLISH CONDITIONS, THE COOLEST PLACE IN TOWN WAS A TUNNEL 200 FEET BELOW THE SURFACE OF LAKE ERIE.

GAMBLING WITH LIFE IN ORDER TO REMAIN EMPLOYED WAS AN UNSPOKEN JOB REQUIREMENT FOR THE SANDHOGS. THE SIZE OF EACH MAN'S GAMBLE WAS ROUGHLY EQUAL TO HIS OWN PERSONAL LEVEL OF DESPERATION. HAD IT NOT BEEN FOR THE MISADVENTURES OF POVERTY, PERHAPS THESE TUNNEL MEN WOULD HAVE SWEATED OUT THE SUMMER HEAT ONSHORE WITH COLD GLASSES OF BEER IN THE DIVE BARS OF WHISKEY ISLAND AND IRISHTOWN BEND. SADLY, THE MERE PROMISE OF A FEW EXTRA DOLLARS WAS ENOUGH INCENTIVE TO TEMPT RATIONAL MEN DOWN A SHAFT AND INTO A TUNNEL WHERE THE SPECTRES OF CATASTROPHE AND DEATH, AIDED AND ABETTED BY CITY LEADERS' DEPRAVED INDIFFERENCE TOWARD WORKER SAFETY, WERE WAITING FOR THEM TO ARRIVE.

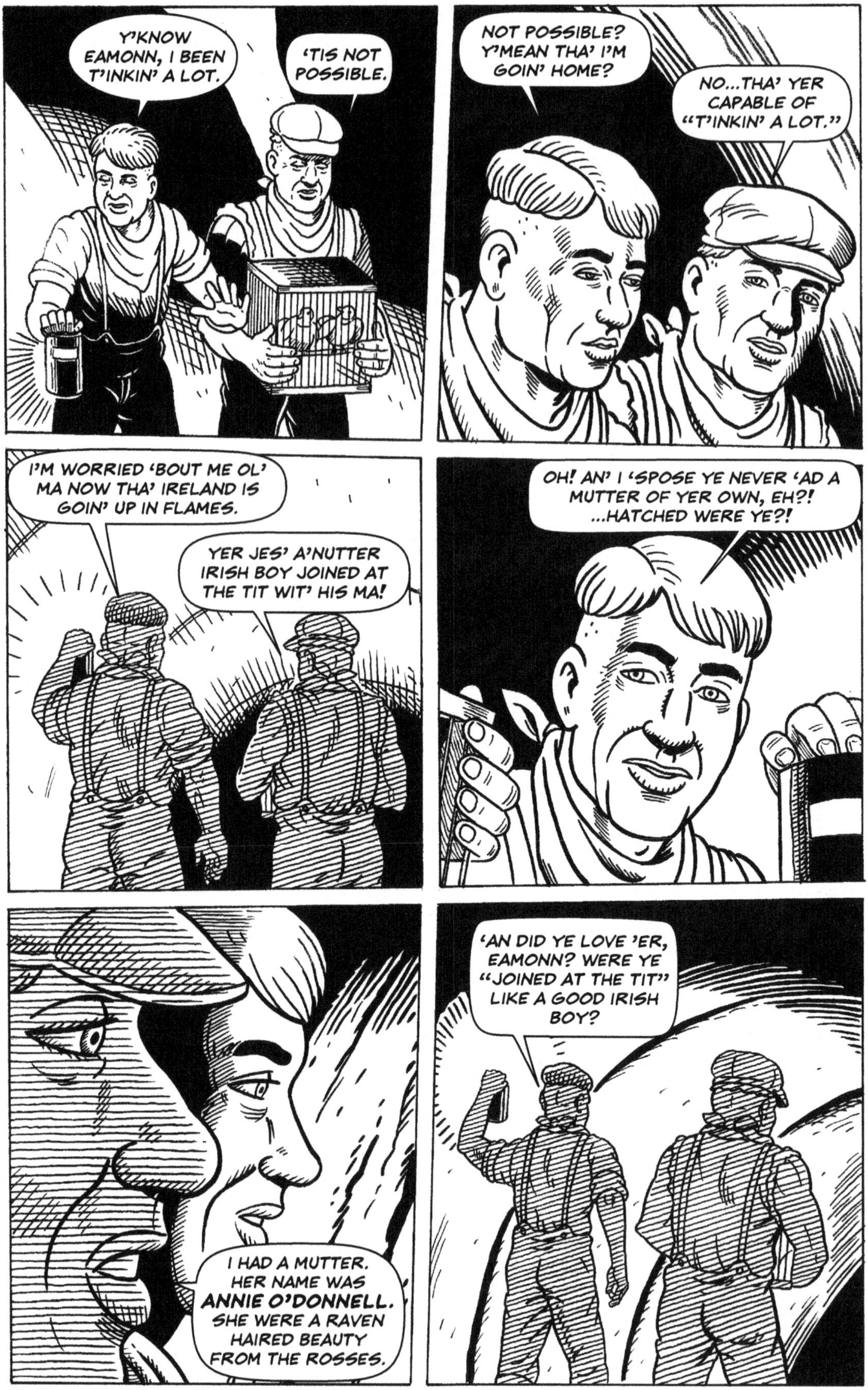
Y'KNOW EAMONN, I BEEN T'INKIN' A LOT.
'TIS NOT POSSIBLE.
NOT POSSIBLE? Y'MEAN THA' I'M GOIN' HOME?
NO...THA' YER CAPABLE OF "T'INKIN' A LOT."
I'M WORRIED 'BOUT ME OL' MA NOW THA' IRELAND IS GOIN' UP IN FLAMES.
YER JES' A'NUTTER IRISH BOY JOINED AT THE TIT WIT' HIS MA!
OH! AN' I 'SPOSE YE NEVER 'AD A MUTTER OF YER OWN, EH?! ...HATCHED WERE YE?!
I HAD A MUTTER. HER NAME WAS ANNIE O'DONNELL. SHE WERE A RAVEN HAIRED BEAUTY FROM THE ROSSES.
'AN DID YE LOVE 'ER, EAMONN? WERE YE "JOINED AT THE TIT" LIKE A GOOD IRISH BOY?

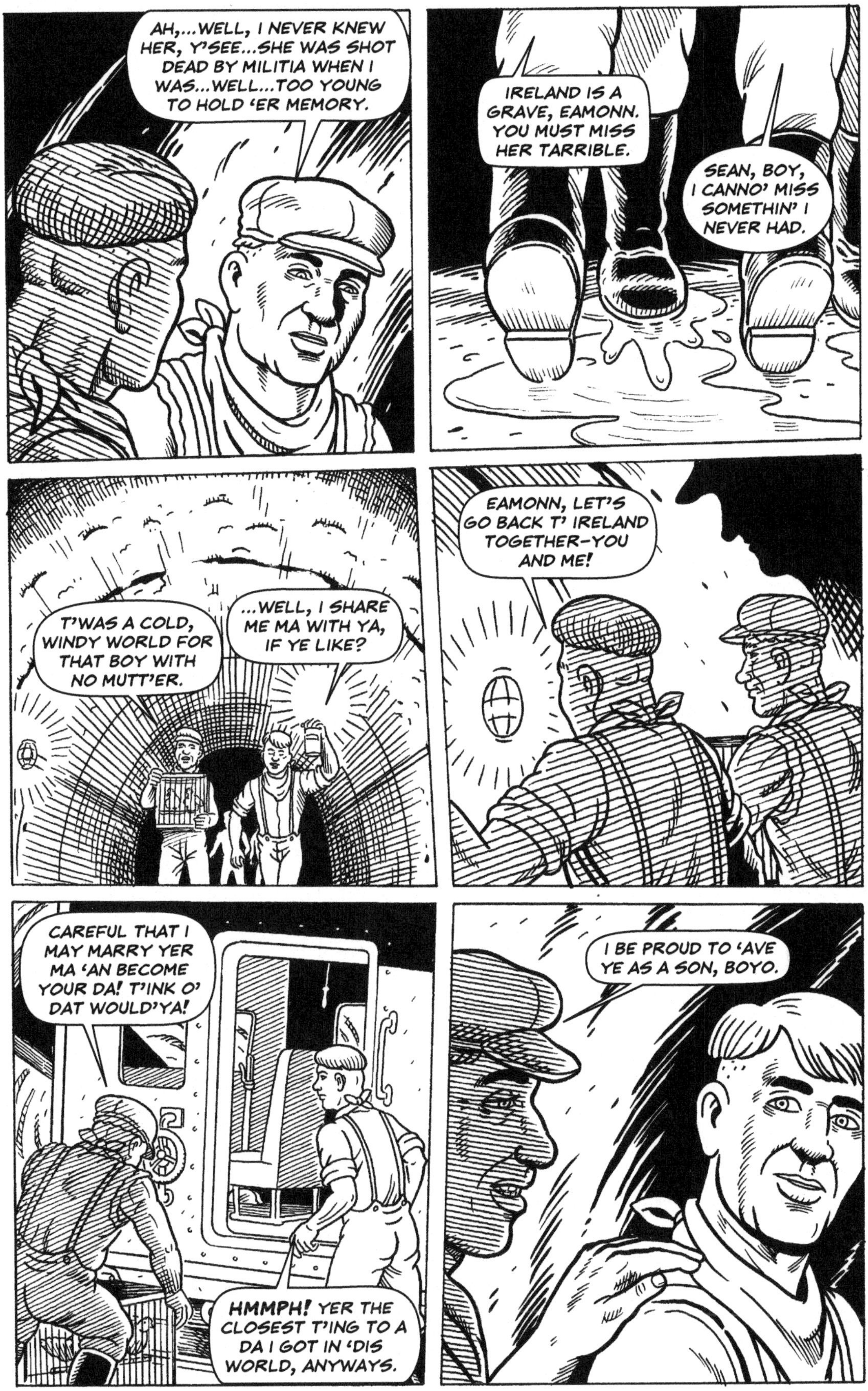
AH,...WELL, I NEVER KNEW HER, Y'SEE...SHE WAS SHOT DEAD BY MILITIA WHEN I WAS...WELL...TOO YOUNG TO HOLD 'ER MEMORY.
IRELAND IS A GRAVE, EAMONN. YOU MUST MISS HER TARRIBLE.
SEAN, BOY, I CANNO' MISS SOMETHIN' I NEVER HAD.
T'WAS A COLD, WINDY WORLD FOR THAT BOY WITH NO MUTT'ER.
...WELL, I SHARE ME MA WITH YA, IF YE LIKE?
EAMONN, LET'S GO BACK T' IRELAND TOGETHER-YOU AND ME!
CAREFUL THAT I MAY MARRY YER MA 'AN BECOME YOUR DA! T'INK O' DAT WOULD'YA!
HMMPH! YER THE CLOSEST T'ING TO A DA I GOT IN 'DIS WORLD, ANYWAYS.
I BE PROUD TO 'AVE YE AS A SON, BOYO.

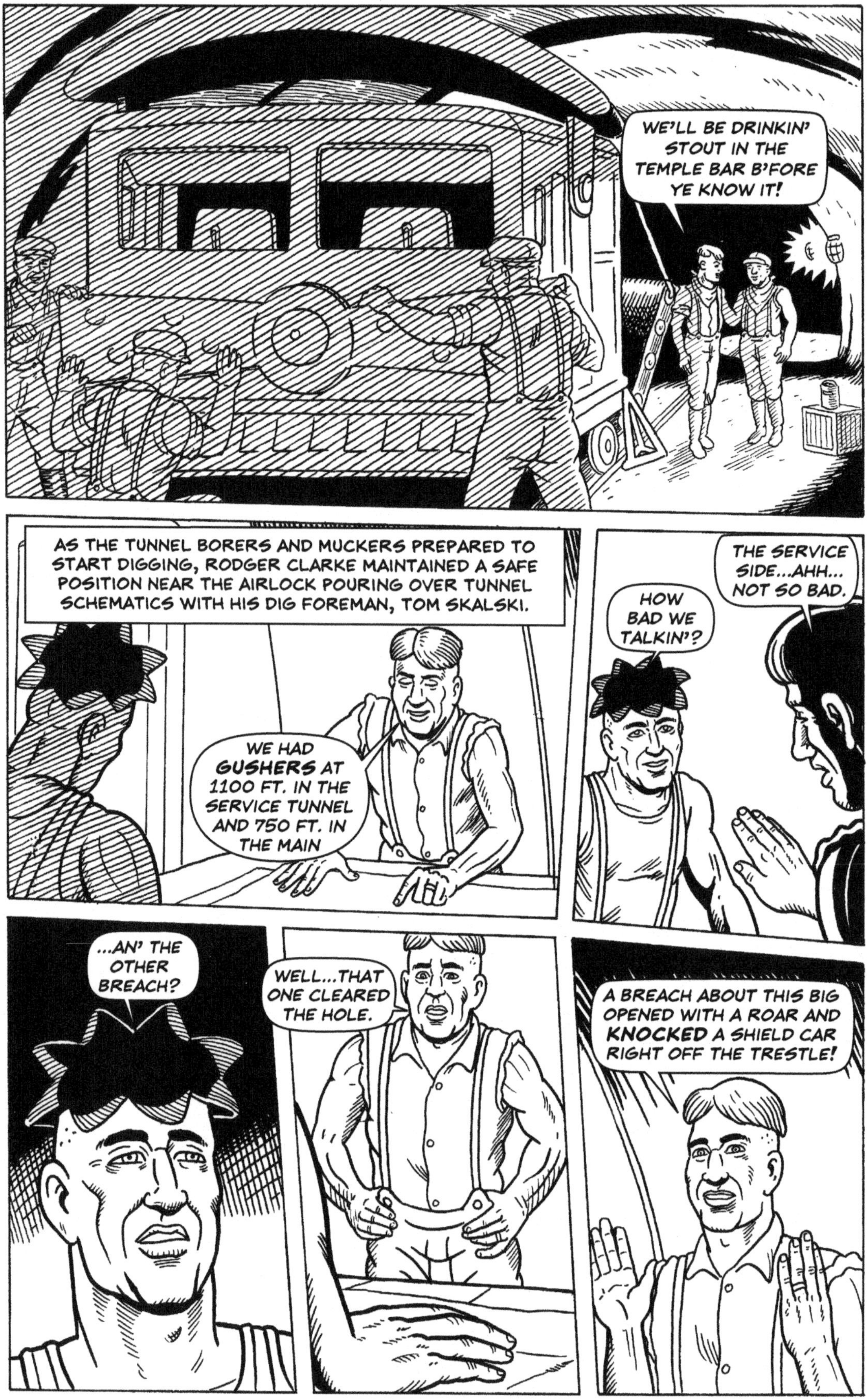
WE'LL BE DRINKIN' STOUT IN THE TEMPLE BAR B'FORE YE KNOW IT!
AS THE TUNNEL BORERS AND MUCKERS PREPARED TO START DIGGING, RODGER CLARKE MAINTAINED A SAFE POSITION NEAR THE AIRLOCK POURING OVER TUNNEL SCHEMATICS WITH HIS DIG FOREMAN, TOM SKALSKI.
WE HAD GUSHERS AT 1100 FT. IN THE SERVICE TUNNEL AND 750 FT. IN THE MAIN
HOW BAD WE TALKIN'?
THE SERVICE SIDE...AHH... NOT SO BAD.
...AN' THE OTHER BREACH?
WELL...THAT ONE CLEARED THE HOLE.
A BREACH ABOUT THIS BIG OPENED WITH A ROAR AND KNOCKED A SHIELD CAR RIGHT OFF THE TRESTLE!

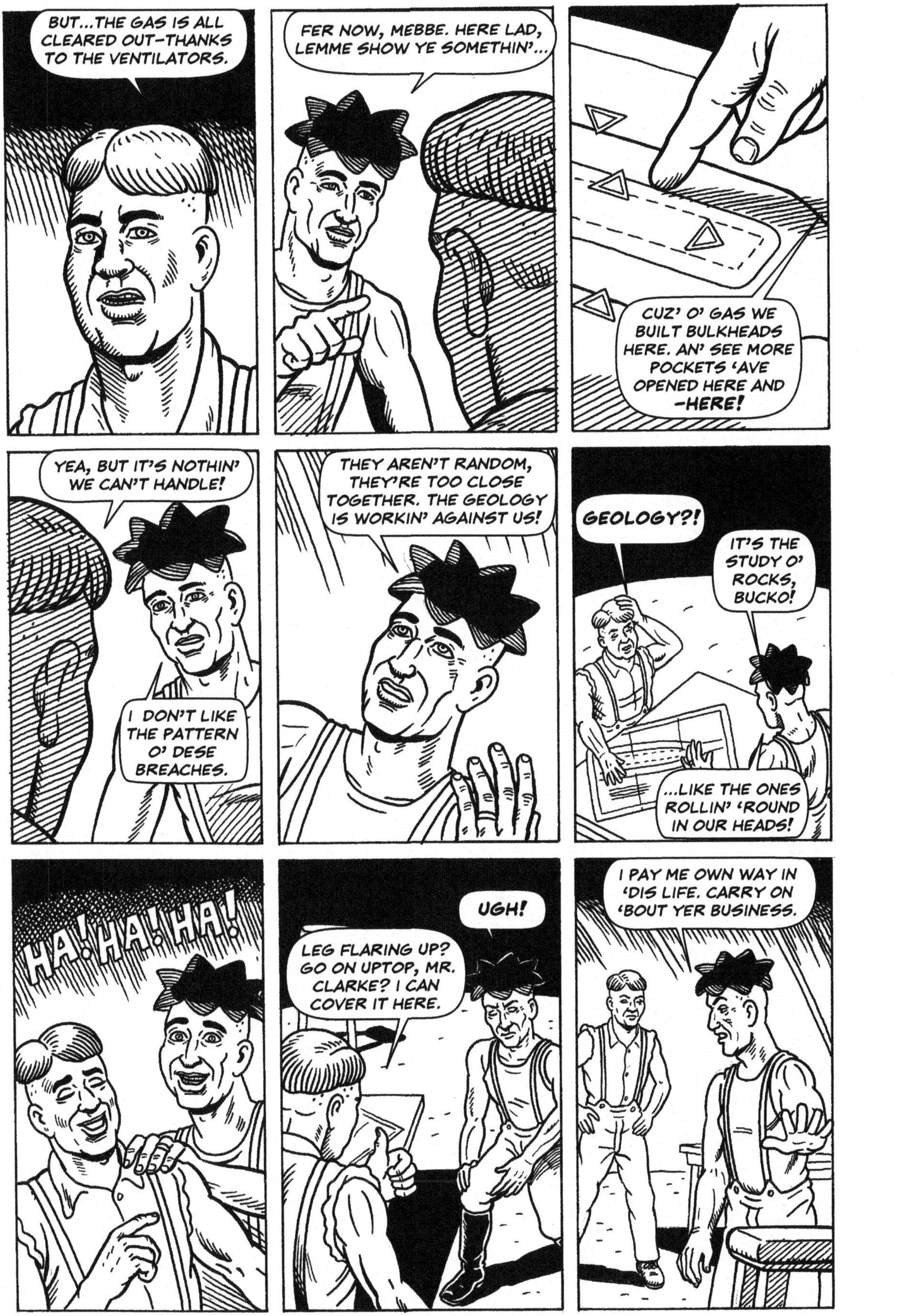
BUT...THE GAS IS ALL CLEARED OUT–THANKS TO THE VENTILATORS.
FER NOW, MEBBE. HERE LAD, LEMME SHOW YE SOMETHIN'...
CUZ' O' GAS WE BUILT BULKHEADS HERE. AN' SEE MORE POCKETS 'AVE OPENED HERE AND –HERE!
YEA, BUT IT'S NOTHIN' WE CAN'T HANDLE!
I DON'T LIKE THE PATTERN O' DESE BREACHES.
THEY AREN'T RANDOM, THEY'RE TOO CLOSE TOGETHER. THE GEOLOGY IS WORKIN' AGAINST US!
GEOLOGY?!
IT'S THE STUDY O' ROCKS, BUCKO!
...LIKE THE ONES ROLLIN' 'ROUND IN OUR HEADS!
HA! HA! HA!
UGH!
LEG FLARING UP? GO ON UPTOP, MR. CLARKE? I CAN COVER IT HERE.
I PAY ME OWN WAY IN 'DIS LIFE. CARRY ON 'BOUT YER BUSINESS.

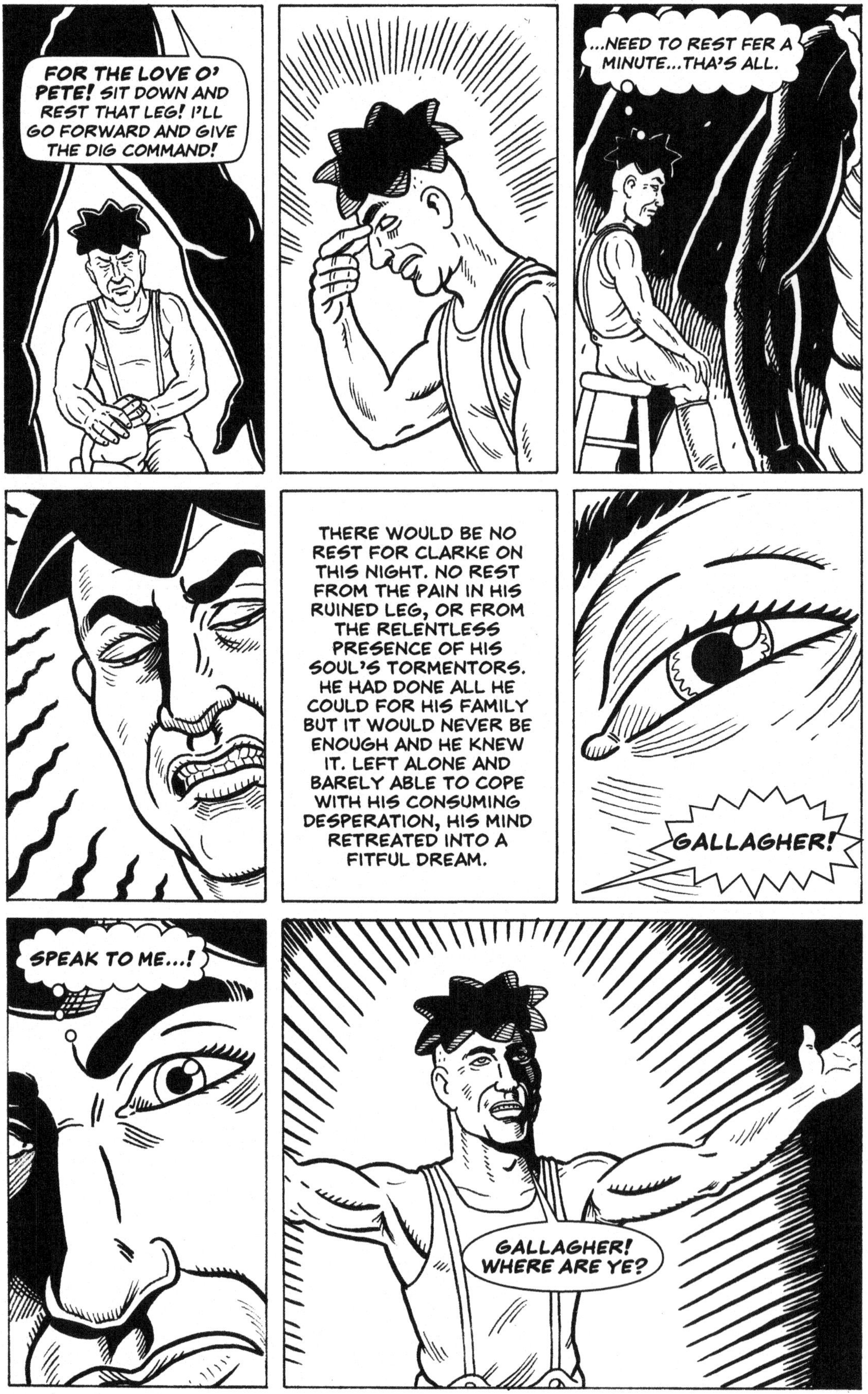
FOR THE LOVE O' PETE! SIT DOWN AND REST THAT LEG! I'LL GO FORWARD AND GIVE THE DIG COMMAND!
...NEED TO REST FER A MINUTE...THA'S ALL.
THERE WOULD BE NO REST FOR CLARKE ON THIS NIGHT. NO REST FROM THE PAIN IN HIS RUINED LEG, OR FROM THE RELENTLESS PRESENCE OF HIS SOUL'S TORMENTORS. HE HAD DONE ALL HE COULD FOR HIS FAMILY BUT IT WOULD NEVER BE ENOUGH AND HE KNEW IT. LEFT ALONE AND BARELY ABLE TO COPE WITH HIS CONSUMING DESPERATION, HIS MIND RETREATED INTO A FITFUL DREAM.
GALLAGHER!
SPEAK TO ME...!
GALLAGHER! WHERE ARE YE?

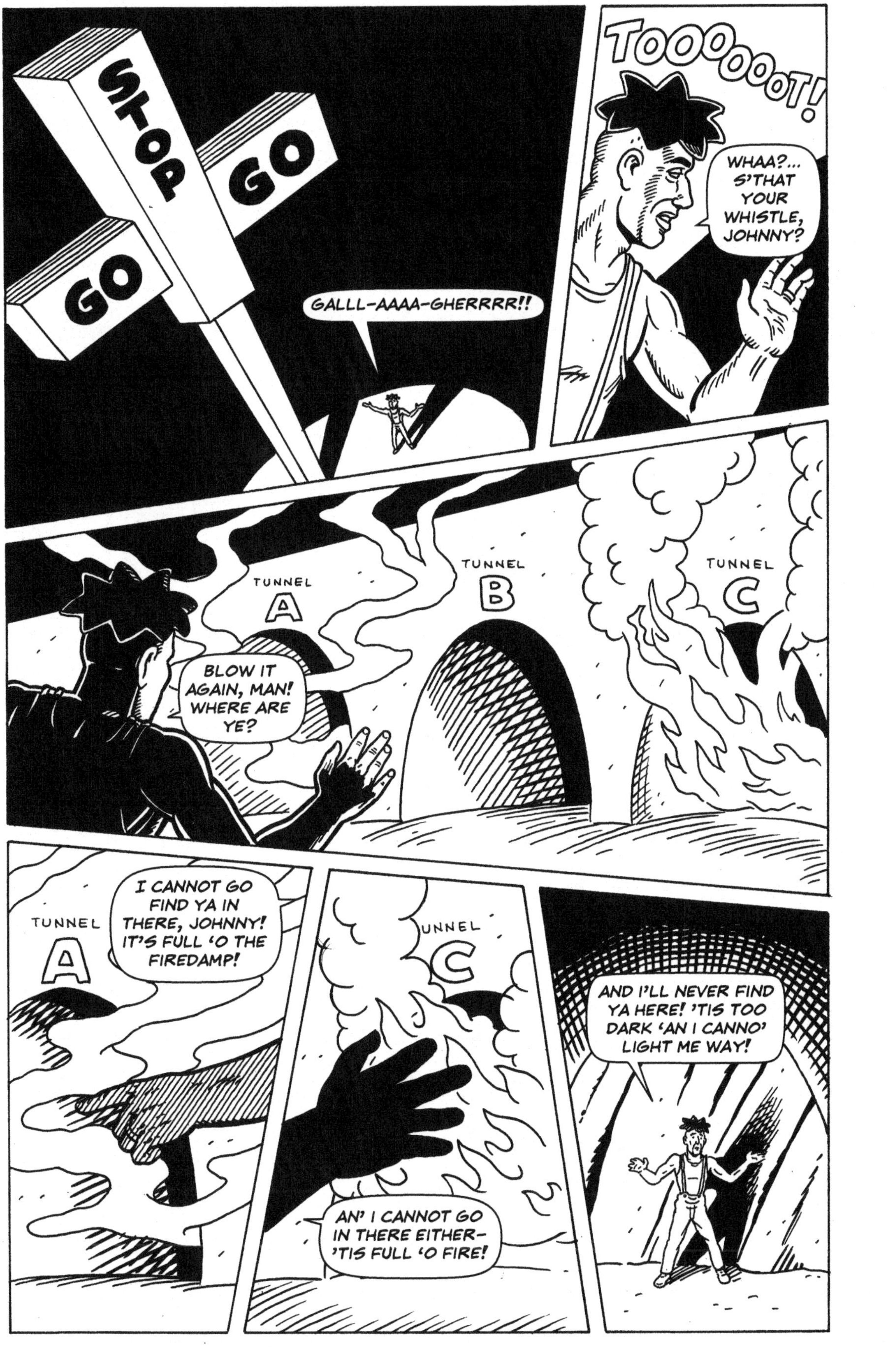
STOP
GO
GO
GALLL-AAAA-GHERRRR!!
TOOOOOOOT!
WHAA?... S'THAT YOUR WHISTLE, JOHNNY?
TUNNEL A
TUNNEL B
TUNNEL C
BLOW IT AGAIN, MAN! WHERE ARE YE?
TUNNEL A
I CANNOT GO FIND YA IN THERE, JOHNNY! IT'S FULL 'O THE FIREDAMP!
UNNEL C
AN' I CANNOT GO IN THERE EITHER- 'TIS FULL 'O FIRE!
AND I'LL NEVER FIND YA HERE! 'TIS TOO DARK 'AN I CANNO' LIGHT ME WAY!

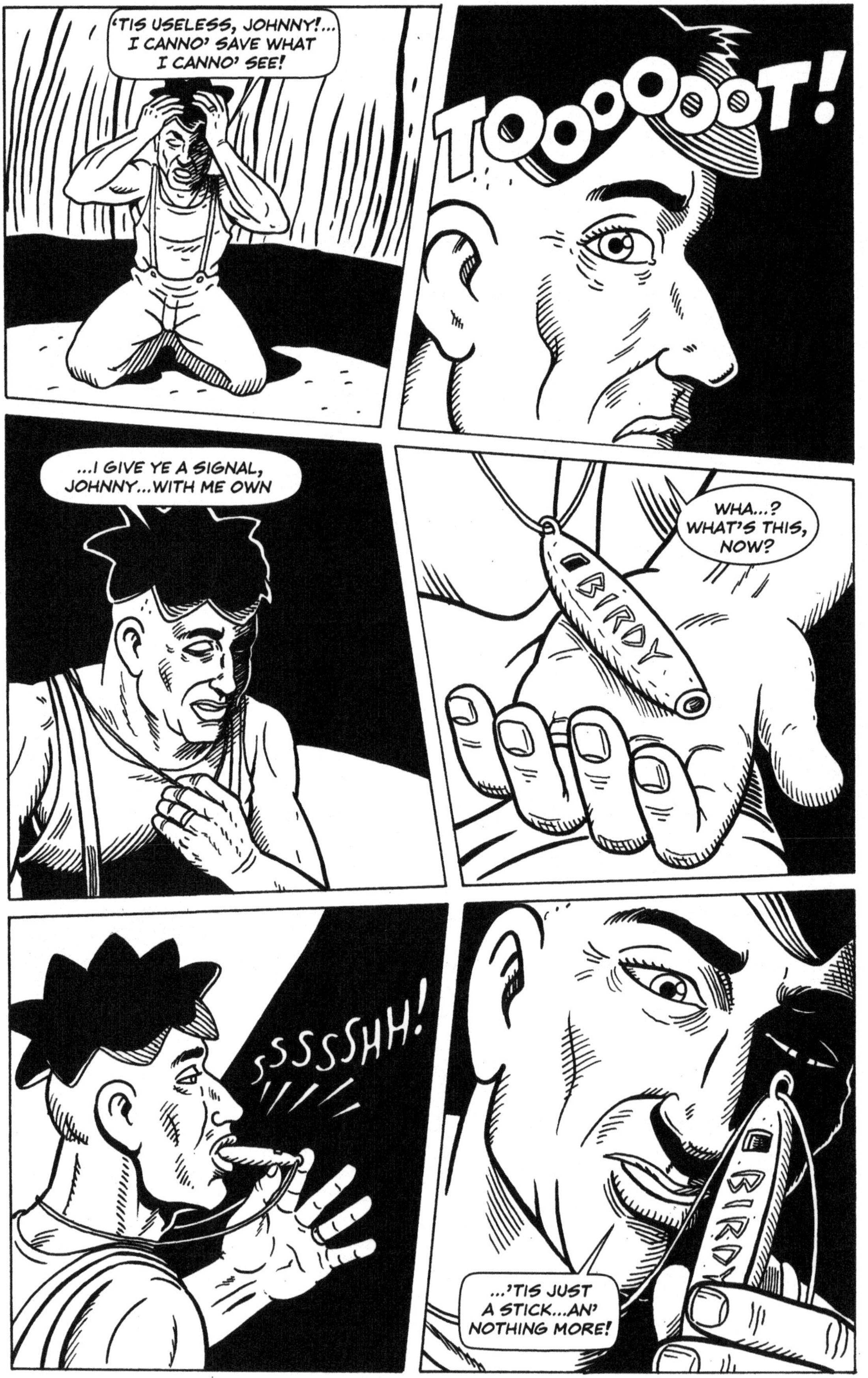

'TIS USELESS, JOHNNY!... I CANNO' SAVE WHAT I CANNO' SEE!
TOOOOOOT!
...I GIVE YE A SIGNAL, JOHNNY...WITH ME OWN
WHA...? WHAT'S THIS, NOW?
BIRDY
SSSSSHH!
BIRDY
...'TIS JUST A STICK...AN' NOTHING MORE!

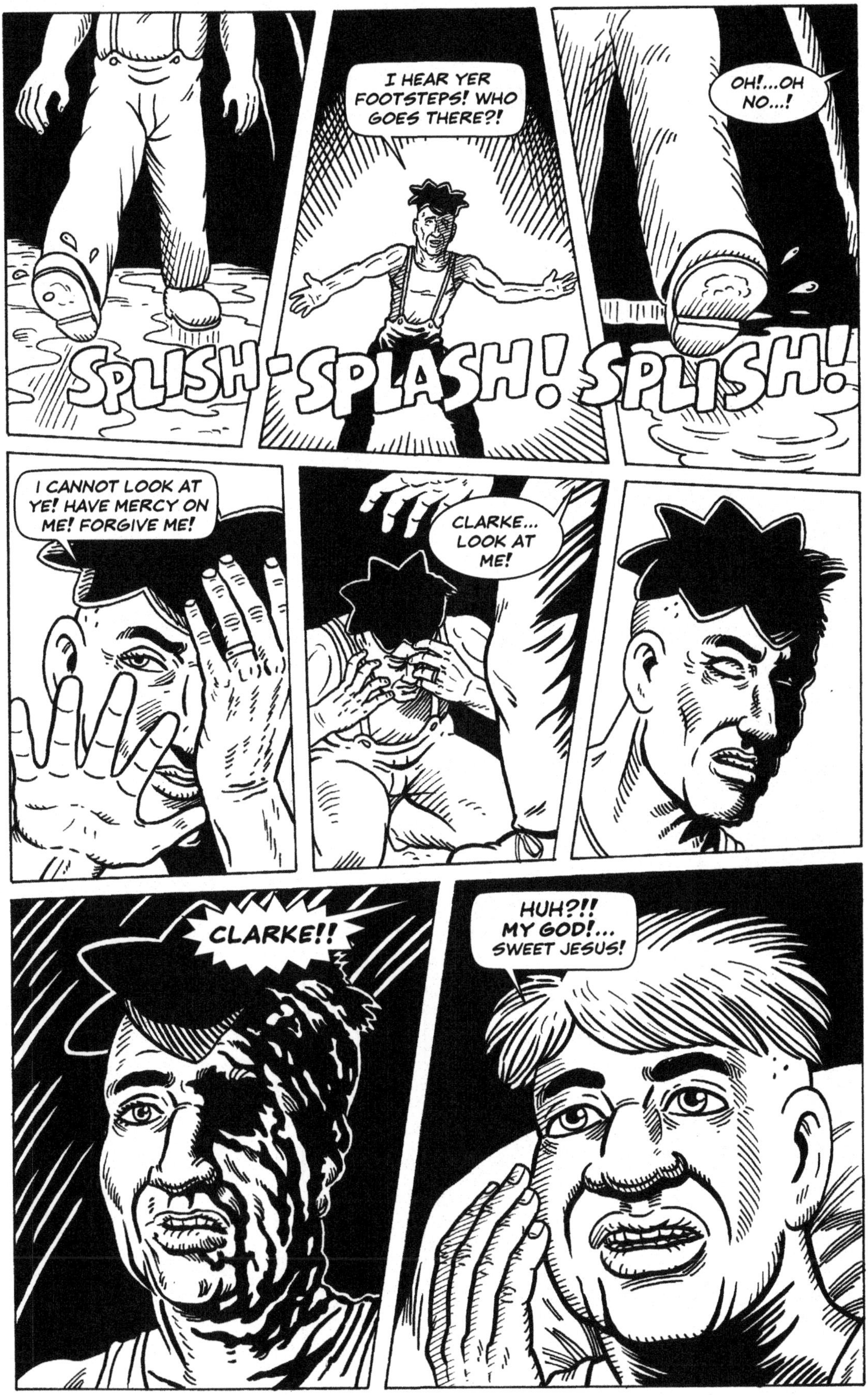
I HEAR YER FOOTSTEPS! WHO GOES THERE?!
OH!...OH NO...!
SPLISH-SPLASH! SPLISH!
I CANNOT LOOK AT YE! HAVE MERCY ON ME! FORGIVE ME!
CLARKE... LOOK AT ME!
CLARKE!!
HUH?!! MY GOD!... SWEET JESUS!

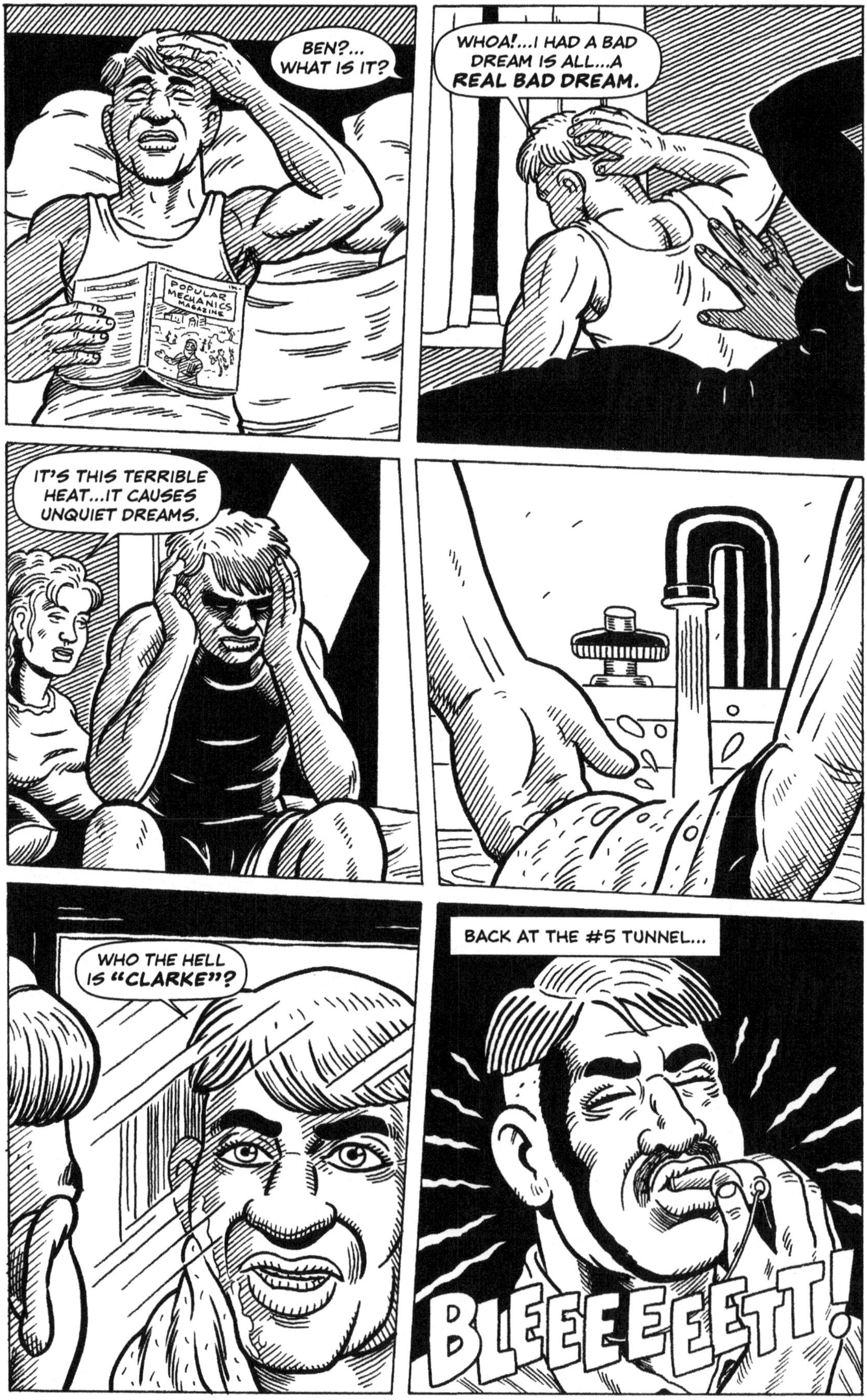
BEN?... WHAT IS IT?
POPULAR MECHANICS MAGAZINE
WHOA!...I HAD A BAD DREAM IS ALL...A **REAL BAD DREAM.**
IT'S THIS TERRIBLE HEAT...IT CAUSES UNQUIET DREAMS.
WHO THE HELL IS **"CLARKE"?**
BACK AT THE #5 TUNNEL...
BLEEEEEETT!

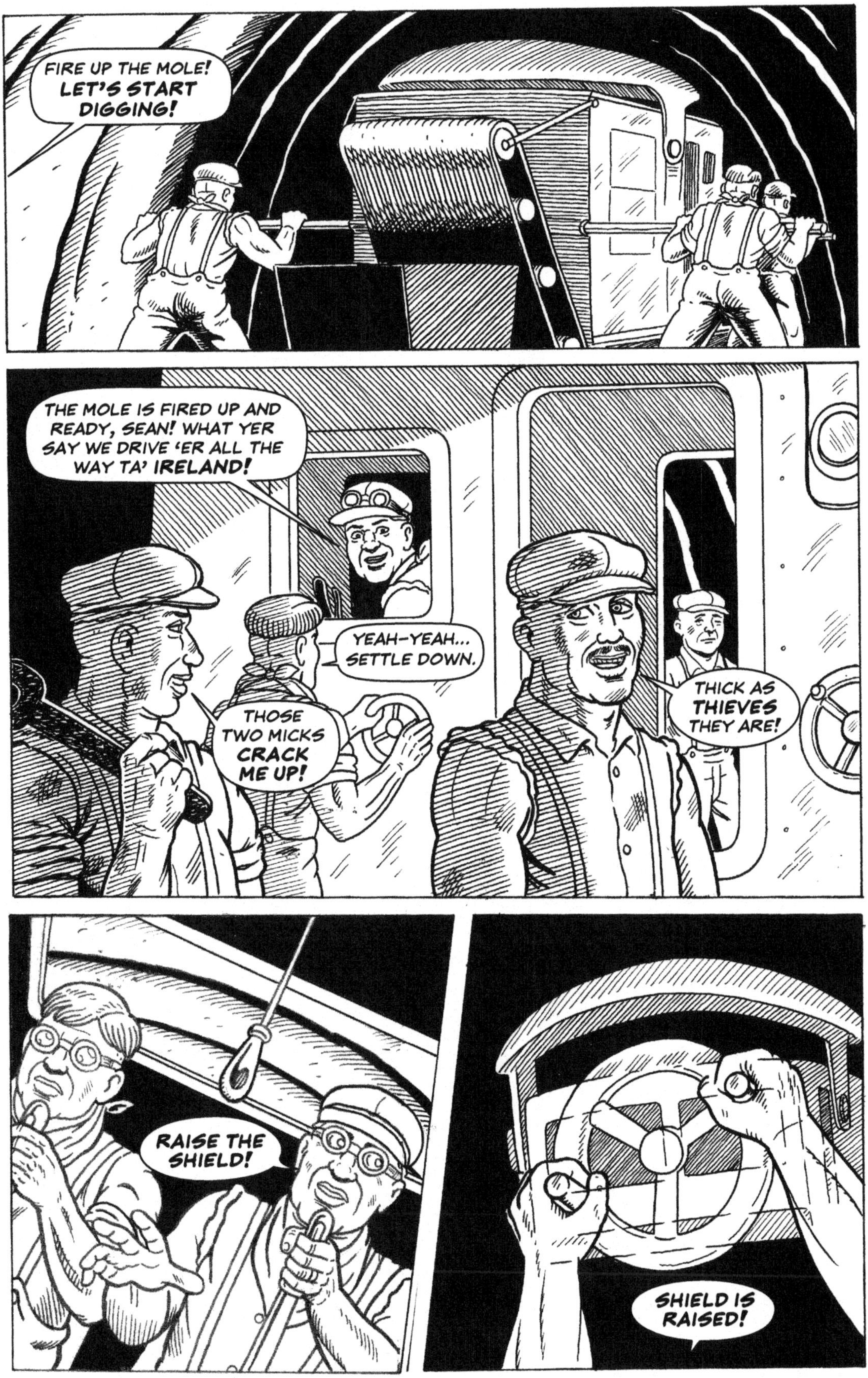
FIRE UP THE MOLE! LET'S START DIGGING!
THE MOLE IS FIRED UP AND READY, SEAN! WHAT YER SAY WE DRIVE 'ER ALL THE WAY TA' IRELAND!
YEAH-YEAH... SETTLE DOWN.
THOSE TWO MICKS CRACK ME UP!
THICK AS THIEVES THEY ARE!
RAISE THE SHIELD!
SHIELD IS RAISED!

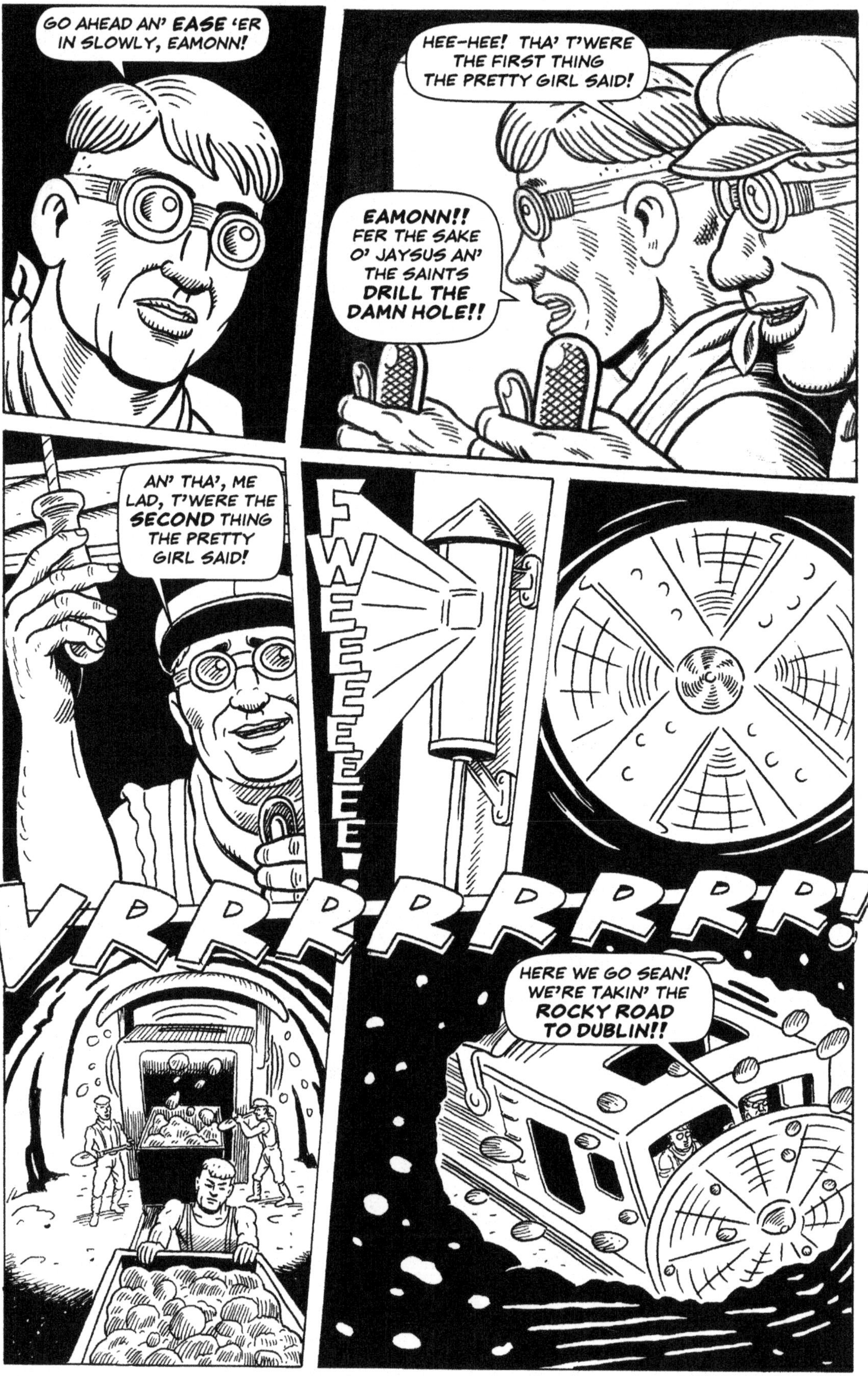
GO AHEAD AN' EASE 'ER IN SLOWLY, EAMONN!
HEE-HEE! THA' T'WERE THE FIRST THING THE PRETTY GIRL SAID!
EAMONN!! FER THE SAKE O' JAYSUS AN' THE SAINTS DRILL THE DAMN HOLE!!
AN' THA', ME LAD, T'WERE THE SECOND THING THE PRETTY GIRL SAID!
FWEEEEEEEE!
VRRRRRRRR!
HERE WE GO SEAN! WE'RE TAKIN' THE ROCKY ROAD TO DUBLIN!!

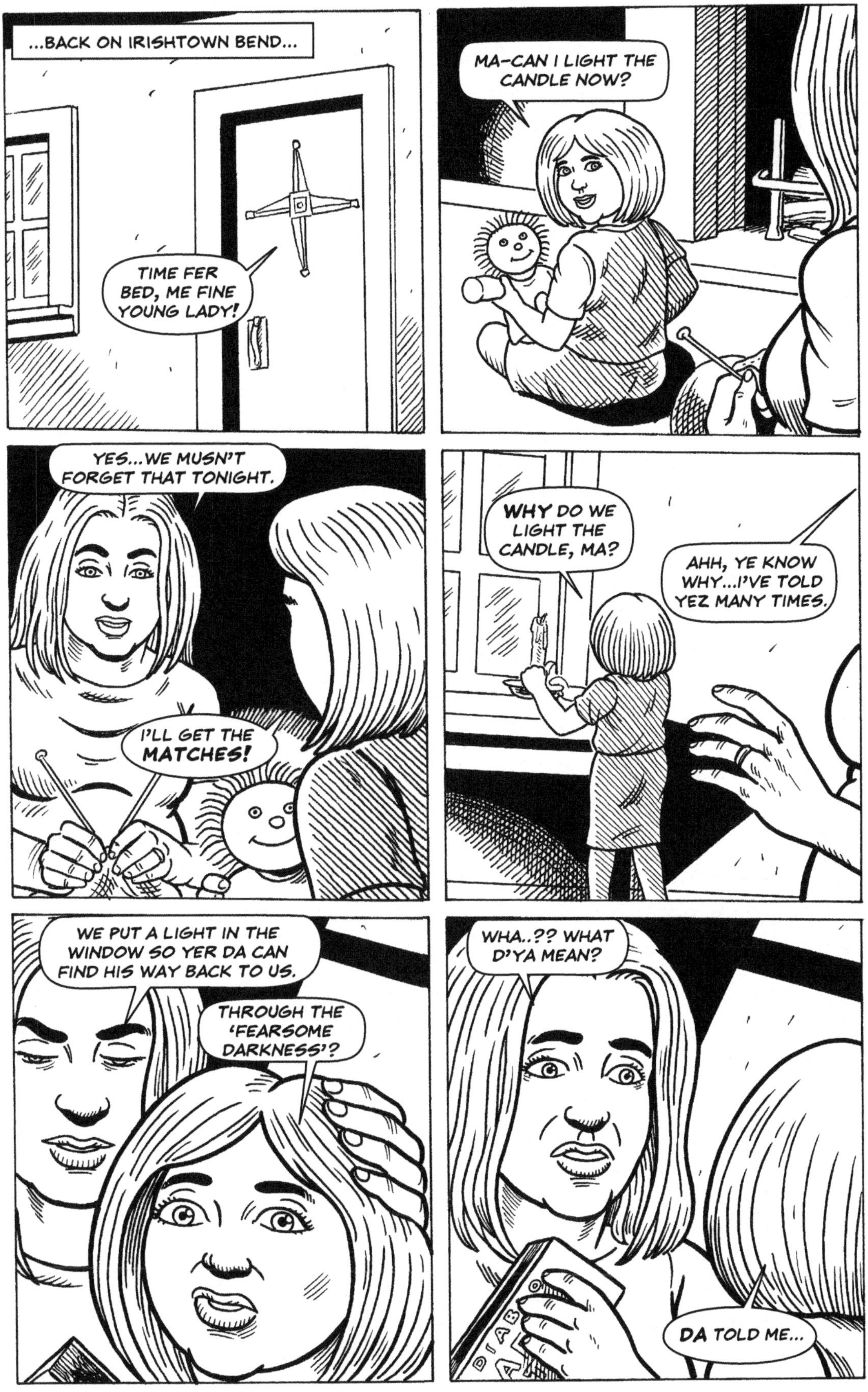
...BACK ON IRISHTOWN BEND...
TIME FER BED, ME FINE YOUNG LADY!
MA–CAN I LIGHT THE CANDLE NOW?
YES...WE MUSN'T FORGET THAT TONIGHT.
I'LL GET THE MATCHES!
WHY DO WE LIGHT THE CANDLE, MA?
AHH, YE KNOW WHY...I'VE TOLD YEZ MANY TIMES.
WE PUT A LIGHT IN THE WINDOW SO YER DA CAN FIND HIS WAY BACK TO US.
THROUGH THE 'FEARSOME DARKNESS'?
WHA..?? WHAT D'YA MEAN?
DA TOLD ME...

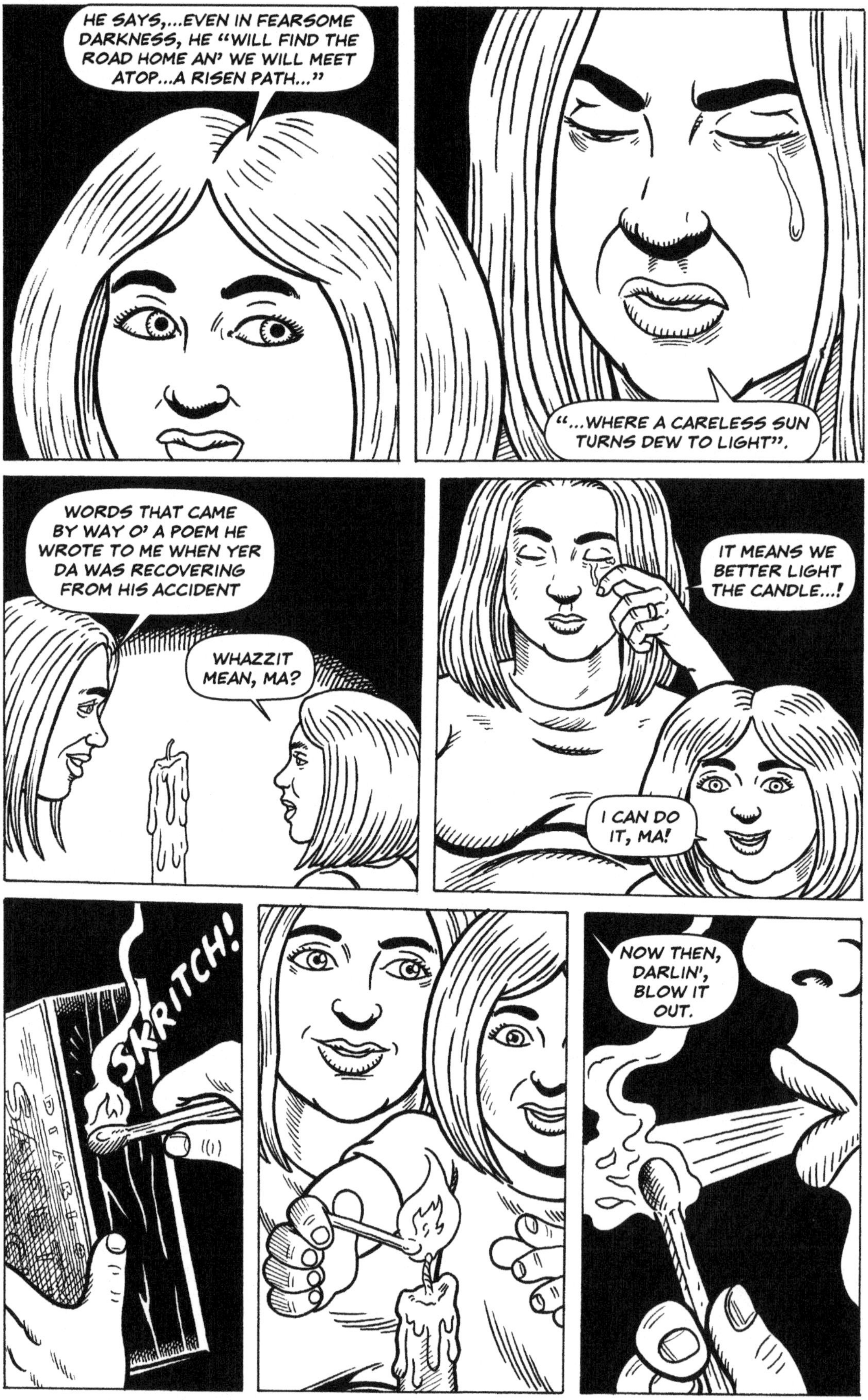
HE SAYS,...EVEN IN FEARSOME DARKNESS, HE "WILL FIND THE ROAD HOME AN' WE WILL MEET ATOP...A RISEN PATH..."
"...WHERE A CARELESS SUN TURNS DEW TO LIGHT".
WORDS THAT CAME BY WAY O' A POEM HE WROTE TO ME WHEN YER DA WAS RECOVERING FROM HIS ACCIDENT
WHAZZIT MEAN, MA?
IT MEANS WE BETTER LIGHT THE CANDLE...!
I CAN DO IT, MA!
SKRITCH!
NOW THEN, DARLIN', BLOW IT OUT.

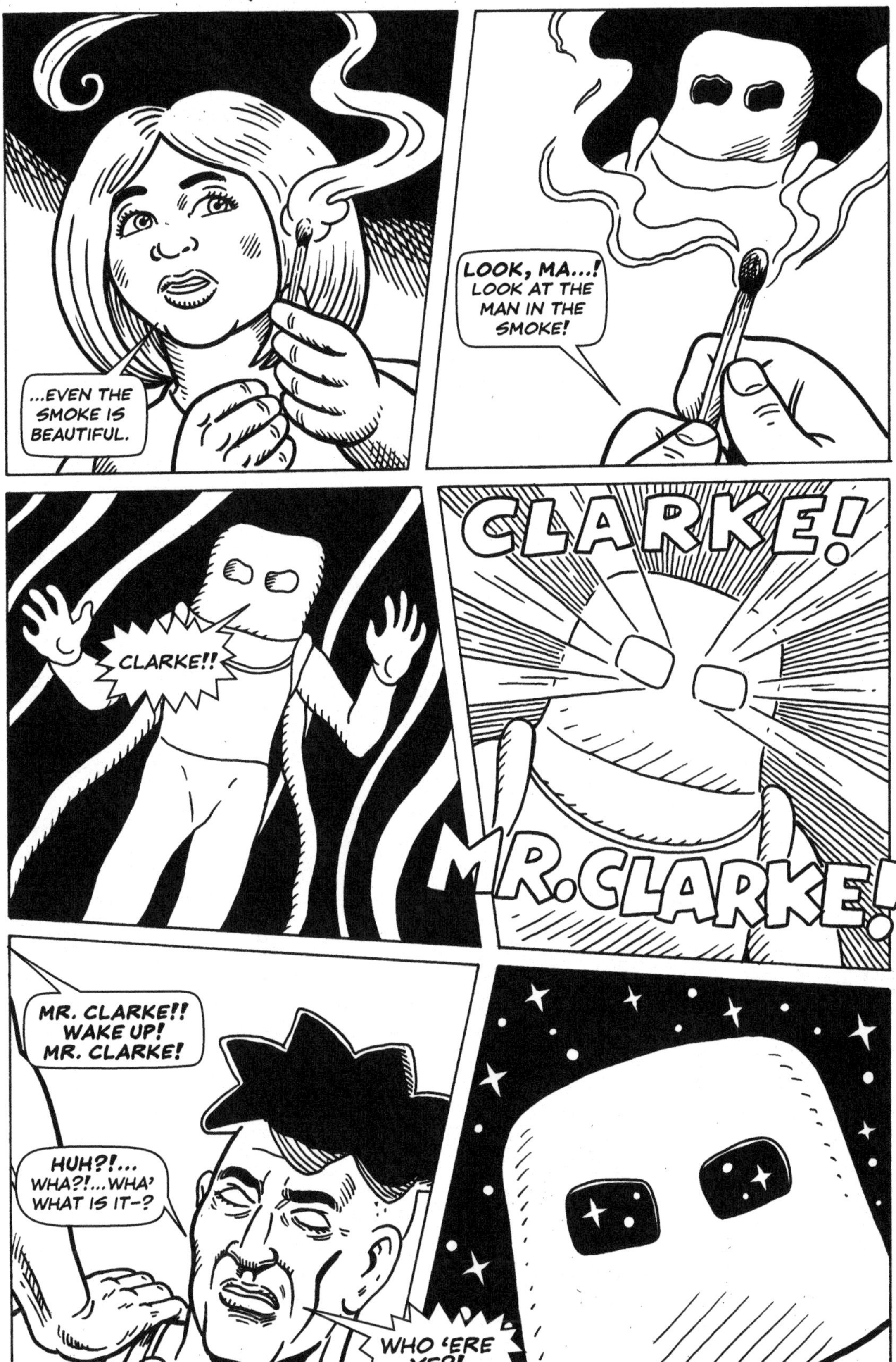
...EVEN THE SMOKE IS BEAUTIFUL.
LOOK, MA...! LOOK AT THE MAN IN THE SMOKE!
CLARKE!!
CLARKE!
MR. CLARKE!
MR. CLARKE!! WAKE UP! MR. CLARKE!
HUH?!... WHA?!...WHA' WHAT IS IT-?
WHO 'ERE YE?!

IT'S BORELLI!... MR. CLARKE!...ME! JOE BORELLI!

BORELLI! UGH... SORRY! I MUSTA DOZED OFF FER A SECOND!

MR. CLARKE!... SERVICE TUNNEL! COME QUICK!

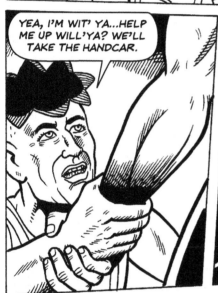

YEA, I'M WIT' YA...HELP ME UP WILL'YA? WE'LL TAKE THE HANDCAR.

TUNNEL FACE

CLARKE WONDERED IF THE HOODED MAN IN HIS DREAM WAS AN OMEN **BUT** WHAT HE SAW NEXT SHOOK HIM STRAIGHT TO HIS BONES!

AH...I SEES YA, OL' FRIEND. YER WIT' ME TONIGHT, AREN'T YE?

WHEN BORELLI DIDN'T SHARE THE SPECTRAL VISION, CLARKE SUDDENLY REALIZED THAT IT WAS MEANT FOR HIM ONLY...

163

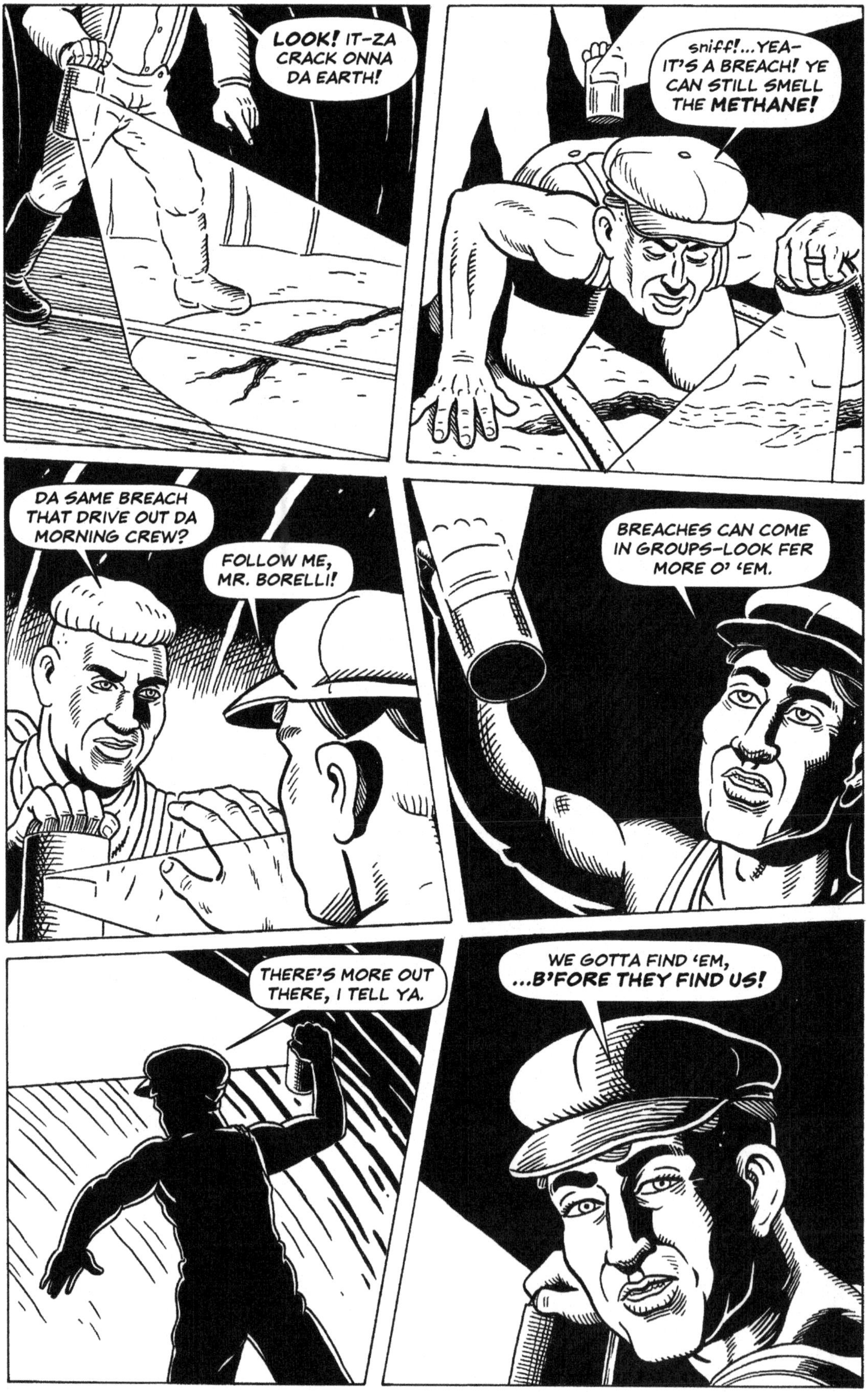
LOOK! IT-ZA CRACK ONNA DA EARTH!
sniff!...YEA- IT'S A BREACH! YE CAN STILL SMELL THE METHANE!
DA SAME BREACH THAT DRIVE OUT DA MORNING CREW?
FOLLOW ME, MR. BORELLI!
BREACHES CAN COME IN GROUPS–LOOK FER MORE O' 'EM.
THERE'S MORE OUT THERE, I TELL YA.
WE GOTTA FIND 'EM, ...B'FORE THEY FIND US!

CHAPTER 7: "GONE...THEN GONE AGAIN"
MEANWHILE, AT THE HOME OF WILHELM AND AGNES VAN DYKE
SNORE!
ZZZZZZZ
TOM SWIFT AND HIS BIG TUNNEL BY VICTOR APPLETON
TOM SWIFT AND HIS BIG TUNNEL BY VICTOR APPLETON

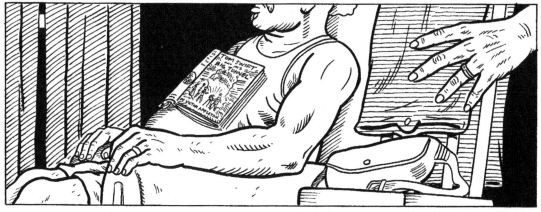

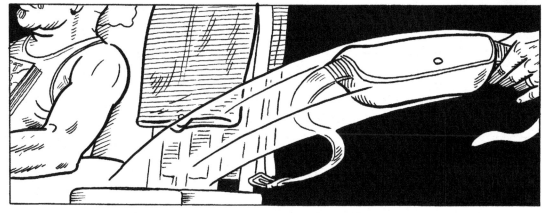

AN' **NOW** WE SEE WHAT THE GOBSHITE IS HOLDIN' BACK ON US...

ZZZZZZZZ

JAYSUS, MARY AND JOSEPH!!

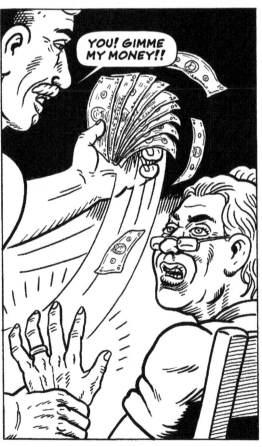

YOU! GIMME MY MONEY!!

DIS IS MONEY TO PAY THE SANDHOGS!!

WADD'YA MEAN? 'TIS THE JOB O' THE WATERWORKS TO PAY 'EM!

166

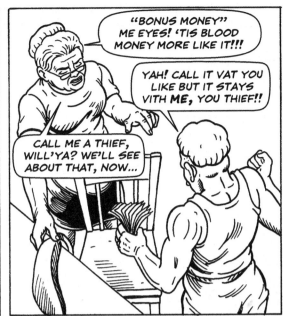

167

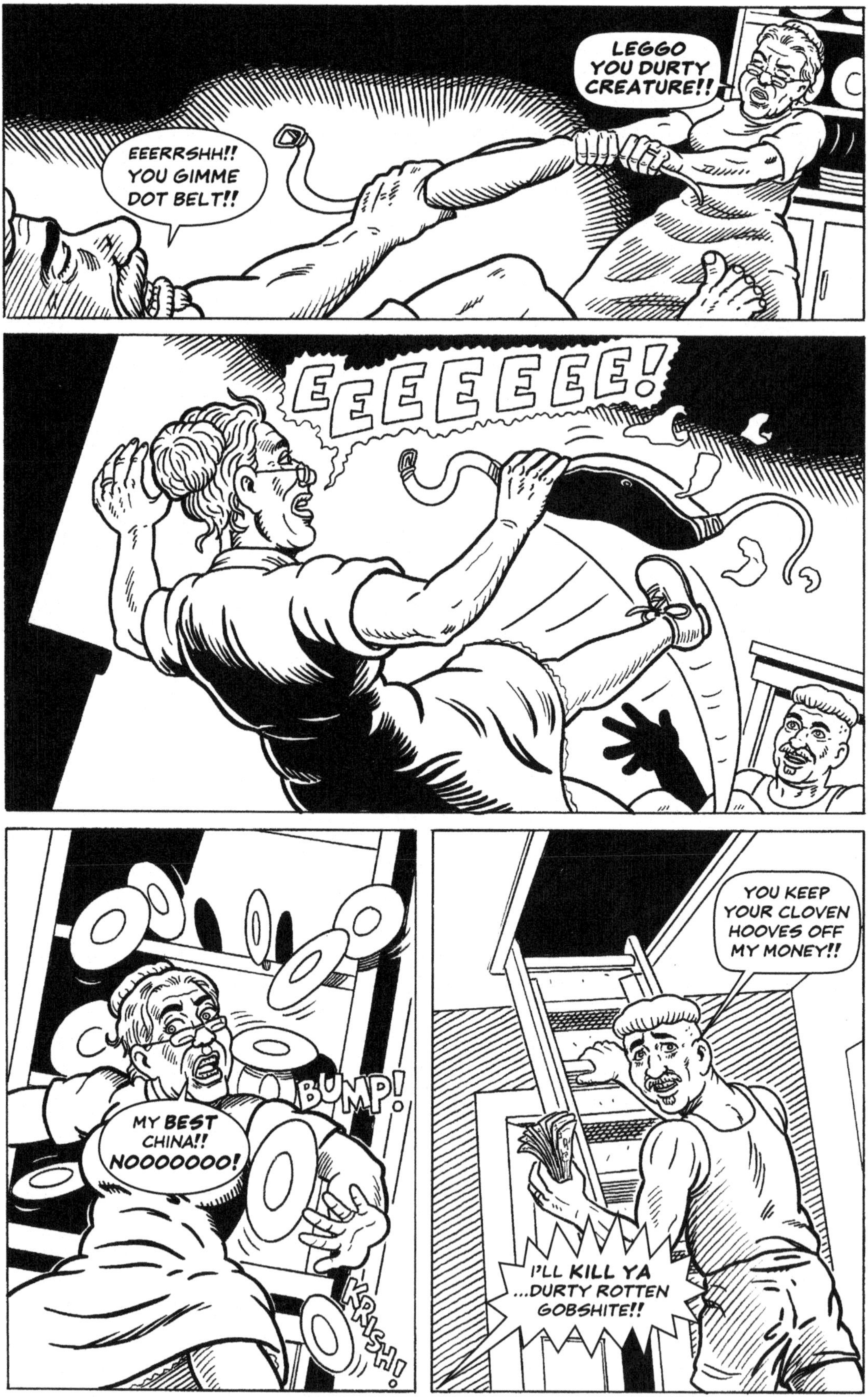
LEGGO YOU DURTY CREATURE!!
EEERRSHH!! YOU GIMME DOT BELT!!
EEEEEEE!
BUMP!
MY BEST CHINA!! NOOOOOOO!
KRISH!
YOU KEEP YOUR CLOVEN HOOVES OFF MY MONEY!!
I'LL KILL YA ...DURTY ROTTEN GOBSHITE!!

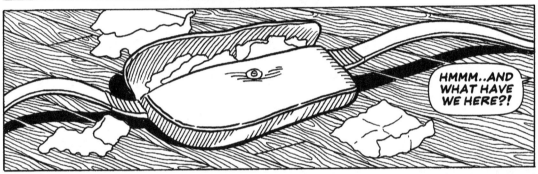

169

172

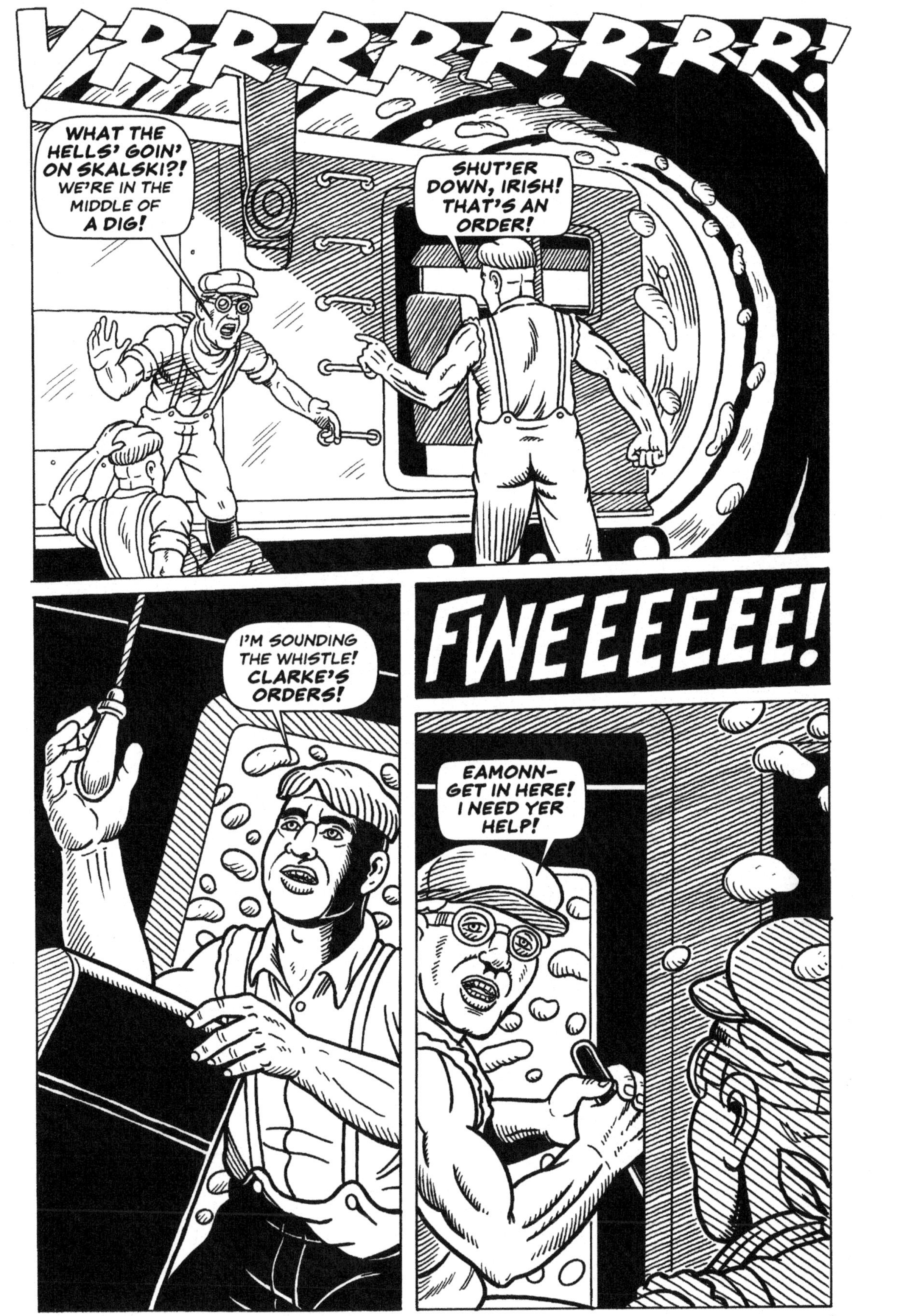
V-R-R-R-R-R-R-R-R-R-R!
WHAT THE HELLS' GOIN' ON SKALSKI?! WE'RE IN THE MIDDLE OF A DIG!
SHUT'ER DOWN, IRISH! THAT'S AN ORDER!
I'M SOUNDING THE WHISTLE! CLARKE'S ORDERS!
FWEEEEEE!
EAMONN- GET IN HERE! I NEED YER HELP!

174

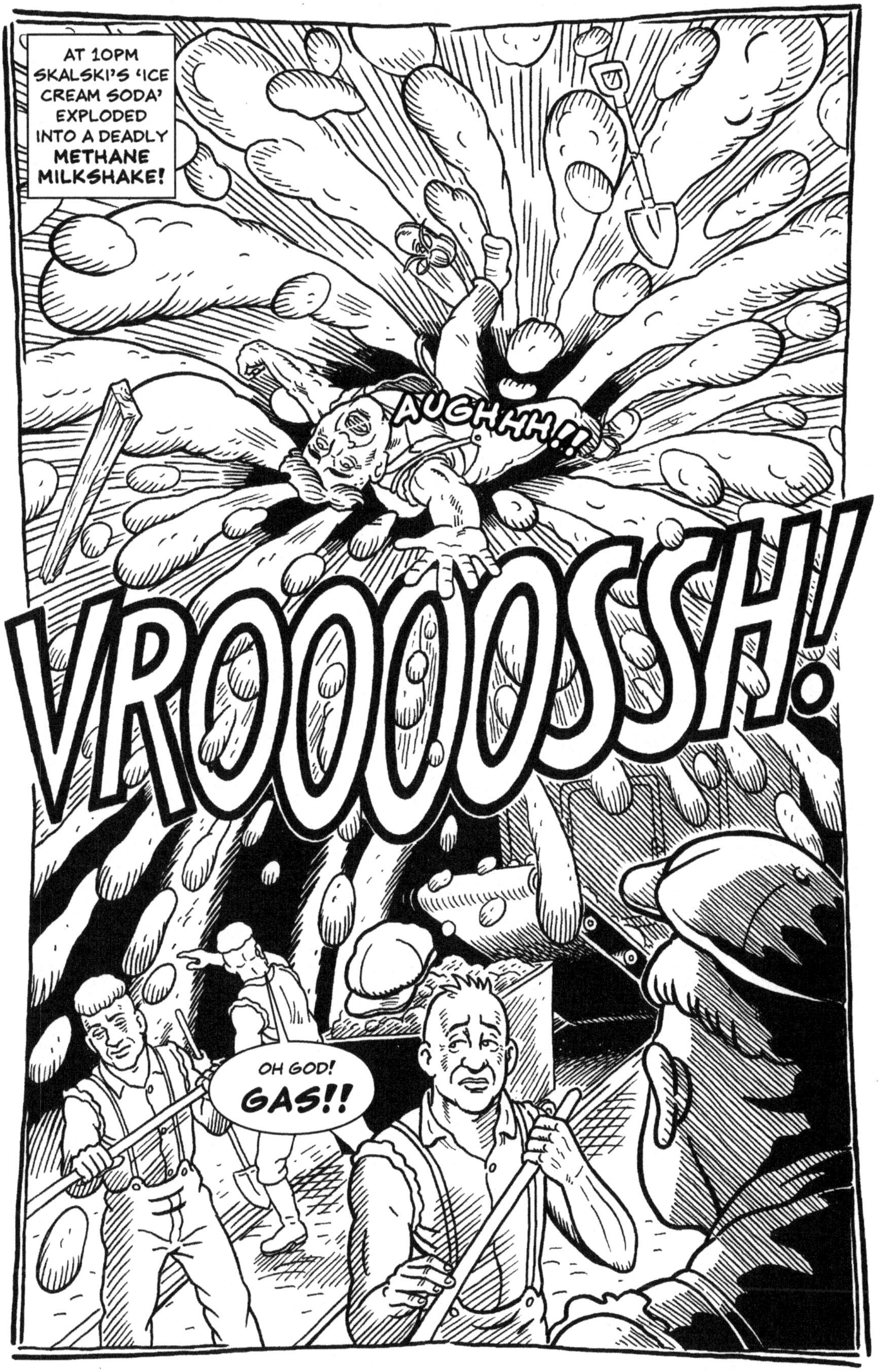
AT 10PM SKALSKI'S 'ICE CREAM SODA' EXPLODED INTO A DEADLY **METHANE MILKSHAKE!**
AUGHHH!!
VROOOOSSH!
OH GOD! **GAS!!**

UNHH!

NO! OH NO!!
AIEEEEEEEE!

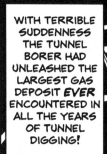

WITH TERRIBLE SUDDENNESS THE TUNNEL BORER HAD UNLEASHED THE LARGEST GAS DEPOSIT *EVER* ENCOUNTERED IN ALL THE YEARS OF TUNNEL DIGGING!

AND WITH THE GAS CAME *THE DEATH ANGELS!*

OOOOH

OOOOH

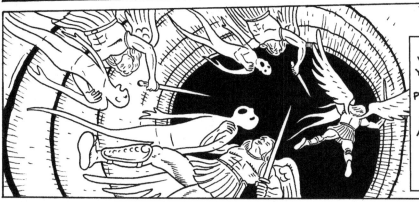

AND THEN WITHIN SECONDS, YEARS OF SHARED DESPERATION, POVERTY AND FEAR WAS *GONE.* ONLY DARKNESS AND LONELY CALM AWAITED THE SOULS SWEPT AWAY BY THE ANGELS.

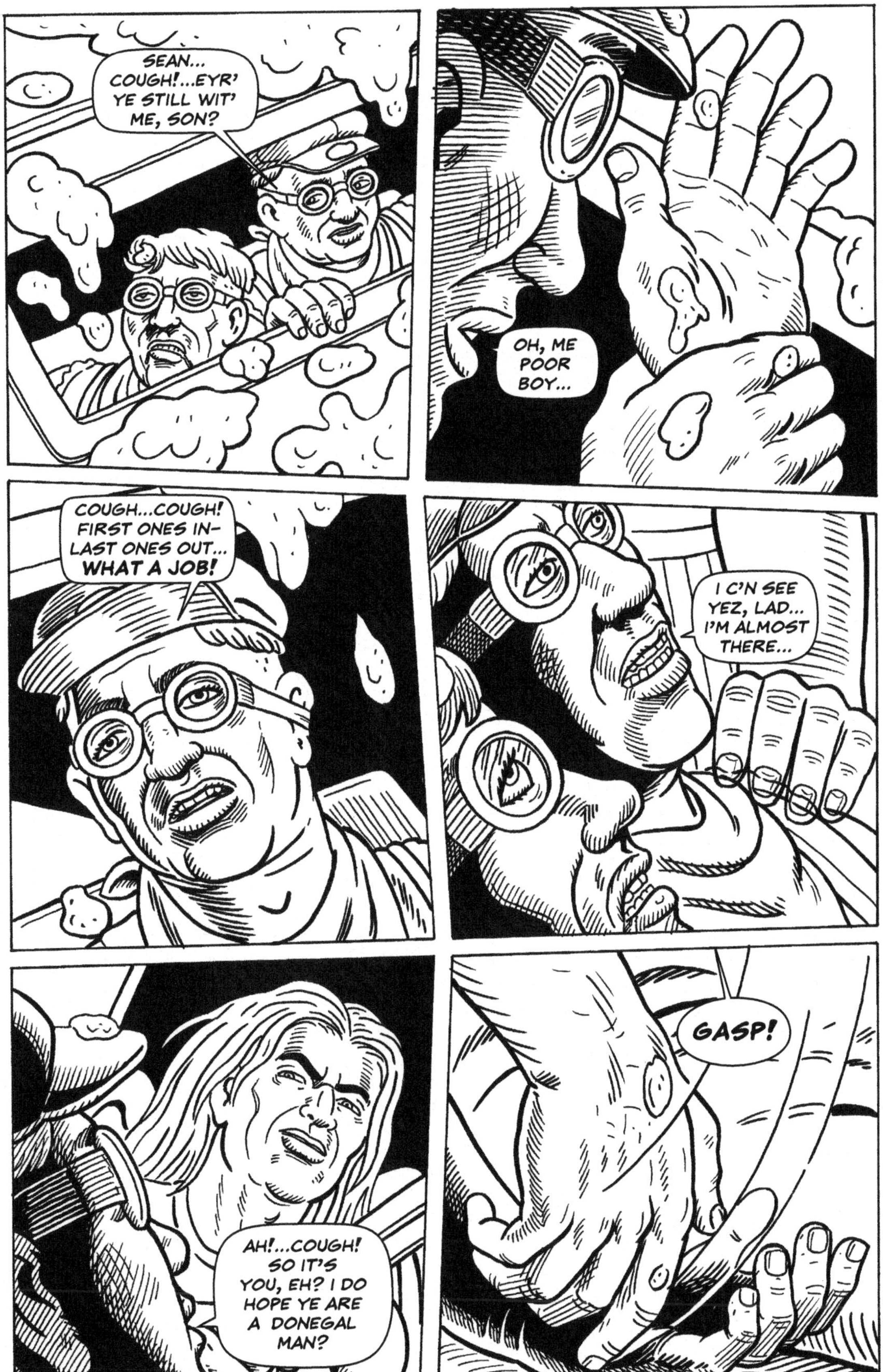
SEAN... COUGH!...EYR' YE STILL WIT' ME, SON?
OH, ME POOR BOY...
COUGH...COUGH! FIRST ONES IN-LAST ONES OUT... WHAT A JOB!
I C'N SEE YEZ, LAD... I'M ALMOST THERE...
AH!...COUGH! SO IT'S YOU, EH? I DO HOPE YE ARE A DONEGAL MAN?
GASP!

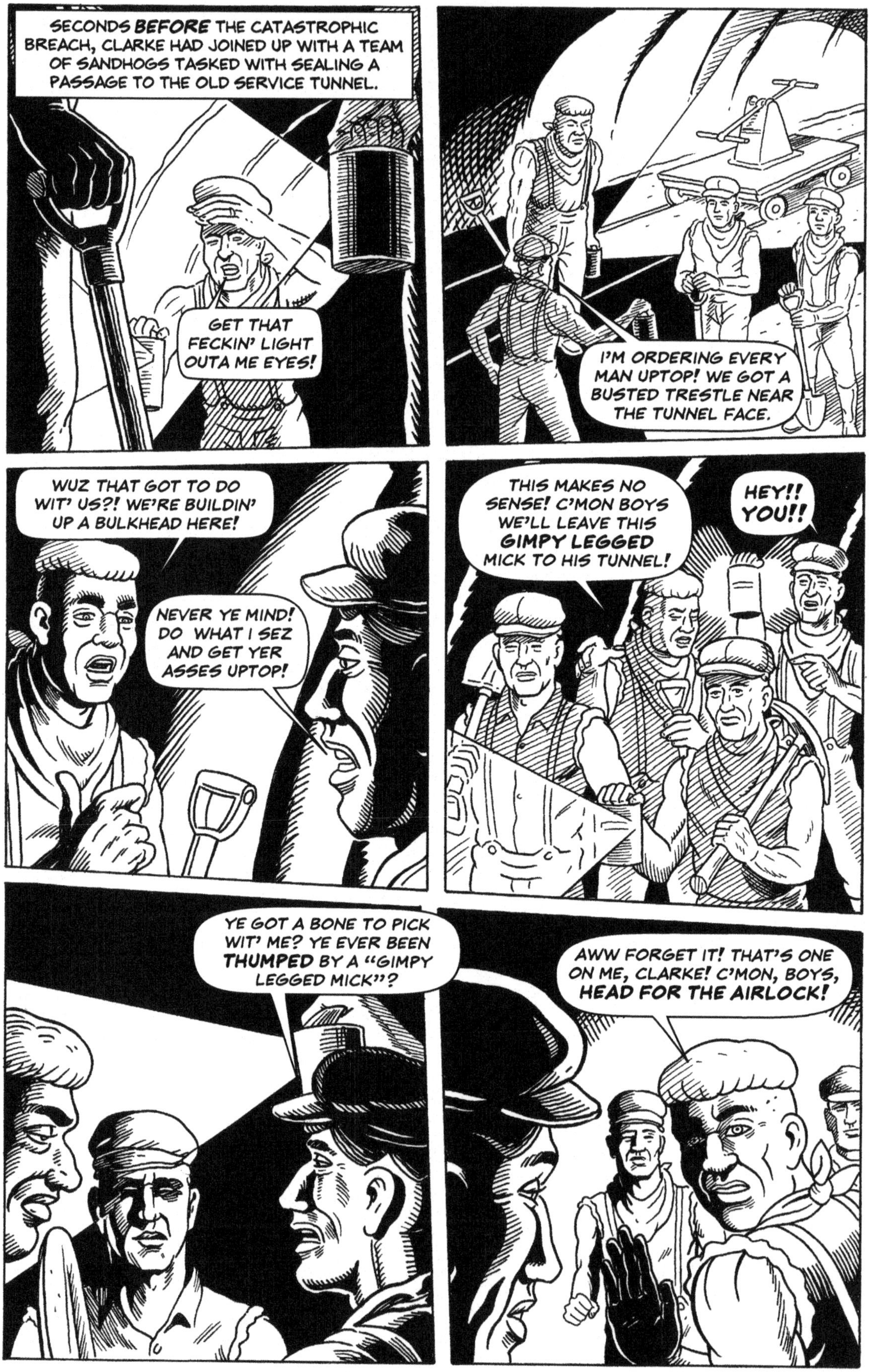
SECONDS BEFORE THE CATASTROPHIC BREACH, CLARKE HAD JOINED UP WITH A TEAM OF SANDHOGS TASKED WITH SEALING A PASSAGE TO THE OLD SERVICE TUNNEL.
GET THAT FECKIN' LIGHT OUTA ME EYES!
I'M ORDERING EVERY MAN UPTOP! WE GOT A BUSTED TRESTLE NEAR THE TUNNEL FACE.
WUZ THAT GOT TO DO WIT' US?! WE'RE BUILDIN' UP A BULKHEAD HERE!
NEVER YE MIND! DO WHAT I SEZ AND GET YER ASSES UPTOP!
THIS MAKES NO SENSE! C'MON BOYS WE'LL LEAVE THIS GIMPY LEGGED MICK TO HIS TUNNEL!
HEY!! YOU!!
YE GOT A BONE TO PICK WIT' ME? YE EVER BEEN THUMPED BY A "GIMPY LEGGED MICK"?
AWW FORGET IT! THAT'S ONE ON ME, CLARKE! C'MON, BOYS, HEAD FOR THE AIRLOCK!

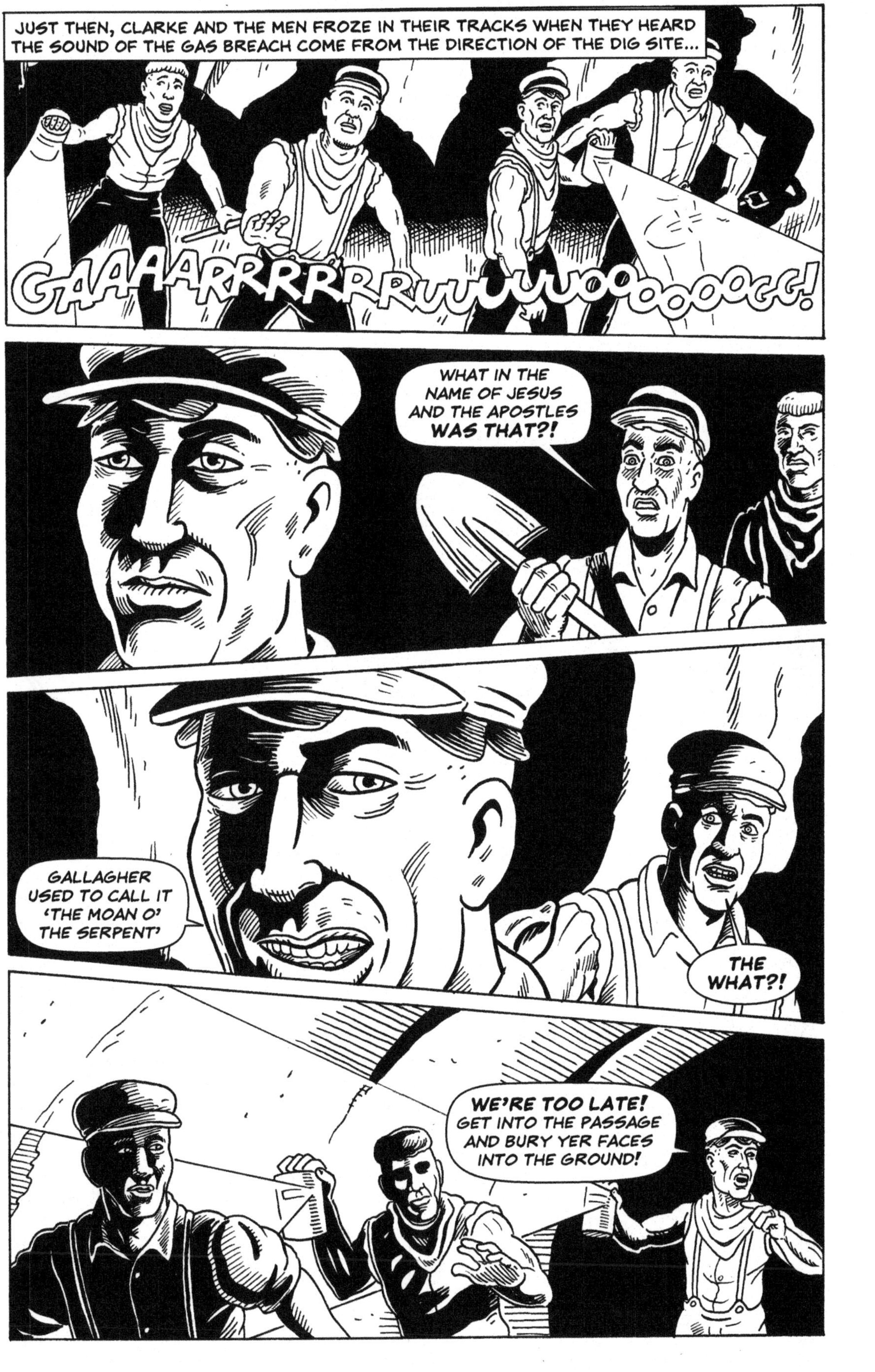
JUST THEN, CLARKE AND THE MEN FROZE IN THEIR TRACKS WHEN THEY HEARD THE SOUND OF THE GAS BREACH COME FROM THE DIRECTION OF THE DIG SITE...
GAAAARRRRRRUUUUUOOOOOOOGG!
WHAT IN THE NAME OF JESUS AND THE APOSTLES WAS THAT?!
GALLAGHER USED TO CALL IT 'THE MOAN O' THE SERPENT'
THE WHAT?!
WE'RE TOO LATE! GET INTO THE PASSAGE AND BURY YER FACES INTO THE GROUND!

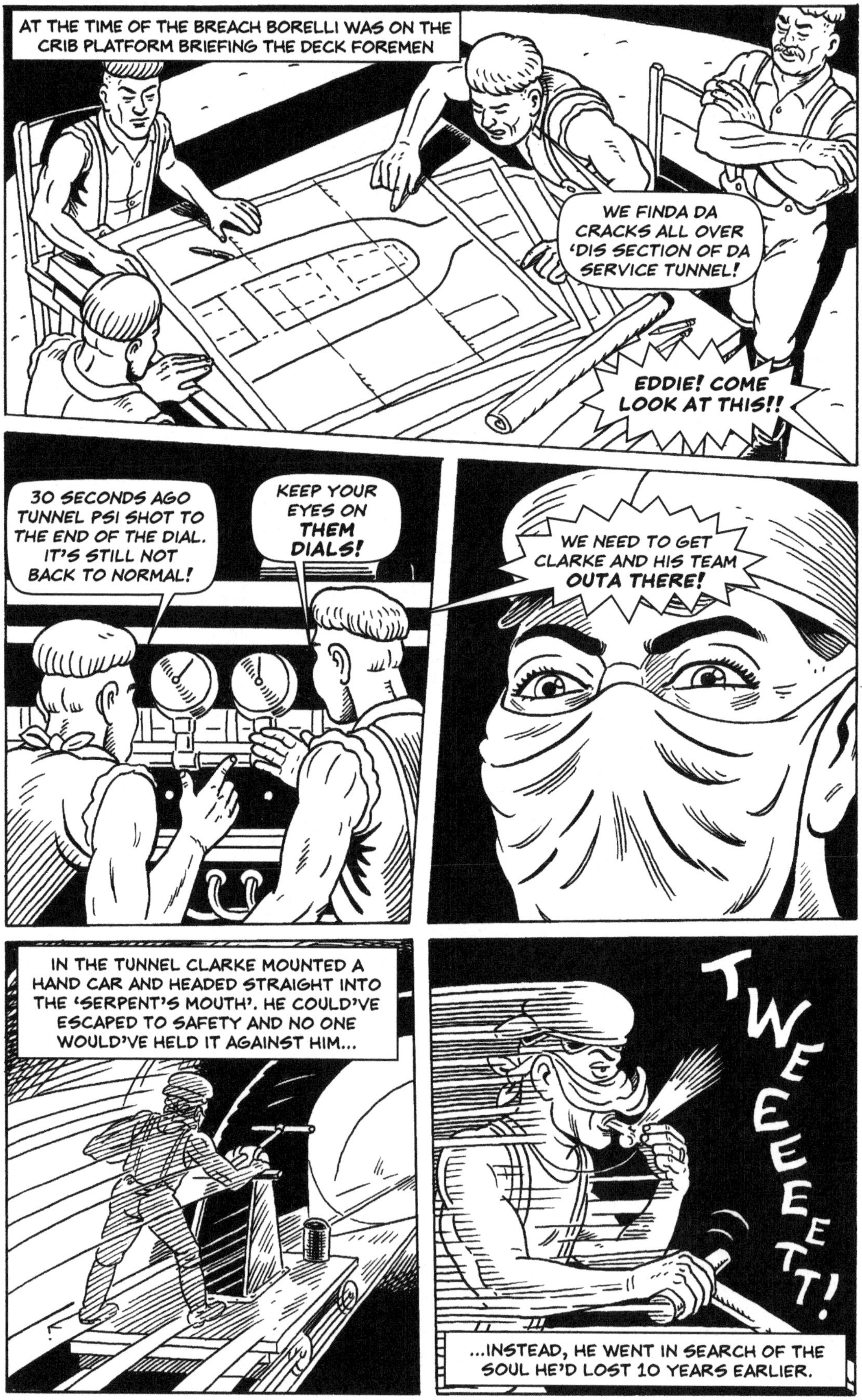
AT THE TIME OF THE BREACH BORELLI WAS ON THE CRIB PLATFORM BRIEFING THE DECK FOREMEN
WE FINDA DA CRACKS ALL OVER 'DIS SECTION OF DA SERVICE TUNNEL!
EDDIE! COME LOOK AT THIS!!
30 SECONDS AGO TUNNEL PSI SHOT TO THE END OF THE DIAL. IT'S STILL NOT BACK TO NORMAL!
KEEP YOUR EYES ON THEM DIALS!
WE NEED TO GET CLARKE AND HIS TEAM OUTA THERE!
IN THE TUNNEL CLARKE MOUNTED A HAND CAR AND HEADED STRAIGHT INTO THE 'SERPENT'S MOUTH'. HE COULD'VE ESCAPED TO SAFETY AND NO ONE WOULD'VE HELD IT AGAINST HIM...
TWEEEEETT!
...INSTEAD, HE WENT IN SEARCH OF THE SOUL HE'D LOST 10 YEARS EARLIER.

182

183

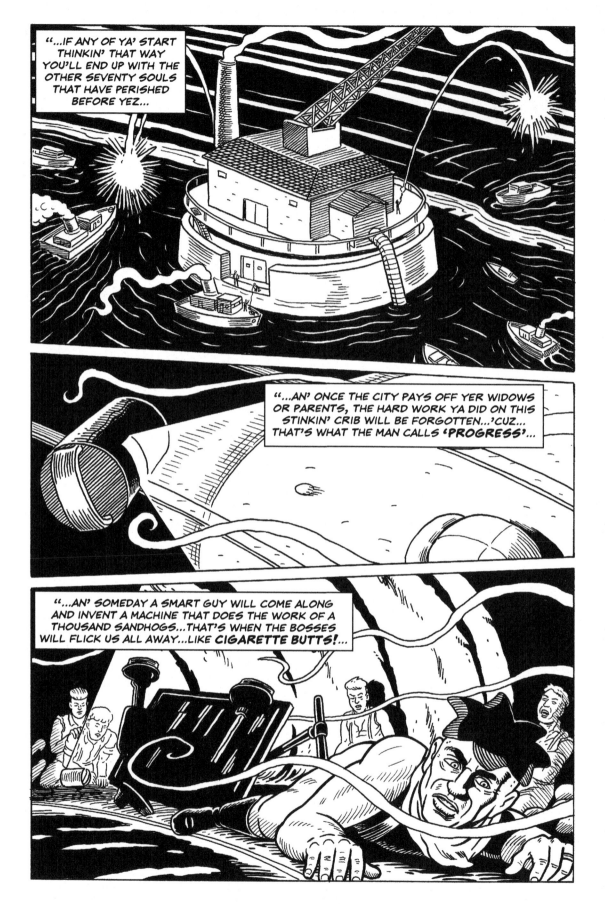

184

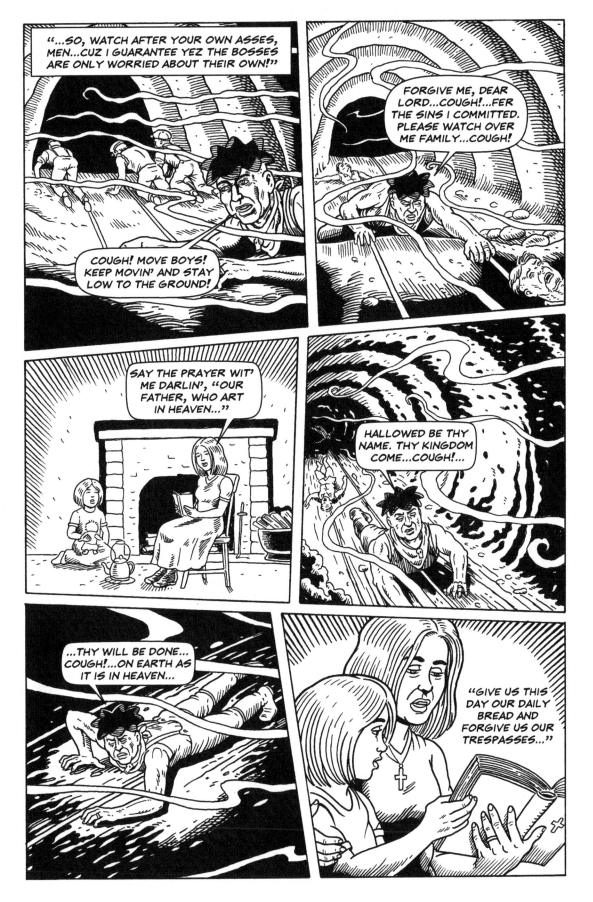

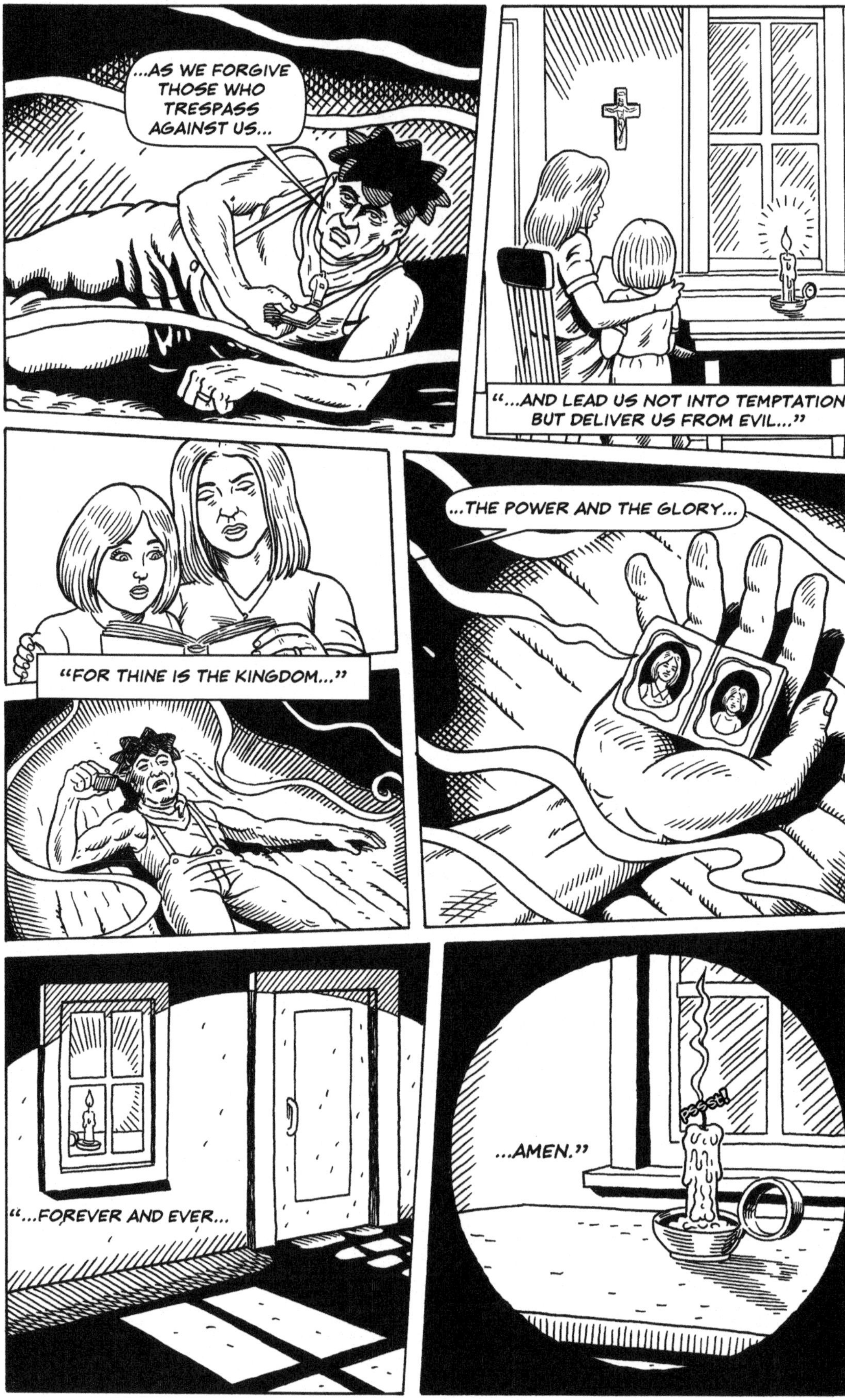
...AS WE FORGIVE THOSE WHO TRESPASS AGAINST US...
"...AND LEAD US NOT INTO TEMPTATION BUT DELIVER US FROM EVIL..."
"FOR THINE IS THE KINGDOM..."
...THE POWER AND THE GLORY...
"...FOREVER AND EVER...
...AMEN."
PSSST!

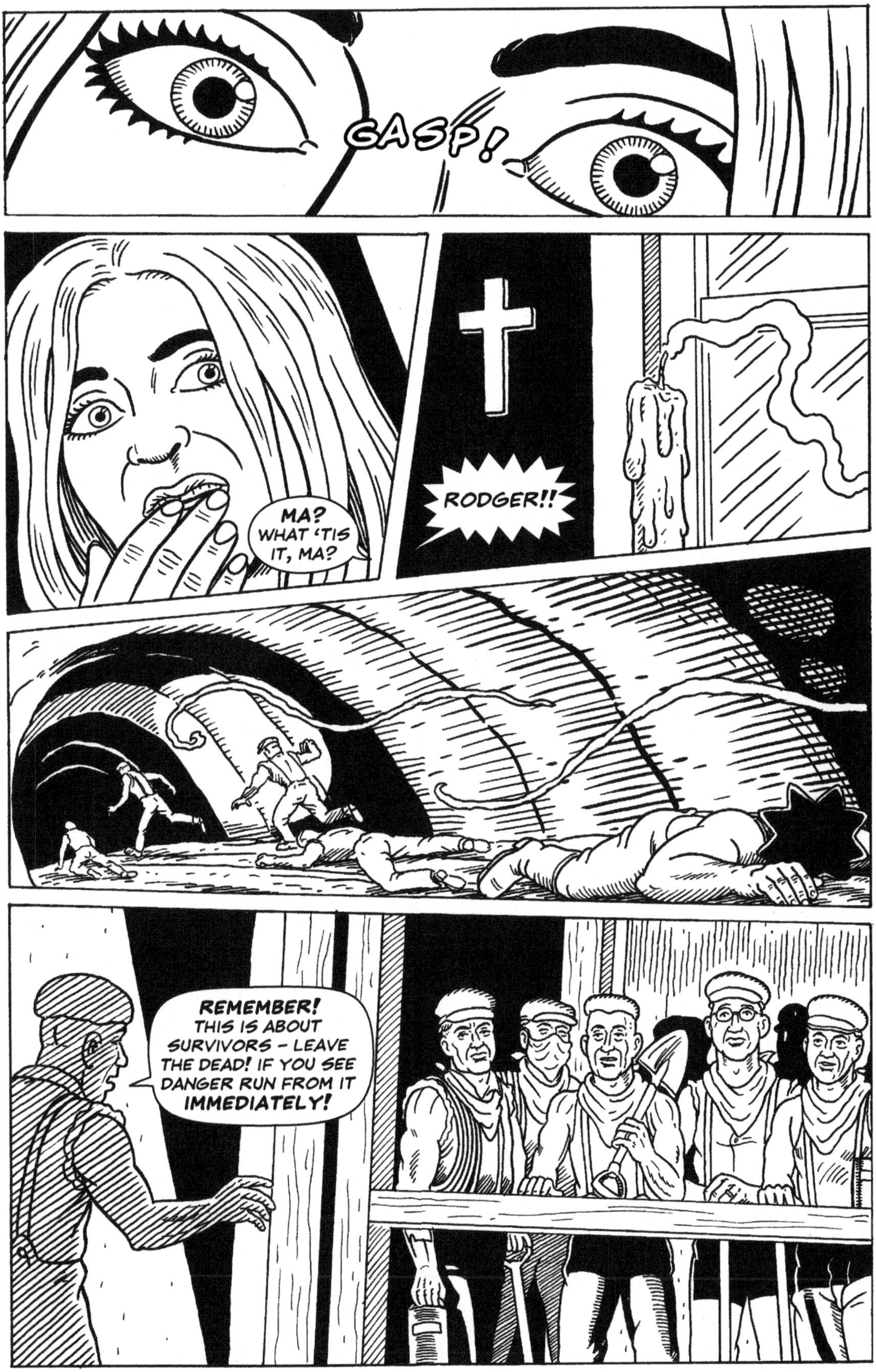
GASP!
MA? WHAT 'TIS IT, MA?
RODGER!!
REMEMBER! THIS IS ABOUT SURVIVORS - LEAVE THE DEAD! IF YOU SEE DANGER RUN FROM IT IMMEDIATELY!

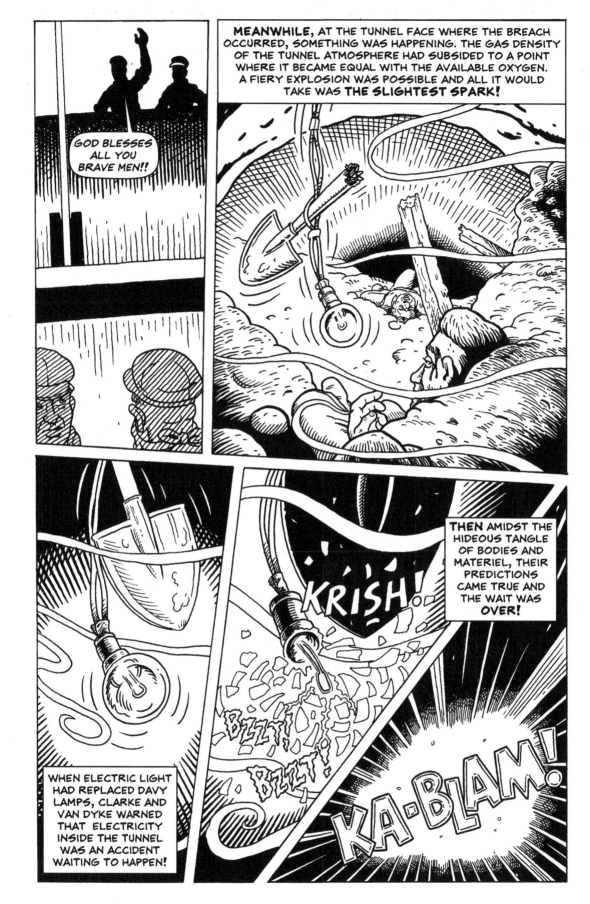

MEANWHILE, AT THE TUNNEL FACE WHERE THE BREACH OCCURRED, SOMETHING WAS HAPPENING. THE GAS DENSITY OF THE TUNNEL ATMOSPHERE HAD SUBSIDED TO A POINT WHERE IT BECAME EQUAL WITH THE AVAILABLE OXYGEN. A FIERY EXPLOSION WAS POSSIBLE AND ALL IT WOULD TAKE WAS **THE SLIGHTEST SPARK!**

GOD BLESSES ALL YOU BRAVE MEN!!

THEN AMIDST THE HIDEOUS TANGLE OF BODIES AND MATERIEL, THEIR PREDICTIONS CAME TRUE AND THE WAIT WAS **OVER!**

KRISH!

BZZT! BZZT!

KA-BLAM!

WHEN ELECTRIC LIGHT HAD REPLACED DAVY LAMPS, CLARKE AND VAN DYKE WARNED THAT ELECTRICITY INSIDE THE TUNNEL WAS AN ACCIDENT WAITING TO HAPPEN!

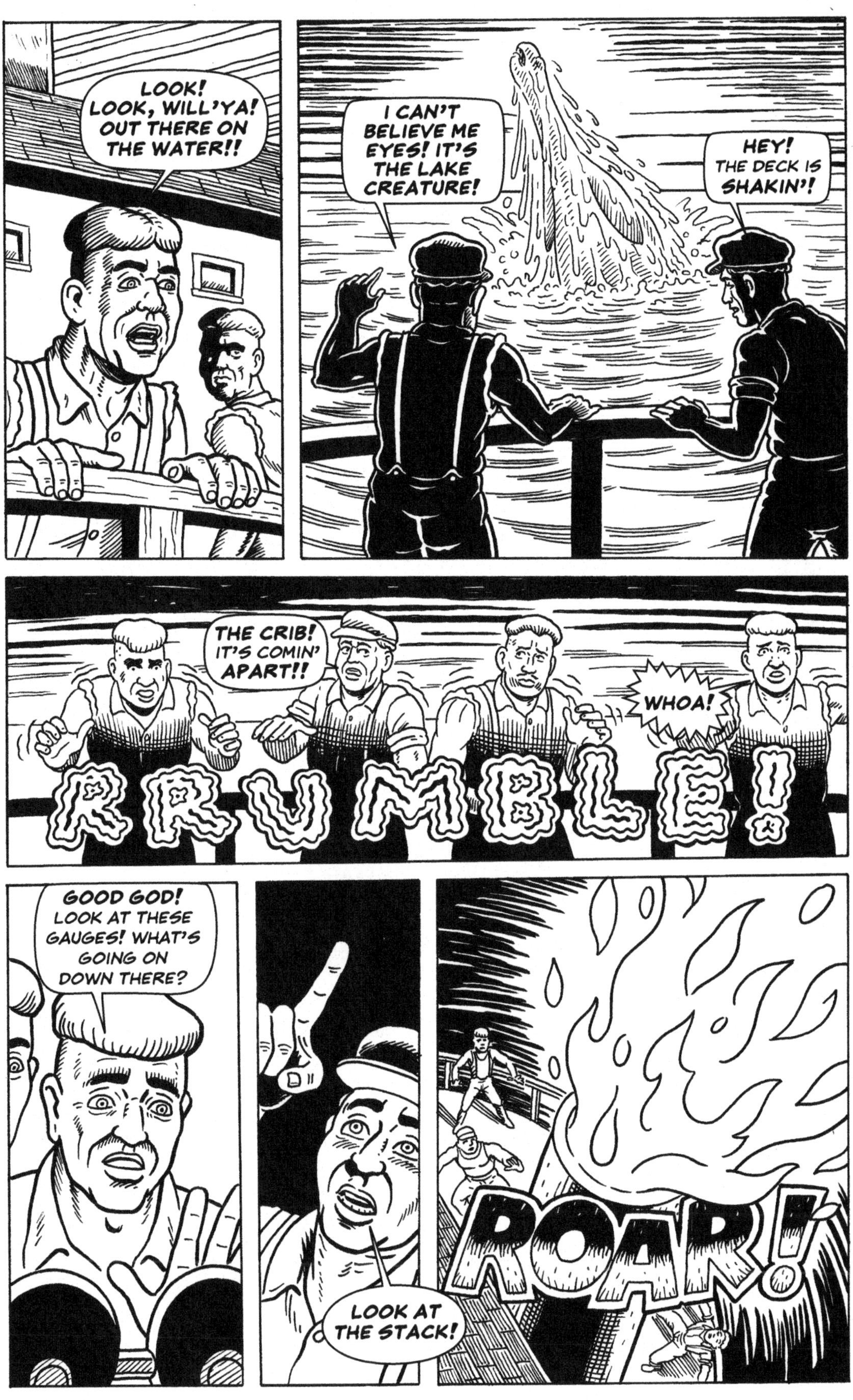
LOOK! LOOK, WILL'YA! OUT THERE ON THE WATER!!
I CAN'T BELIEVE ME EYES! IT'S THE LAKE CREATURE!
HEY! THE DECK IS SHAKIN'!
THE CRIB! IT'S COMIN' APART!!
WHOA!
RRUMBLE!
GOOD GOD! LOOK AT THESE GAUGES! WHAT'S GOING ON DOWN THERE?
LOOK AT THE STACK!
ROAR!

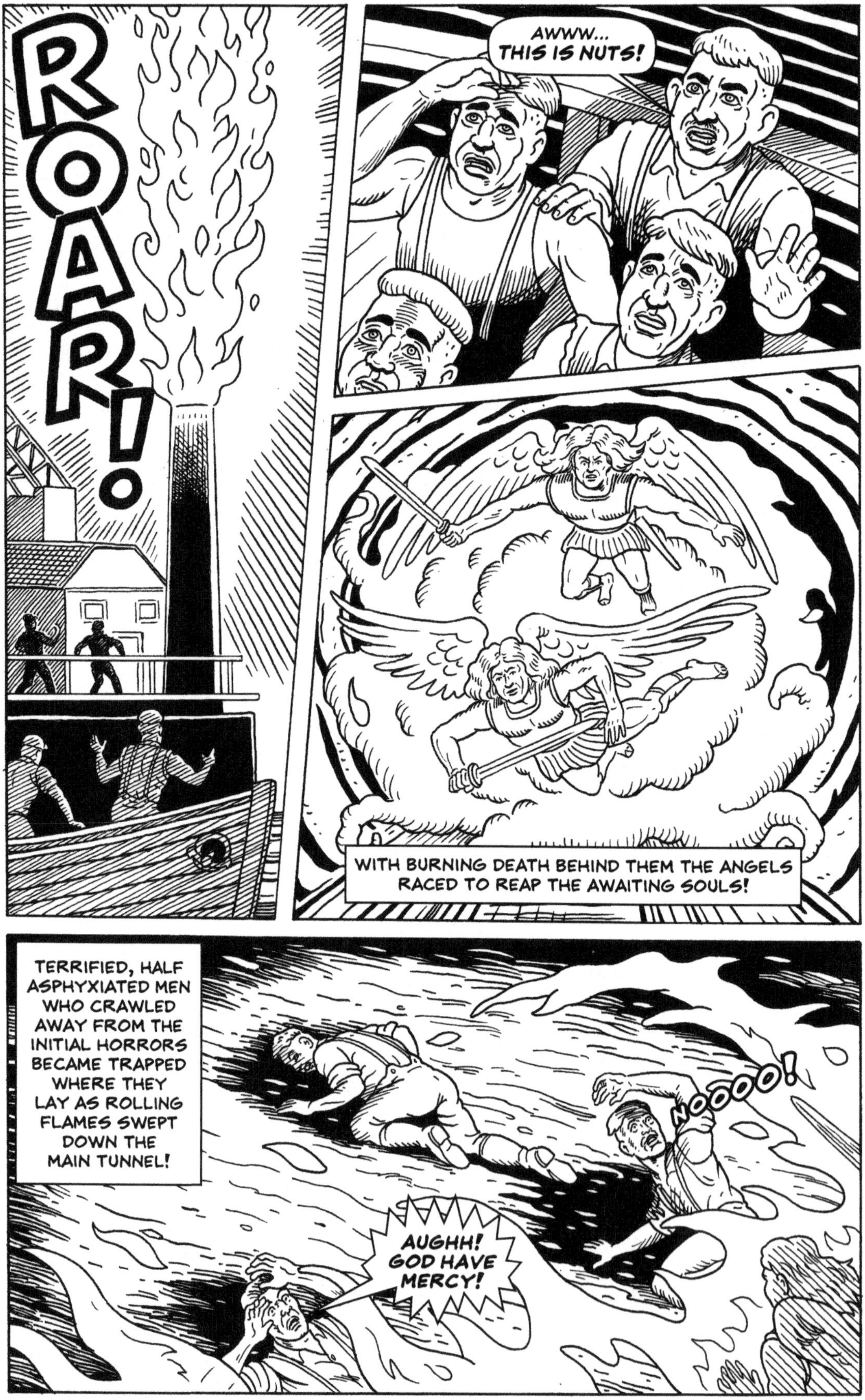
ROAR!
AWWW... THIS IS NUTS!
WITH BURNING DEATH BEHIND THEM THE ANGELS RACED TO REAP THE AWAITING SOULS!
TERRIFIED, HALF ASPHYXIATED MEN WHO CRAWLED AWAY FROM THE INITIAL HORRORS BECAME TRAPPED WHERE THEY LAY AS ROLLING FLAMES SWEPT DOWN THE MAIN TUNNEL!
NOOOO!
AUGHH! GOD HAVE MERCY!

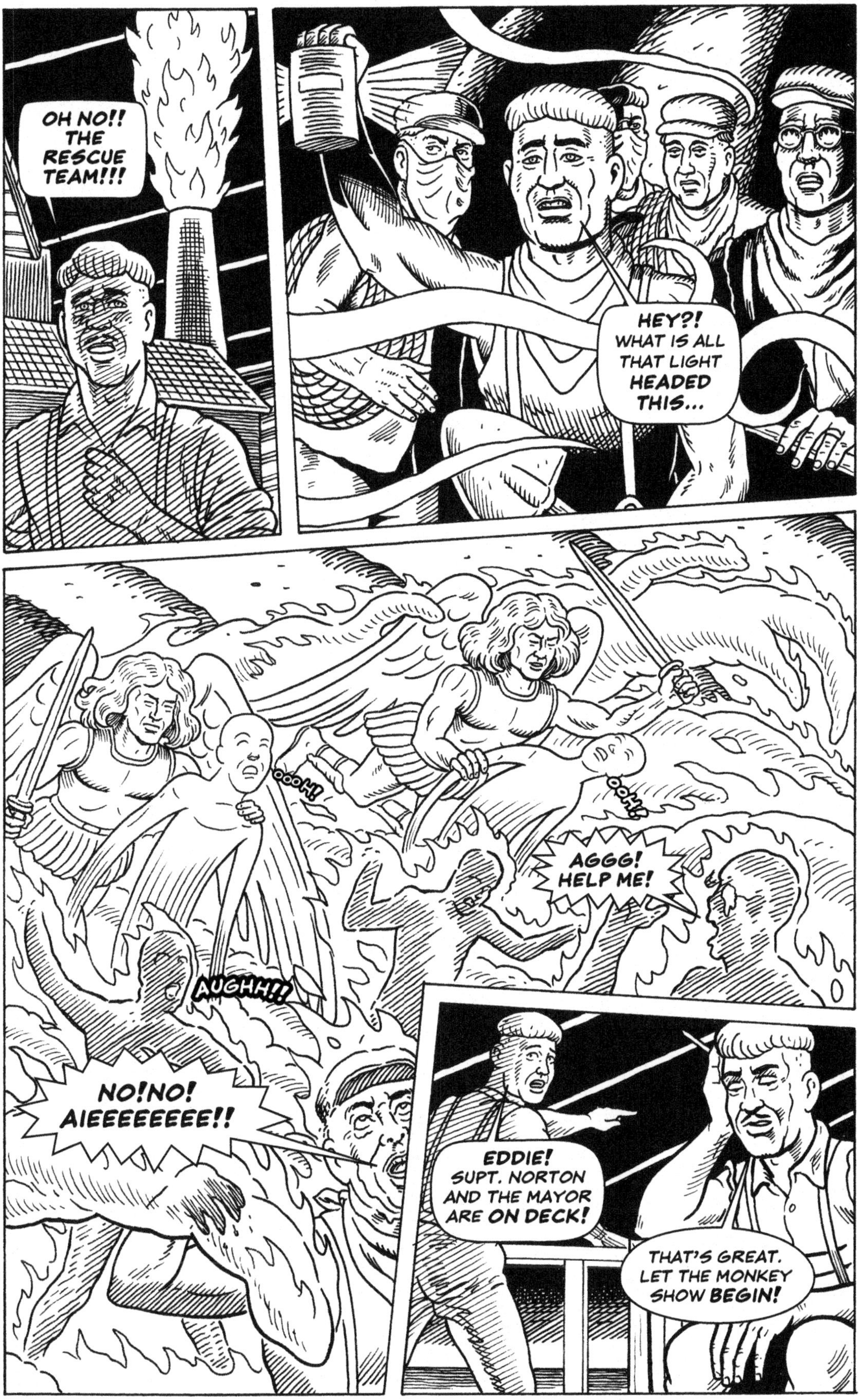
OH NO!! THE RESCUE TEAM!!!
HEY?! WHAT IS ALL THAT LIGHT HEADED THIS...
OOOH!
OOH!
AGGG! HELP ME!
AUGHH!!
NO!NO! AIEEEEEEE!!
EDDIE! SUPT. NORTON AND THE MAYOR ARE ON DECK!
THAT'S GREAT. LET THE MONKEY SHOW BEGIN!

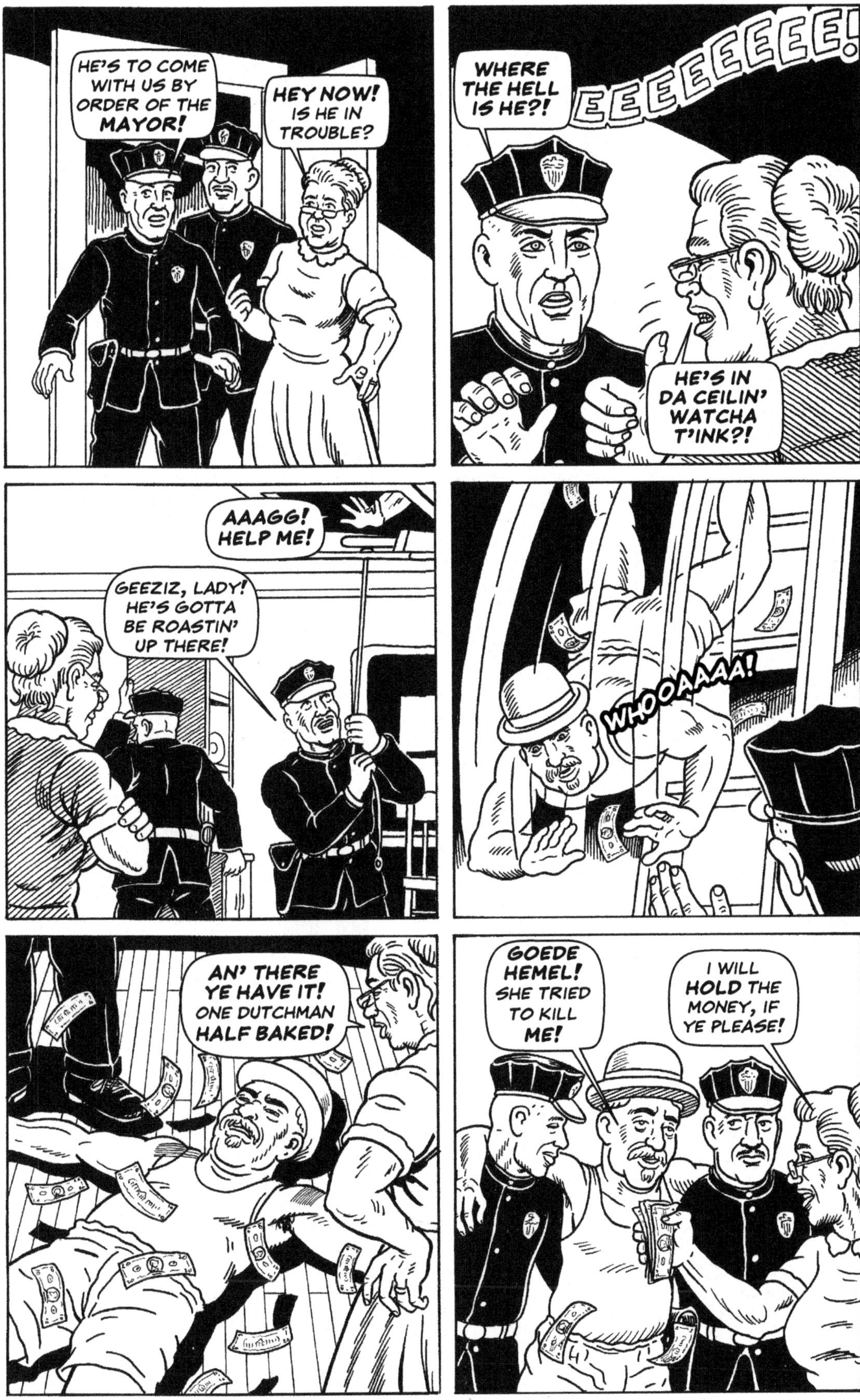
HE'S TO COME WITH US BY ORDER OF THE MAYOR!
HEY NOW! IS HE IN TROUBLE?
WHERE THE HELL IS HE?!
EEEEEEEEE!
HE'S IN DA CEILIN' WATCHA T'INK?!
AAAGG! HELP ME!
GEEZIZ, LADY! HE'S GOTTA BE ROASTIN' UP THERE!
WHOOAAAA!
AN' THERE YE HAVE IT! ONE DUTCHMAN HALF BAKED!
GOEDE HEMEL! SHE TRIED TO KILL ME!
I WILL HOLD THE MONEY, IF YE PLEASE!

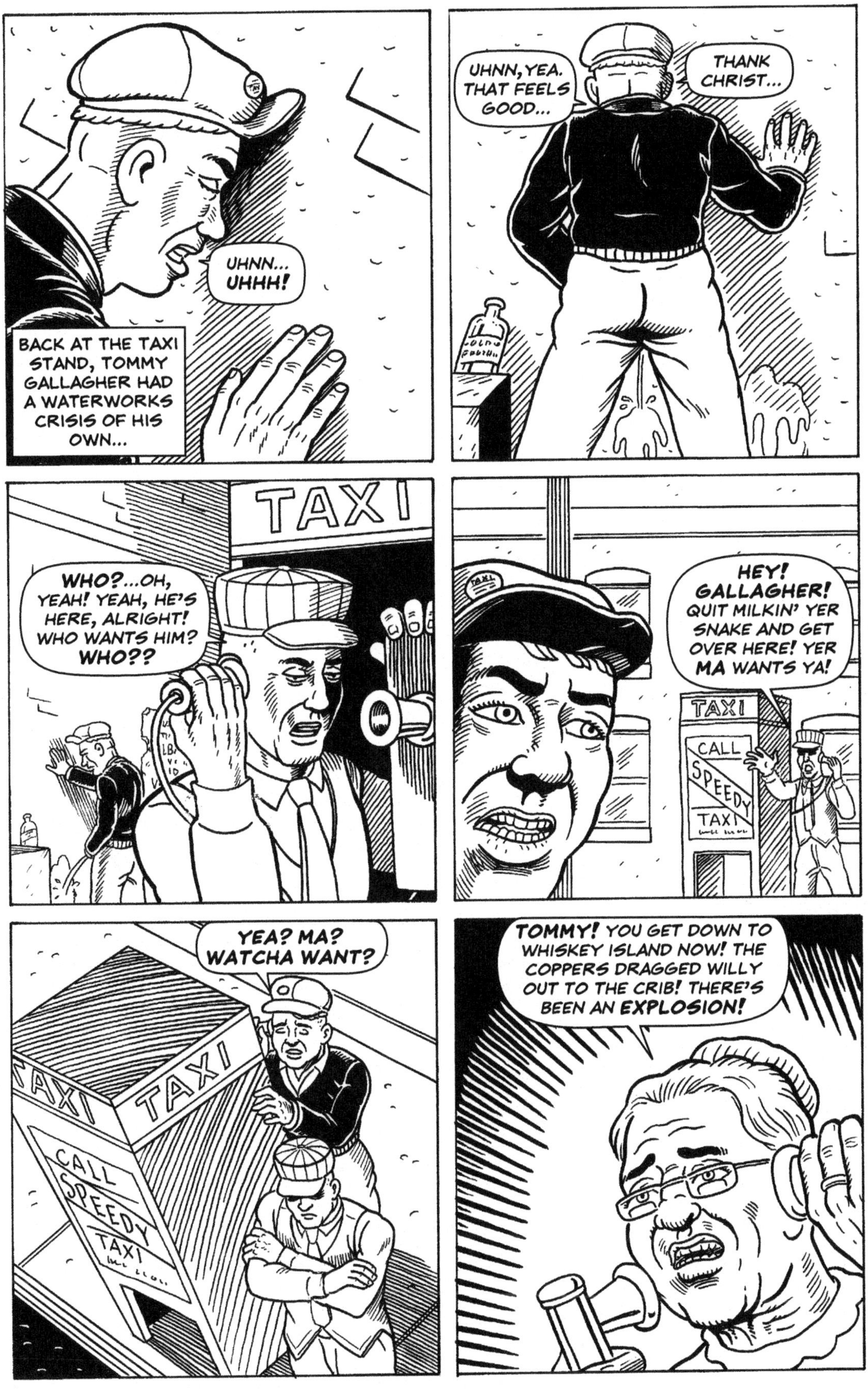
UHNN... UHHH!
BACK AT THE TAXI STAND, TOMMY GALLAGHER HAD A WATERWORKS CRISIS OF HIS OWN...
UHNN, YEA. THAT FEELS GOOD...
THANK CHRIST...
TAXI
WHO?...OH, YEAH! YEAH, HE'S HERE, ALRIGHT! WHO WANTS HIM? WHO??
HEY! GALLAGHER! QUIT MILKIN' YER SNAKE AND GET OVER HERE! YER MA WANTS YA!
TAXI
CALL SPEEDY TAXI
YEA? MA? WATCHA WANT?
TAXI
TAXI
CALL SPEEDY TAXI
TOMMY! YOU GET DOWN TO WHISKEY ISLAND NOW! THE COPPERS DRAGGED WILLY OUT TO THE CRIB! THERE'S BEEN AN EXPLOSION!

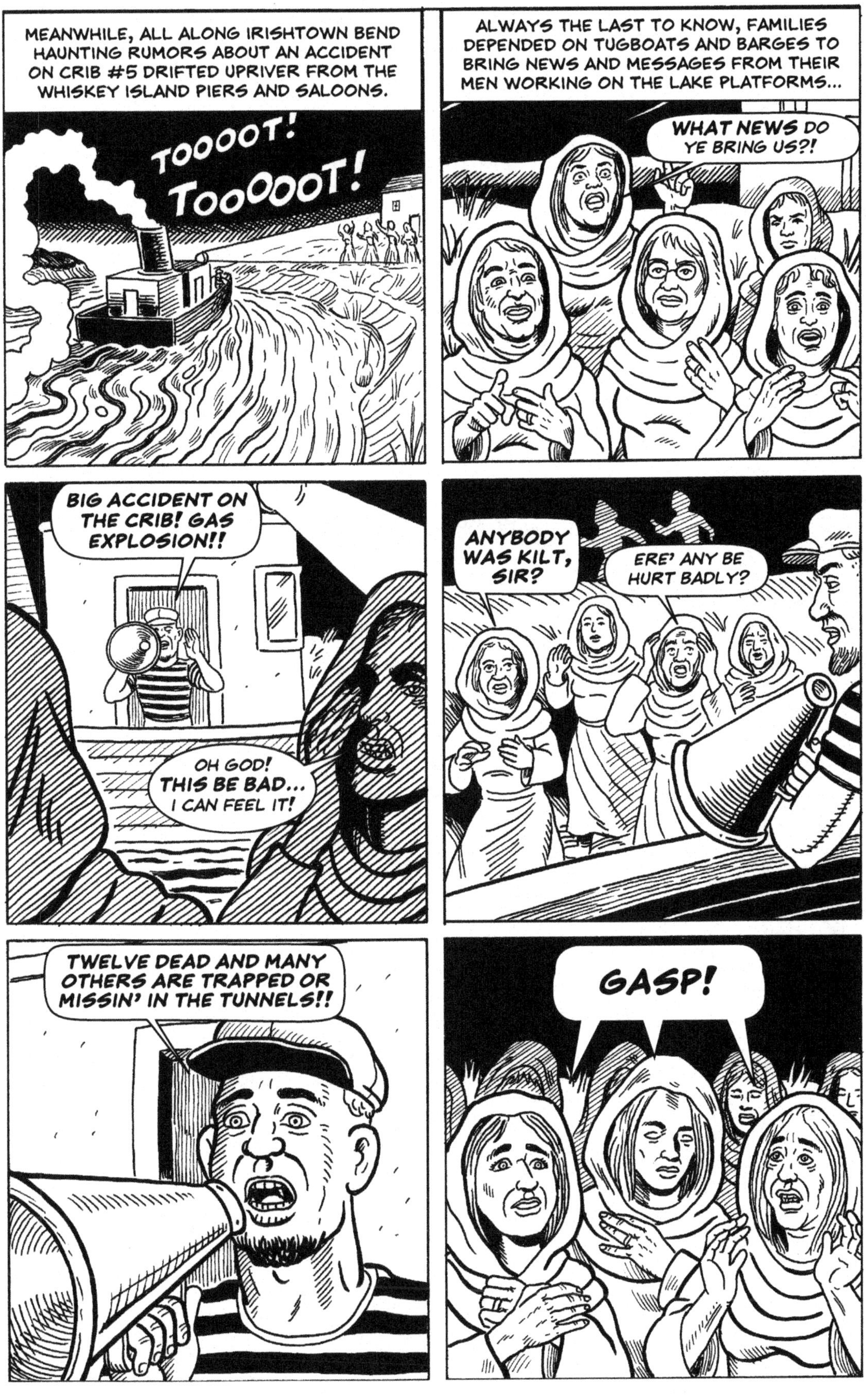
MEANWHILE, ALL ALONG IRISHTOWN BEND HAUNTING RUMORS ABOUT AN ACCIDENT ON CRIB #5 DRIFTED UPRIVER FROM THE WHISKEY ISLAND PIERS AND SALOONS.
TOOOOT! TOOOOOT!
ALWAYS THE LAST TO KNOW, FAMILIES DEPENDED ON TUGBOATS AND BARGES TO BRING NEWS AND MESSAGES FROM THEIR MEN WORKING ON THE LAKE PLATFORMS...
WHAT NEWS DO YE BRING US?!
BIG ACCIDENT ON THE CRIB! GAS EXPLOSION!!
OH GOD! THIS BE BAD... I CAN FEEL IT!
ANYBODY WAS KILT, SIR?
ERE' ANY BE HURT BADLY?
TWELVE DEAD AND MANY OTHERS ARE TRAPPED OR MISSIN' IN THE TUNNELS!!
GASP!

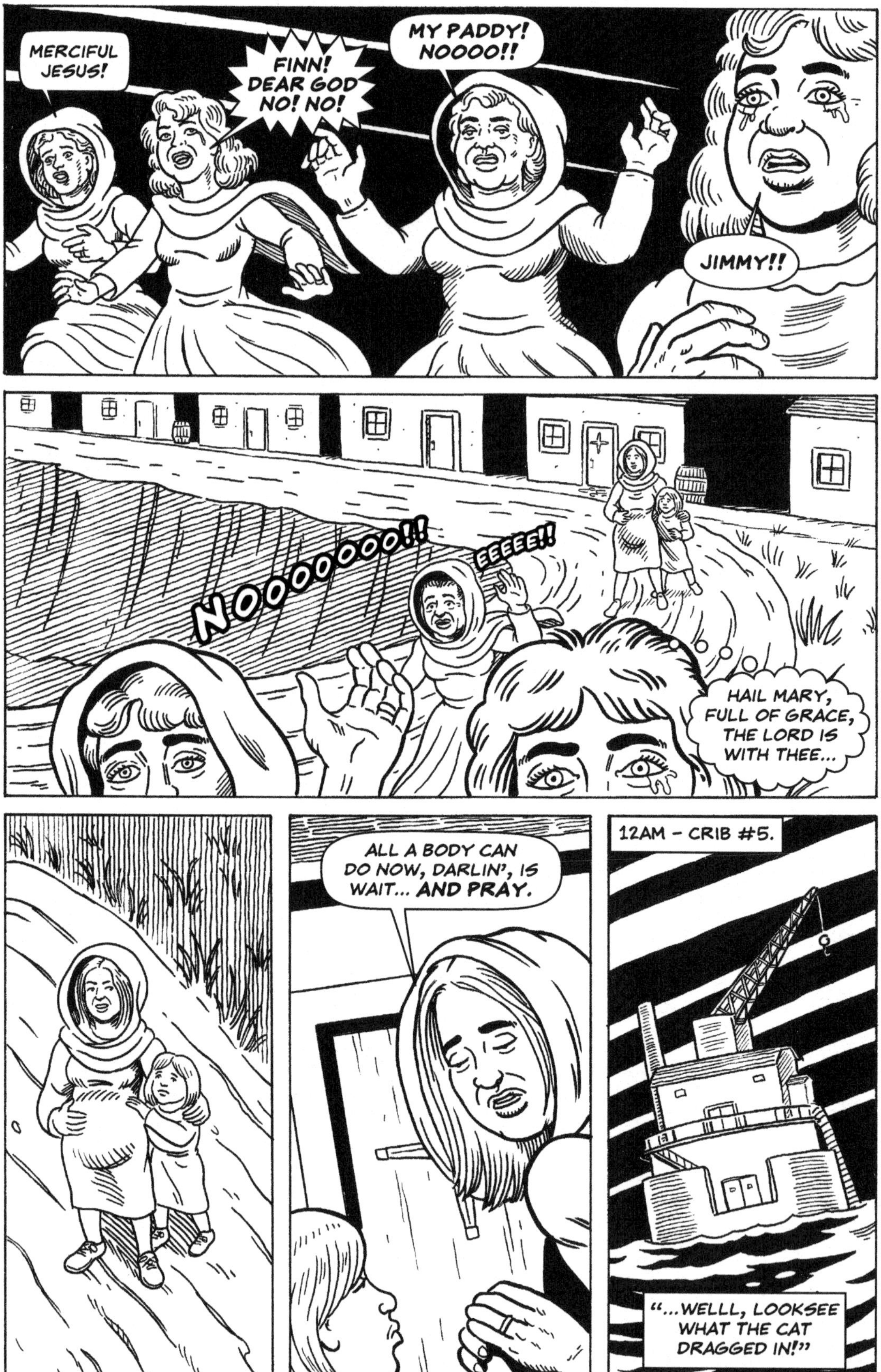
MERCIFUL JESUS!
FINN! DEAR GOD NO! NO!
MY PADDY! NOOOO!!
JIMMY!!
NOOOOOOO!!
EEEEE!!
HAIL MARY, FULL OF GRACE, THE LORD IS WITH THEE...
ALL A BODY CAN DO NOW, DARLIN', IS WAIT... AND PRAY.
12AM – CRIB #5.
"...WELLL, LOOKSEE WHAT THE CAT DRAGGED IN!"

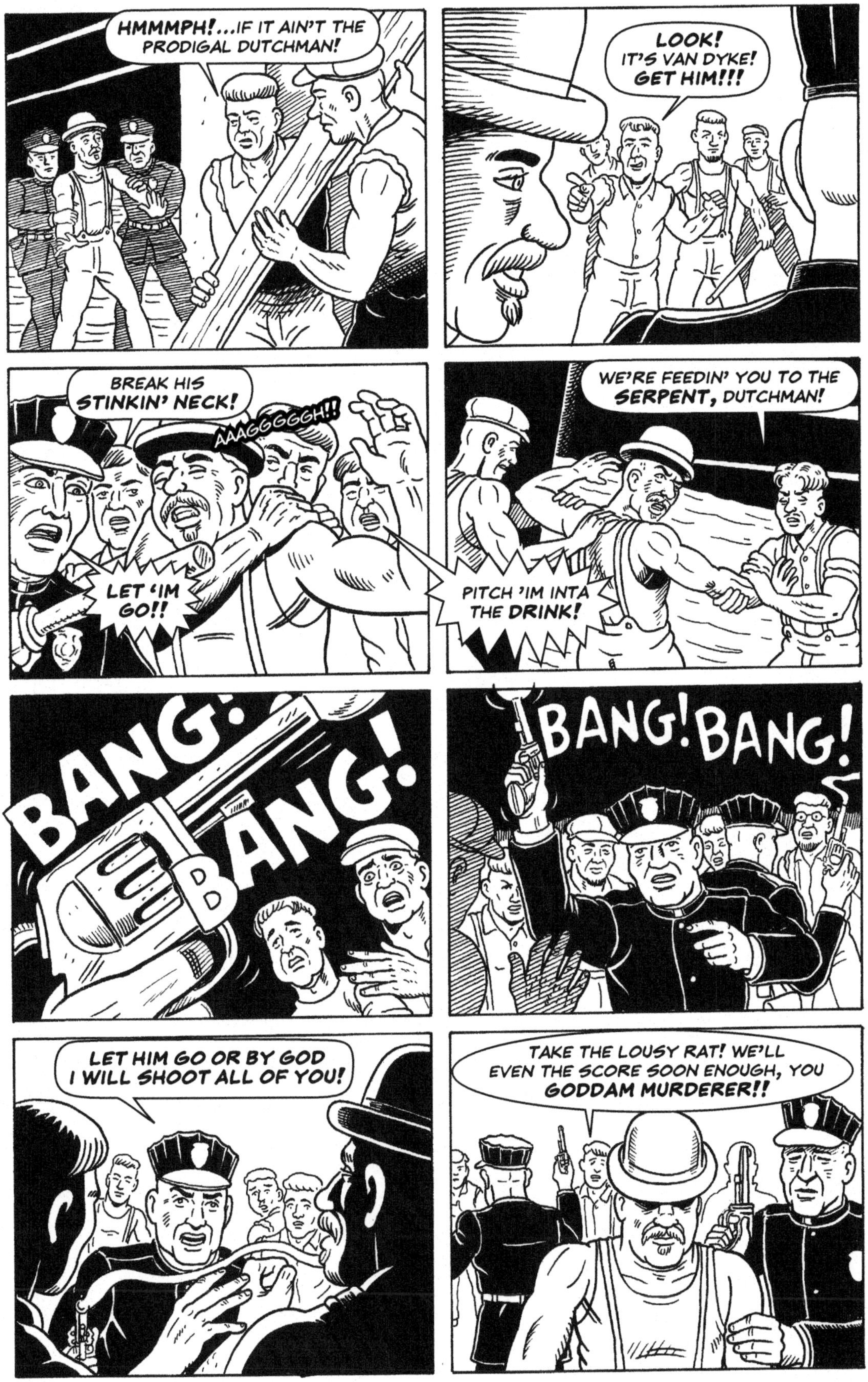
HMMMPH!...IF IT AIN'T THE PRODIGAL DUTCHMAN!
LOOK! IT'S VAN DYKE! GET HIM!!!
BREAK HIS STINKIN' NECK!
AAAGGGGGH!!
LET 'IM GO!!
PITCH 'IM INTA THE DRINK!
WE'RE FEEDIN' YOU TO THE SERPENT, DUTCHMAN!
BANG! BANG!
BANG! BANG!
LET HIM GO OR BY GOD I WILL SHOOT ALL OF YOU!
TAKE THE LOUSY RAT! WE'LL EVEN THE SCORE SOON ENOUGH, YOU GODDAM MURDERER!!

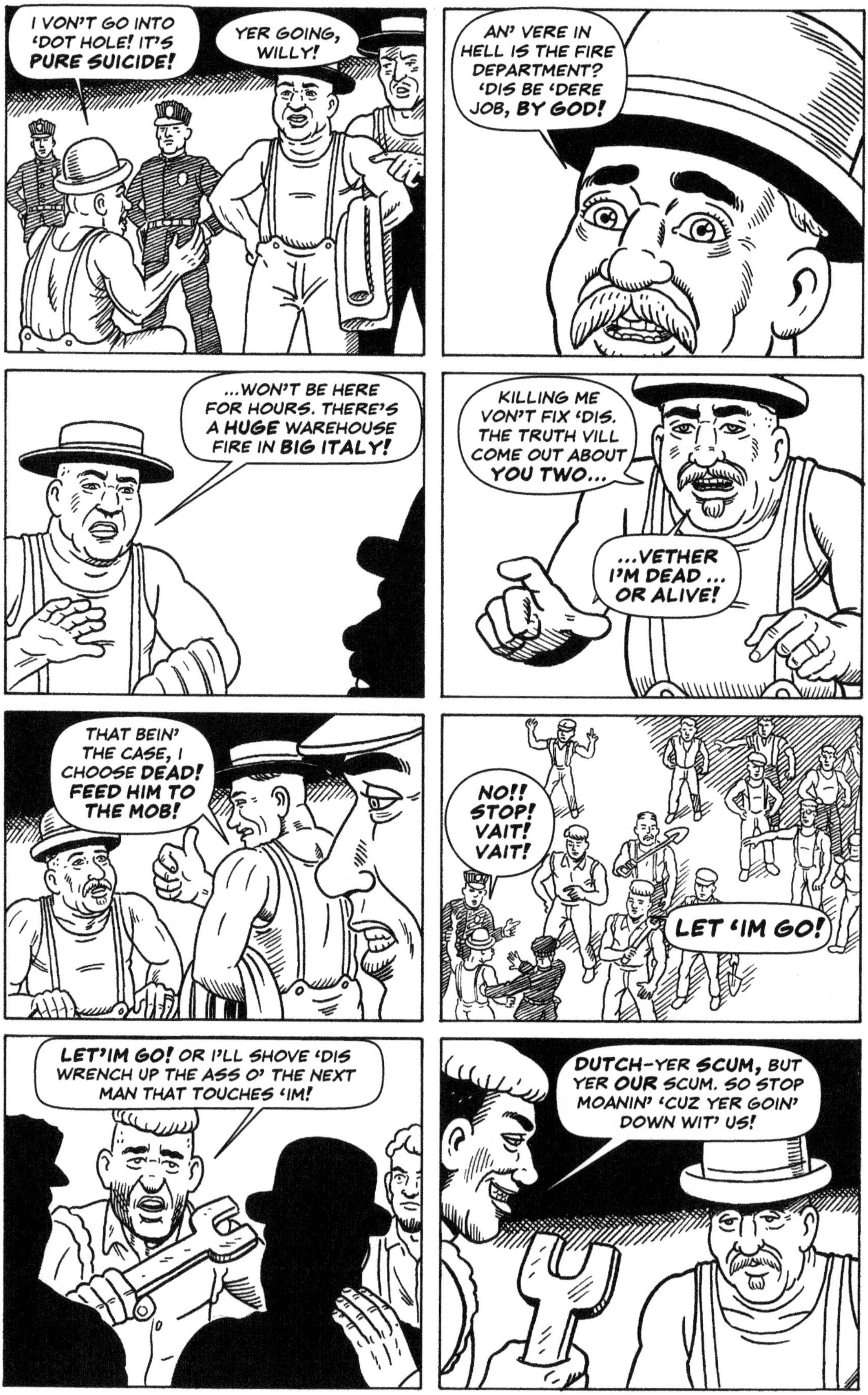
I VON'T GO INTO 'DOT HOLE! IT'S PURE SUICIDE!
YER GOING, WILLY!
AN' VERE IN HELL IS THE FIRE DEPARTMENT? 'DIS BE 'DERE JOB, BY GOD!
...WON'T BE HERE FOR HOURS. THERE'S A HUGE WAREHOUSE FIRE IN BIG ITALY!
KILLING ME VON'T FIX 'DIS. THE TRUTH VILL COME OUT ABOUT YOU TWO...
...VETHER I'M DEAD ... OR ALIVE!
THAT BEIN' THE CASE, I CHOOSE DEAD! FEED HIM TO THE MOB!
NO!! STOP! VAIT! VAIT!
LET 'IM GO!
LET'IM GO! OR I'LL SHOVE 'DIS WRENCH UP THE ASS O' THE NEXT MAN THAT TOUCHES 'IM!
DUTCH-YER SCUM, BUT YER OUR SCUM. SO STOP MOANIN' 'CUZ YER GOIN' DOWN WIT' US!

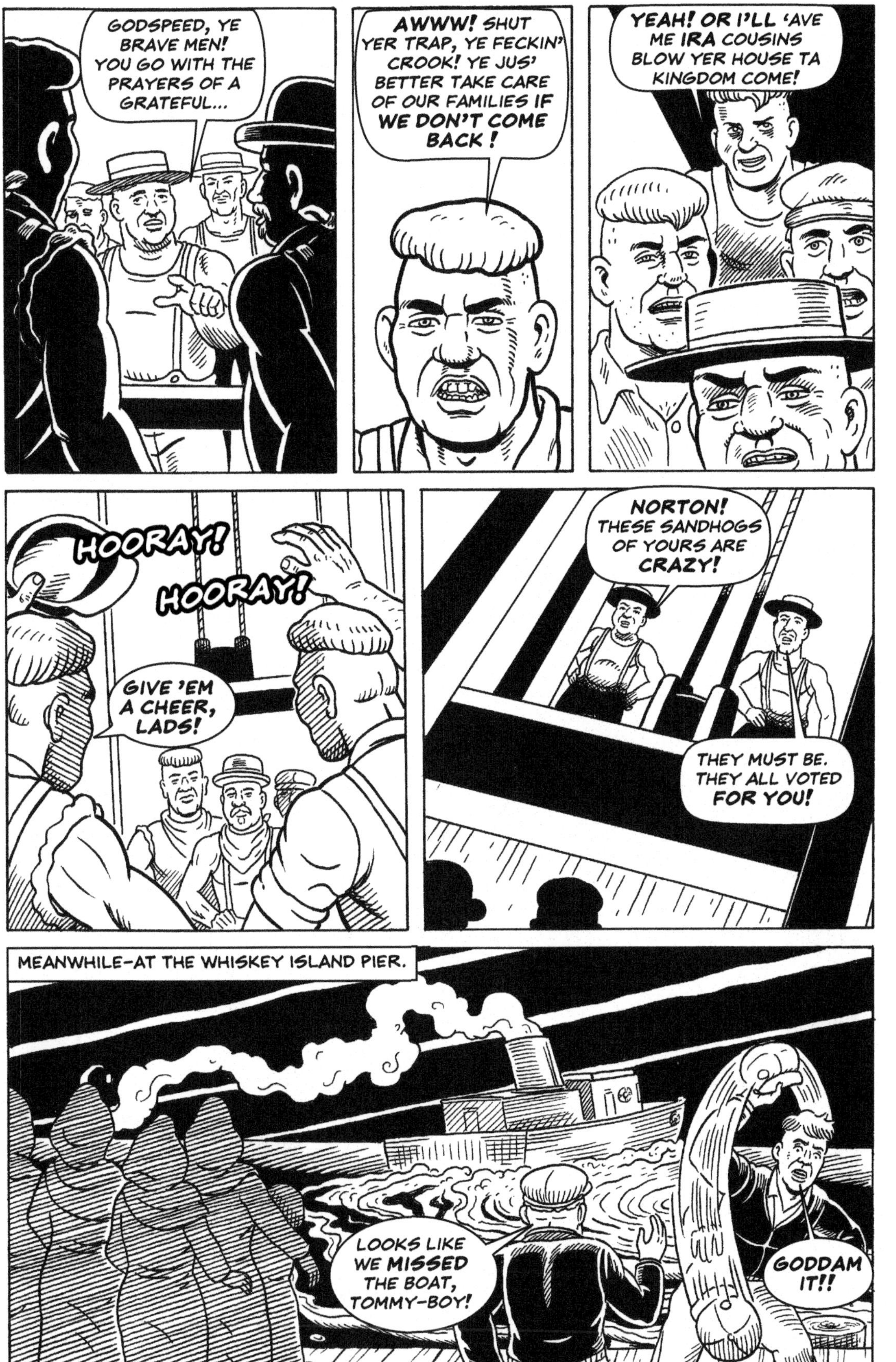
GODSPEED, YE BRAVE MEN! YOU GO WITH THE PRAYERS OF A GRATEFUL...
AWWW! SHUT YER TRAP, YE FECKIN' CROOK! YE JUS' BETTER TAKE CARE OF OUR FAMILIES IF WE DON'T COME BACK!
YEAH! OR I'LL 'AVE ME IRA COUSINS BLOW YER HOUSE TA KINGDOM COME!
HOORAY!
HOORAY!
GIVE 'EM A CHEER, LADS!
NORTON! THESE SANDHOGS OF YOURS ARE CRAZY!
THEY MUST BE. THEY ALL VOTED FOR YOU!
MEANWHILE-AT THE WHISKEY ISLAND PIER.
LOOKS LIKE WE MISSED THE BOAT, TOMMY-BOY!
GODDAM IT!!

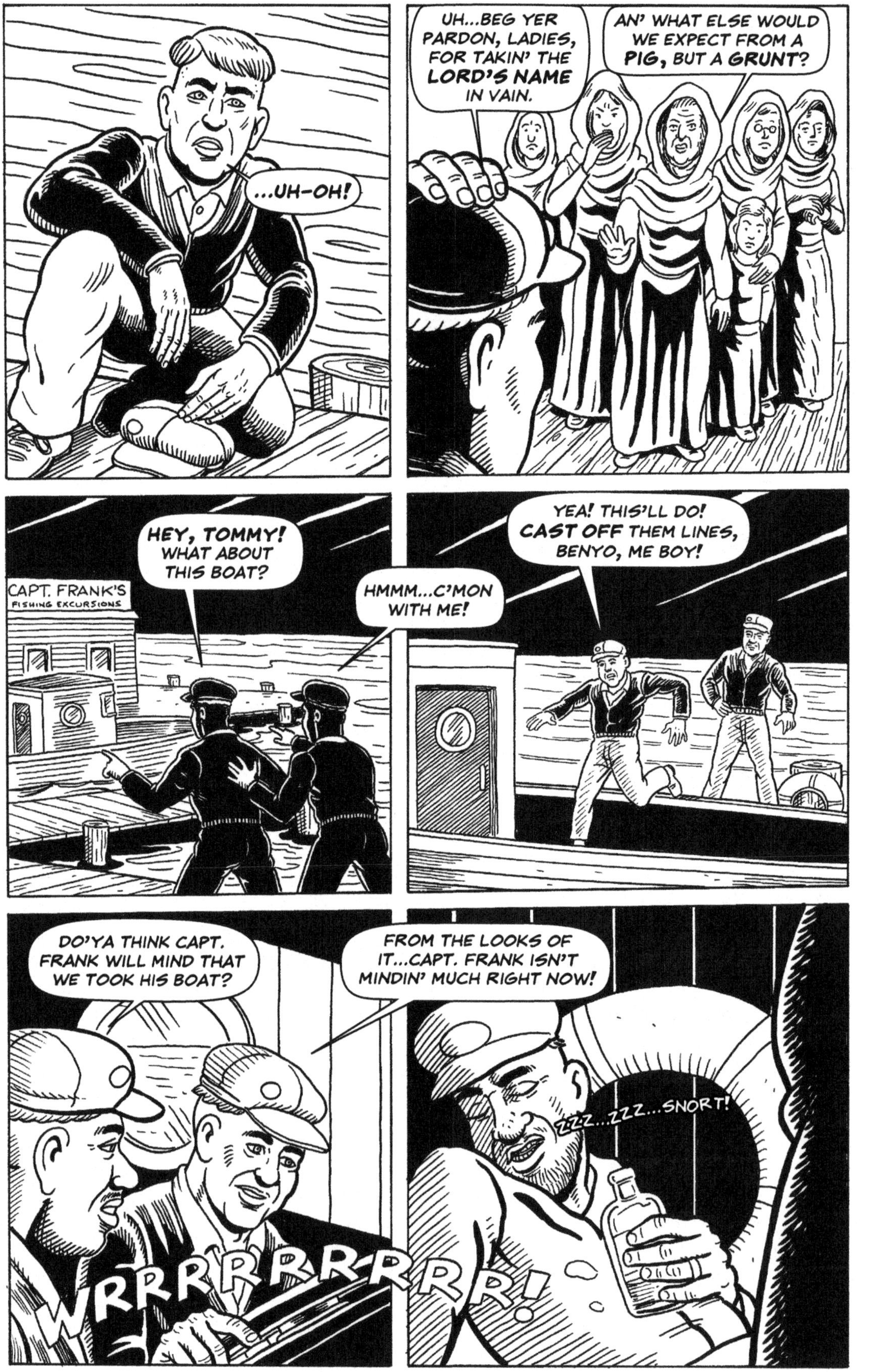
...UH-OH!
UH...BEG YER PARDON, LADIES, FOR TAKIN' THE LORD'S NAME IN VAIN.
AN' WHAT ELSE WOULD WE EXPECT FROM A PIG, BUT A GRUNT?
CAPT. FRANK'S FISHING EXCURSIONS
HEY, TOMMY! WHAT ABOUT THIS BOAT?
HMMM...C'MON WITH ME!
YEA! THIS'LL DO! CAST OFF THEM LINES, BENYO, ME BOY!
DO'YA THINK CAPT. FRANK WILL MIND THAT WE TOOK HIS BOAT?
FROM THE LOOKS OF IT...CAPT. FRANK ISN'T MINDIN' MUCH RIGHT NOW!
WRRRRRRRRRRR!
ZZZ...ZZZ...SNORT!

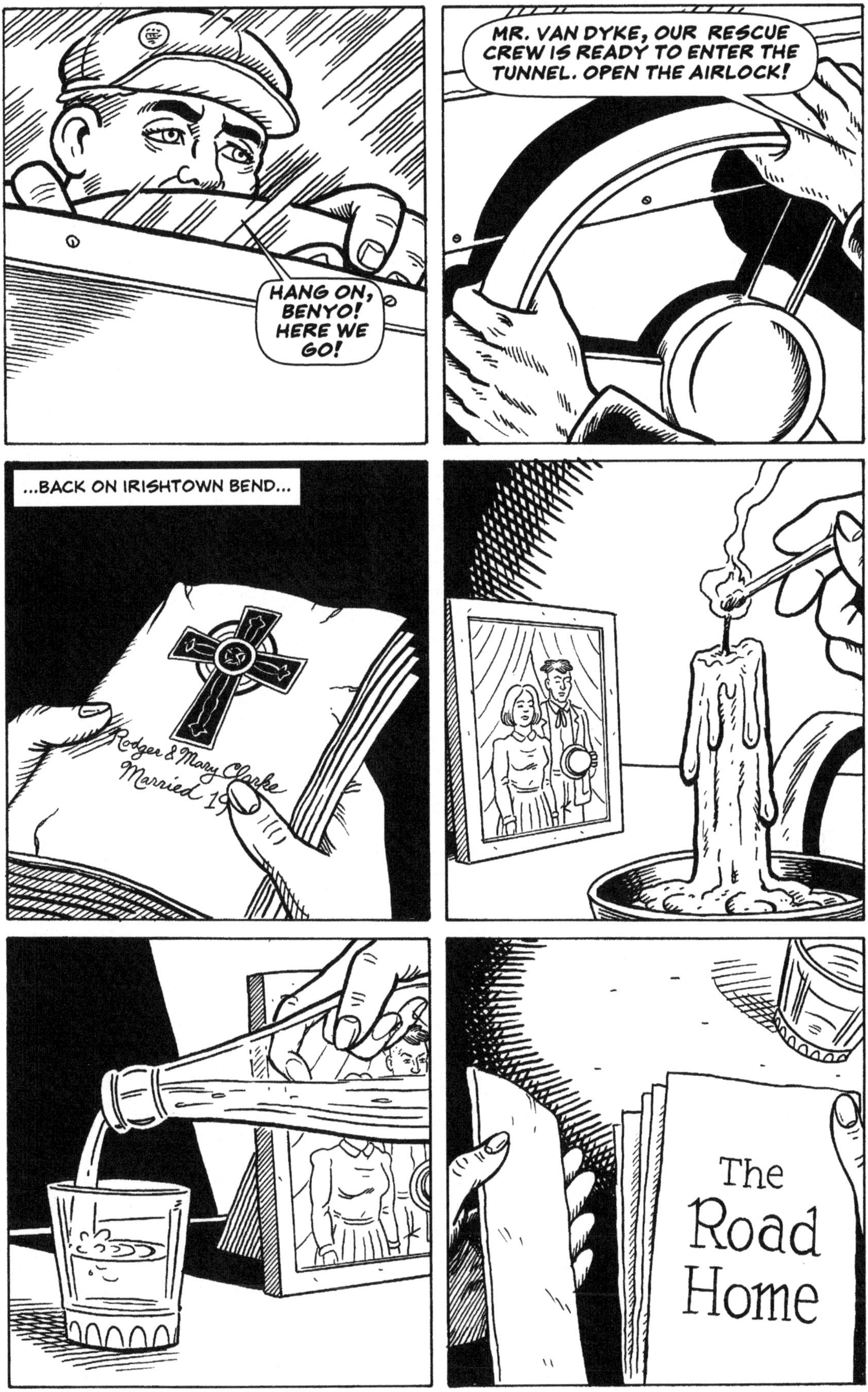
HANG ON, BENYO! HERE WE GO!
MR. VAN DYKE, OUR RESCUE CREW IS READY TO ENTER THE TUNNEL. OPEN THE AIRLOCK!
...BACK ON IRISHTOWN BEND...
Rodger & Mary Clarke
Married 19
The Road Home

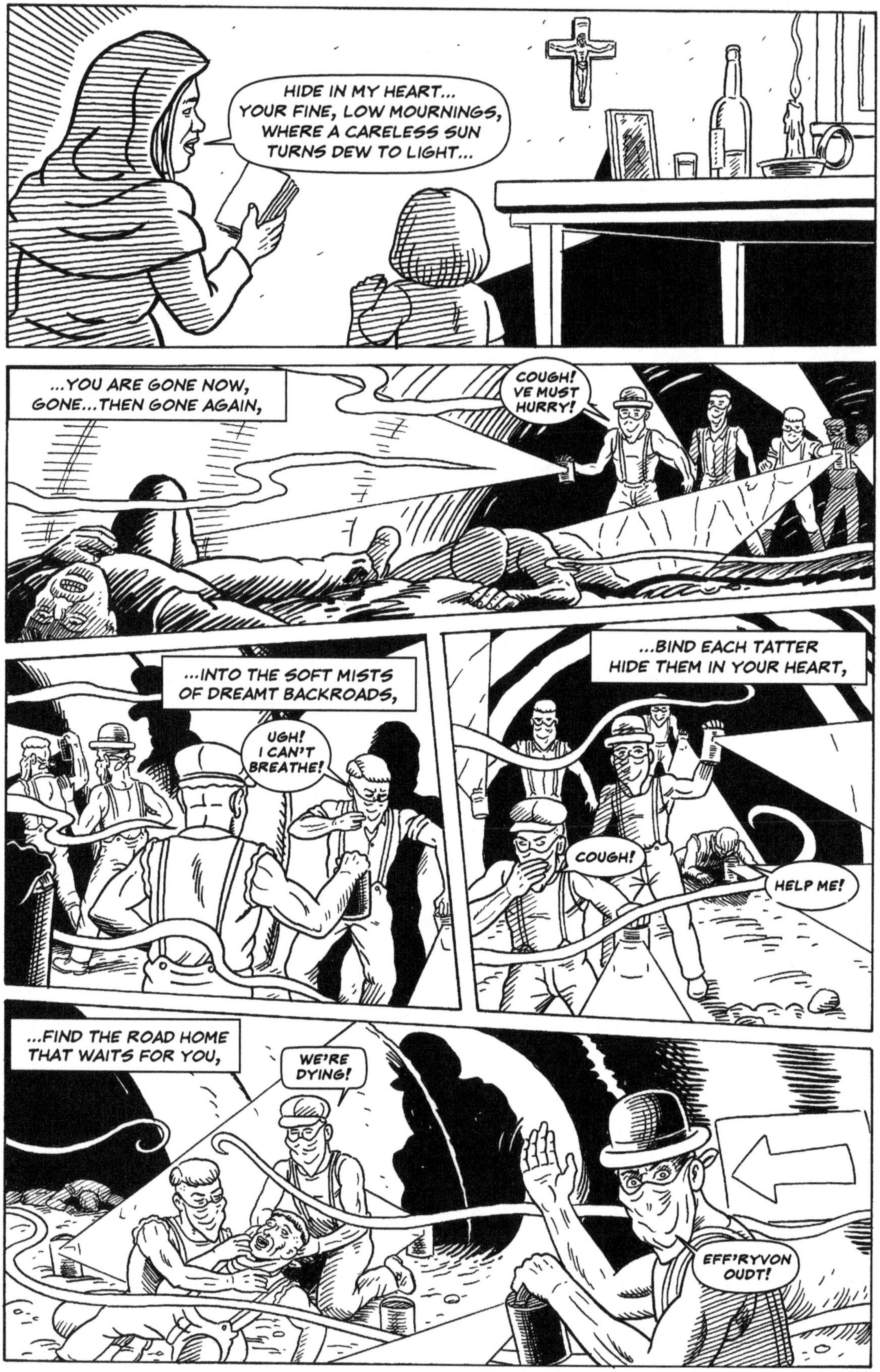
HIDE IN MY HEART... YOUR FINE, LOW MOURNINGS, WHERE A CARELESS SUN TURNS DEW TO LIGHT...
...YOU ARE GONE NOW, GONE...THEN GONE AGAIN,
COUGH! VE MUST HURRY!
...INTO THE SOFT MISTS OF DREAMT BACKROADS,
UGH! I CAN'T BREATHE!
...BIND EACH TATTER HIDE THEM IN YOUR HEART,
COUGH!
HELP ME!
...FIND THE ROAD HOME THAT WAITS FOR YOU,
WE'RE DYING!
EFF'RYVON OUDT!

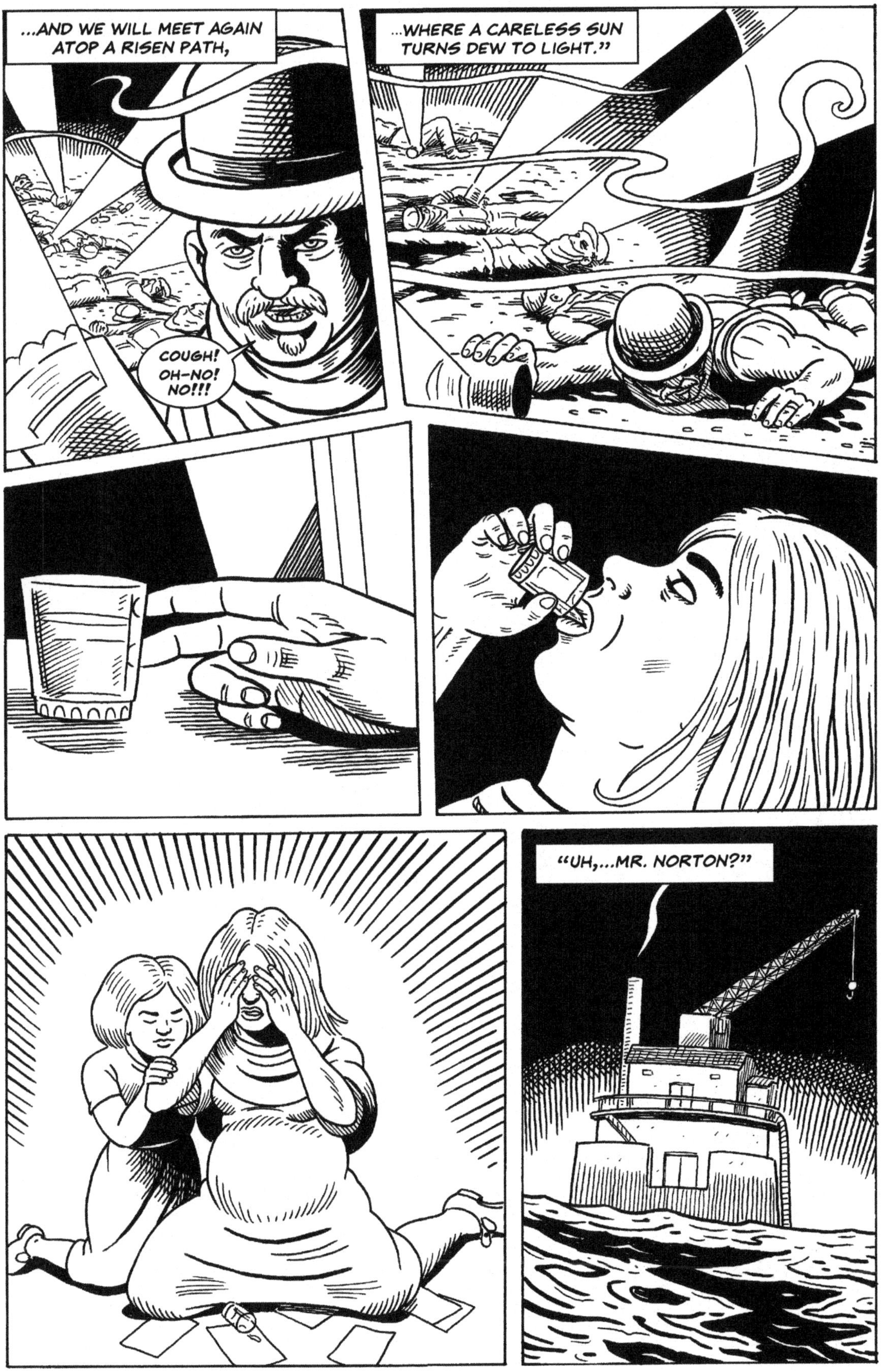
...AND WE WILL MEET AGAIN ATOP A RISEN PATH,
COUGH! OH-NO! NO!!!
...WHERE A CARELESS SUN TURNS DEW TO LIGHT."
"UH,...MR. NORTON?"

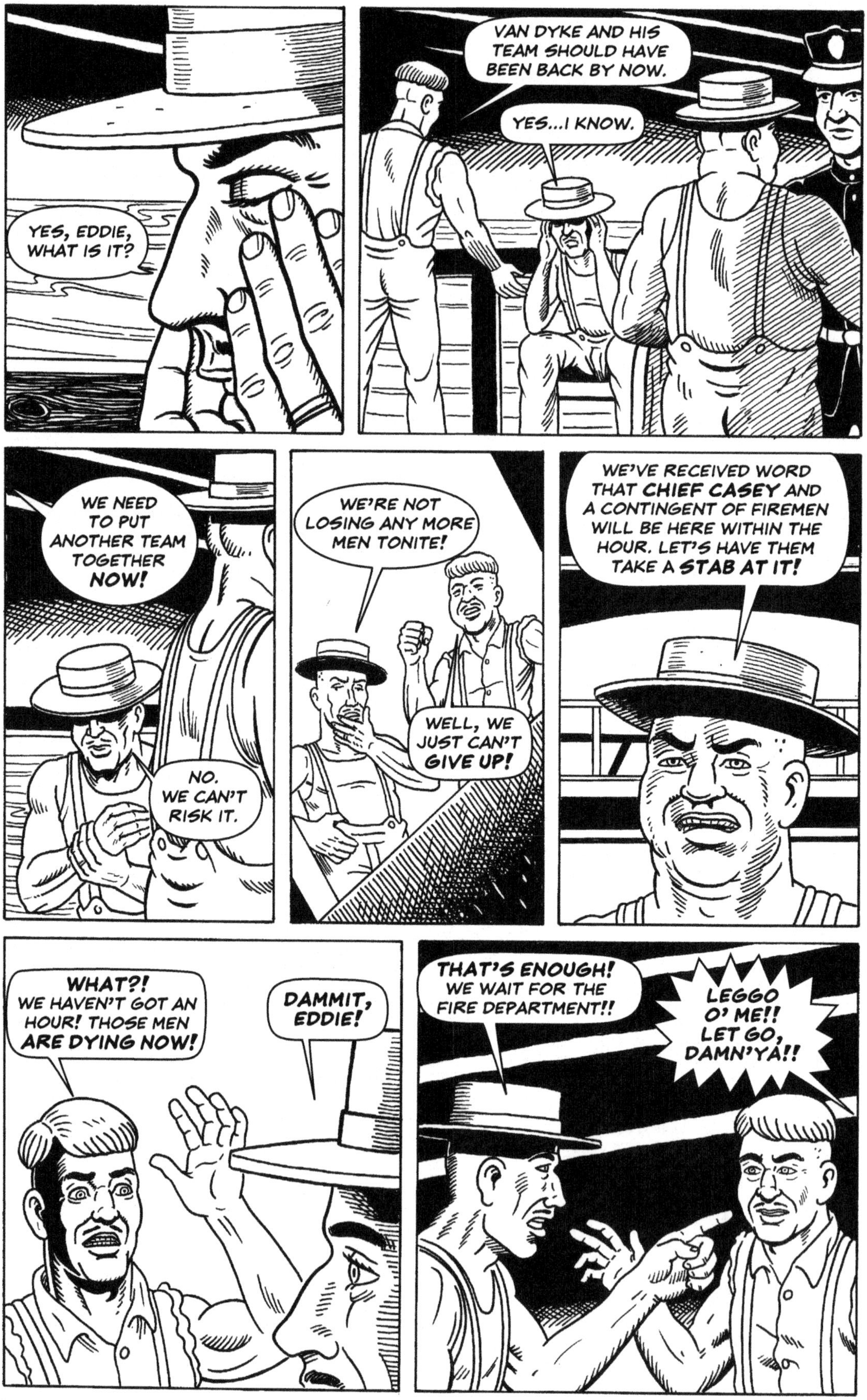
YES, EDDIE, WHAT IS IT?
VAN DYKE AND HIS TEAM SHOULD HAVE BEEN BACK BY NOW.
YES...I KNOW.
WE NEED TO PUT ANOTHER TEAM TOGETHER NOW!
NO. WE CAN'T RISK IT.
WE'RE NOT LOSING ANY MORE MEN TONITE!
WELL, WE JUST CAN'T GIVE UP!
WE'VE RECEIVED WORD THAT CHIEF CASEY AND A CONTINGENT OF FIREMEN WILL BE HERE WITHIN THE HOUR. LET'S HAVE THEM TAKE A STAB AT IT!
WHAT?! WE HAVEN'T GOT AN HOUR! THOSE MEN ARE DYING NOW!
DAMMIT, EDDIE!
THAT'S ENOUGH! WE WAIT FOR THE FIRE DEPARTMENT!!
LEGGO O' ME!! LET GO, DAMN'YA!!

HEY! MR. NORTON!!

GEEZIZ! WHAT'S HE DOING HERE?!

WHERE'S WILLY? MY MA SAYS YOU GUYS ARE TRYIN' TO KILL HIM!

HE'S IN THE TUNNEL.

HE LED A RESCUE TEAM DOWN AN HOUR AGO.

WHAT?!

TOMMY, I'M GOING TO LEVEL WITH YOU BUT YOU MUST STAY CALM! CAN YOU DO THAT?

SURE, I S'POSE.

BECAUSE I HAVE NEWS THAT YOU'LL HAVE TO TAKE LIKE A MAN.

C'MON 'N SPILL IT ALREADY!

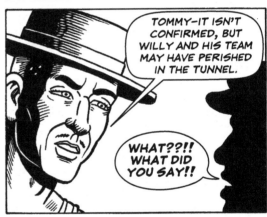

TOMMY—IT ISN'T CONFIRMED, BUT WILLY AND HIS TEAM MAY HAVE PERISHED IN THE TUNNEL.

WHAT??!! WHAT DID YOU SAY!!

WE THINK THEY WERE OVERCOME BY THE GAS. IF TRUE, THEN HE DIED A HERO!

NO!! NO!!

WILLY! NOOOOOOO!!

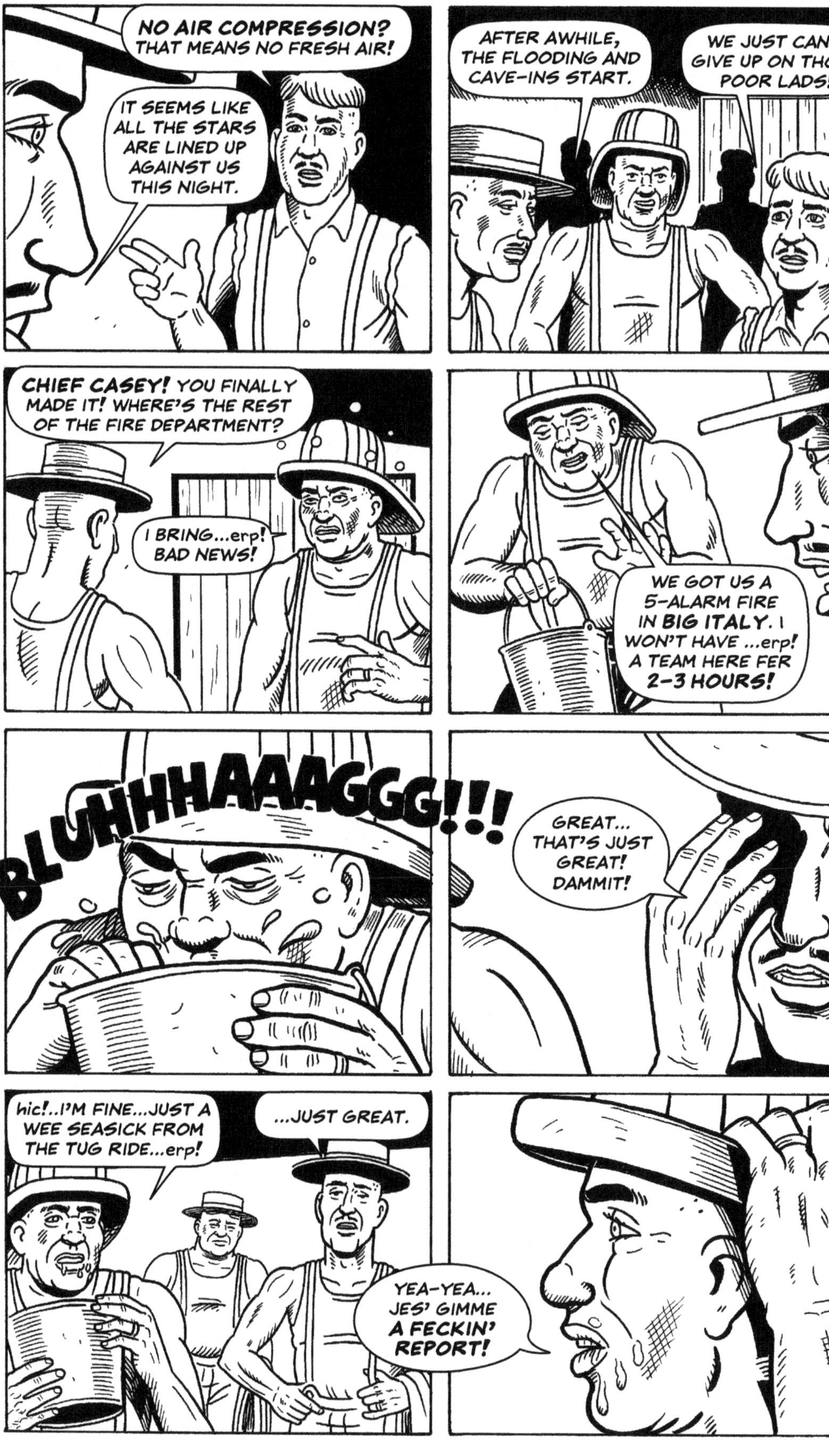
NO AIR COMPRESSION? THAT MEANS NO FRESH AIR!
IT SEEMS LIKE ALL THE STARS ARE LINED UP AGAINST US THIS NIGHT.
AFTER AWHILE, THE FLOODING AND CAVE-INS START.
WE JUST CAN'T GIVE UP ON THOSE POOR LADS!
CHIEF CASEY! YOU FINALLY MADE IT! WHERE'S THE REST OF THE FIRE DEPARTMENT?
I BRING...erp! BAD NEWS!
WE GOT US A 5-ALARM FIRE IN BIG ITALY. I WON'T HAVE ...erp! A TEAM HERE FER 2-3 HOURS!
BLUHHHAAAGGG!!!
GREAT... THAT'S JUST GREAT! DAMMIT!
hic!..I'M FINE...JUST A WEE SEASICK FROM THE TUG RIDE...erp!
...JUST GREAT.
YEA-YEA... JES' GIMME A FECKIN' REPORT!

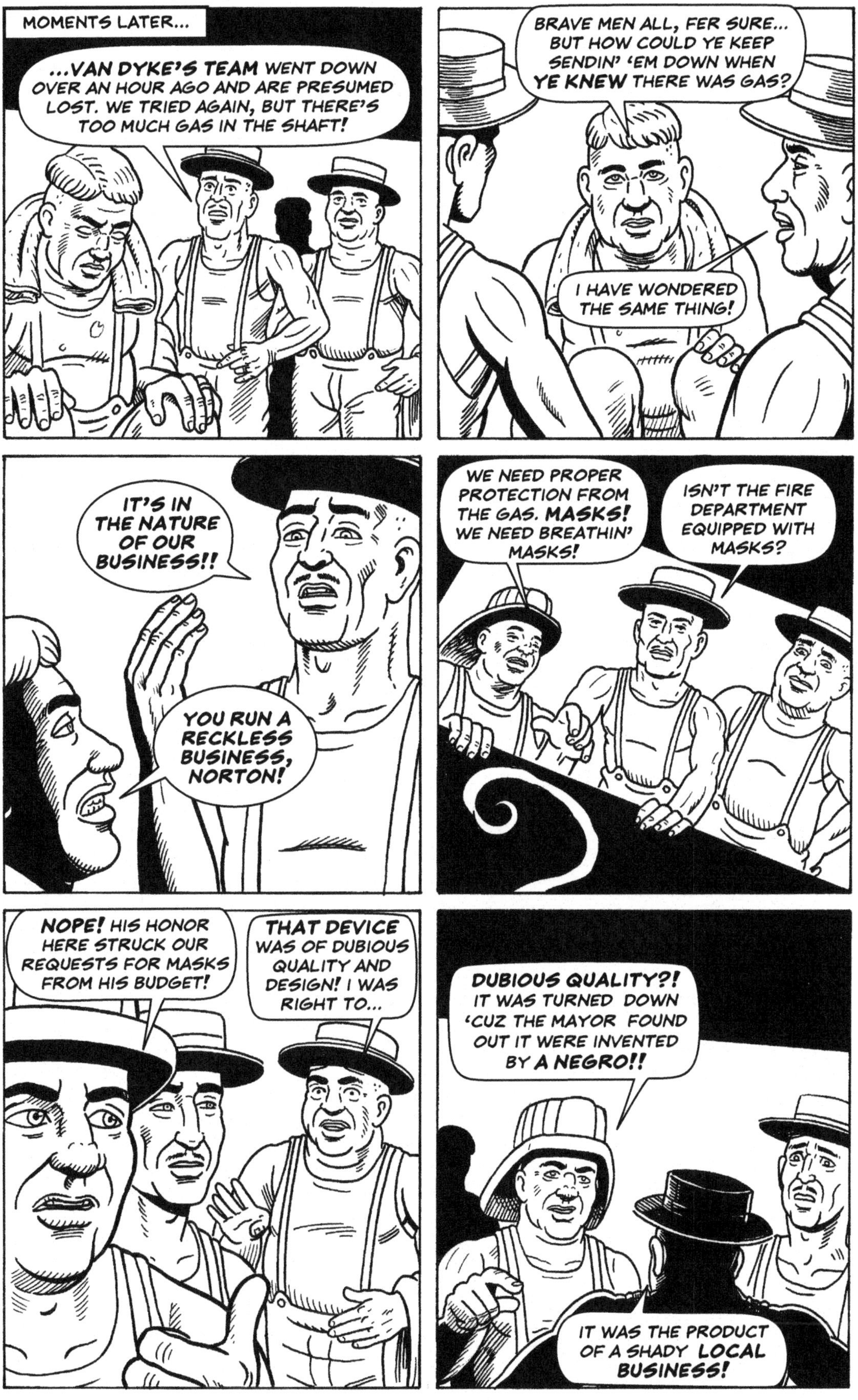
MOMENTS LATER...
...VAN DYKE'S TEAM WENT DOWN OVER AN HOUR AGO AND ARE PRESUMED LOST. WE TRIED AGAIN, BUT THERE'S TOO MUCH GAS IN THE SHAFT!
BRAVE MEN ALL, FER SURE... BUT HOW COULD YE KEEP SENDIN' 'EM DOWN WHEN YE KNEW THERE WAS GAS?
I HAVE WONDERED THE SAME THING!
IT'S IN THE NATURE OF OUR BUSINESS!!
YOU RUN A RECKLESS BUSINESS, NORTON!
WE NEED PROPER PROTECTION FROM THE GAS. MASKS! WE NEED BREATHIN' MASKS!
ISN'T THE FIRE DEPARTMENT EQUIPPED WITH MASKS?
NOPE! HIS HONOR HERE STRUCK OUR REQUESTS FOR MASKS FROM HIS BUDGET!
THAT DEVICE WAS OF DUBIOUS QUALITY AND DESIGN! I WAS RIGHT TO...
DUBIOUS QUALITY?! IT WAS TURNED DOWN 'CUZ THE MAYOR FOUND OUT IT WERE INVENTED BY A NEGRO!!
IT WAS THE PRODUCT OF A SHADY LOCAL BUSINESS!

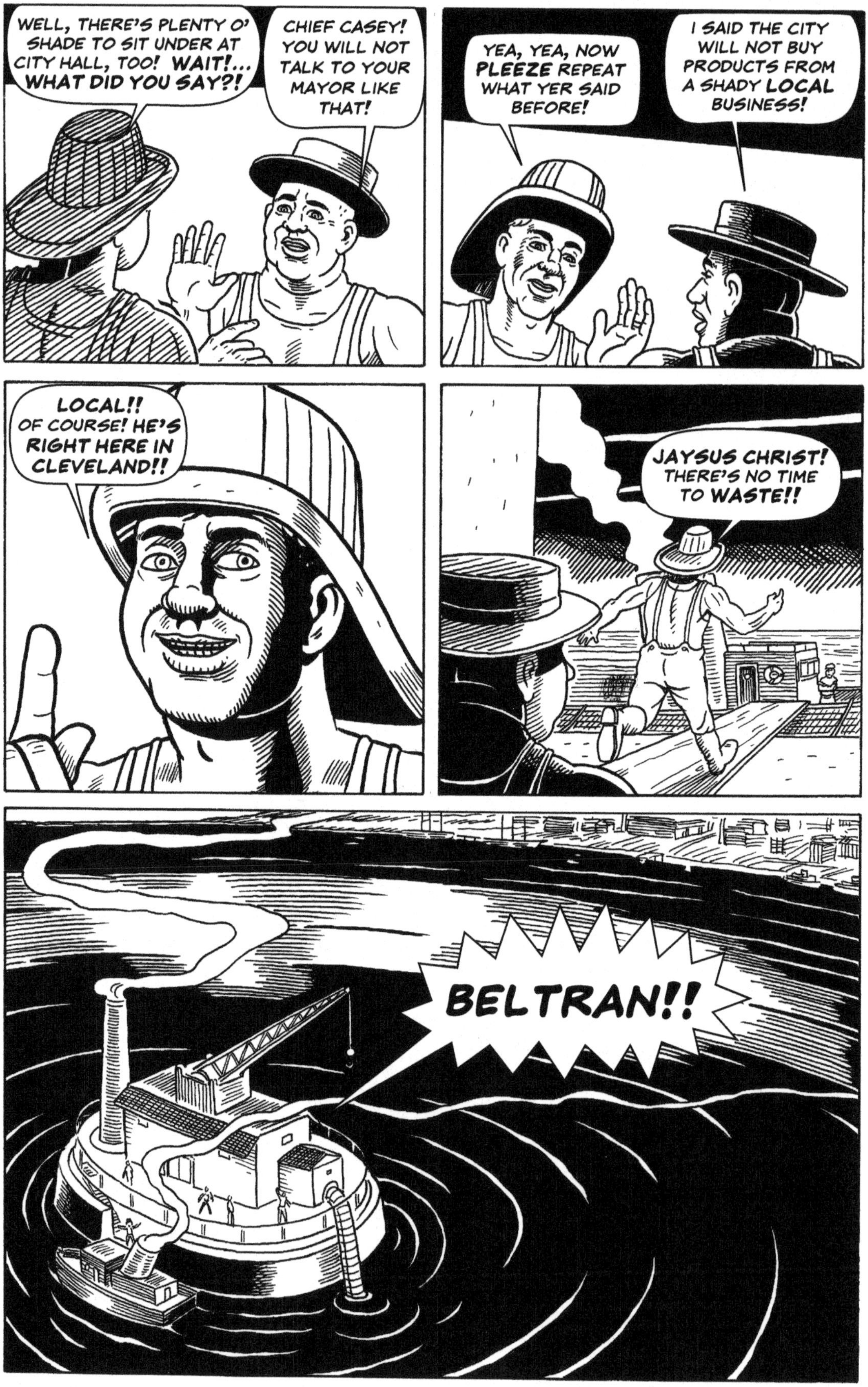
WELL, THERE'S PLENTY O' SHADE TO SIT UNDER AT CITY HALL, TOO! WAIT!... WHAT DID YOU SAY?!
CHIEF CASEY! YOU WILL NOT TALK TO YOUR MAYOR LIKE THAT!
YEA, YEA, NOW PLEEZE REPEAT WHAT YER SAID BEFORE!
I SAID THE CITY WILL NOT BUY PRODUCTS FROM A SHADY LOCAL BUSINESS!
LOCAL!! OF COURSE! HE'S RIGHT HERE IN CLEVELAND!!
JAYSUS CHRIST! THERE'S NO TIME TO WASTE!!
BELTRAN!!

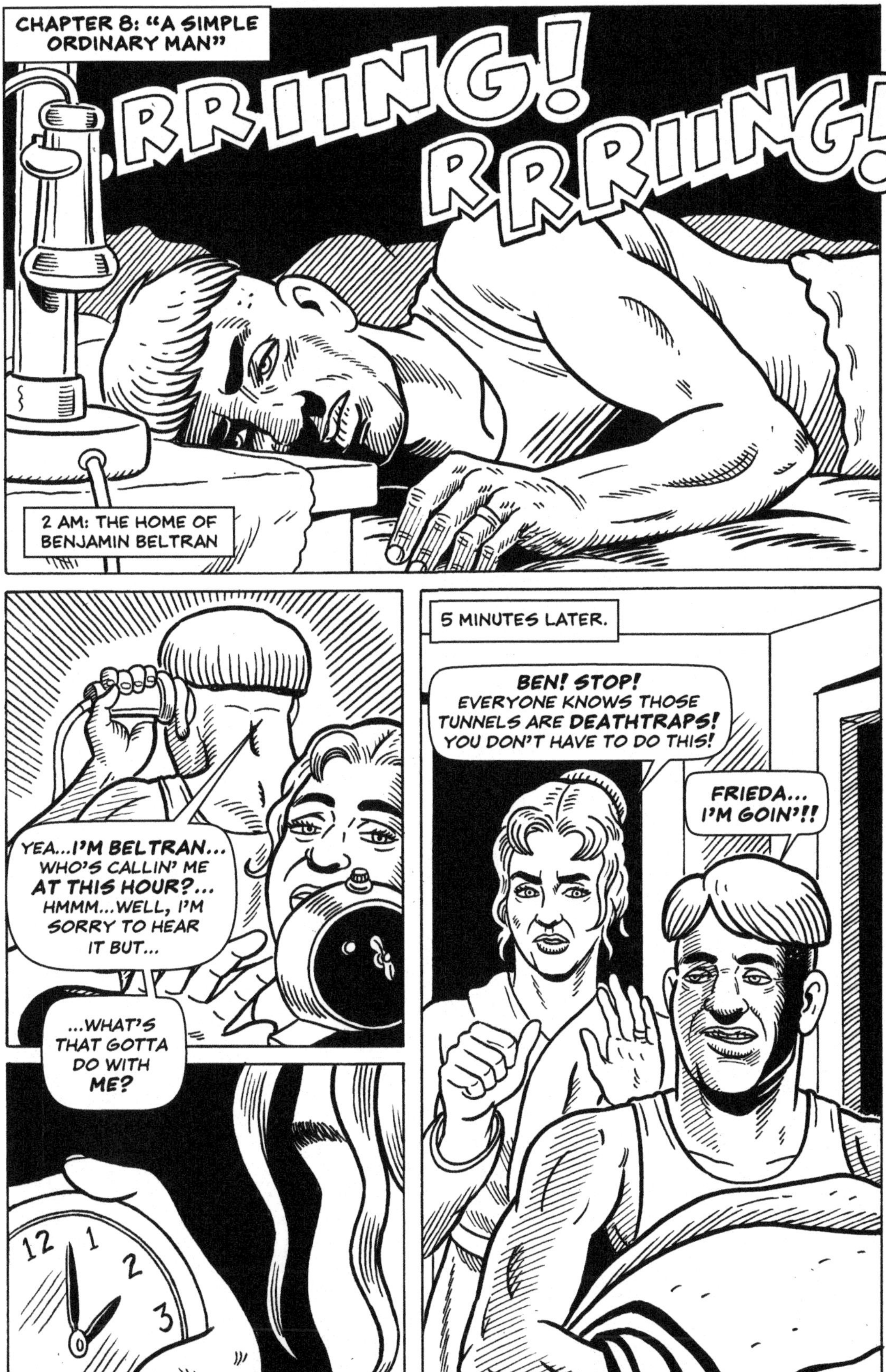
CHAPTER 8: "A SIMPLE ORDINARY MAN"
RRIING! RRRIING!
2 AM: THE HOME OF BENJAMIN BELTRAN
YEA...I'M BELTRAN... WHO'S CALLIN' ME AT THIS HOUR?... HMMM...WELL, I'M SORRY TO HEAR IT BUT...
...WHAT'S THAT GOTTA DO WITH ME?
5 MINUTES LATER.
BEN! STOP! EVERYONE KNOWS THOSE TUNNELS ARE DEATHTRAPS! YOU DON'T HAVE TO DO THIS!
FRIEDA... I'M GOIN'!!

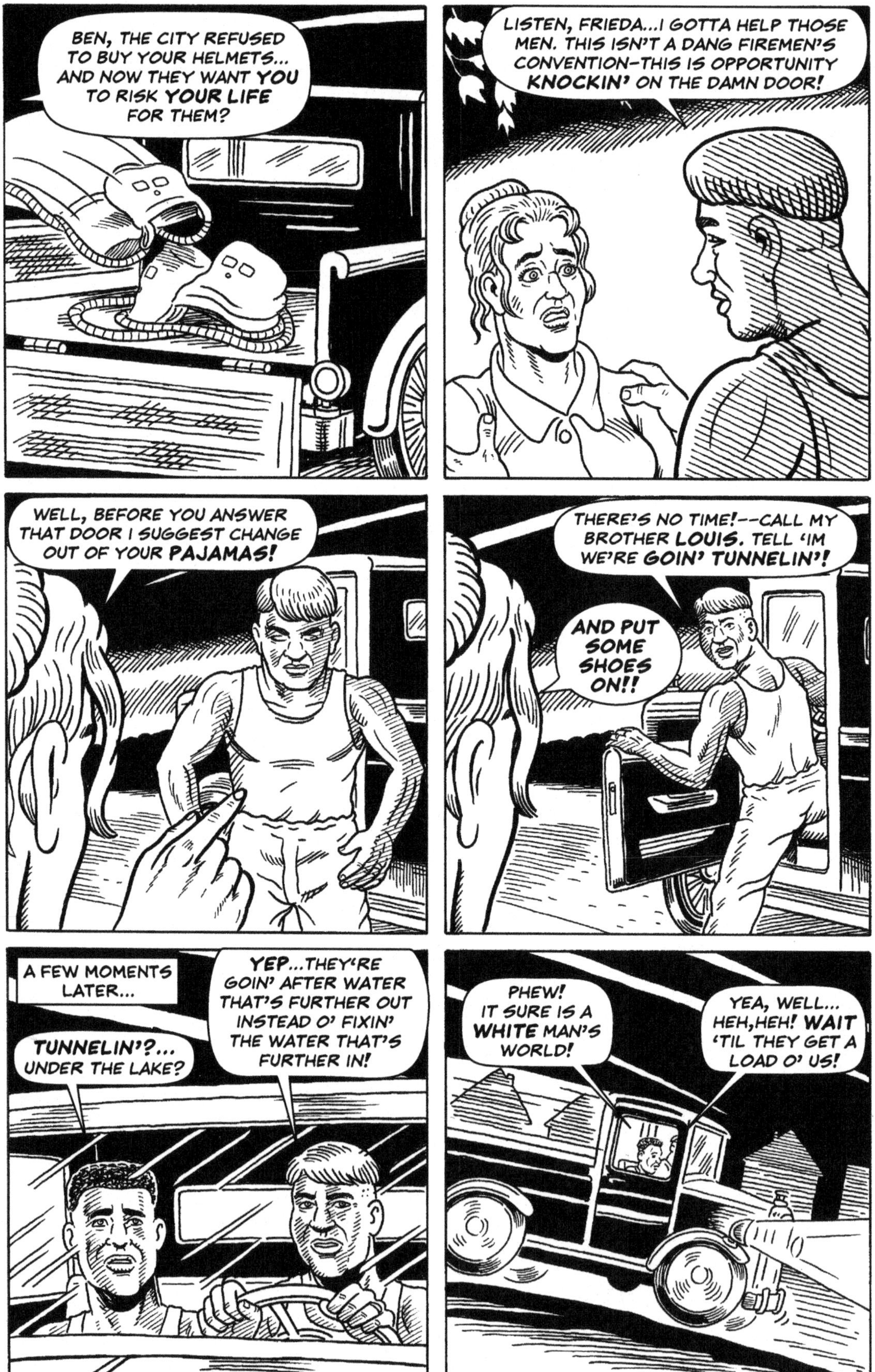
BEN, THE CITY REFUSED TO BUY YOUR HELMETS... AND NOW THEY WANT YOU TO RISK YOUR LIFE FOR THEM?
LISTEN, FRIEDA...I GOTTA HELP THOSE MEN. THIS ISN'T A DANG FIREMEN'S CONVENTION–THIS IS OPPORTUNITY KNOCKIN' ON THE DAMN DOOR!
WELL, BEFORE YOU ANSWER THAT DOOR I SUGGEST CHANGE OUT OF YOUR PAJAMAS!
THERE'S NO TIME!--CALL MY BROTHER LOUIS. TELL 'IM WE'RE GOIN' TUNNELIN'!
AND PUT SOME SHOES ON!!
A FEW MOMENTS LATER...
TUNNELIN'?... UNDER THE LAKE?
YEP...THEY'RE GOIN' AFTER WATER THAT'S FURTHER OUT INSTEAD O' FIXIN' THE WATER THAT'S FURTHER IN!
PHEW! IT SURE IS A WHITE MAN'S WORLD!
YEA, WELL... HEH,HEH! WAIT 'TIL THEY GET A LOAD O' US!

217

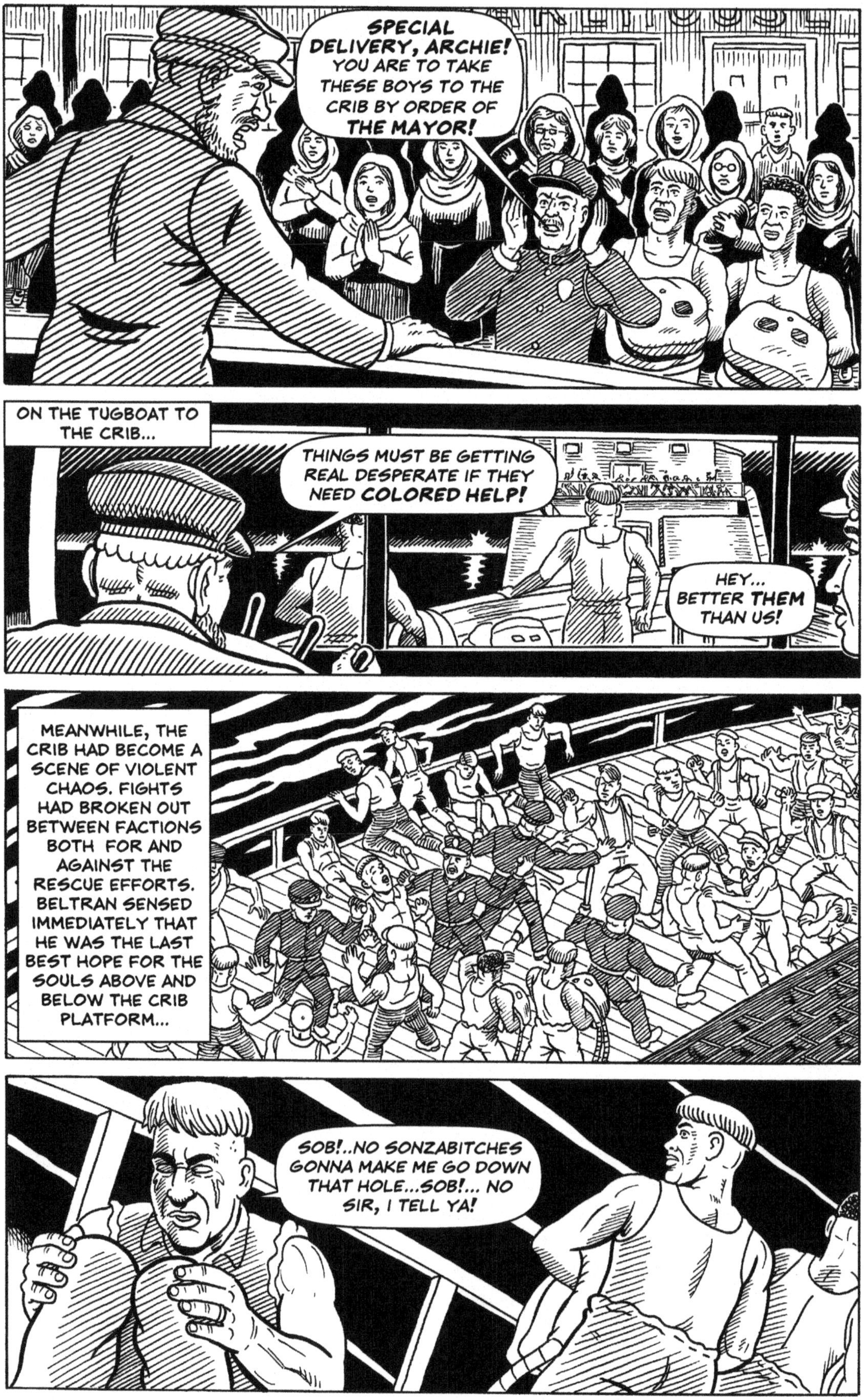

SPECIAL DELIVERY, ARCHIE! YOU ARE TO TAKE THESE BOYS TO THE CRIB BY ORDER OF THE MAYOR!
ON THE TUGBOAT TO THE CRIB...
THINGS MUST BE GETTING REAL DESPERATE IF THEY NEED COLORED HELP!
HEY... BETTER THEM THAN US!
MEANWHILE, THE CRIB HAD BECOME A SCENE OF VIOLENT CHAOS. FIGHTS HAD BROKEN OUT BETWEEN FACTIONS BOTH FOR AND AGAINST THE RESCUE EFFORTS. BELTRAN SENSED IMMEDIATELY THAT HE WAS THE LAST BEST HOPE FOR THE SOULS ABOVE AND BELOW THE CRIB PLATFORM...
SOB!..NO SONZABITCHES GONNA MAKE ME GO DOWN THAT HOLE...SOB!... NO SIR, I TELL YA!

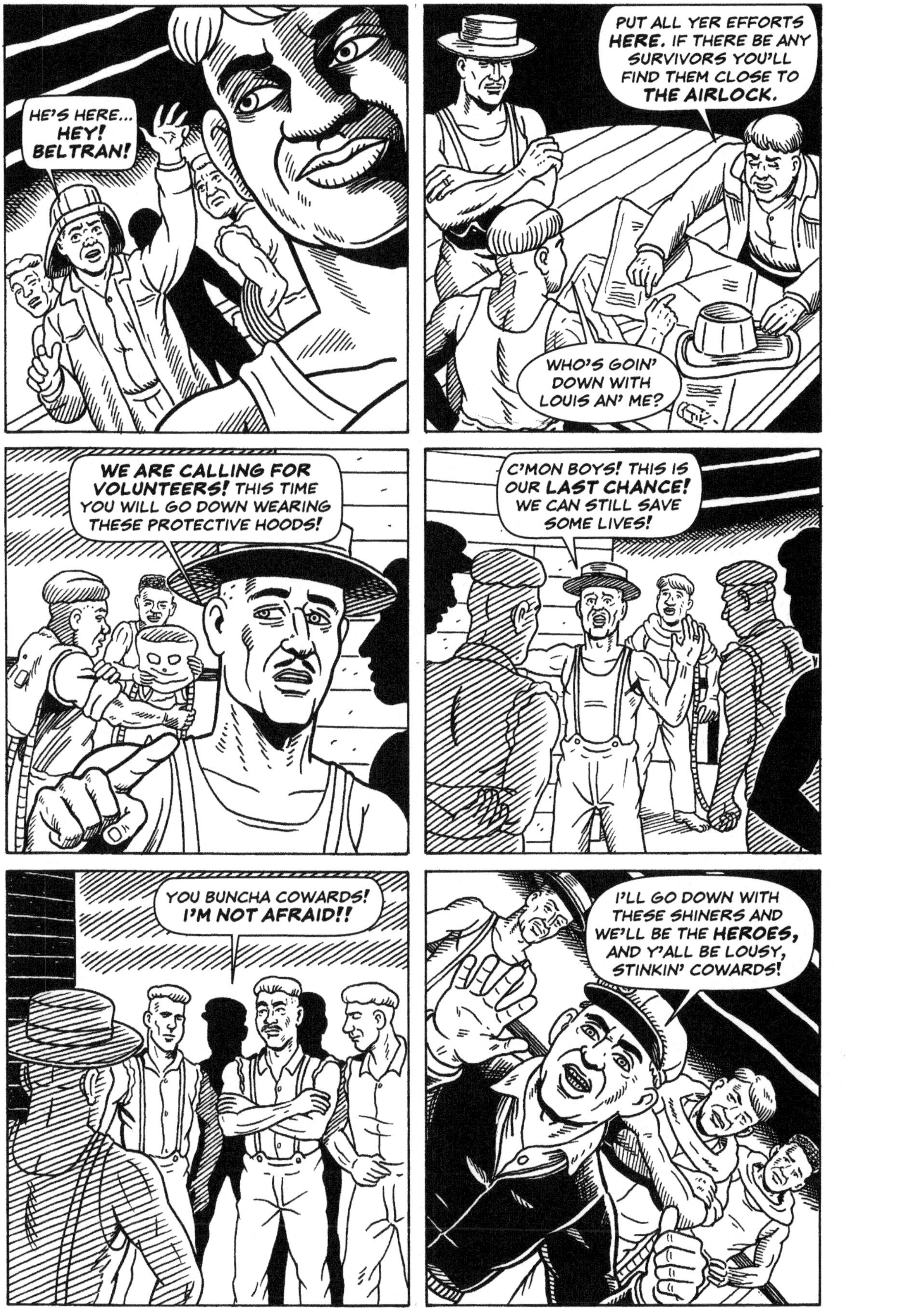
HE'S HERE... HEY! BELTRAN!
PUT ALL YER EFFORTS HERE. IF THERE BE ANY SURVIVORS YOU'LL FIND THEM CLOSE TO THE AIRLOCK.
WHO'S GOIN' DOWN WITH LOUIS AN' ME?
WE ARE CALLING FOR VOLUNTEERS! THIS TIME YOU WILL GO DOWN WEARING THESE PROTECTIVE HOODS!
C'MON BOYS! THIS IS OUR LAST CHANCE! WE CAN STILL SAVE SOME LIVES!
YOU BUNCHA COWARDS! I'M NOT AFRAID!!
I'LL GO DOWN WITH THESE SHINERS AND WE'LL BE THE HEROES, AND Y'ALL BE LOUSY, STINKIN' COWARDS!

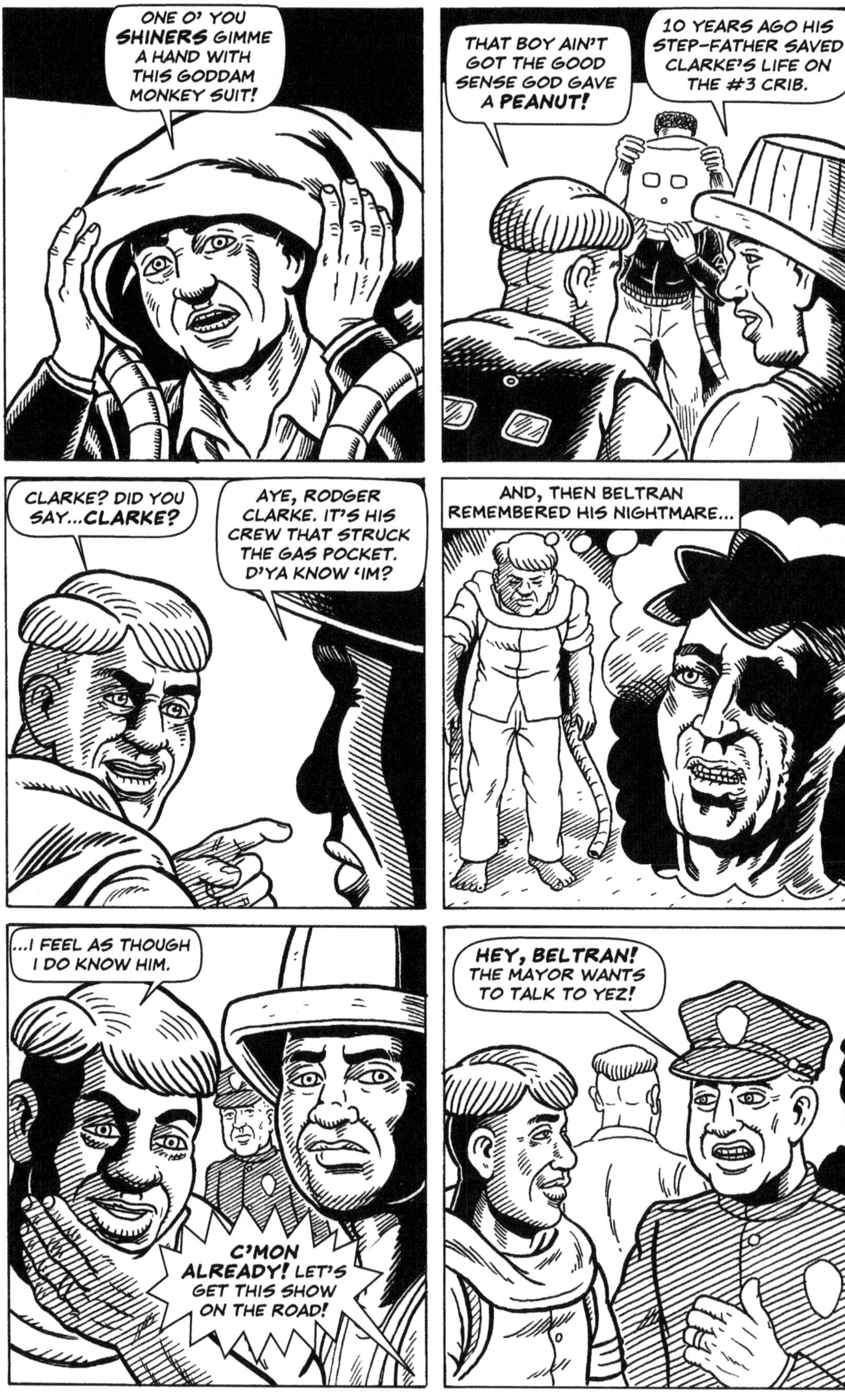
ONE O' YOU SHINERS GIMME A HAND WITH THIS GODDAM MONKEY SUIT!
THAT BOY AIN'T GOT THE GOOD SENSE GOD GAVE A PEANUT!
10 YEARS AGO HIS STEP-FATHER SAVED CLARKE'S LIFE ON THE #3 CRIB.
CLARKE? DID YOU SAY...CLARKE?
AYE, RODGER CLARKE. IT'S HIS CREW THAT STRUCK THE GAS POCKET. D'YA KNOW 'IM?
AND, THEN BELTRAN REMEMBERED HIS NIGHTMARE...
...I FEEL AS THOUGH I DO KNOW HIM.
C'MON ALREADY! LET'S GET THIS SHOW ON THE ROAD!
HEY, BELTRAN! THE MAYOR WANTS TO TALK TO YEZ!

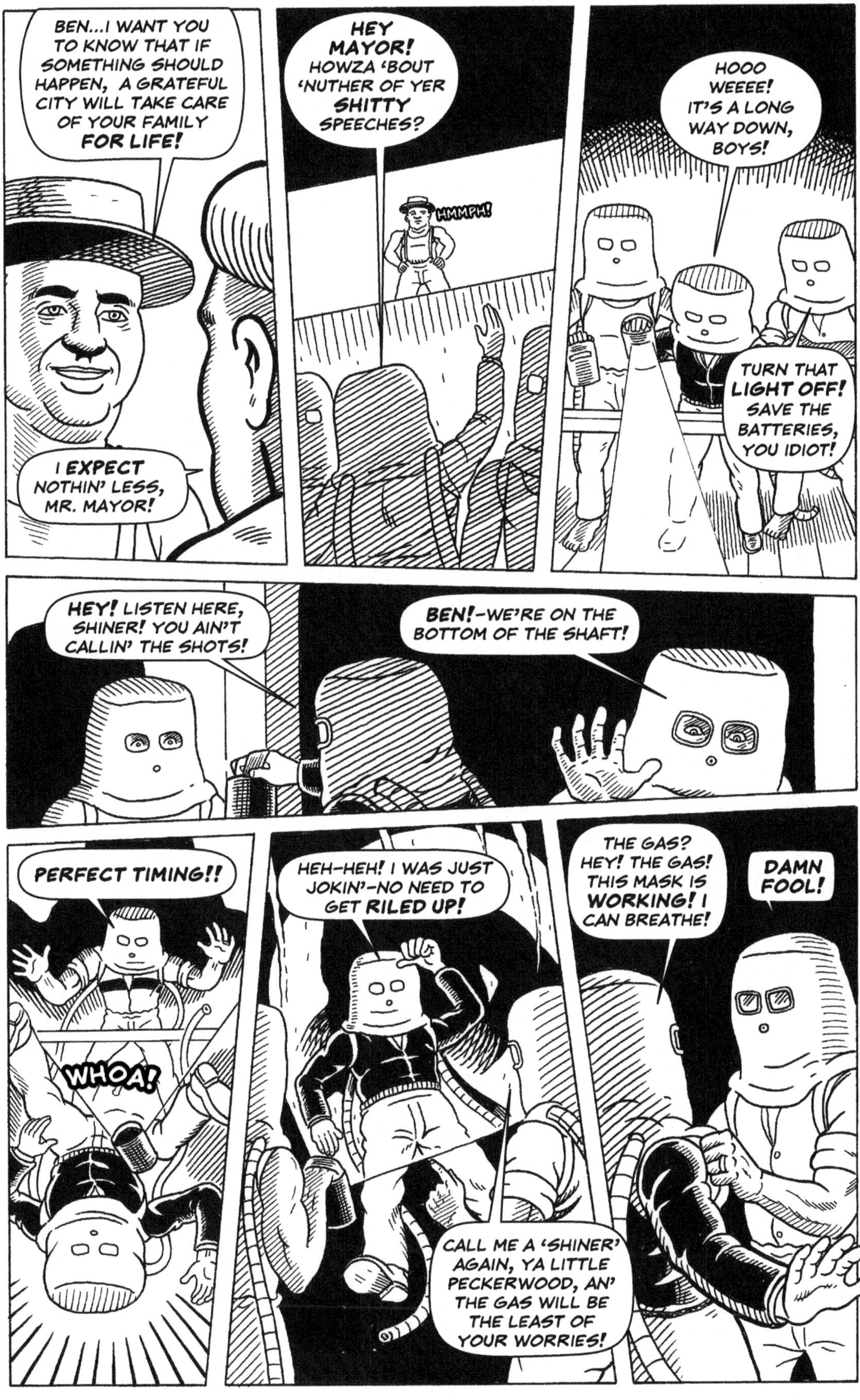
BEN...I WANT YOU TO KNOW THAT IF SOMETHING SHOULD HAPPEN, A GRATEFUL CITY WILL TAKE CARE OF YOUR FAMILY FOR LIFE!
I EXPECT NOTHIN' LESS, MR. MAYOR!
HEY MAYOR! HOWZA 'BOUT 'NUTHER OF YER SHITTY SPEECHES?
HMMPH!
HOOO WEEEE! IT'S A LONG WAY DOWN, BOYS!
TURN THAT LIGHT OFF! SAVE THE BATTERIES, YOU IDIOT!
HEY! LISTEN HERE, SHINER! YOU AIN'T CALLIN' THE SHOTS!
BEN!-WE'RE ON THE BOTTOM OF THE SHAFT!
PERFECT TIMING!!
WHOA!
HEH-HEH! I WAS JUST JOKIN'-NO NEED TO GET RILED UP!
CALL ME A 'SHINER' AGAIN, YA LITTLE PECKERWOOD, AN' THE GAS WILL BE THE LEAST OF YOUR WORRIES!
THE GAS? HEY! THE GAS! THIS MASK IS WORKING! I CAN BREATHE!
DAMN FOOL!

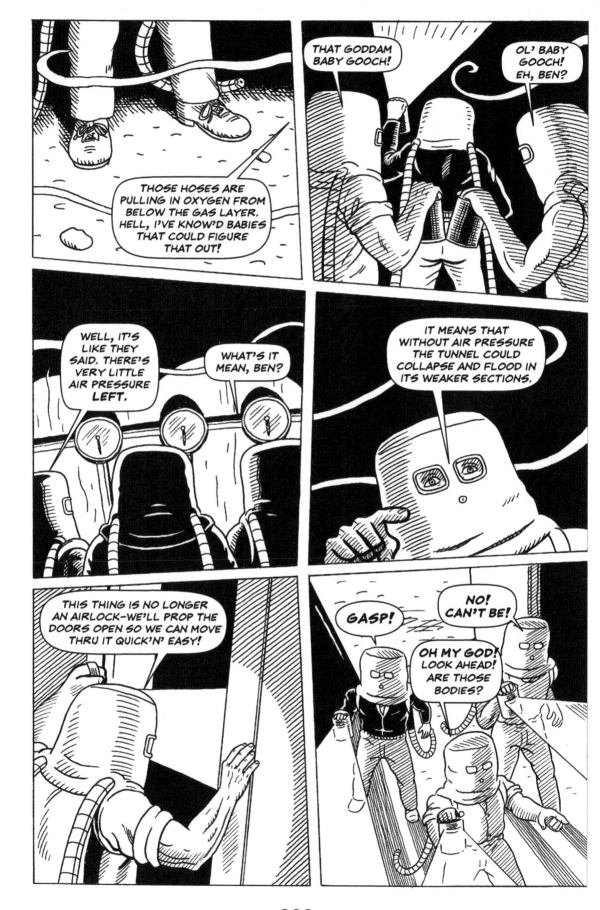

222

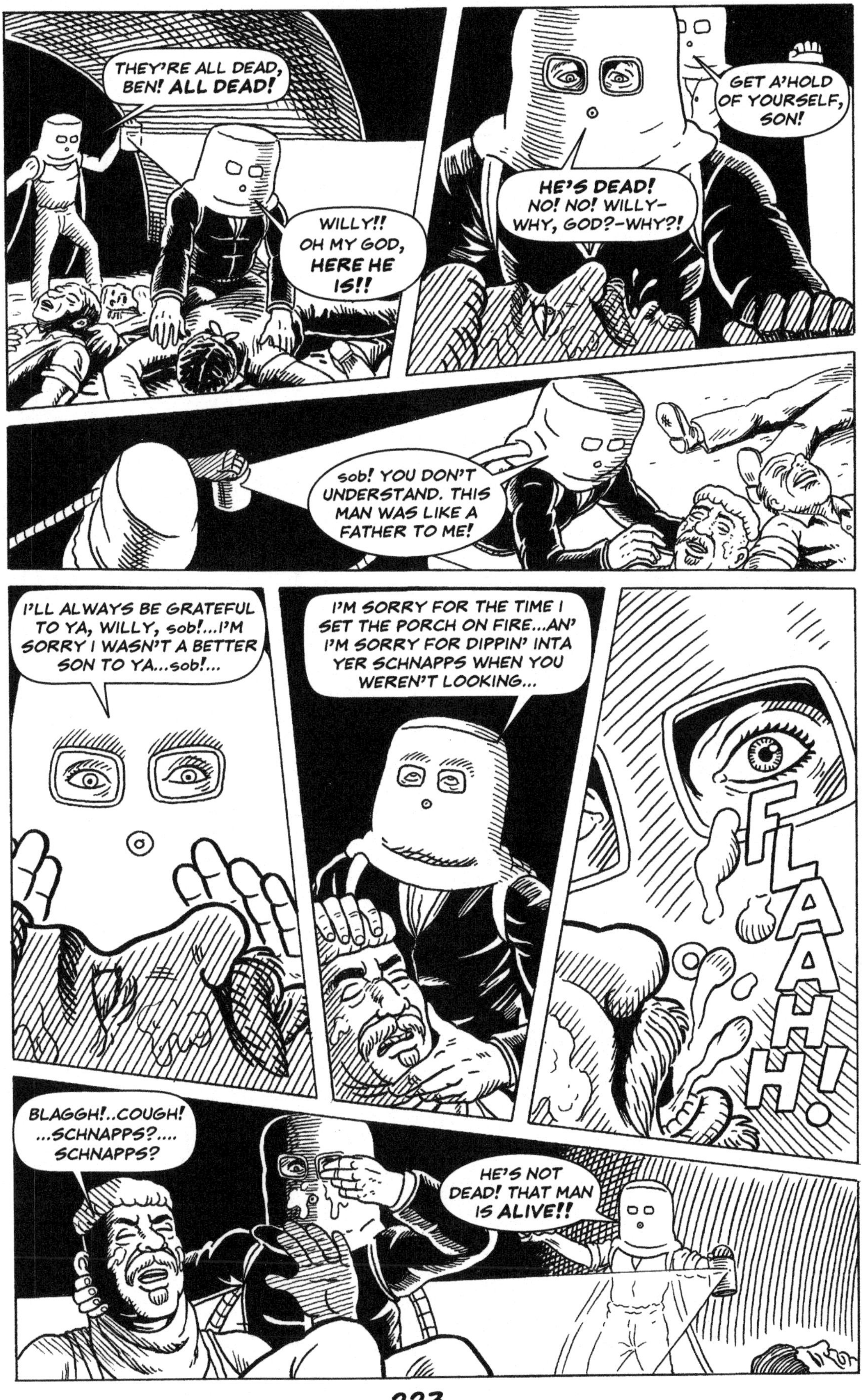
THEY'RE ALL DEAD, BEN! ALL DEAD!
WILLY!! OH MY GOD, HERE HE IS!!
GET A'HOLD OF YOURSELF, SON!
HE'S DEAD! NO! NO! WILLY- WHY, GOD?-WHY?!
sob! YOU DON'T UNDERSTAND. THIS MAN WAS LIKE A FATHER TO ME!
I'LL ALWAYS BE GRATEFUL TO YA, WILLY, sob!...I'M SORRY I WASN'T A BETTER SON TO YA...sob!...
I'M SORRY FOR THE TIME I SET THE PORCH ON FIRE...AN' I'M SORRY FOR DIPPIN' INTA YER SCHNAPPS WHEN YOU WEREN'T LOOKING...
FLAAHH!
BLAGGH!..COUGH! ...SCHNAPPS?.... SCHNAPPS?
HE'S NOT DEAD! THAT MAN IS ALIVE!!

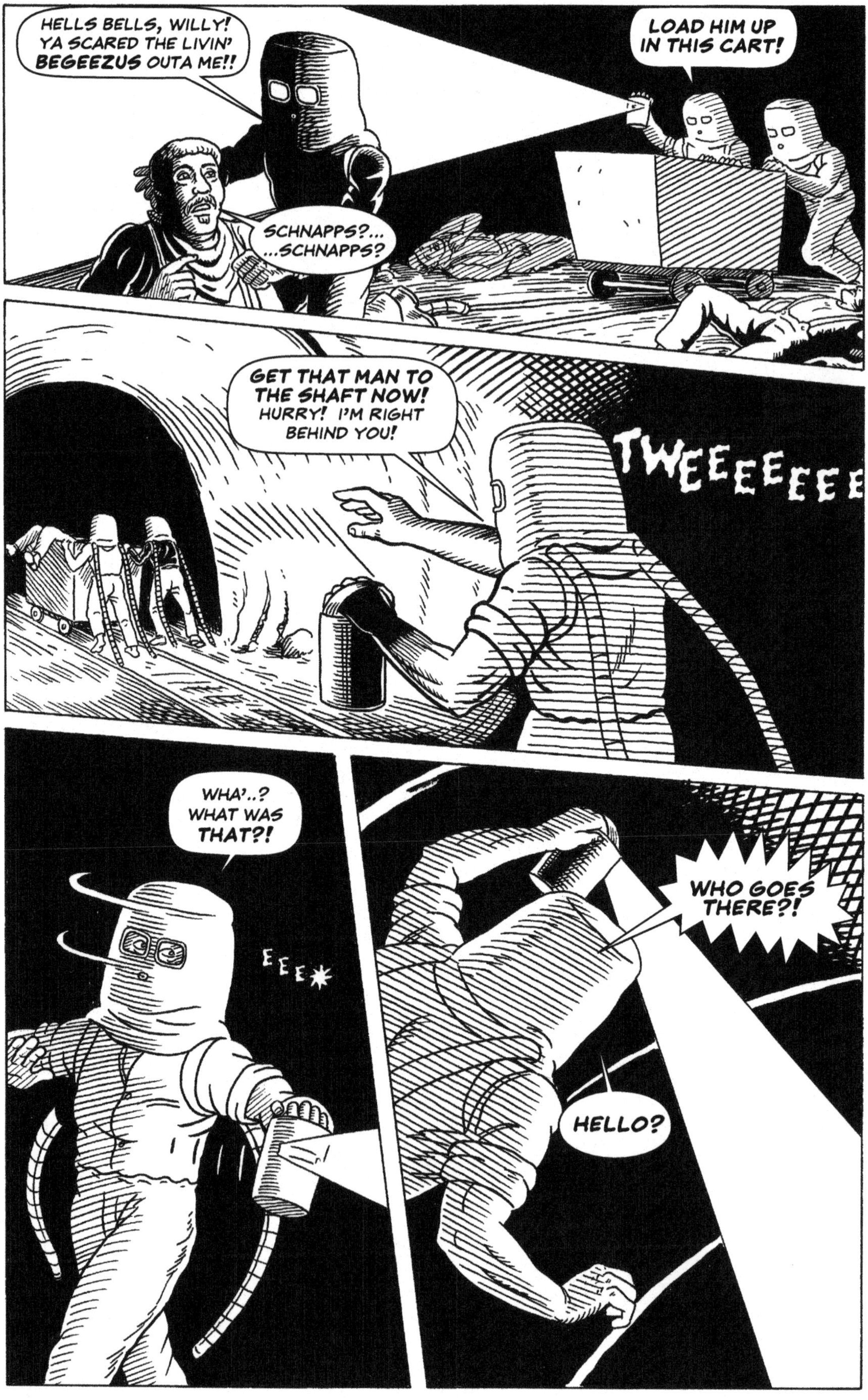
HELLS BELLS, WILLY! YA SCARED THE LIVIN' BEGEEZUS OUTA ME!!
LOAD HIM UP IN THIS CART!
SCHNAPPS?... ...SCHNAPPS?
GET THAT MAN TO THE SHAFT NOW! HURRY! I'M RIGHT BEHIND YOU!
TWEEEEEEE
WHA'..? WHAT WAS THAT?!
EEE
WHO GOES THERE?!
HELLO?

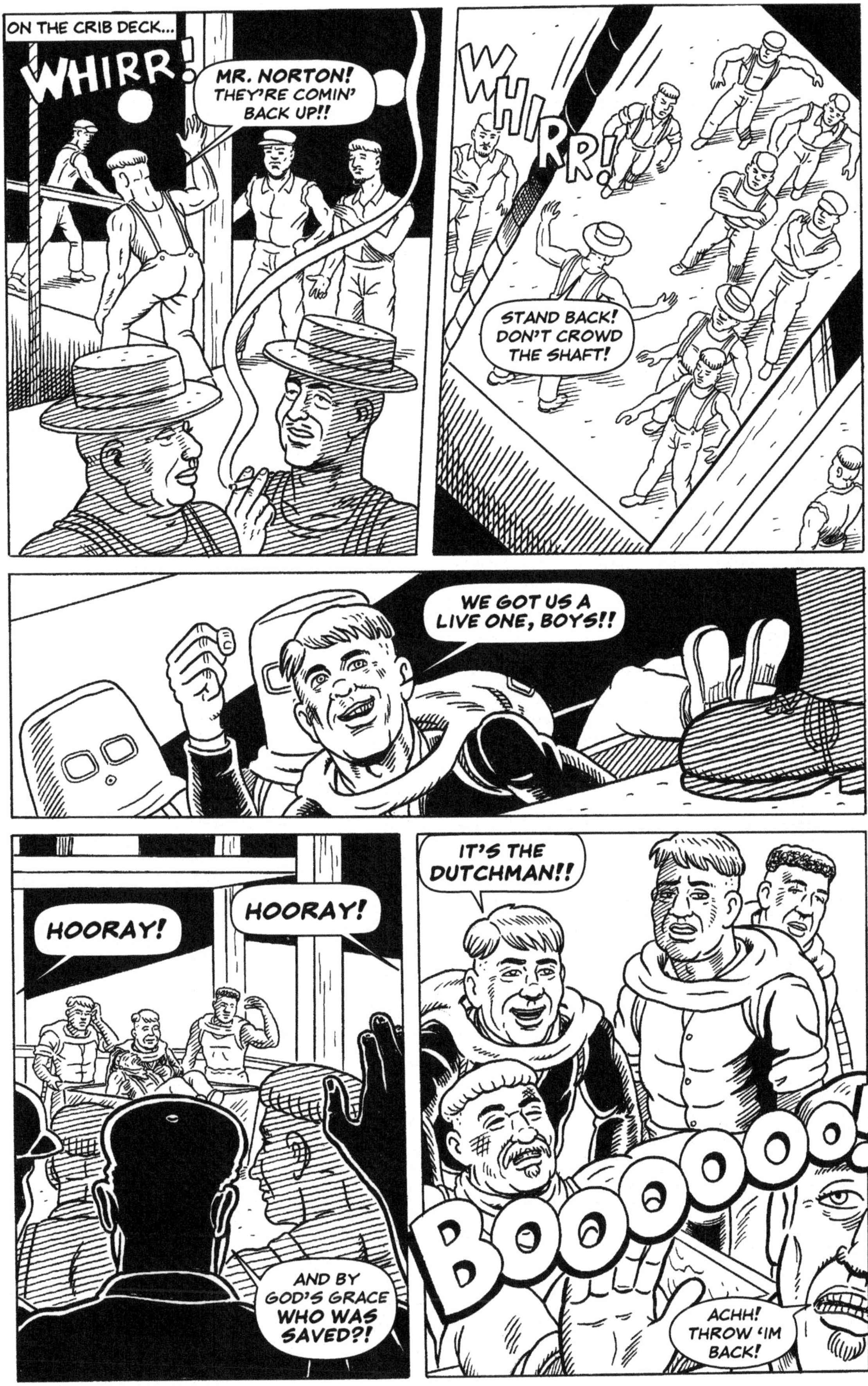
ON THE CRIB DECK...
WHIRR!
MR. NORTON! THEY'RE COMIN' BACK UP!!
WHIRR!
STAND BACK! DON'T CROWD THE SHAFT!
WE GOT US A LIVE ONE, BOYS!!
HOORAY!
HOORAY!
AND BY GOD'S GRACE WHO WAS SAVED?!
IT'S THE DUTCHMAN!!
BOOOOOOO!
ACHH! THROW 'IM BACK!

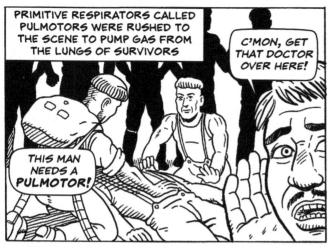

PRIMITIVE RESPIRATORS CALLED PULMOTORS WERE RUSHED TO THE SCENE TO PUMP GAS FROM THE LUNGS OF SURVIVORS

C'MON, GET THAT DOCTOR OVER HERE!

THIS MAN NEEDS A PULMOTOR!

IF HE MADE IT THERE COULD BE OTHERS, LET'S GO!

I GOT WHAT I CAME FOR. I AIN'T GOIN' BACK DOWN THERE!

BELTRAN! GIVE ME YOUR REPORT!

THERE'S MORE LIVE ONES DOWN THERE, I'M SURE OF IT!

YOUR BROTHER SAYS THEY'RE ALL DEAD!

THEN LET'S HAVE A TEAM BRING UP THE DEAD WHILE I GO DEEPER DOWN THE TUNNEL!

OK, LADS...THE HELMET WORKS! BELTRAN AIN'T EVEN A SANDHOG AND HE'S WILLIN' TO GO BACK DOWN. WHO'S GONNA HELP HIM?!

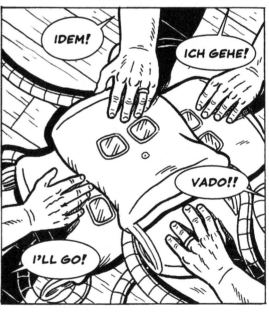

IDEM!

ICH GEHE!

VADO!!

I'LL GO!

ON BELTRAN'S SECOND DESCENT HIS TEAM REMOVED SEVERAL DEAD BODIES BEFORE CLOUDS OF GAS FORCED THEM TO RETREAT. IT HAD BECOME CLEAR THAT THEIR ONLY HOPE OF FINDING MORE SURVIVORS REQUIRED THEM TO VENTURE FARTHER AND FASTER INTO THE CRIPPLED TUNNEL.

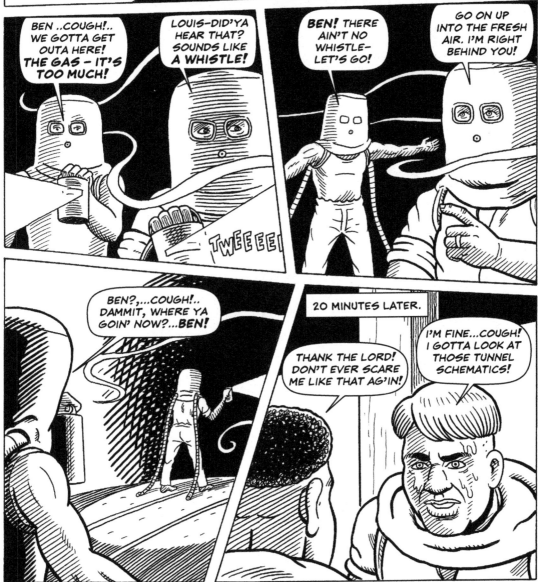

BEN ..COUGH!.. WE GOTTA GET OUTA HERE! THE GAS – IT'S TOO MUCH!

LOUIS–DID'YA HEAR THAT? SOUNDS LIKE A WHISTLE!

TWEEEEE!

BEN! THERE AIN'T NO WHISTLE– LET'S GO!

GO ON UP INTO THE FRESH AIR. I'M RIGHT BEHIND YOU!

BEN?,...COUGH!.. DAMMIT, WHERE YA GOIN' NOW?...BEN!

20 MINUTES LATER.

THANK THE LORD! DON'T EVER SCARE ME LIKE THAT AG'IN!

I'M FINE...COUGH! I GOTTA LOOK AT THOSE TUNNEL SCHEMATICS!

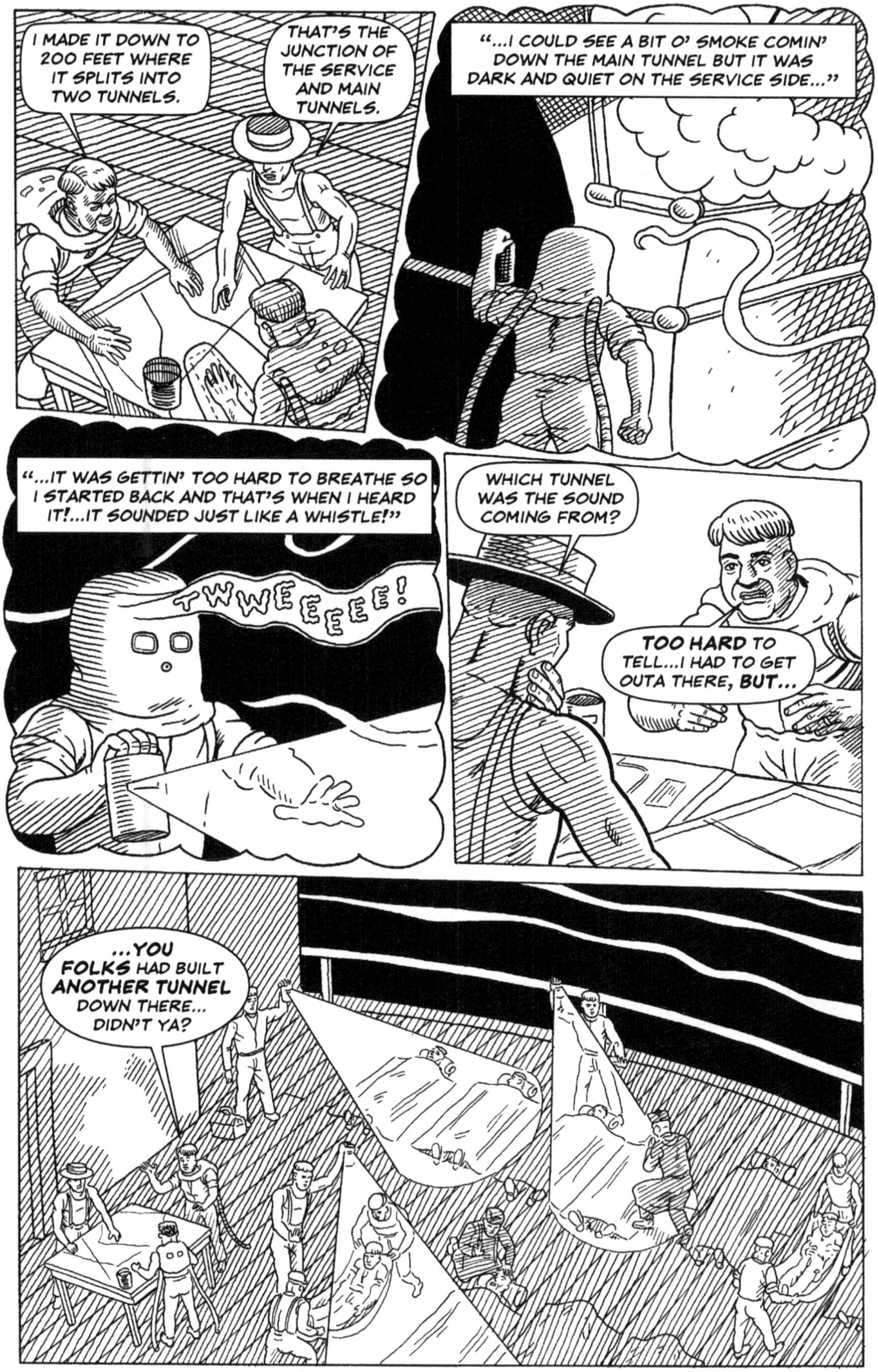
I MADE IT DOWN TO 200 FEET WHERE IT SPLITS INTO TWO TUNNELS.
THAT'S THE JUNCTION OF THE SERVICE AND MAIN TUNNELS.
"...I COULD SEE A BIT O' SMOKE COMIN' DOWN THE MAIN TUNNEL BUT IT WAS DARK AND QUIET ON THE SERVICE SIDE..."
"...IT WAS GETTIN' TOO HARD TO BREATHE SO I STARTED BACK AND THAT'S WHEN I HEARD IT!...IT SOUNDED JUST LIKE A WHISTLE!"
TWWEEEEE!
WHICH TUNNEL WAS THE SOUND COMING FROM?
TOO HARD TO TELL...I HAD TO GET OUTA THERE, BUT...
...YOU FOLKS HAD BUILT ANOTHER TUNNEL DOWN THERE... DIDN'T YA?

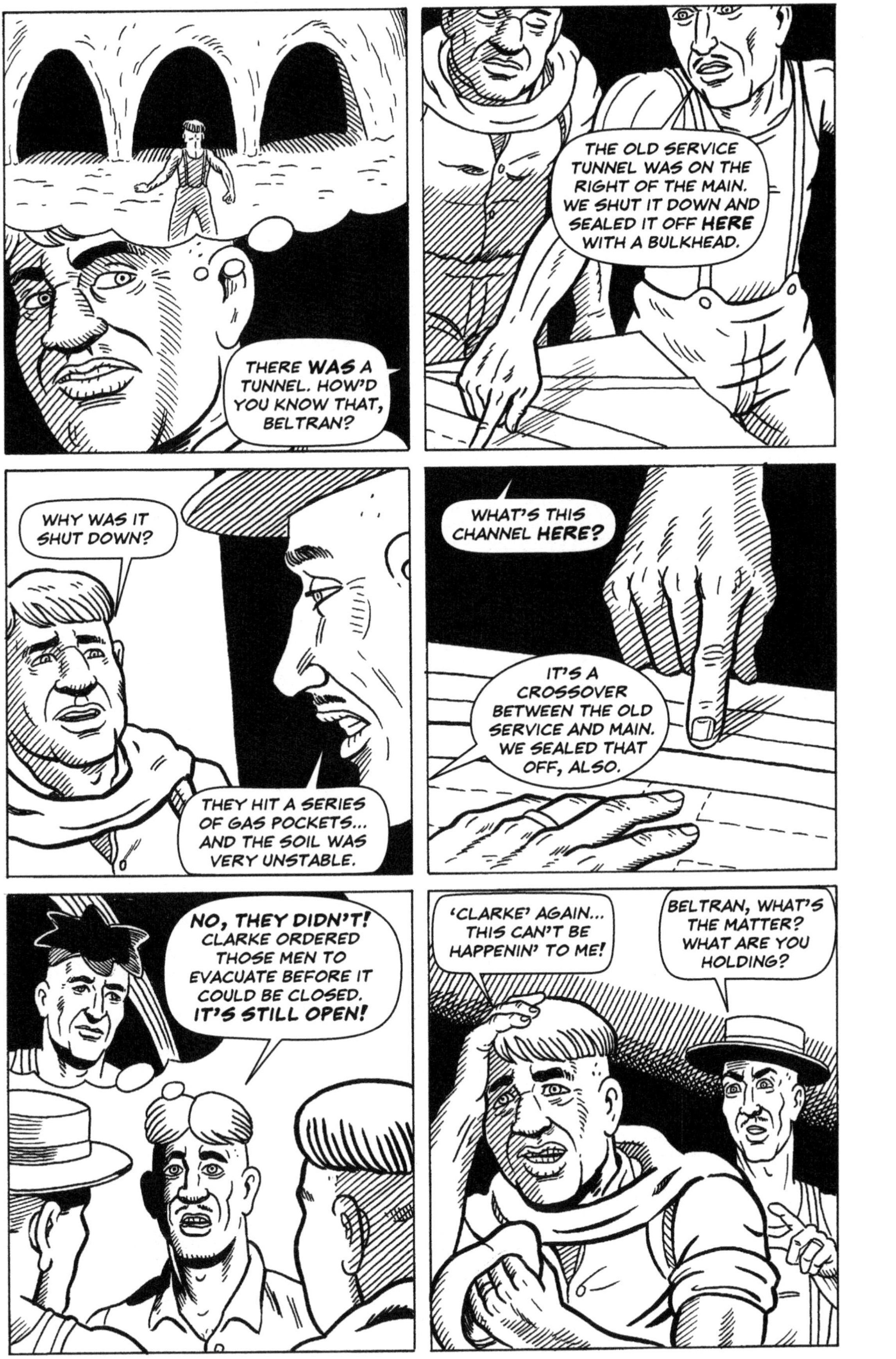
THERE **WAS** A TUNNEL. HOW'D YOU KNOW THAT, BELTRAN?
THE OLD SERVICE TUNNEL WAS ON THE RIGHT OF THE MAIN. WE SHUT IT DOWN AND SEALED IT OFF **HERE** WITH A BULKHEAD.
WHY WAS IT SHUT DOWN?
THEY HIT A SERIES OF GAS POCKETS... AND THE SOIL WAS VERY UNSTABLE.
WHAT'S THIS CHANNEL **HERE?**
IT'S A CROSSOVER BETWEEN THE OLD SERVICE AND MAIN. WE SEALED THAT OFF, ALSO.
NO, THEY DIDN'T! CLARKE ORDERED THOSE MEN TO EVACUATE BEFORE IT COULD BE CLOSED. **IT'S STILL OPEN!**
'CLARKE' AGAIN... THIS CAN'T BE HAPPENIN' TO ME!
BELTRAN, WHAT'S THE MATTER? WHAT ARE YOU HOLDING?

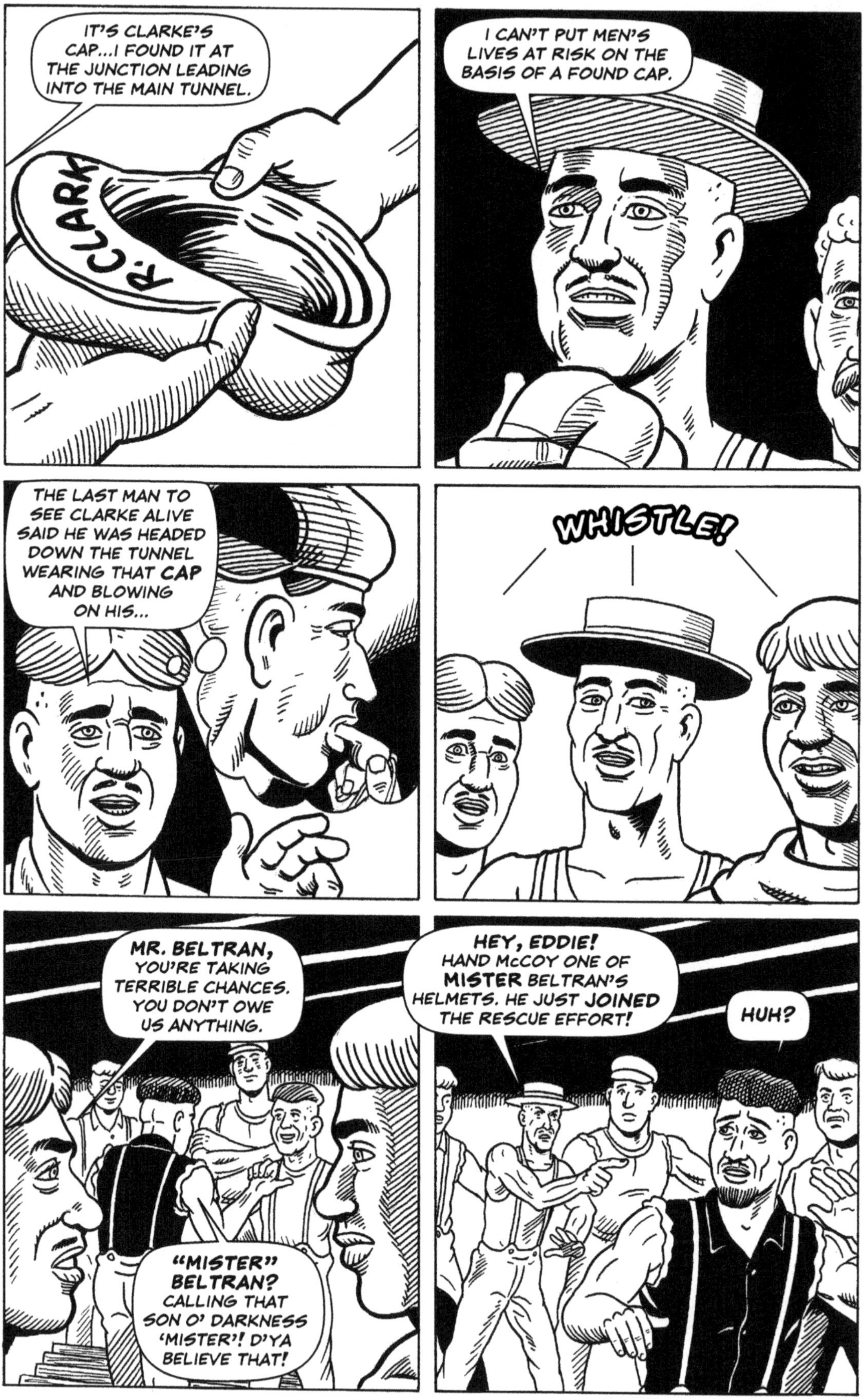
IT'S CLARKE'S CAP...I FOUND IT AT THE JUNCTION LEADING INTO THE MAIN TUNNEL.
R. CLARK
I CAN'T PUT MEN'S LIVES AT RISK ON THE BASIS OF A FOUND CAP.
THE LAST MAN TO SEE CLARKE ALIVE SAID HE WAS HEADED DOWN THE TUNNEL WEARING THAT CAP AND BLOWING ON HIS...
WHISTLE!
MR. BELTRAN, YOU'RE TAKING TERRIBLE CHANCES. YOU DON'T OWE US ANYTHING.
"MISTER" BELTRAN? CALLING THAT SON O' DARKNESS 'MISTER'! D'YA BELIEVE THAT!
HEY, EDDIE! HAND McCOY ONE OF MISTER BELTRAN'S HELMETS. HE JUST JOINED THE RESCUE EFFORT!
HUH?

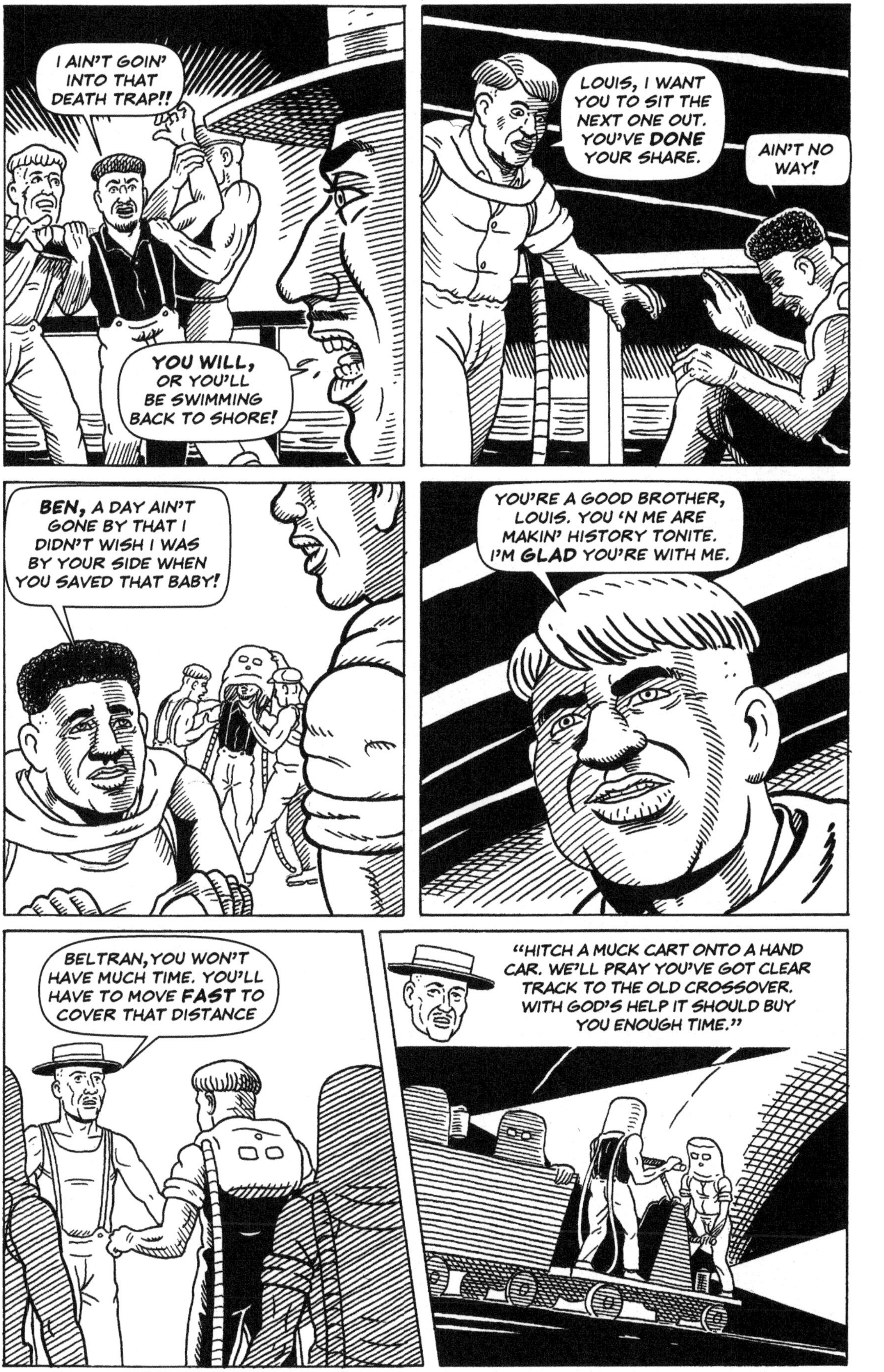
I AIN'T GOIN' INTO THAT DEATH TRAP!!
YOU WILL, OR YOU'LL BE SWIMMING BACK TO SHORE!
LOUIS, I WANT YOU TO SIT THE NEXT ONE OUT. YOU'VE DONE YOUR SHARE.
AIN'T NO WAY!
BEN, A DAY AIN'T GONE BY THAT I DIDN'T WISH I WAS BY YOUR SIDE WHEN YOU SAVED THAT BABY!
YOU'RE A GOOD BROTHER, LOUIS. YOU 'N ME ARE MAKIN' HISTORY TONITE. I'M GLAD YOU'RE WITH ME.
BELTRAN, YOU WON'T HAVE MUCH TIME. YOU'LL HAVE TO MOVE FAST TO COVER THAT DISTANCE
"HITCH A MUCK CART ONTO A HAND CAR. WE'LL PRAY YOU'VE GOT CLEAR TRACK TO THE OLD CROSSOVER. WITH GOD'S HELP IT SHOULD BUY YOU ENOUGH TIME."

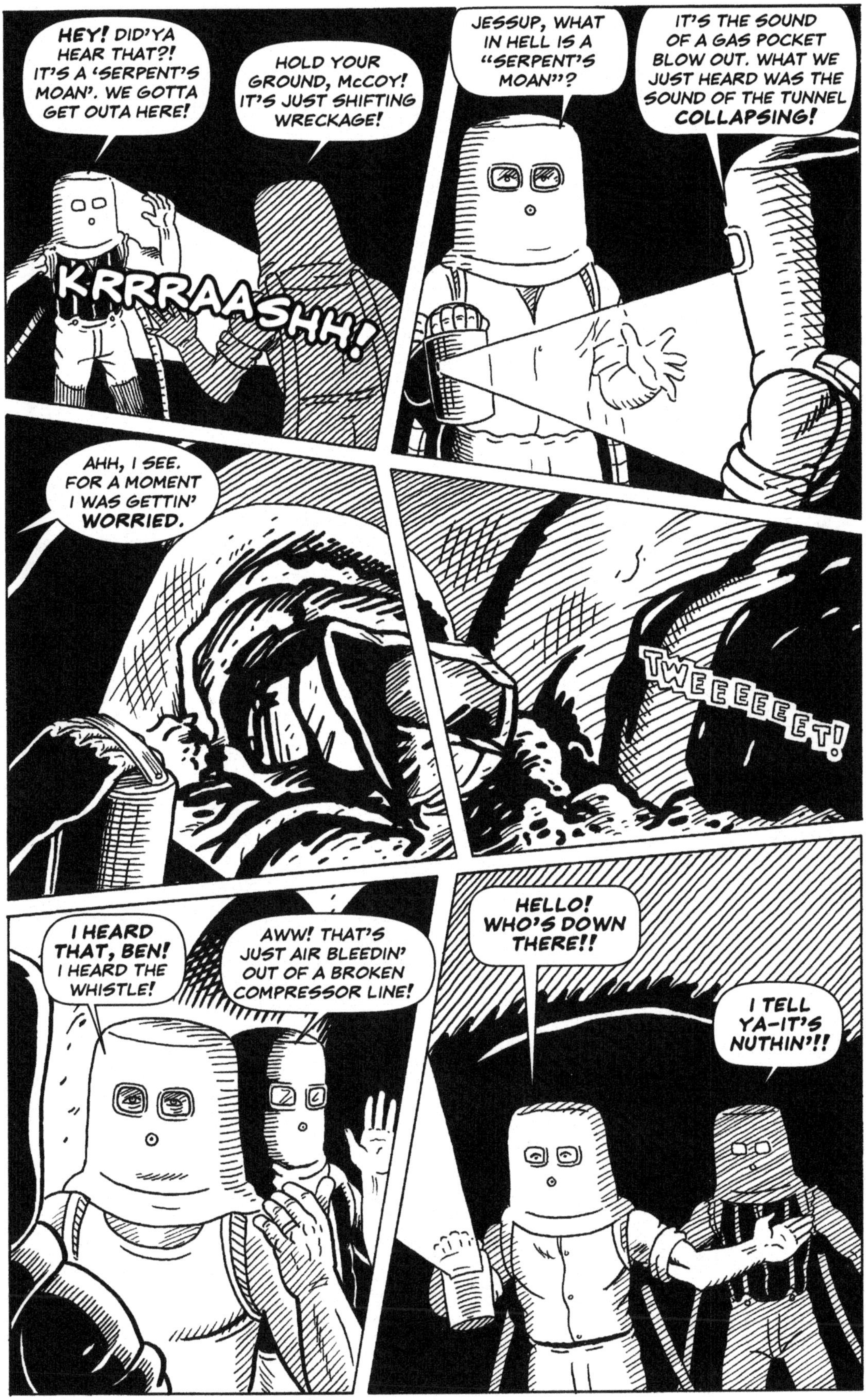
HEY! DID'YA HEAR THAT?! IT'S A 'SERPENT'S MOAN'. WE GOTTA GET OUTA HERE!
HOLD YOUR GROUND, McCOY! IT'S JUST SHIFTING WRECKAGE!
KRRRAASHH!
JESSUP, WHAT IN HELL IS A "SERPENT'S MOAN"?
IT'S THE SOUND OF A GAS POCKET BLOW OUT. WHAT WE JUST HEARD WAS THE SOUND OF THE TUNNEL COLLAPSING!
AHH, I SEE. FOR A MOMENT I WAS GETTIN' WORRIED.
TWEEEEEEET!
I HEARD THAT, BEN! I HEARD THE WHISTLE!
AWW! THAT'S JUST AIR BLEEDIN' OUT OF A BROKEN COMPRESSOR LINE!
HELLO! WHO'S DOWN THERE!!
I TELL YA-IT'S NUTHIN'!!

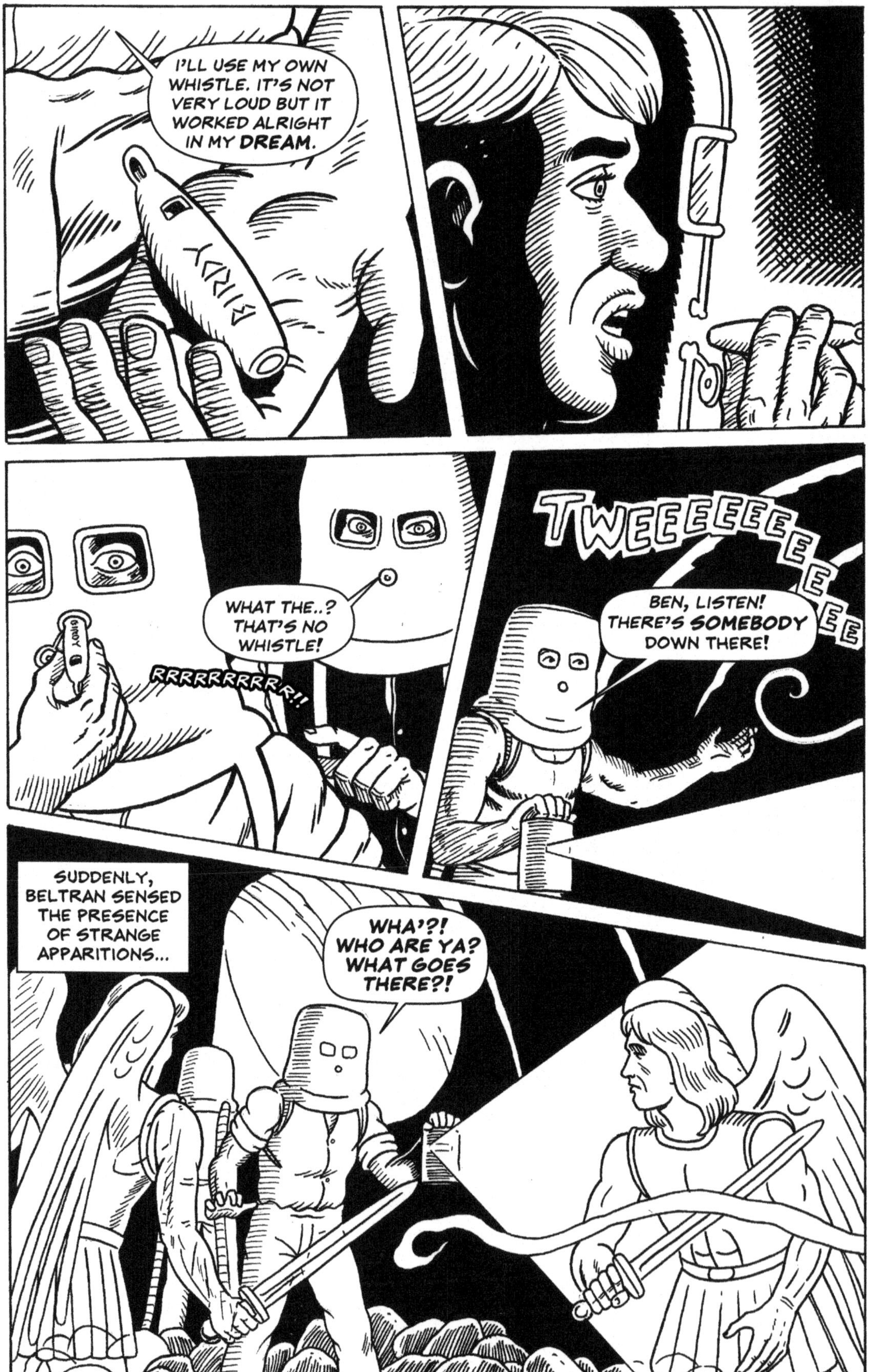
I'LL USE MY OWN WHISTLE. IT'S NOT VERY LOUD BUT IT WORKED ALRIGHT IN MY DREAM.
WHAT THE..? THAT'S NO WHISTLE!
RRRRRRRRRR!!
TWEEEEEEEEEEEEE
BEN, LISTEN! THERE'S SOMEBODY DOWN THERE!
SUDDENLY, BELTRAN SENSED THE PRESENCE OF STRANGE APPARITIONS...
WHA'?! WHO ARE YA? WHAT GOES THERE?!

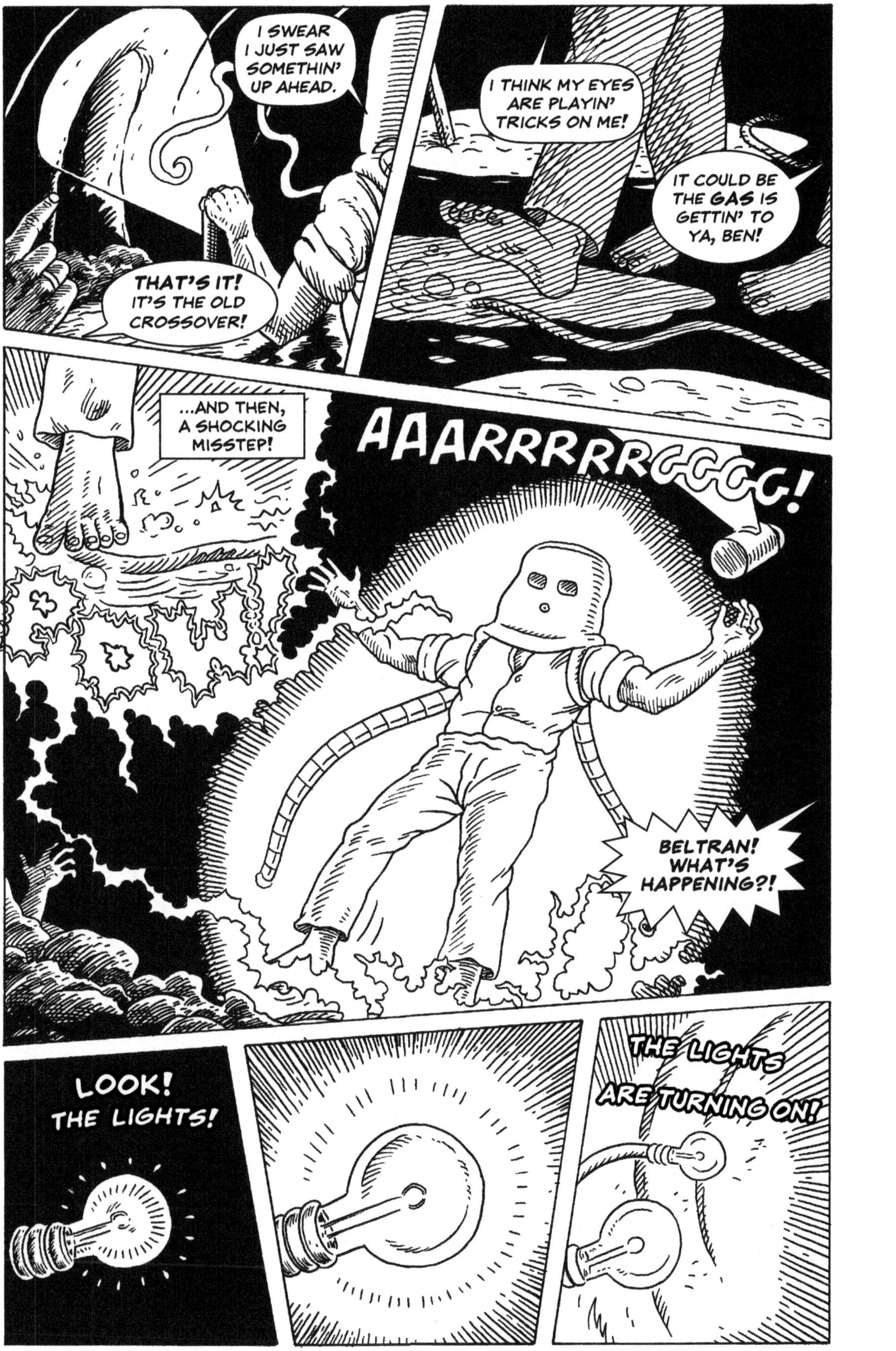
I SWEAR I JUST SAW SOMETHIN' UP AHEAD.
THAT'S IT! IT'S THE OLD CROSSOVER!
I THINK MY EYES ARE PLAYIN' TRICKS ON ME!
IT COULD BE THE GAS IS GETTIN' TO YA, BEN!
...AND THEN, A SHOCKING MISSTEP!
AAARRRRRRGGGG!
BELTRAN! WHAT'S HAPPENING?!
LOOK! THE LIGHTS!
THE LIGHTS ARE TURNING ON!

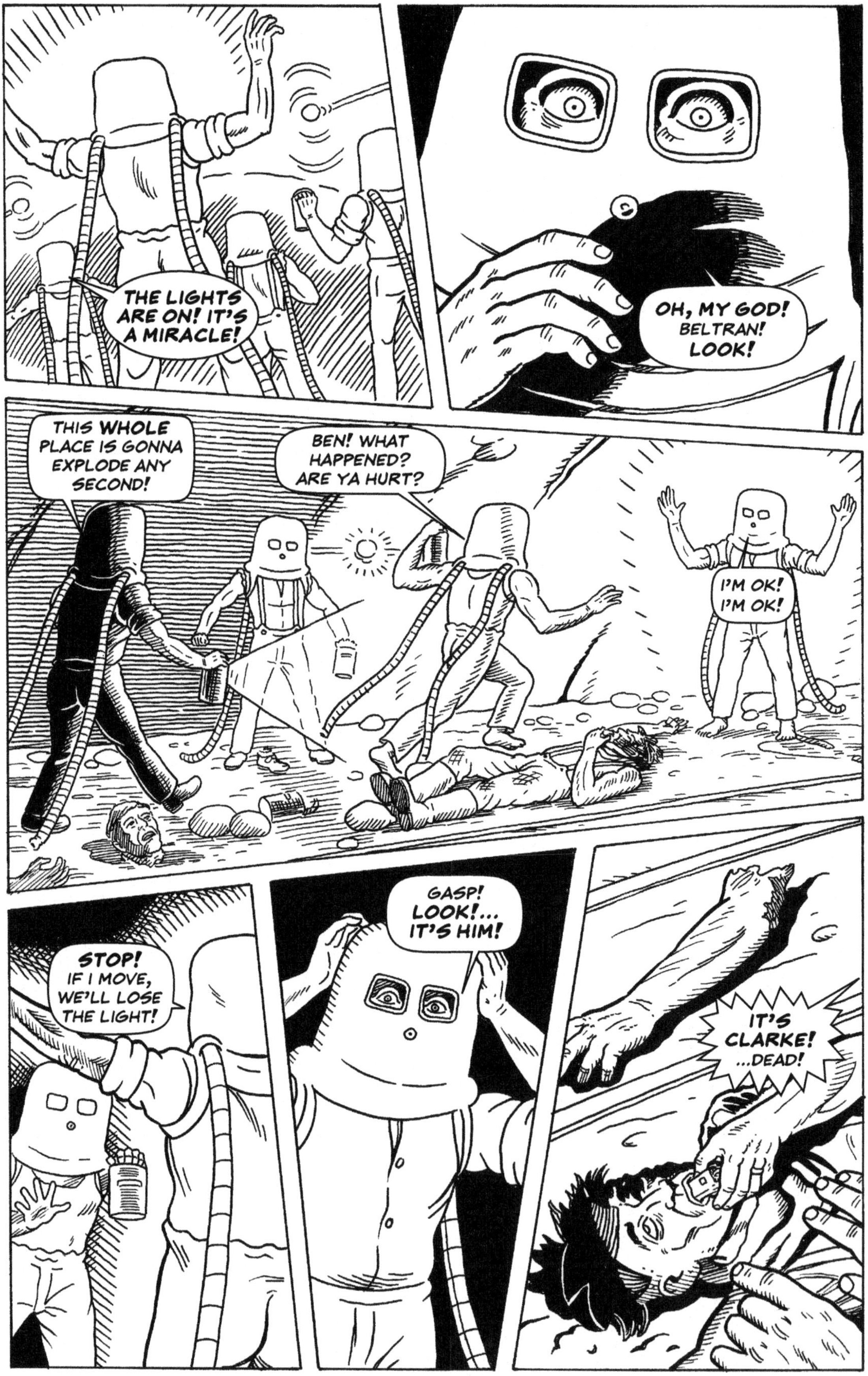

THE LIGHTS ARE ON! IT'S A MIRACLE!
OH, MY GOD! BELTRAN! LOOK!
THIS WHOLE PLACE IS GONNA EXPLODE ANY SECOND!
BEN! WHAT HAPPENED? ARE YA HURT?
I'M OK! I'M OK!
STOP! IF I MOVE, WE'LL LOSE THE LIGHT!
GASP! LOOK!... IT'S HIM!
IT'S CLARKE! ...DEAD!

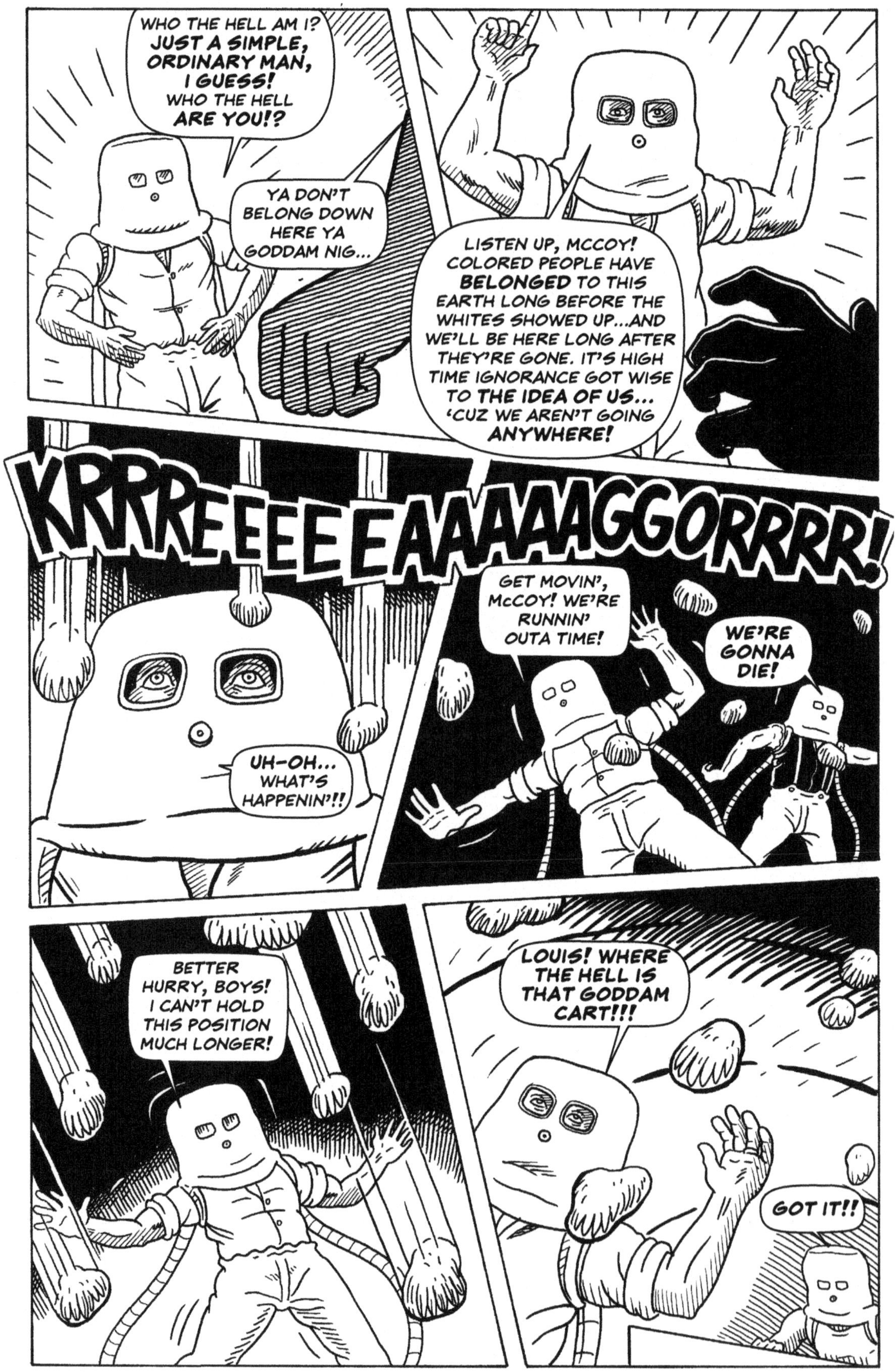
WHO THE HELL AM I? JUST A SIMPLE, ORDINARY MAN, I GUESS! WHO THE HELL ARE YOU!?
YA DON'T BELONG DOWN HERE YA GODDAM NIG...
LISTEN UP, MCCOY! COLORED PEOPLE HAVE BELONGED TO THIS EARTH LONG BEFORE THE WHITES SHOWED UP...AND WE'LL BE HERE LONG AFTER THEY'RE GONE. IT'S HIGH TIME IGNORANCE GOT WISE TO THE IDEA OF US... 'CUZ WE AREN'T GOING ANYWHERE!
KRRREEEEAAAAAGGORRRRR!
UH-OH... WHAT'S HAPPENIN'!!
GET MOVIN', McCOY! WE'RE RUNNIN' OUTA TIME!
WE'RE GONNA DIE!
BETTER HURRY, BOYS! I CAN'T HOLD THIS POSITION MUCH LONGER!
LOUIS! WHERE THE HELL IS THAT GODDAM CART!!!
GOT IT!!

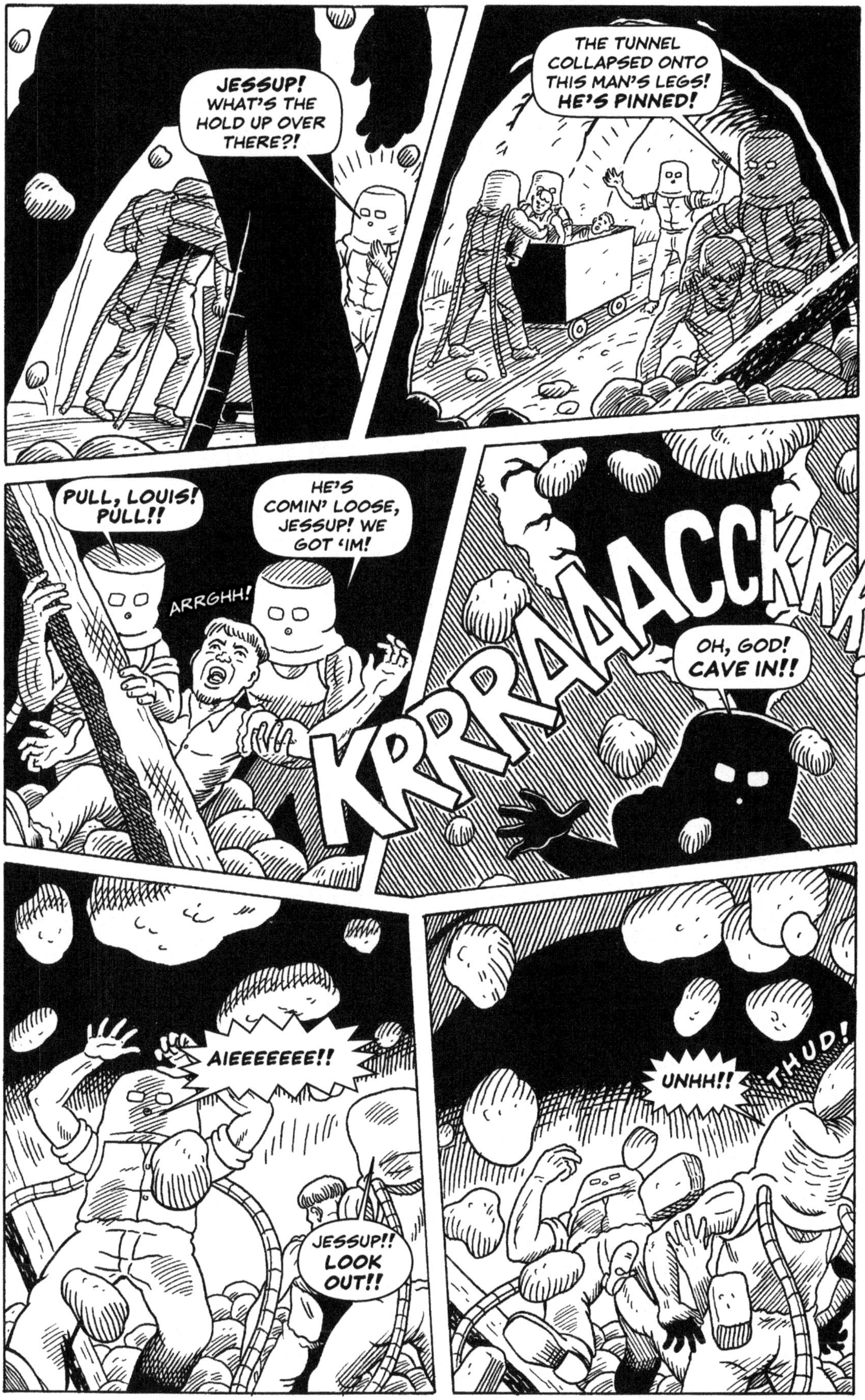
JESSUP! WHAT'S THE HOLD UP OVER THERE?!
THE TUNNEL COLLAPSED ONTO THIS MAN'S LEGS! HE'S PINNED!
PULL, LOUIS! PULL!!
HE'S COMIN' LOOSE, JESSUP! WE GOT 'IM!
ARRGHH!
KRRRAAACCKKK!
OH, GOD! CAVE IN!!
AIEEEEEEE!!
JESSUP!! LOOK OUT!!
UNHH!!
THUD!

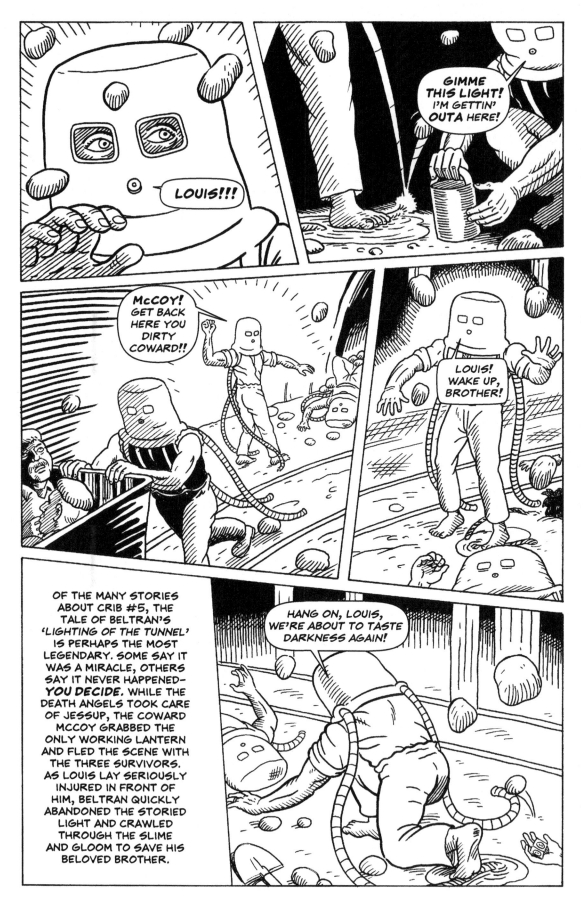

OF THE MANY STORIES
ABOUT CRIB #5, THE
TALE OF BELTRAN'S
'LIGHTING OF THE TUNNEL'
IS PERHAPS THE MOST
LEGENDARY. SOME SAY IT
WAS A MIRACLE, OTHERS
SAY IT NEVER HAPPENED—
YOU DECIDE. WHILE THE
DEATH ANGELS TOOK CARE
OF JESSUP, THE COWARD
MCCOY GRABBED THE
ONLY WORKING LANTERN
AND FLED THE SCENE WITH
THE THREE SURVIVORS.
AS LOUIS LAY SERIOUSLY
INJURED IN FRONT OF
HIM, BELTRAN QUICKLY
ABANDONED THE STORIED
LIGHT AND CRAWLED
THROUGH THE SLIME
AND GLOOM TO SAVE HIS
BELOVED BROTHER.

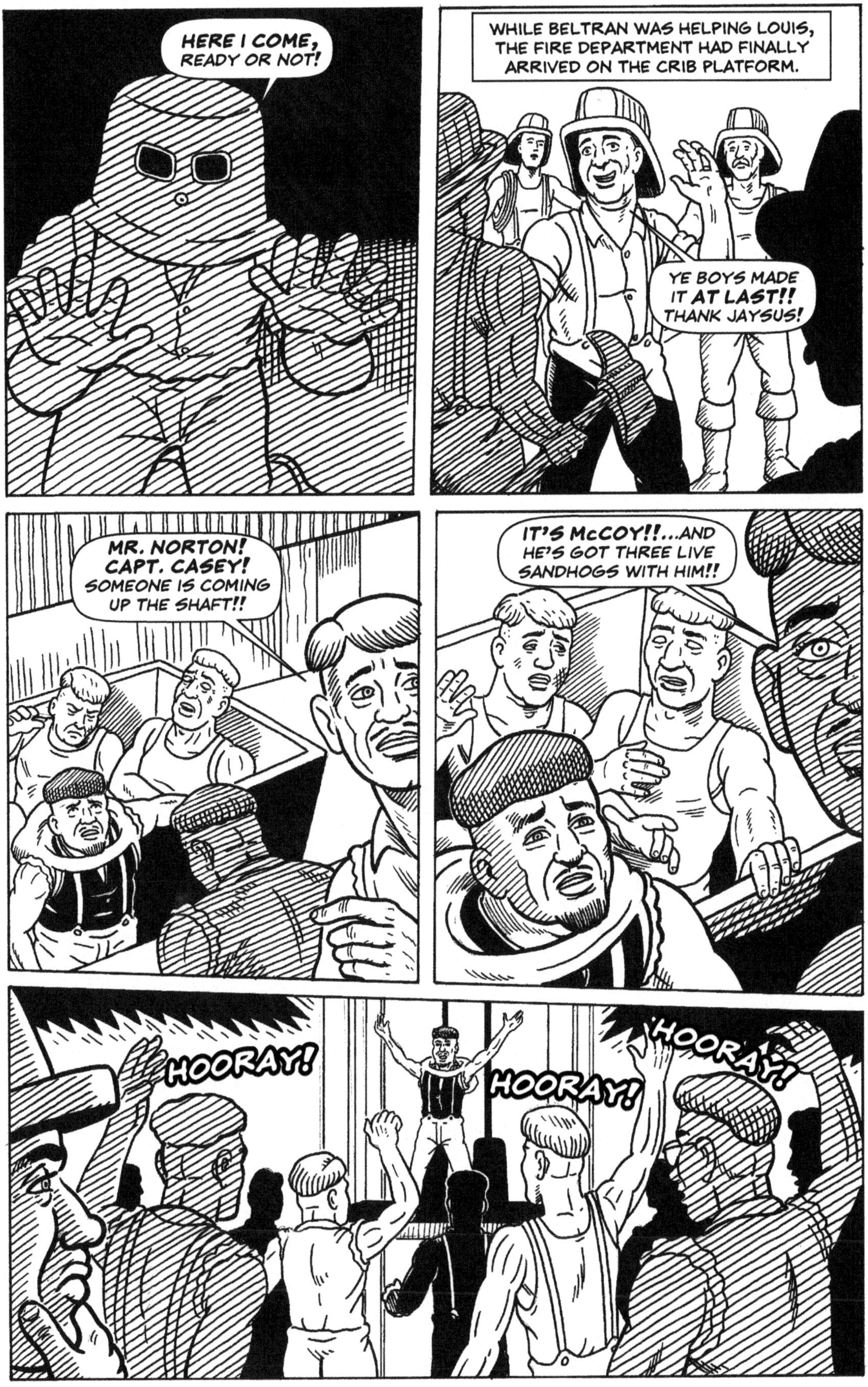
HERE I COME, READY OR NOT!
WHILE BELTRAN WAS HELPING LOUIS, THE FIRE DEPARTMENT HAD FINALLY ARRIVED ON THE CRIB PLATFORM.
YE BOYS MADE IT AT LAST!! THANK JAYSUS!
MR. NORTON! CAPT. CASEY! SOMEONE IS COMING UP THE SHAFT!!
IT'S McCOY!!...AND HE'S GOT THREE LIVE SANDHOGS WITH HIM!!
HOORAY!
HOORAY!
HOORAY!

YOUNG MAN, I'M GOING TO PIN A MEDAL ON YOUR CHEST!

HOLD YER HORSES!

WHERE'S THE REST O' YER TEAM? WHERE'S BELTRAN?

I WAS ABOUT TO TELL YA... JESSUP AND ANOTHER GUY WERE KILLED IN A CAVE-IN. IT WAS HORRIBLE!

AND...THE BELTRANS? WHAT O' THEM? SPIT IT OUT!

BELTRAN'S BROTHER WAS HURT, BUT BOTH WERE ALIVE WHEN I LAST SAW 'EM.

Y'MEAN YE LEFT 'EM?

YE DESERTED 'EM DIDN'T YE?!

COUGH!... THAT MCCOY IS A COWARD!

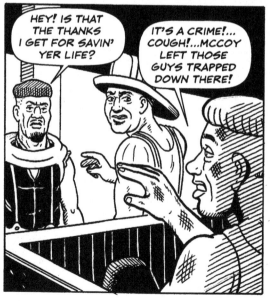

HEY! IS THAT THE THANKS I GET FOR SAVIN' YER LIFE?

IT'S A CRIME!... COUGH!...MCCOY LEFT THOSE GUYS TRAPPED DOWN THERE!

LOOK, I HAD TO SAVE THESE MEN, RIGHT? WHAT'S THE USE IN ALL O' US DYIN'?

WELL, BOYO, GET THAT HOOD ON 'CUZ YER GOIN' BACK DOWN THERE!

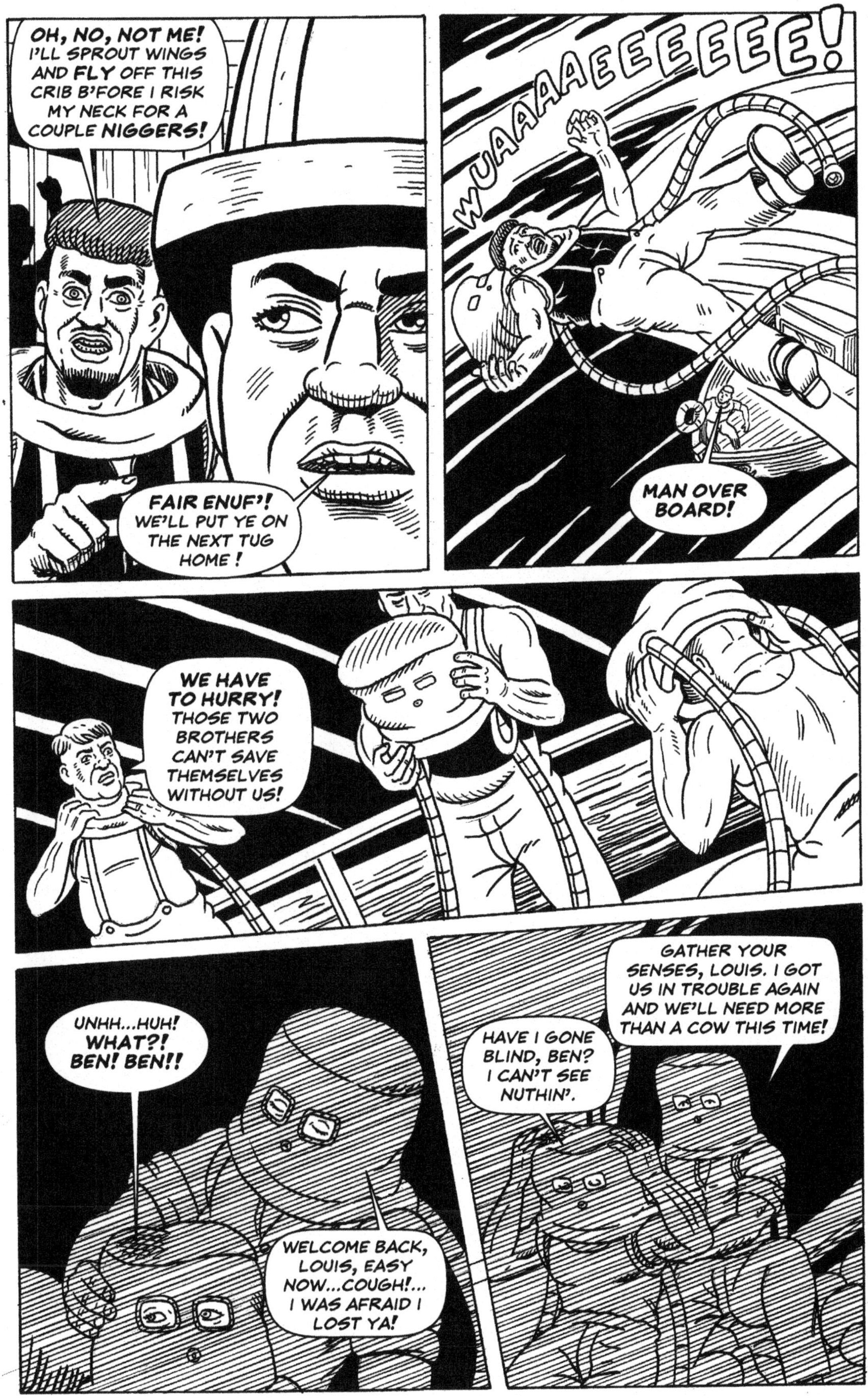
OH, NO, NOT ME! I'LL SPROUT WINGS AND FLY OFF THIS CRIB B'FORE I RISK MY NECK FOR A COUPLE NIGGERS!
FAIR ENUF'! WE'LL PUT YE ON THE NEXT TUG HOME!
WUAAAAEEEEEEE!
MAN OVER BOARD!
WE HAVE TO HURRY! THOSE TWO BROTHERS CAN'T SAVE THEMSELVES WITHOUT US!
UNHH...HUH! WHAT?! BEN! BEN!!
WELCOME BACK, LOUIS, EASY NOW...COUGH!... I WAS AFRAID I LOST YA!
GATHER YOUR SENSES, LOUIS. I GOT US IN TROUBLE AGAIN AND WE'LL NEED MORE THAN A COW THIS TIME!
HAVE I GONE BLIND, BEN? I CAN'T SEE NUTHIN'.

244

245

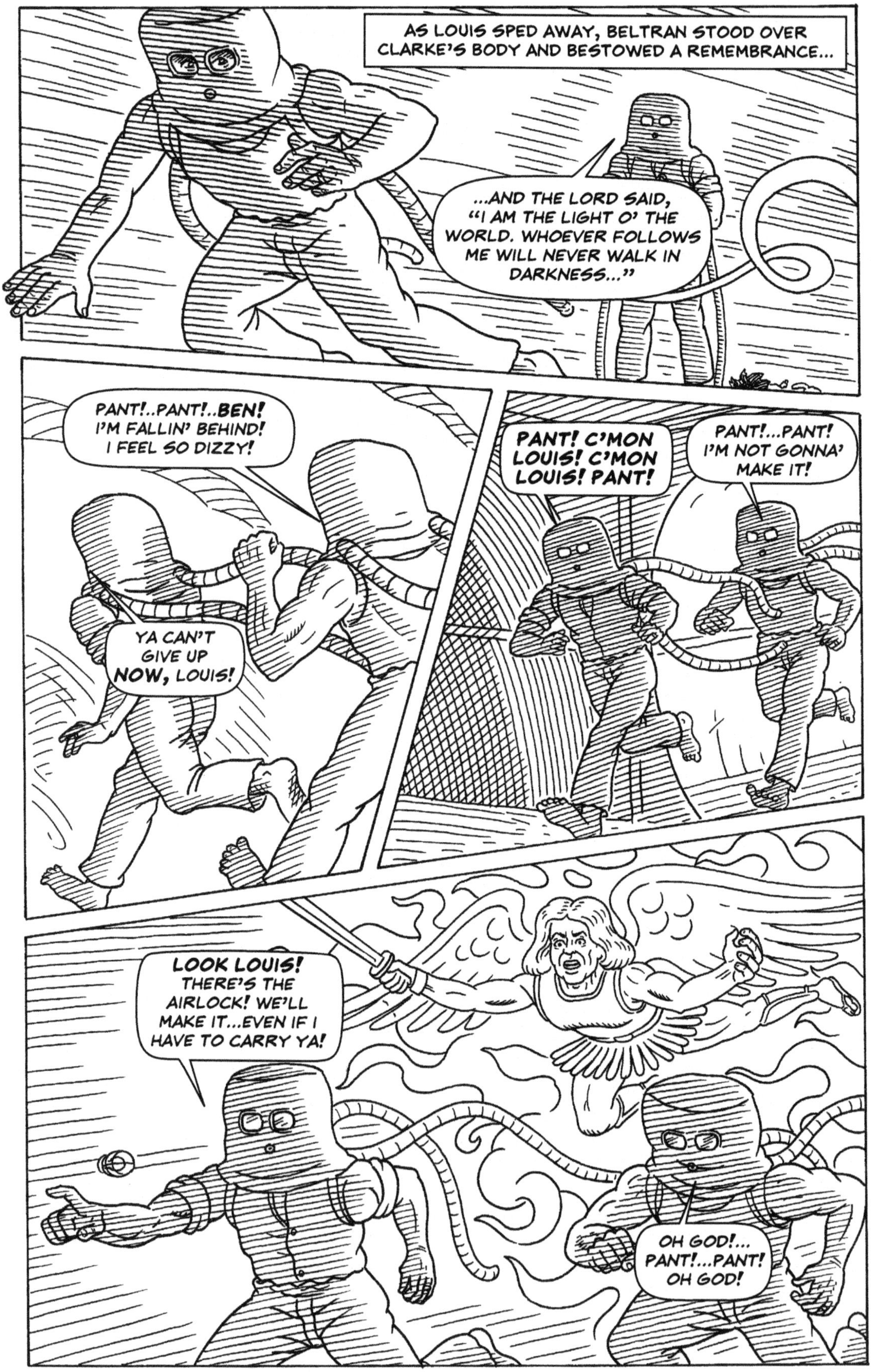
AS LOUIS SPED AWAY, BELTRAN STOOD OVER CLARKE'S BODY AND BESTOWED A REMEMBRANCE...
...AND THE LORD SAID, "I AM THE LIGHT O' THE WORLD. WHOEVER FOLLOWS ME WILL NEVER WALK IN DARKNESS..."
PANT!..PANT!..BEN! I'M FALLIN' BEHIND! I FEEL SO DIZZY!
YA CAN'T GIVE UP NOW, LOUIS!
PANT! C'MON LOUIS! C'MON LOUIS! PANT!
PANT!...PANT! I'M NOT GONNA' MAKE IT!
LOOK LOUIS! THERE'S THE AIRLOCK! WE'LL MAKE IT...EVEN IF I HAVE TO CARRY YA!
OH GOD!... PANT!...PANT! OH GOD!

247

UPON LANDING ON THE FLOOR OF THE SHAFT CASEY AND HIS MEN HEADED DIRECTLY INTO THE AIRLOCK...

TO AIRLOCK

...AND, WITHOUT A MOMENT TO SPARE...

I'LL **TAKE** THIS MAN ME'SELF! PANT!...I OWE 'IM THAT MUCH!

... THE FIREMEN HAD WRESTLED BOTH BROTHERS FROM THE OUTSTRETCHED ARMS OF THE DEATH ANGELS...

WE NEED A **PULMOTOR!** C'MON, THIS MAN NEEDS HELP!

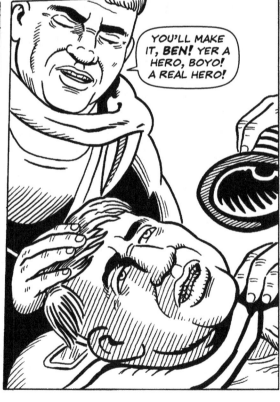

YOU'LL MAKE IT, **BEN!** YER A HERO, BOYO! A REAL HERO!

CHAPTER 9: AFTERMATH:
"THE SIGNIFICANCE OF THINGS AS LARGE AS LAKES"

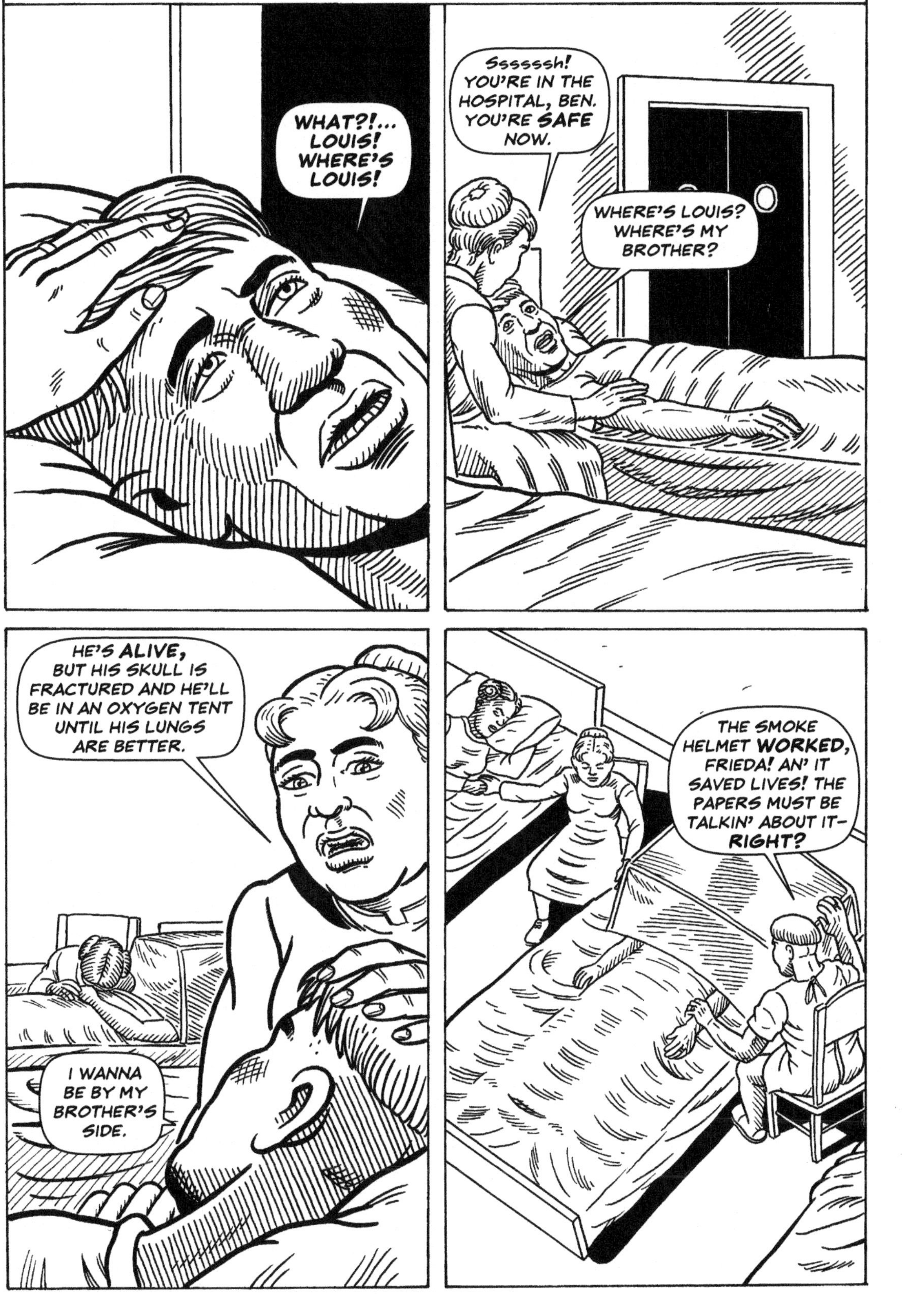
WHAT?!... LOUIS! WHERE'S LOUIS!
Sssssh! YOU'RE IN THE HOSPITAL, BEN. YOU'RE SAFE NOW.
WHERE'S LOUIS? WHERE'S MY BROTHER?
HE'S ALIVE, BUT HIS SKULL IS FRACTURED AND HE'LL BE IN AN OXYGEN TENT UNTIL HIS LUNGS ARE BETTER.
I WANNA BE BY MY BROTHER'S SIDE.
THE SMOKE HELMET WORKED, FRIEDA! AN' IT SAVED LIVES! THE PAPERS MUST BE TALKIN' ABOUT IT- RIGHT?

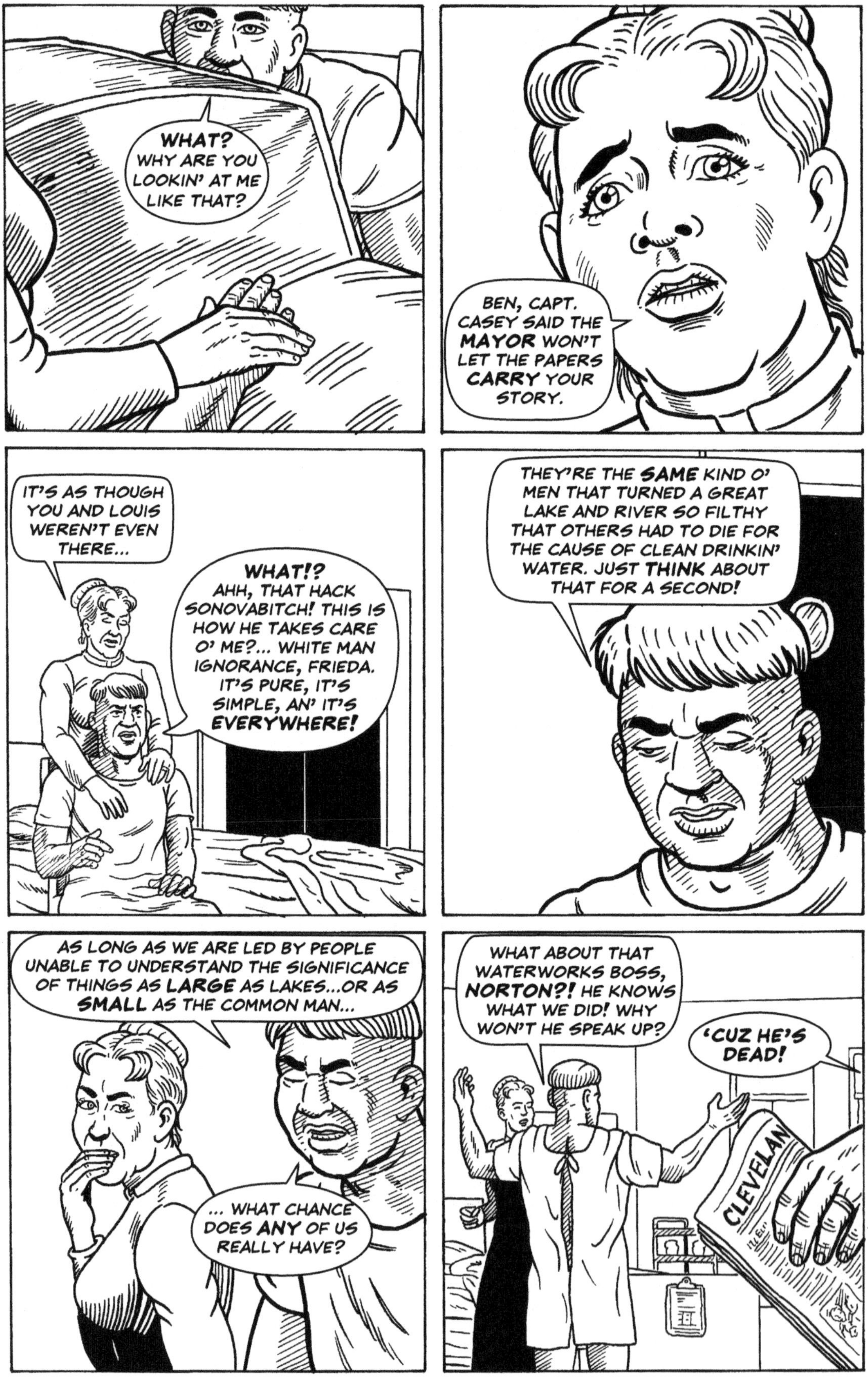
WHAT? WHY ARE YOU LOOKIN' AT ME LIKE THAT?
BEN, CAPT. CASEY SAID THE MAYOR WON'T LET THE PAPERS CARRY YOUR STORY.
IT'S AS THOUGH YOU AND LOUIS WEREN'T EVEN THERE...
WHAT!? AHH, THAT HACK SONOVABITCH! THIS IS HOW HE TAKES CARE O' ME?... WHITE MAN IGNORANCE, FRIEDA. IT'S PURE, IT'S SIMPLE, AN' IT'S EVERYWHERE!
THEY'RE THE SAME KIND O' MEN THAT TURNED A GREAT LAKE AND RIVER SO FILTHY THAT OTHERS HAD TO DIE FOR THE CAUSE OF CLEAN DRINKIN' WATER. JUST THINK ABOUT THAT FOR A SECOND!
AS LONG AS WE ARE LED BY PEOPLE UNABLE TO UNDERSTAND THE SIGNIFICANCE OF THINGS AS LARGE AS LAKES...OR AS SMALL AS THE COMMON MAN...
... WHAT CHANCE DOES ANY OF US REALLY HAVE?
WHAT ABOUT THAT WATERWORKS BOSS, NORTON?! HE KNOWS WHAT WE DID! WHY WON'T HE SPEAK UP?
'CUZ HE'S DEAD!
CLEVELAN

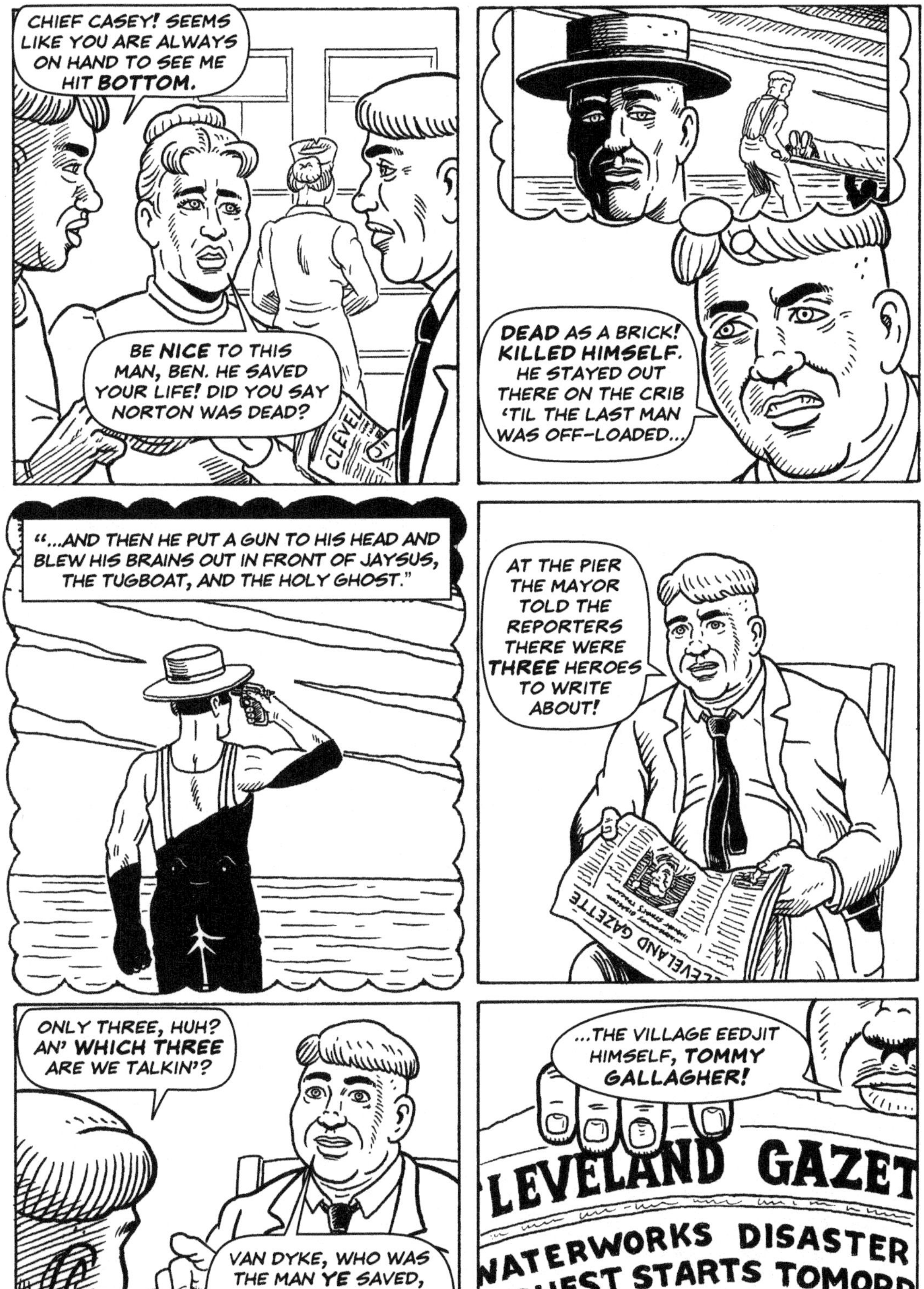
CHIEF CASEY! SEEMS LIKE YOU ARE ALWAYS ON HAND TO SEE ME HIT BOTTOM.
BE NICE TO THIS MAN, BEN. HE SAVED YOUR LIFE! DID YOU SAY NORTON WAS DEAD?
DEAD AS A BRICK! KILLED HIMSELF. HE STAYED OUT THERE ON THE CRIB 'TIL THE LAST MAN WAS OFF-LOADED...
"...AND THEN HE PUT A GUN TO HIS HEAD AND BLEW HIS BRAINS OUT IN FRONT OF JAYSUS, THE TUGBOAT, AND THE HOLY GHOST."
AT THE PIER THE MAYOR TOLD THE REPORTERS THERE WERE THREE HEROES TO WRITE ABOUT!
ONLY THREE, HUH? AN' WHICH THREE ARE WE TALKIN'?
VAN DYKE, WHO WAS THE MAN YE SAVED, McCOY, THE ROTTEN SKUNK WHO DESERTED YE, AN' LAST BUT NOT LEAST...
...THE VILLAGE EEDJIT HIMSELF, TOMMY GALLAGHER!
LEVELAND GAZET
WATERWORKS DISASTER
INQUEST STARTS TOMORR
TUNNEL HERO TO TESTIFY
Thomas Van Dyke

253

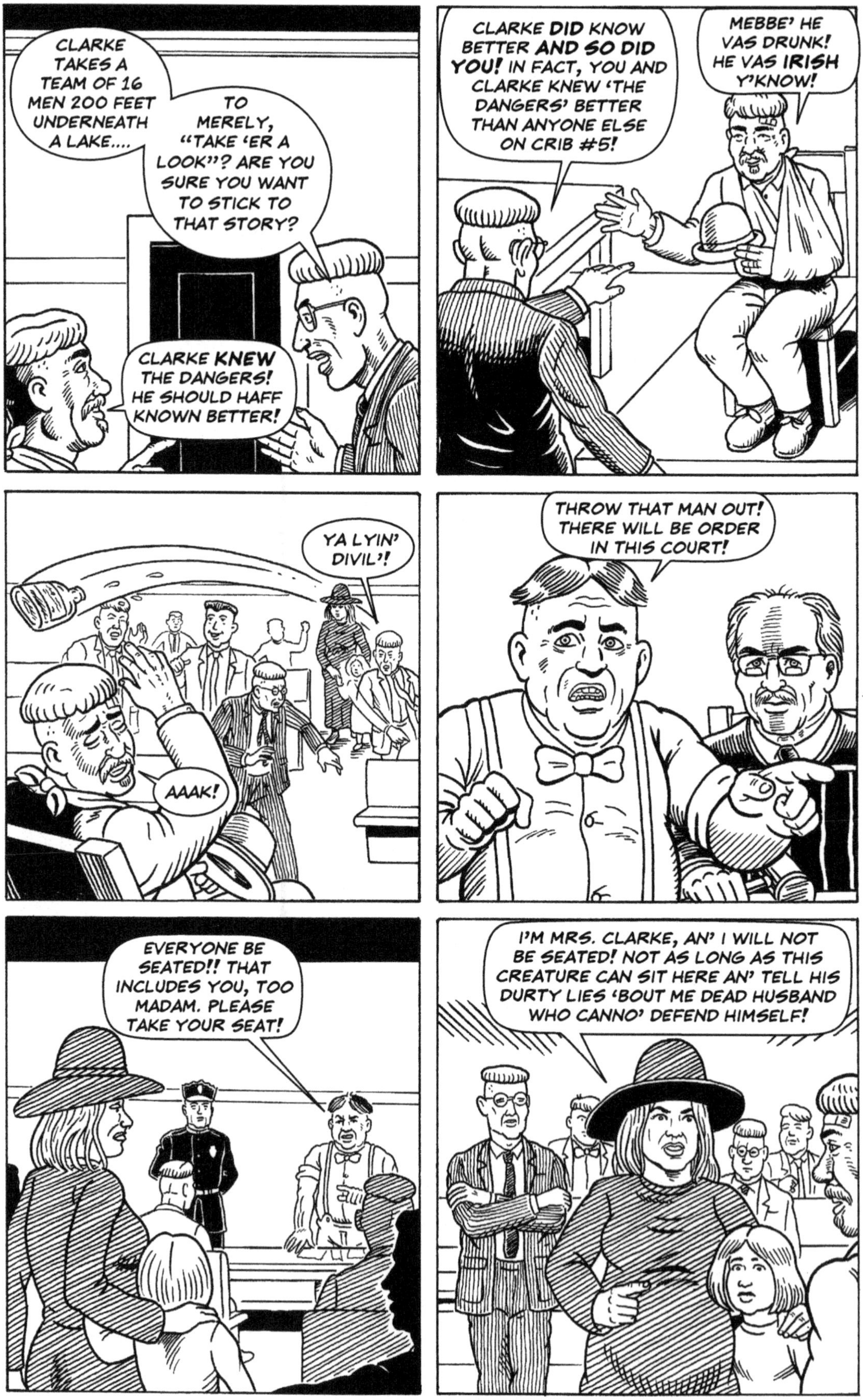
CLARKE TAKES A TEAM OF 16 MEN 200 FEET UNDERNEATH A LAKE....
TO MERELY, "TAKE 'ER A LOOK"? ARE YOU SURE YOU WANT TO STICK TO THAT STORY?
CLARKE KNEW THE DANGERS! HE SHOULD HAFF KNOWN BETTER!
CLARKE DID KNOW BETTER AND SO DID YOU! IN FACT, YOU AND CLARKE KNEW 'THE DANGERS' BETTER THAN ANYONE ELSE ON CRIB #5!
MEBBE' HE VAS DRUNK! HE VAS IRISH Y'KNOW!
YA LYIN' DIVIL'!
AAAK!
THROW THAT MAN OUT! THERE WILL BE ORDER IN THIS COURT!
EVERYONE BE SEATED!! THAT INCLUDES YOU, TOO MADAM. PLEASE TAKE YOUR SEAT!
I'M MRS. CLARKE, AN' I WILL NOT BE SEATED! NOT AS LONG AS THIS CREATURE CAN SIT HERE AN' TELL HIS DURTY LIES 'BOUT ME DEAD HUSBAND WHO CANNO' DEFEND HIMSELF!

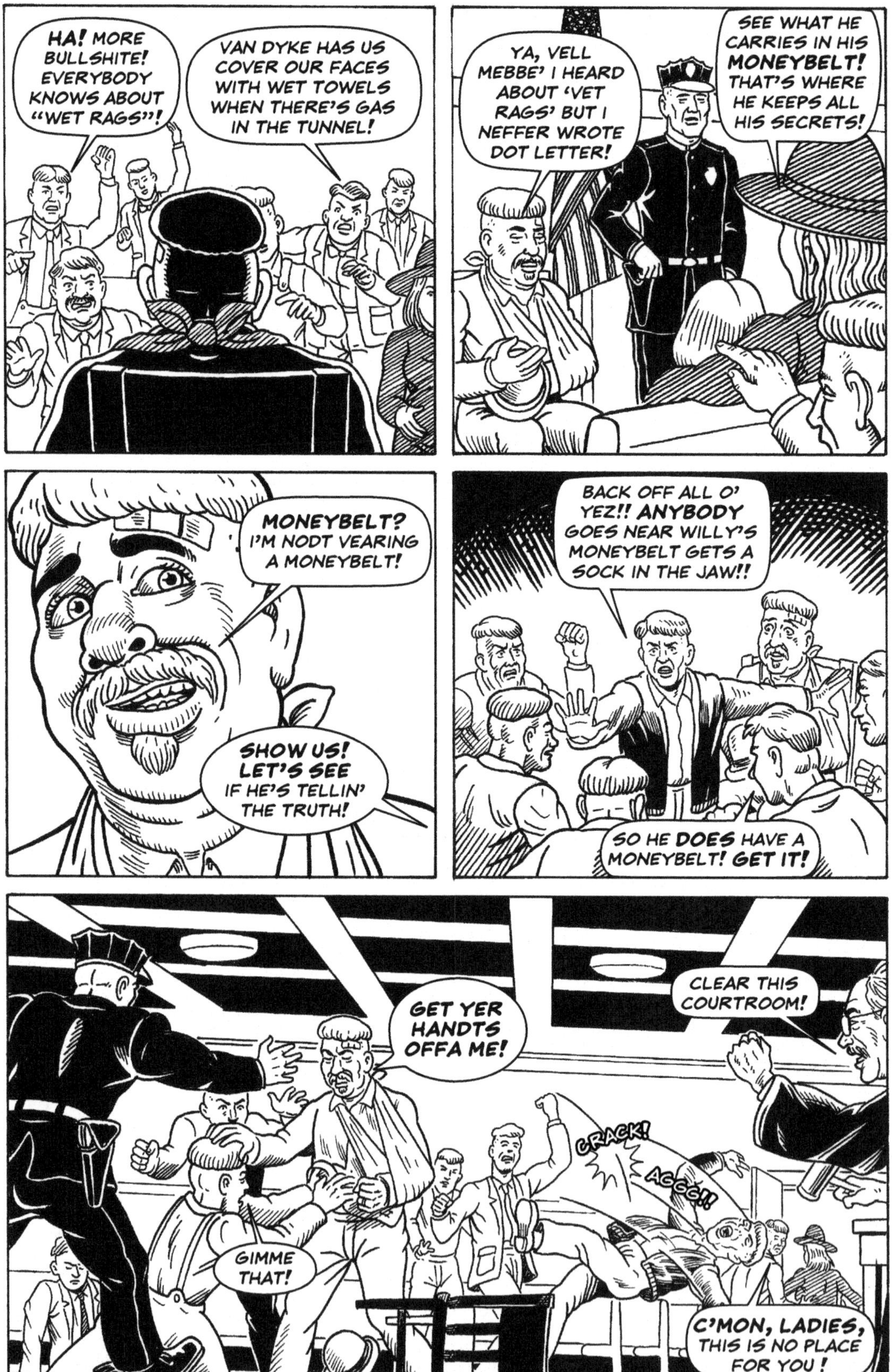
HA! MORE BULLSHITE! EVERYBODY KNOWS ABOUT "WET RAGS"!
VAN DYKE HAS US COVER OUR FACES WITH WET TOWELS WHEN THERE'S GAS IN THE TUNNEL!
YA, VELL MEBBE' I HEARD ABOUT 'VET RAGS' BUT I NEFFER WROTE DOT LETTER!
SEE WHAT HE CARRIES IN HIS MONEYBELT! THAT'S WHERE HE KEEPS ALL HIS SECRETS!
MONEYBELT? I'M NODT VEARING A MONEYBELT!
SHOW US! LET'S SEE IF HE'S TELLIN' THE TRUTH!
BACK OFF ALL O' YEZ!! ANYBODY GOES NEAR WILLY'S MONEYBELT GETS A SOCK IN THE JAW!!
SO HE DOES HAVE A MONEYBELT! GET IT!
GET YER HANDTS OFFA ME!
CLEAR THIS COURTROOM!
CRACK!
AGGG!!
GIMME THAT!
C'MON, LADIES, THIS IS NO PLACE FOR YOU!

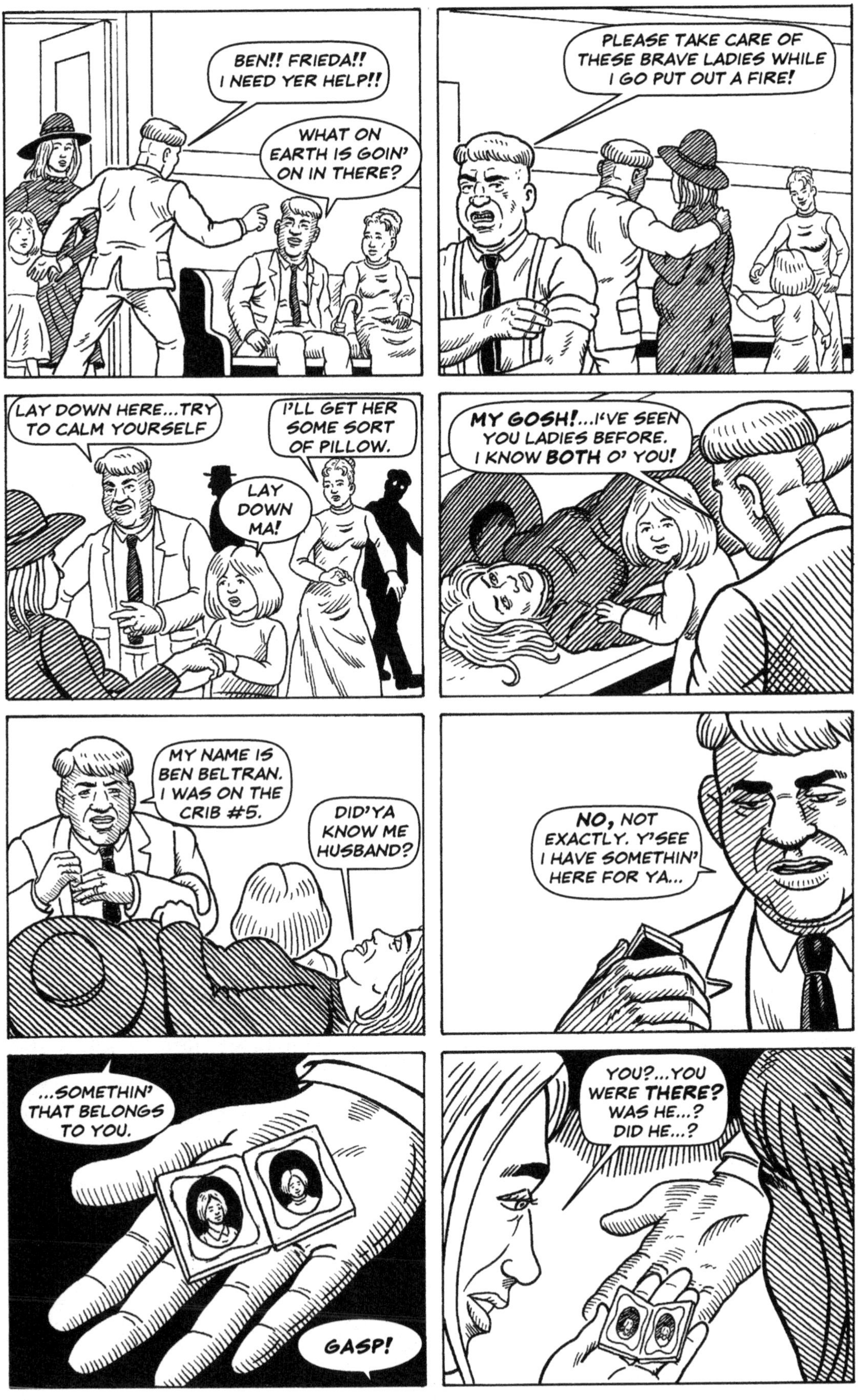
BEN!! FRIEDA!! I NEED YER HELP!!
WHAT ON EARTH IS GOIN' ON IN THERE?
PLEASE TAKE CARE OF THESE BRAVE LADIES WHILE I GO PUT OUT A FIRE!
LAY DOWN HERE...TRY TO CALM YOURSELF
I'LL GET HER SOME SORT OF PILLOW.
LAY DOWN MA!
MY GOSH!...I'VE SEEN YOU LADIES BEFORE. I KNOW BOTH O' YOU!
MY NAME IS BEN BELTRAN. I WAS ON THE CRIB #5.
DID'YA KNOW ME HUSBAND?
NO, NOT EXACTLY. Y'SEE I HAVE SOMETHIN' HERE FOR YA...
...SOMETHIN' THAT BELONGS TO YOU.
GASP!
YOU?...YOU WERE THERE? WAS HE...? DID HE...?

HE WAS CLUTCHIN' THIS IN HIS HAND. YOU **BOTH** WERE IN HIS LAST THOUGHTS. I HOPE YOU DON'T MIND I BROUGHT IT BACK.

YE BROUGHT US HIS LAST MOMENTS ON EARTH...THAT'S EVERYTHIN' FER US.

SHE'S SO PALE. LET'S HAVE HER LAY DOWN AGAIN.

30 MINUTES LATER

BEN!...I NEED A WORD WIT'YA PLEASE.

THERE YOU GO. THAT'S BETTER.

IT'S OVER, BEN. THE INQUEST IS **CLOSED**.

WHAT?! WITHOUT MY TESTIMONY?

THE TUNNEL BOYS RIPPED AWAY VAN DYKE'S CLOTHES TO GET AT HIS INFERNAL **MONEYBELT**...

EUREKA!

...THE MAYOR AND JUDGE LOOKED THRU IT AN' FOUND ALL MANNER O' THINGS: MONEY, NOTES, AN' A LEDGER LIST O' PAYOFFS...

...THE WRITIN' ON THE LEDGER MATCHED VAN DYKE'S NOTE TO CLARKE, PROVIN' THEY **KNEW** THERE WAS GAS IN THE TUNNEL.

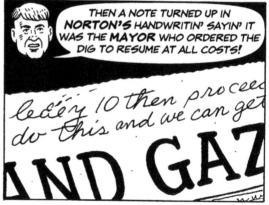

THEN A NOTE TURNED UP IN **NORTON'S** HANDWRITIN' SAYIN' IT WAS THE **MAYOR** WHO ORDERED THE DIG TO RESUME AT ALL COSTS!

258

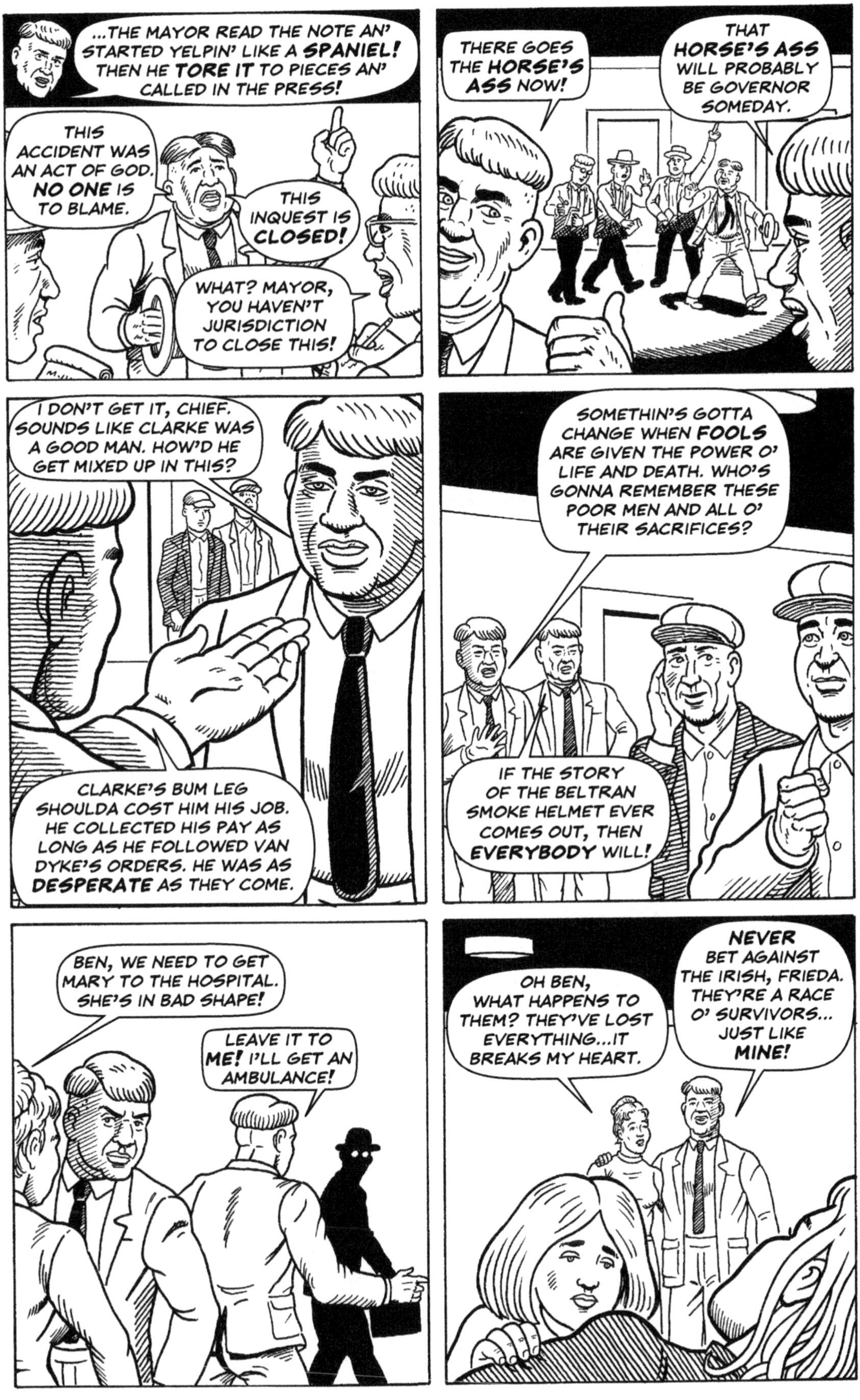
...THE MAYOR READ THE NOTE AN' STARTED YELPIN' LIKE A SPANIEL! THEN HE TORE IT TO PIECES AN' CALLED IN THE PRESS!
THIS ACCIDENT WAS AN ACT OF GOD. NO ONE IS TO BLAME.
THIS INQUEST IS CLOSED!
WHAT? MAYOR, YOU HAVEN'T JURISDICTION TO CLOSE THIS!
THERE GOES THE HORSE'S ASS NOW!
THAT HORSE'S ASS WILL PROBABLY BE GOVERNOR SOMEDAY.
I DON'T GET IT, CHIEF. SOUNDS LIKE CLARKE WAS A GOOD MAN. HOW'D HE GET MIXED UP IN THIS?
CLARKE'S BUM LEG SHOULDA COST HIM HIS JOB. HE COLLECTED HIS PAY AS LONG AS HE FOLLOWED VAN DYKE'S ORDERS. HE WAS AS DESPERATE AS THEY COME.
SOMETHIN'S GOTTA CHANGE WHEN FOOLS ARE GIVEN THE POWER O' LIFE AND DEATH. WHO'S GONNA REMEMBER THESE POOR MEN AND ALL O' THEIR SACRIFICES?
IF THE STORY OF THE BELTRAN SMOKE HELMET EVER COMES OUT, THEN EVERYBODY WILL!
BEN, WE NEED TO GET MARY TO THE HOSPITAL. SHE'S IN BAD SHAPE!
LEAVE IT TO ME! I'LL GET AN AMBULANCE!
OH BEN, WHAT HAPPENS TO THEM? THEY'VE LOST EVERYTHING...IT BREAKS MY HEART.
NEVER BET AGAINST THE IRISH, FRIEDA. THEY'RE A RACE O' SURVIVORS... JUST LIKE MINE!

YOUNG MISS, I'D LIKE TO GIVE YOU SOMETHIN'.

WHAT IS IT?

JUS' AN OL' WHISTLE TO CARRY FOR GOOD LUCK.

BIRDY

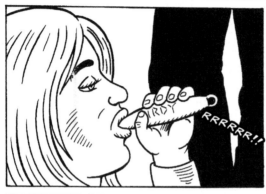

RRRRRR!!

BIRDY

UH-OH, IT'S BUSTED!

TREAT 'ER LIKE FINE CHINA, LADS.

IT'S A SPECIAL WHISTLE, DARLIN'.

ONLY YOUR DADDY CAN HEAR IT. WHENEVER YOU ARE AFRAID OR LONELY, BLOW ON THE WHISTLE AND YOU'LL FEEL HIM RIGHT BESIDE YOU.

THEY NEED HELP. I'M GOING TO THE HOSPITAL WITH THEM.

BEN, I GOTTA GO. I DID PUT IN ANUTTER REQUEST FER THE SMOKE HELMETS. LET'S HOPE FER THE BEST AN' EXPECT THE WORST, EH, BOYO?

OK, CHIEF, AN' BY THE WAY, **THANK YOU** FOR SAVIN' MY LIFE.

AHHH....IT'LL BE NICE TO SLEEP IN MY OWN BED TONITE...EH...?

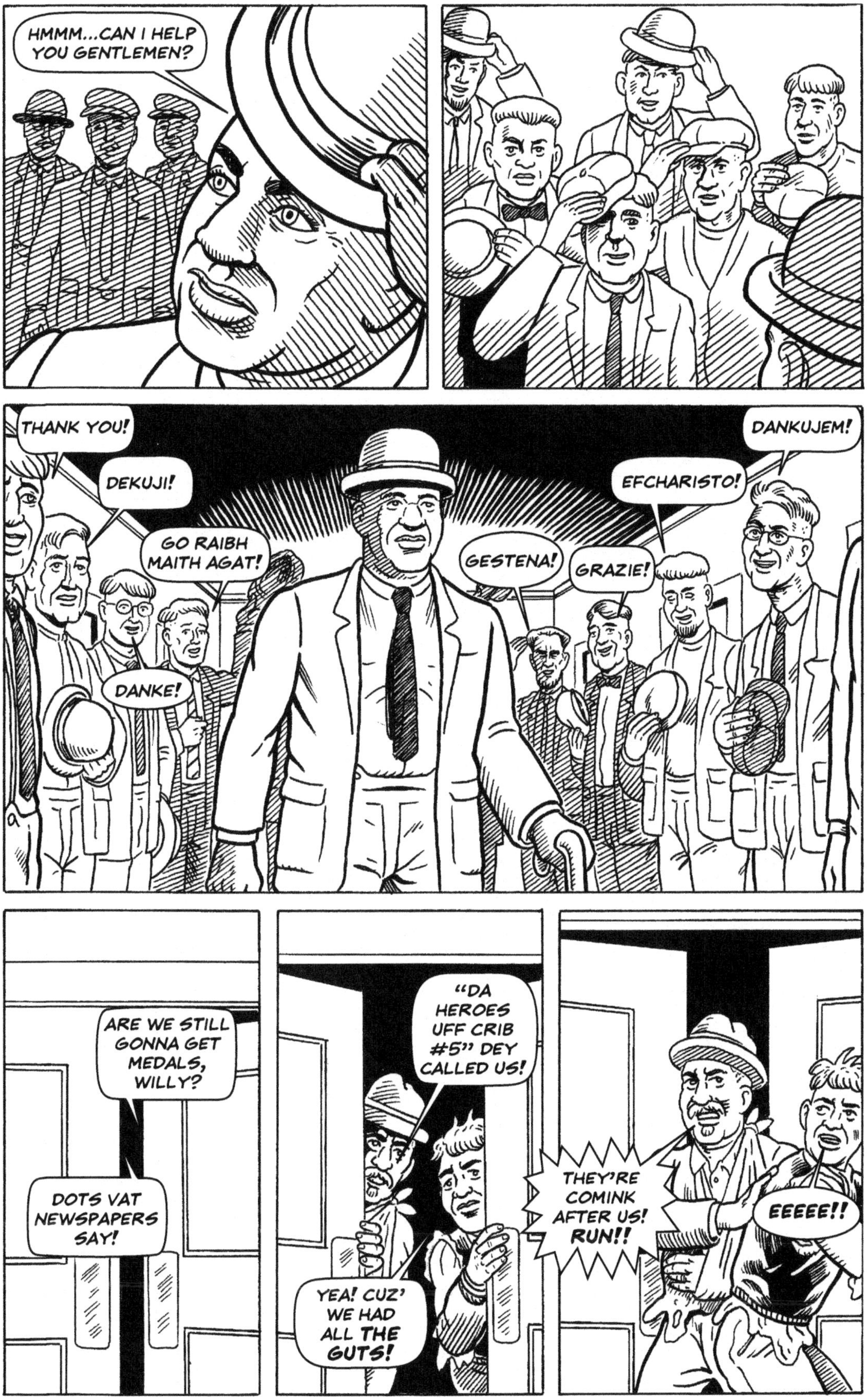
HMMM...CAN I HELP YOU GENTLEMEN?
THANK YOU!
DEKUJI!
GO RAIBH MAITH AGAT!
DANKE!
GESTENA!
GRAZIE!
EFCHARISTO!
DANKUJEM!
ARE WE STILL GONNA GET MEDALS, WILLY?
DOTS VAT NEWSPAPERS SAY!
"DA HEROES UFF CRIB #5" DEY CALLED US!
YEA! CUZ' WE HAD ALL THE GUTS!
THEY'RE COMINK AFTER US! RUN!!
EEEEE!!

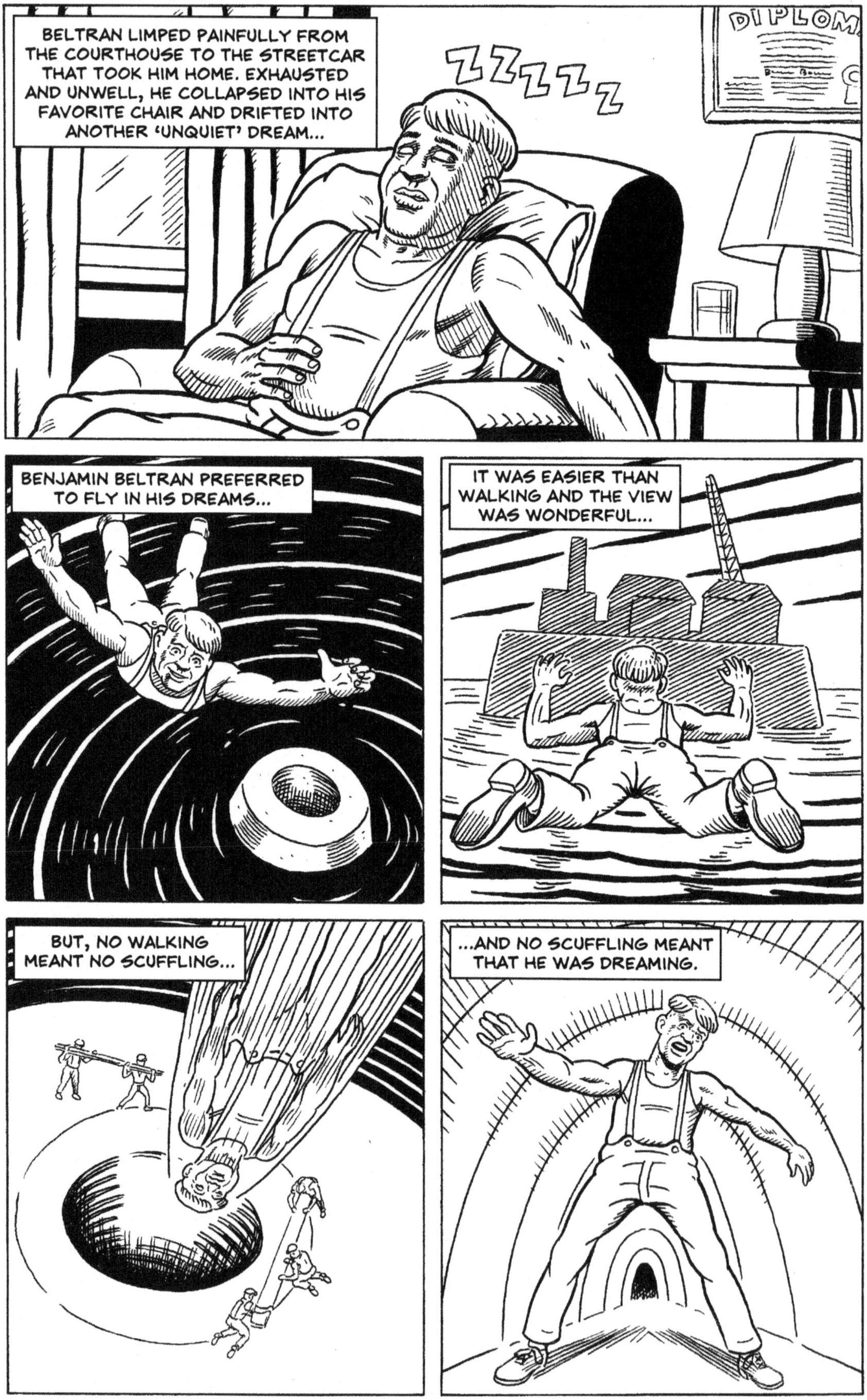
BELTRAN LIMPED PAINFULLY FROM THE COURTHOUSE TO THE STREETCAR THAT TOOK HIM HOME. EXHAUSTED AND UNWELL, HE COLLAPSED INTO HIS FAVORITE CHAIR AND DRIFTED INTO ANOTHER 'UNQUIET' DREAM...
ZZZZZZ
DIPLOM
BENJAMIN BELTRAN PREFERRED TO FLY IN HIS DREAMS...
IT WAS EASIER THAN WALKING AND THE VIEW WAS WONDERFUL...
BUT, NO WALKING MEANT NO SCUFFLING...
...AND NO SCUFFLING MEANT THAT HE WAS DREAMING.

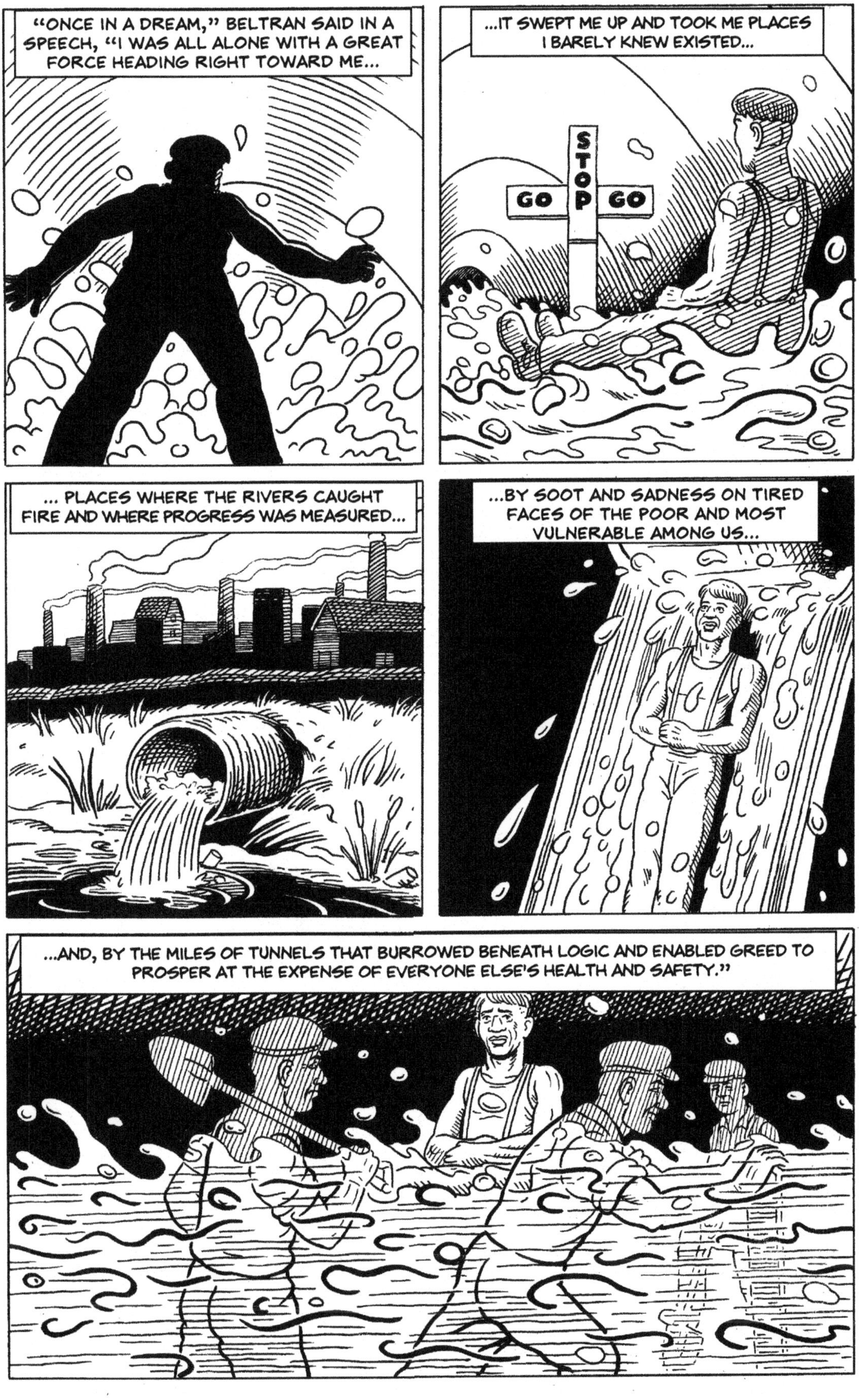
"ONCE IN A DREAM," BELTRAN SAID IN A SPEECH, "I WAS ALL ALONE WITH A GREAT FORCE HEADING RIGHT TOWARD ME...
...IT SWEPT ME UP AND TOOK ME PLACES I BARELY KNEW EXISTED...
STOP
GO
GO
... PLACES WHERE THE RIVERS CAUGHT FIRE AND WHERE PROGRESS WAS MEASURED...
...BY SOOT AND SADNESS ON TIRED FACES OF THE POOR AND MOST VULNERABLE AMONG US...
...AND, BY THE MILES OF TUNNELS THAT BURROWED BENEATH LOGIC AND ENABLED GREED TO PROSPER AT THE EXPENSE OF EVERYONE ELSE'S HEALTH AND SAFETY."

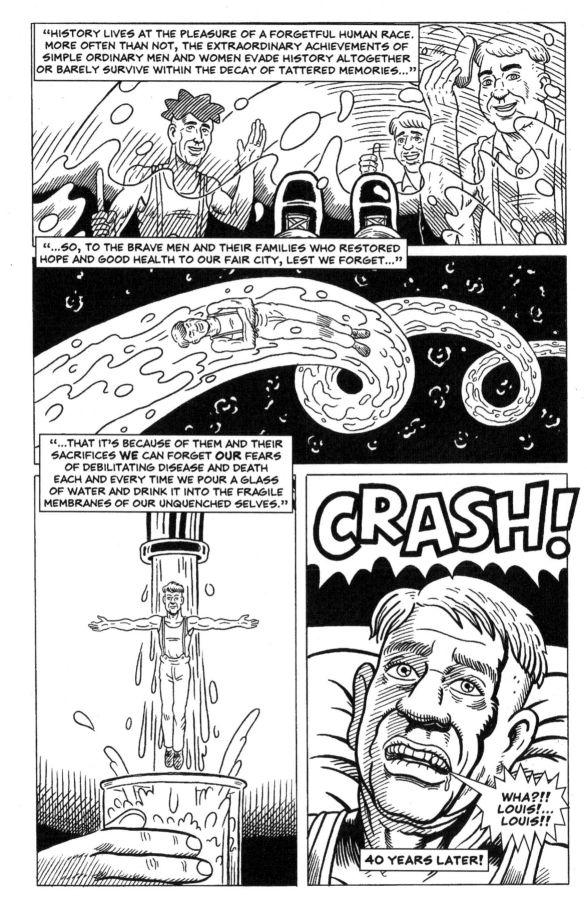

"HISTORY LIVES AT THE PLEASURE OF A FORGETFUL HUMAN RACE. MORE OFTEN THAN NOT, THE EXTRAORDINARY ACHIEVEMENTS OF SIMPLE ORDINARY MEN AND WOMEN EVADE HISTORY ALTOGETHER OR BARELY SURVIVE WITHIN THE DECAY OF TATTERED MEMORIES..."

"...SO, TO THE BRAVE MEN AND THEIR FAMILIES WHO RESTORED HOPE AND GOOD HEALTH TO OUR FAIR CITY, LEST WE FORGET..."

"...THAT IT'S BECAUSE OF THEM AND THEIR SACRIFICES WE CAN FORGET OUR FEARS OF DEBILITATING DISEASE AND DEATH EACH AND EVERY TIME WE POUR A GLASS OF WATER AND DRINK IT INTO THE FRAGILE MEMBRANES OF OUR UNQUENCHED SELVES."

CRASH!

WHA?!! LOUIS!... LOUIS!!

40 YEARS LATER!

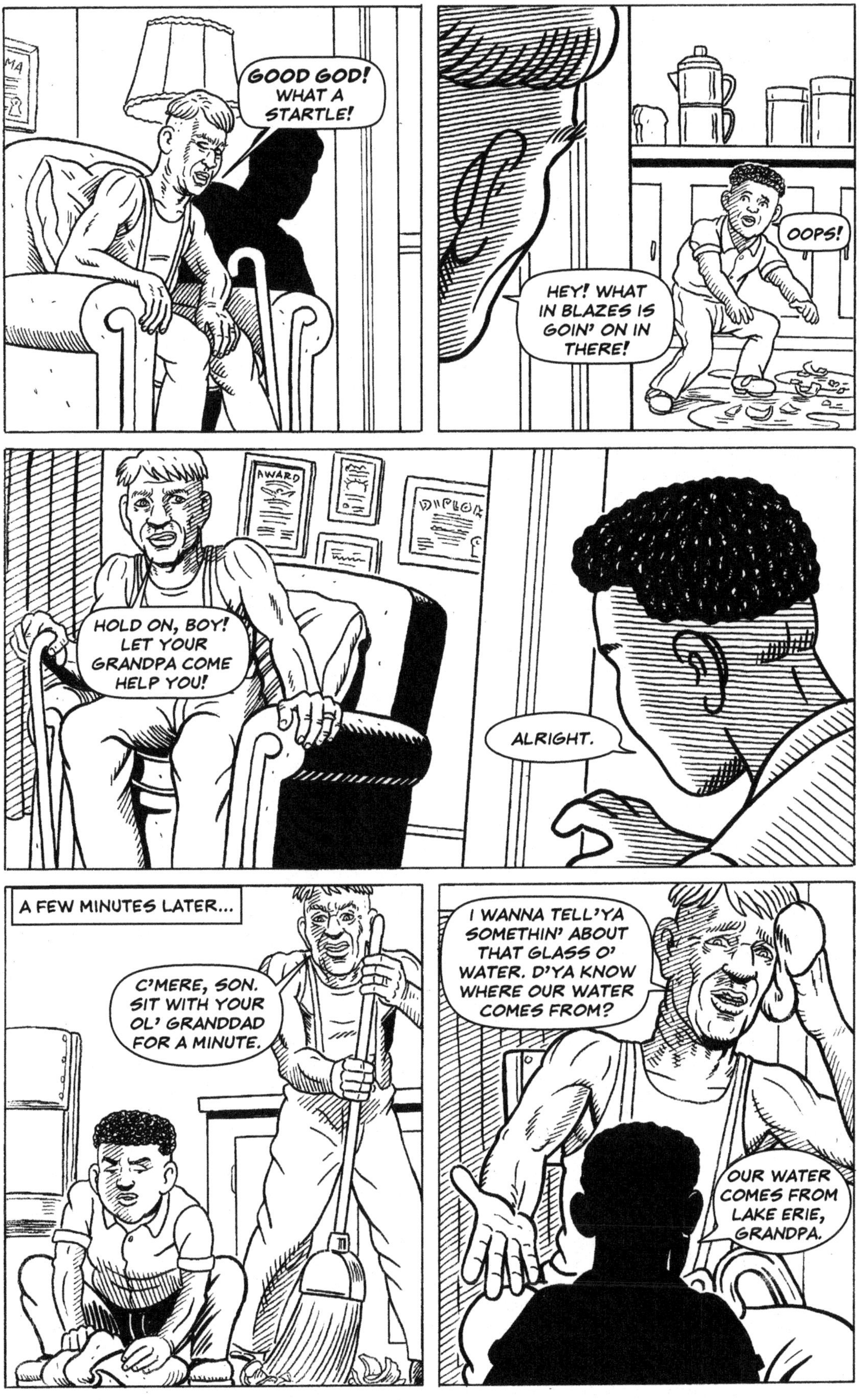
GOOD GOD! WHAT A STARTLE!
HEY! WHAT IN BLAZES IS GOIN' ON IN THERE!
OOPS!
HOLD ON, BOY! LET YOUR GRANDPA COME HELP YOU!
ALRIGHT.
A FEW MINUTES LATER...
C'MERE, SON. SIT WITH YOUR OL' GRANDDAD FOR A MINUTE.
I WANNA TELL'YA SOMETHIN' ABOUT THAT GLASS O' WATER. D'YA KNOW WHERE OUR WATER COMES FROM?
OUR WATER COMES FROM LAKE ERIE, GRANDPA.

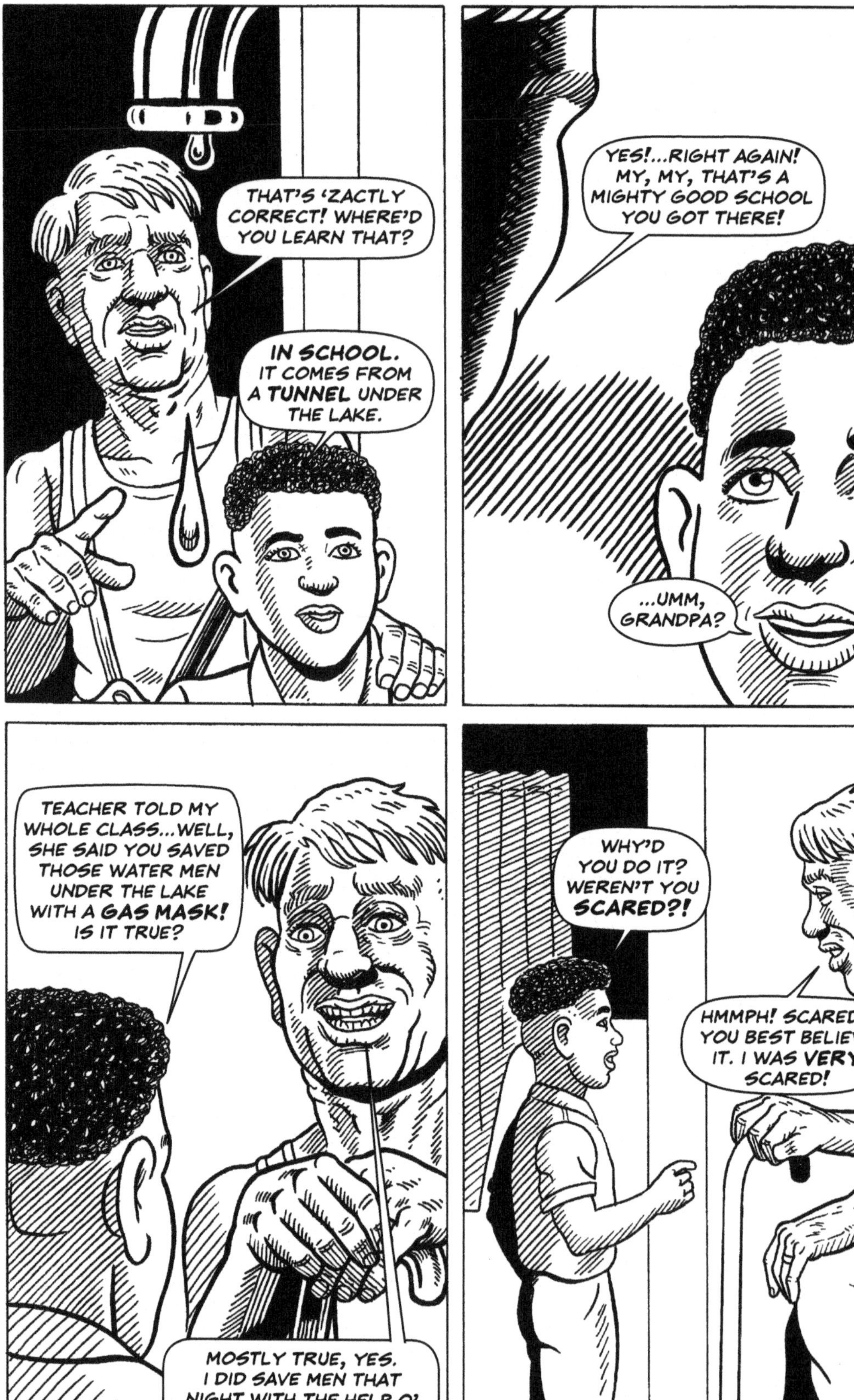
THAT'S 'ZACTLY CORRECT! WHERE'D YOU LEARN THAT?
IN SCHOOL. IT COMES FROM A TUNNEL UNDER THE LAKE.
YES!...RIGHT AGAIN! MY, MY, THAT'S A MIGHTY GOOD SCHOOL YOU GOT THERE!
...UMM, GRANDPA?
TEACHER TOLD MY WHOLE CLASS...WELL, SHE SAID YOU SAVED THOSE WATER MEN UNDER THE LAKE WITH A GAS MASK! IS IT TRUE?
MOSTLY TRUE, YES. I DID SAVE MEN THAT NIGHT WITH THE HELP O' YOUR GREAT UNCLE LOUIS... GOD REST HIS SOUL.
WHY'D YOU DO IT? WEREN'T YOU SCARED?!
HMMPH! SCARED? YOU BEST BELIEVE IT. I WAS VERY SCARED!

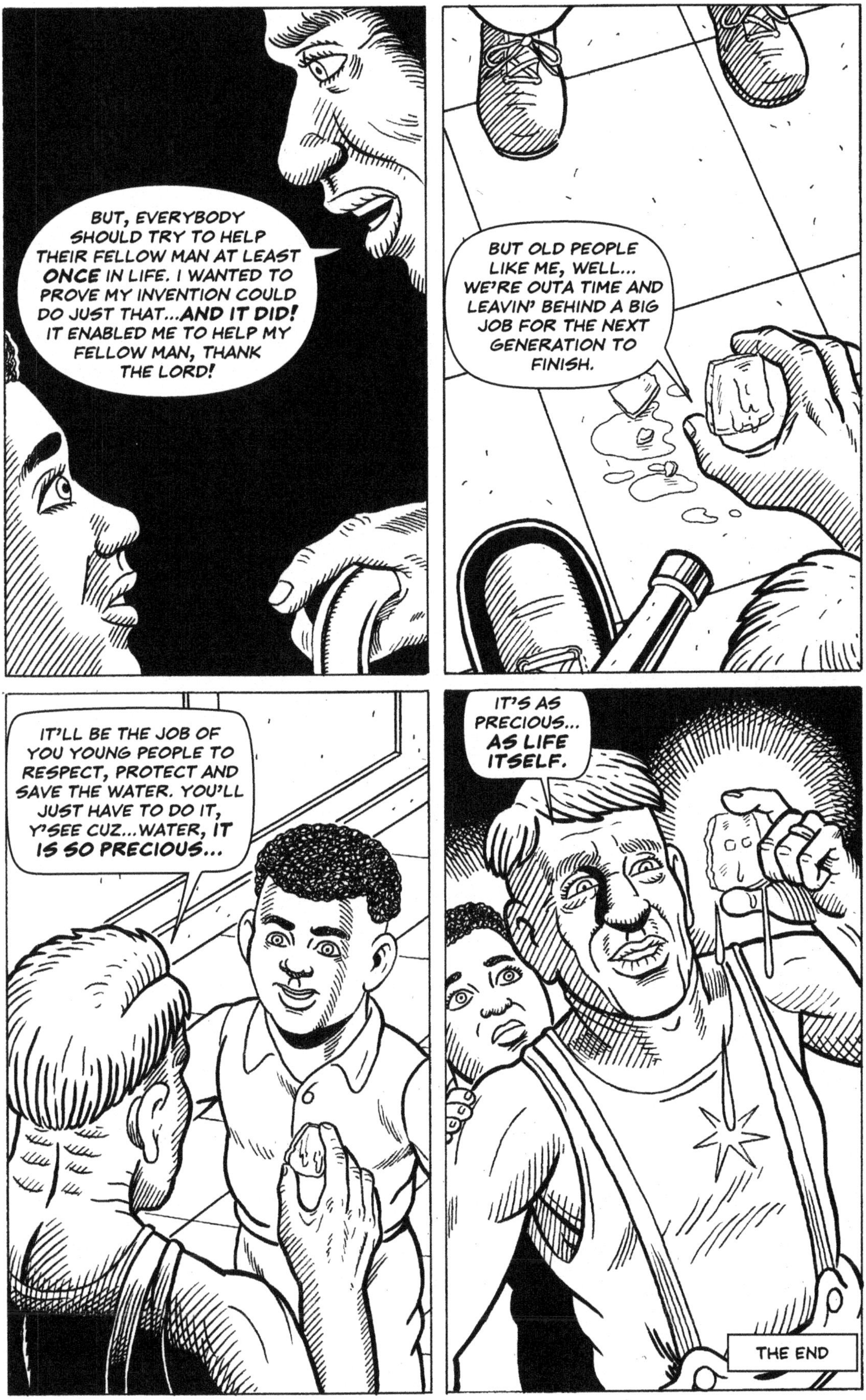
BUT, EVERYBODY SHOULD TRY TO HELP THEIR FELLOW MAN AT LEAST ONCE IN LIFE. I WANTED TO PROVE MY INVENTION COULD DO JUST THAT...AND IT DID! IT ENABLED ME TO HELP MY FELLOW MAN, THANK THE LORD!
BUT OLD PEOPLE LIKE ME, WELL... WE'RE OUTA TIME AND LEAVIN' BEHIND A BIG JOB FOR THE NEXT GENERATION TO FINISH.
IT'LL BE THE JOB OF YOU YOUNG PEOPLE TO RESPECT, PROTECT AND SAVE THE WATER. YOU'LL JUST HAVE TO DO IT, Y'SEE CUZ...WATER, IT IS SO PRECIOUS...
IT'S AS PRECIOUS... AS LIFE ITSELF.
THE END

CPSIA information can be obtained
at www.ICGtesting.com
Printed in the USA
LVOW06*2038301117
558157LV00026B/480/P